Tracing the Evidence

Studies in Biblical Literature

Hemchand Gossai
General Editor

Vol. 102

PETER LANG
New York • Washington, D.C./Baltimore • Bern
Frankfurt am Main • Berlin • Brussels • Vienna • Oxford

Mary Anna Bader

Tracing the Evidence

Dinah in Post-Hebrew Bible Literature

PETER LANG
New York • Washington, D.C./Baltimore • Bern
Frankfurt am Main • Berlin • Brussels • Vienna • Oxford

Library of Congress Cataloging-in-Publication Data

Bader, Mary Anna.
Tracing the evidence: Dinah in post-Hebrew Bible literature / Mary Anna Bader.
p. cm. — (Studies in biblical literature; v. 102)
Includes bibliographical references and index.
1. Dinah (Biblical figure). 2. Women in the Bible. 3. Women
in rabbinical literature. 4. Bible. O.T. Genesis XXXIV—
Criticism, interpretation, etc. I. Title.
BS580.D55B33   222′.11092—dc22   2007051178
ISBN 978-0-8204-8853-0
ISSN 1089-0645

Bibliographic information published by **Die Deutsche Bibliothek**.
Die Deutsche Bibliothek lists this publication in the "Deutsche
Nationalbibliografie"; detailed bibliographic data is available
on the Internet at http://dnb.ddb.de/.

The paper in this book meets the guidelines for permanence and durability
of the Committee on Production Guidelines for Book Longevity
of the Council of Library Resources.

© 2008 Peter Lang Publishing, Inc., New York
29 Broadway, 18th floor, New York, NY 10006
www.peterlang.com

All rights reserved.
Reprint or reproduction, even partially, in all forms such as microfilm,
xerography, microfiche, microcard, and offset strictly prohibited.

Printed in Germany

Table OF Contents

Editor's Preface...vii
Acknowledgments ix
Permission Acknowledgments xi

Introduction xiii

Chapter 1. Dinah in *The Legends of the Jews* 1
    Conclusions 26

Chapter 2. Dinah in Midrashic Texts from the Ninth Century C.E. and Earlier..........29
    Introduction to Midrash...29
    Genesis Rabbah...30
    Leviticus Rabbah 49
    Pirqe Rabbi Eliezer 50
    Ecclesiastes Rabbah..53
    Tanhuma..54
    Conclusions 66

Chapter 3. Dinah in the *Targumim* 69
    Introduction to the *Targumim* 69
    Introduction to *Targum Neofiti I*....................................69
    Introduction to *Targum Onqelos*...................................76

Introduction to *Targum Pseudo-Jonathan* 79
Introduction to *Targum Job* 84
Conclusions 86

Chapter 4. Dinah in the Pseudepigrapha 89
Introduction to the Pseudepigrapha 89
The *Testaments of the Twelve Patriarchs* 90
Testament of Job 95
Liber antiquitatum biblicarum 97
Joseph and Aseneth 99
Theodotus 102
Jubilees 106
Demetrius the Chronographer 110
Conclusions about the Pseudepigrapha 112

Chapter 5. Dinah in Apocryphal/Deuterocanonical Writings 115
Judith 115
4 Maccabees 137
Conclusions 141

Chapter 6. Dinah in Philo and Josephus 143
Philo 143
Josephus 155
Conclusions 160

Conclusion 163

Notes 171
Bibliography 205
Index 211

Editor's Preface

More than ever the horizons in biblical literature are being expanded beyond that which is immediately imagined; important new methodological, theological, and hermeneutical directions are being explored, often resulting in significant contributions to the world of biblical scholarship. It is an exciting time for the academy as engagement in biblical studies continues to be heightened.

This series seeks to make available to scholars and institutions, scholarship of a high order, and which will make a significant contribution to the ongoing biblical discourse. This series includes established and innovative directions, covering general and particular areas in biblical study. For every volume considered for this series, we explore the question as to whether the study will push the horizons of biblical scholarship. The answer must be yes for inclusion.

In this volume Mary Bader has presented a post HB scholarly mosaic on Dinah. Following up on her book *Sexual Violation in the Hebrew Bible: A Multi-Methodological Study of Genesis 34 and 2 Samuel 13*, Bader explores a number of post HB texts and traditions in order to examine the manner in which Dinah is presented and in so doing she seeks to create a more complete portrait of Dinah. Bader focuses in particular on Louis Ginzberg's *Legends of the Jews, Midrashim, Targumim*, Pseudepigrapha, Apocryphal/Deuterocanonical books, together with the writings of Josephus and Philo. In addition to "filling in gaps" in the Dinah story, Bader paints a complex portrait of Dinah that is deeply interwoven in the fabric of the HB. Dinah's story as it is broadly examined here, is one that continues to have relevance and resonance with contemporary readers, and this book will provide for scholars compelling reasons to revisit Dinah in a way that is certain to expand our thinking in significant ways.

The horizon has been expanded.

Hemchand Gossai
Series Editor

Acknowledgments

I am gratefully aware of the many people that have surrounded and supported me writing this second book. I would like to mention specifically the following persons:

Heidi Burns, the Senior Editor at Peter Lang, Bel Air, Maryland. It has been an absolute pleasure to work with you and all the others at Peter Lang. Thank you.

During my time at The College of Wooster, I have been very fortunate to have wonderful chairpersons who have supported and encouraged my writing and publication: Charles (Chuck) Kammer and Madeline Duntley. I also acknowledge my colleagues in the Religious Studies department: Joan Friedman, Jen Graber, Mark Graham, and Ishwar Harris.

One of the wonderful aspects of teaching at a liberal arts college is the opportunity for inter-disciplinary ventures. I wish to thank my colleagues and the Coordinators of the Women's Studies Program, especially Heather Fitz Gibbon and Linda Hults. Under your leadership, I had the gracious gifts of latitude and the encouragement to envision and propose a new course largely based on this developing manuscript.

Others deserving of mention are: R. Stanton (Stan) Hales, the President; Iain Crawford, the Vice President for Academic Affairs; and Shila Garg, the Dean of the Faculty, who have shown their support for this and other projects of mine in many and varied ways. Thank you very much; your expressions of institutional and personal support for me and this book are greatly appreciated.

The Henry Luce Endowment Committee twice awarded me very generous fellowships to support my writing this manuscript in its various stages. I also wish to thank the TS&T (Teaching, Staff, and Tenure) Committee for your encouragement and support of my writing. Special thanks to the Leave Committee which granted me a semester's leave; it was during that time that I wrote a successful book proposal and a significant block of this material. That time also afforded me the opportunity to contemplate the ways in which my research, scholarship, and my teaching inform one another.

Speaking of teaching, I wish to name some of my students. I have worked closely with Rashmi Ekka, who was a Sophomore Research Assistant to me in the Fall of 2006. She worked hard to help assemble the various readings for the course mentioned above, Dinah in Scripture and Literature. This Sophomore Research Assistant program has been yet another means of support that The College of Wooster has provided.

The students who took that first "Dinah course" engaged the texts found in this book in most profound ways. They have been a vital part of my thinking about these stories and their impact upon college students. You will note a few references to their class papers throughout this manuscript. The students in that course, cross-listed as Womens' Studies and Religious Studies, were: Elizabeth Bennett, Hilary Bryant, Shannon Conley, Kristen Cox, Ali Drushal, Joe Francescangeli, Catherine Grandgeorge, Lisa Jackson, Megan Liber, Michelle Lydenberg, Noah Lyons, Katie Magelaner, Taylor McKay, Jazmin McNeal, Emily Neumann, Erin Plant, Broede Young, and Ashley Zervos. It was a joy to work with you! Your insights, questions, and frustrations were valuable voices for me in the dialogue about Dinah. Thank you, most sincerely.

I am surrounded by a host of friends and family. I lovingly acknowledge my family: my mother, Anna Bader; my brother, David Bader, and his family, Brenda, Matt, Heidi, Greg, and Kim; and my sister, Ruth Walker, and her family: David, Courtney, Amber, and Veronica.

I wish to thank Dick Forringer for his love and support! Writing this book in the context of our relationship has been wonderful; it was fun to have a concentrated writing summer of 2007. Thank you for being who you are.

Permission Acknowledgments

A special thank you to the following publishers who granted worldwide rights to reprint their material:

Hendrickson Publishers for:
The Works of Josephus: New Updated Edition, 1987. ISBN 1-56563-167-6
Antiquities of the Jews 1.21.1-3 (pp. 51-52) 2.7.4 (p. 64)
and
The Works of Philo: New Updated Edition, 1993. ISBN 0-943575-93-1
On the Migration of Abraham XXXIX.216-225 (pp. 274-275) VII (p. 256)
On the Change of Names XXXV.186-XXXVI.200 (pp. 357-358)
Allegorical Interpretation VIII:23-27 (pp. 52-53)

Ktav Publishing House for:
Excerpts from *Midrash Tanhuma: S. Buber Rescension*. Translated by John T. Townsend. Vol. 1: Genesis. Hoboken, N.J.: Ktav Publishing House, 1989.

Michael Glazier, Inc. for:
Excerpts from Grossfeld, Bernard. *The Targum Onqelos to Genesis*. The Aramaic Bible, Volume 6. Wilmington, Del.: Michael Glazier, Inc., 1988. Reprinted with permission of Liturgical Press (www.litpress.org).

Excerpts from Maher, Michael. *Targum Pseudo-Jonathan: Genesis*. The Aramaic Bible, Volume 1B. Collegeville, Minn.: Michael Glazier, Inc., 1992. Reprinted with permission of Liturgical Press (www.litpress.org).

Excerpts from Mangan, Céline. *The Targum of Job*. The Aramaic Bible, Volume 15. Collegeville, Minn.: Michael Glazier, Inc., 1991. Reprinted with permission of Liturgical Press (www.litpress.org).

Excerpts from McNamara, Martin. *Targum Neofiti 1: Genesis*. The Aramaic Bible, Volume 1A. Collegeville, Minn.: Michael Glazier, Inc., 1992. Reprinted with permission of Liturgical Press (www.litpress.org).

Sepher-Hermon Press, Inc. for:
Excerpts from *Pirkei De Rabbi Eliezer: The Chapters of Rabbi Eliezer the Great According to the Text of the Manuscript Belonging to Abraham Epstein of Vienna*. Translated by Gerald Friedlander. New York: Hermon Press, 1965.

Soncino Press Ltd. for:
The Midrash Rabbah, edited by Freedman and Simon, 1961, London, Soncino Press Ltd. (vol. 1, pp. 63, 141–42, 157, and 505); (vol. 2, pp. 666–67, 673, 709, 727–44, 771, 785–86, 829, 855, 860, 952–53, and 979); (vol. 4, p. 465); and (vol. 8, p. 268–69).

Introduction

My first book *Sexual Violation in the Hebrew Bible: A Multi-Methodological Study of Genesis 34 and 2 Samuel 13*[1] focused on two Hebrew Bible (HB) narratives involving different kinds of sexual violation against women—Dinah, the daughter of Leah and Jacob, and Tamar, the daughter of Maacah and King David. After writing this book and presenting parts of the book in my teaching at The College of Wooster and as papers at professional conferences, I came to realize how disturbed others and I have remained at the gaps in the biblical narrative.

Speaking from a literary critical point-of-view, Dinah is not well-developed as a character. For example, as I mentioned in *Sexual Violation*, many express wonder and dismay that the HB narrator left so many gaps in Genesis 34; particularly problematic to modern readers is that nothing is said about Dinah's perspective, state of mind, or state of body.[2] The biblical narrator says literally nothing about Dinah's thoughts, feelings, or her reactions to any of what happened with or at Shechem. At the beginning of the story, and it's still true at the end, the reader has no details about why she went out to see the women of the land. One doesn't know if this was the first time she went out to see them or if they had been meeting for years. And most importantly, and most disturbing to modern readers, we have no idea about her "take" on or understanding of the sexual congress which happened with Shechem (was she amenable to it—i.e., was Dinah a complicit partner in it or was it rape?). Lastly, besides the reference in Gen. 46:15, which states that Dinah went down to Egypt with the rest of Jacob's clan, nothing is said about what happened to Dinah after this event at Shechem. These gaps, among other things, beckon a reader into the narrative. There are many unanswered questions.

I am excited to see the extent to which post-HB traditions develop the character of Dinah. As is evident from even a cursory look at the Table of Contents, this book will investigate Dinah traditions in Louis Ginzberg's *Legends of the Jews*, relatively early *Midrashim, Targumim,* Pseudepigrapha, the Apocryphal/Deuterocanonical Books, and Josephus and Philo.

Many of the texts explored in this book portray Dinah and the events surrounding her in markedly different ways than does Genesis 34. For example, the HB has very little to say about what happened to Dinah after this fateful event; the texts explored in this book offer a variety of explanations and suggestions. Some allege that Dinah had become pregnant by Shechem, giving birth to a daughter Aseneth, who later is said to have married Joseph. Other texts offer divergent traditions about Dinah's marriage(s); some make it clear that she had married Shechem, others depict her marrying her brother Simeon, and still others speak of her matrimonial union with Job. These are just a few of the pieces of information one will glean about Dinah in this book.

Ever since I was a little girl, I have loved puzzles. This book may be conceived of presenting different pieces of a puzzle regarding Dinah. As we will see, some of the pieces fit well together; hooked or linked with one another they present a larger unified picture. Some pictures are beautiful; others are still highly disturbing. Some other pieces do not fit together at all. In fact, one may conclude that our exploration of the following texts yields more than one composite picture of Dinah. The texts presented in this book are: *The Legends of the Jews*; *Midrash* which includes, but is not limited to *Genesis (Bereshit) Rabbah*, excerpts from *Leviticus Rabbah* and *Ecclesiastes Rabbah*; Deuterocanonical texts such as the books of Judith and 4 Maccabees; Pseudepigraphic references including, The Testaments of the Twelve Patriarchs (and most specifically the Testaments of Levi and Job), Pseudo-Philo, Joseph and Aseneth, Jubilees, and Theodotus, and Josephus' *Antiquities of the Jews*. In each of these cases, I will provide a brief historical introduction to the book/writing. These various records will be brought into dialogue with one another; I will cross-reference texts in the appropriate places. I will consistently make reference to Genesis 34, which will serve as the touchstone and springboard for our exploration outside of the Hebrew Bible (HB). The following is the HB text:[3]

Genesis 34

(1) And Dinah, the daughter of Leah whom she had borne to Jacob, went out to see the daughters of the land. (2) And Shechem, the son of Hamor the Hivite, the prince of the land, saw her and took her and lay with her and dishonored her. (3) And his very being clung to Dinah, the daughter of Jacob, and he loved the young woman and he spoke to the heart of the young woman. (4) And Shechem said to Hamor, his father, saying, "Get for me this girl as a wife."

(5) When Jacob heard that he had defiled Dinah, his daughter, his sons were with his cattle in the field. And Jacob was silent until their coming. (6) So Hamor, the father of Shechem, went out to Jacob to speak with him. (7) And the sons of

Jacob came from the field. When they heard, the men were deeply grieved and they were very angry because he had committed a heinous offense in Israel by lying with the daughter of Jacob. For such is not to be done.

(8) Hamor spoke with them saying, Shechem, my son, his very being is set on your daughter—please give her to him as a wife." (9) Form marriages with us; you will give your daughters to us, and our daughters you will take for yourselves. (10) You will dwell with us and the land will be in front of you. Dwell and go about (in) it, and take possession of it. (11) Then Shechem said to her father and to her brothers, "Let me find favor in your eyes, and whatever you say to me I will give. (12) Make very great upon me the bride price and the gift and I will give according to what you say to me—just give me the young woman as a wife."

(13) The sons of Jacob answered Shechem and Hamor, his father, and they spoke with deceit because he had defiled Dinah, their sister. (14) They said to them, "We are not able to do this thing, to give our sister to a man who has a foreskin; for that would be a disgrace to us. (15) Only on this condition will we consent to you—that you become as we are—that every male among you be circumcised. (16) Then we will give our daughters to you, and your daughters we will take for ourselves. And we will dwell with you, and we will be as one people. (17) But if you do not listen to us to be circumcised, we will take our daughter and go."

(18) And their words were pleasing in the eyes of Hamor and in the eyes of Shechem, the son of Hamor. (19) And the young man did not hesitate to do the thing because he delighted in the daughter of Jacob. And he was the most distinguished of the house of his father. (20) So Hamor and Shechem, his son, came to the gate of their city and they spoke to the men of their city saying, (21) "These men are sound; they are with us. Let them dwell in the land and go about (in) it—see the land is big enough for them. Let us take their daughters as wives for ourselves and let us give our daughters to them. (22) Only on this condition will the men consent to us to dwell with us to be one people—among us every male is to be circumcised as they are circumcised. (23) Their cattle, their acquisitions, and all their beasts—will they not be ours? Only let us consent to them, and they will dwell with us." (24) All who went out to the gate of his city listened to Hamor and to Shechem, his son. And all the males were circumcised—all who went out to the gate of his city.

(25) And it happened on the third day of their being in pain that two of the sons of Jacob, Simeon and Levi, brothers of Dinah, each took his sword and came upon the city unbeknown. And they killed every male. (26) They killed Hamor and Shechem, his son, with the mouth of the sword. And they took Dinah from the house of Shechem, and they went out. (27) And the sons of Jacob came upon the slain, and they plundered the city because they had defiled their sister.

(28) And their flocks, their herds, and their asses and whatever was in the city and whatever was in the field they took. (29) And all their wealth and all their children and their women they took captive and they plundered—all that was in the house.

(30) And Jacob said to Simeon and to Levi, "You have troubled me to cause me to stink among the inhabitants of the land, the Canaanites and the Perizzites. And I am few in number; they will gather themselves against me and attack me and I will be destroyed–I and my house." (31) But they said, "Should he treat our sister as a whore?"

CHAPTER ONE

Dinah IN *The Legends* OF THE *Jews*

My students and I have found Louis Ginzberg's ongoing narrative to be incredibly engaging. As he sought to construct this metaphorical tapestry, he interwove various traditions and provided a paper trail to the numerous sources from which he gleaned his information. The accessibility of *The Legends of the Jews* merits its inclusion as an excellent point of entry for the modern reader, especially an undergraduate non-Hebrew speaking/reading student. It is an invitation to find one's way to the ancient texts. Additionally, it provides in one location a collection of multivalent references to Dinah, the event at Shechem and hosts of traditions about the aftermath of what happened in Dinah's life. Before delving into *The Legends of the Jews*, the following is background material to Ginzberg and his work.

Louis Ginzberg was born on November 28, 1873, in former Kovno, Lithuania; he moved to the United States in 1899, after earning his Ph.D. at the University of Heidelberg. Ginzberg served on the staff of the *Jewish Encyclopedia*, taught for many years at the Jewish Theological Seminary in Manhattan, and wrote *The Legends of the Jews* from 1909 to 1938. In this seven-volume collection, he pieced together into a continuous narrative a number of *Haggadot*, that is, stories or legends, primarily those about biblical figures. As will soon become evident, Ginzberg derived much of his material the *Midrashim* as well as other sources.[1] Arthur Hertzberg has written, "In his major work *The Legends of the Jews* (7 vols., 1909–1938) he combined hundreds of legends, maxims, and parables from the entire midrashic literature into a continuous narrative taken from the lives of the fathers of the people of Israel, its heroes, and its prophets. ..."[2] Ginzberg's work and reputation earned him the title of a scholar of "Jewish 'Law and Lore'"[3]

Ginzberg's collection *The Legends of the Jews* refers to Dinah numerous times. Much of what is found in *Legends* sounds vaguely reminiscent of the Jewish Scriptures; the basic story line is the same. Dinah went out. Shechem sexually dishonored Dinah; this led to the concomitant revenge which Simeon (alternately spelled "Simon") and Levi, the full maternal brothers of Dinah, took upon

Shechem, the man and the city. While the general plots are very similar, *Legends* presents the reader with new information. Within the collection of stories, there is mention that Dinah had become pregnant as a result of the sexual congress at Shechem and gave birth to a daughter, Asenath. There are many variations and additions to the HB account. Much more is said about the many characters found in Genesis 34.

The most complete narrative about Dinah may be found in *Legends* I:394–403. Please attend to how the characters are developed by the narrator. After an analysis of various parts of speech (verbs, nouns, and adjectives), i.e., the rhetoric used by the narrator, the similarities and difference(s) between the account(s) in *Legends* and in Genesis 34 will be explored.

> [I:394][4] And Jacob, after abiding these many years in a strange land, came to Shechem in peace, unimpaired in mind and body. He had forgotten none of the knowledge he had acquired before; the gifts he gave to Esau did not encroach upon his wealth; the injury inflicted by the angel that wrestled with him had been healed, and likewise his children were sound and healthy.
>
> Jacob entered Shechem on a Friday, late in the afternoon, and his first concern was to lay out the boundaries of the [395] city, that the laws of the Sabbath might not be transgressed. As soon as he was settled in the place, he sent presents to the notables. A man must be grateful to a city from which he derives benefits. No less did the common people enjoy his bounty. For them he opened a market where he sold all wares at low prices.
>
> Also he lost no time in buying a parcel of ground, for it is the duty of every man of substance who comes to the Holy Land from outside to make himself the possessor of the land there. He gave a hundred lambs for his estate, a hundred yearling sheep, and a hundred pieces of money, and received in return a bill of sale, to which he attached his signature, using the letters Yod-He for it. And then he erected an altar to God upon his land, and he said, "Thou art the Lord of all celestial things, and I am the lord of all earthly things." But God said, "Not even the overseer of the synagogue arrogates privileges in the synagogue, and thou assumest lordship with a high hand? Forsooth, on the merrow thy daughter will go abroad, and she shall be humbled."
>
> While Jacob and his sons were sitting in the house of learning, occupied with the study of Torah, Dinah went abroad to see the dancing and singing women, whom Shechem had hired to dance and play in the streets in order to entice her forth. Had she remained at home, nothing would have happened to her. But she was a woman, and all women like to show themselves in the street. When Shechem caught sight of her, he seized her by main force, young though she was, and violated her in beastly fashion.
>
> [396] This misfortune befell Jacob as a punishment for his excessive self-confidence. In his negotiations with Laban, he had used the expression, "My righteousness shall answer for me hereafter," Besides, on his return to Palestine, when he was preparing to meet his brother, he concealed his daughter Dinah in a chest, lest Esau desire to

have her for wife, and he be obliged to give her to him. God spoke to him, saying: "Herein hast thou acted unkindly toward thy brother, and therefore Dinah will have to marry Job, one that is neither circumcised nor a proselyte. Thou didst refuse to give her to one that is circumcised, and one that is uncircumcised will take her. Thou didst refuse to give her to Esau in lawful wedlock, and now she will fall a victim to the ravisher's illicit passion."

When Jacob heard that Shechem had defiled his daughter, he sent twelve servants to fetch Dinah from Shechem's house, but Shechem went out to them with his men, and drove them from his house, and he would not suffer them to come unto Dinah, and he kissed and embraced her before their eyes. Jacob then sent two maidens of his servants' daughters to remain with Dinah in the house of Shechem. Shechem bade three of his friends go to his father Hamor, the son of Haddakum, the son of Pered, and say, "Get me this damsel to wife." Hamor tried at first to persuade his son not to take a Hebrew woman to wife, but when Shechem persisted in his request, he did according to the word of his son, and went forth to communicate with Jacob concerning the matter. In the meanwhile the sons of Jacob returned from the field, and, kindled with wrath, they spoke unto their father, saying, "Surely death is due to this man and [397] his household, because the Lord God of the whole earth commanded Noah and his children that man shall never rob nor commit adultery. Now, behold, Shechem has ravaged and committed fornication with our sister, and not one of all the people of the city spake a word to him." And whilst they were speaking, Hamor came to speak to Jacob the words of his son concerning Dinah, and after he ceased to speak, Shechem himself came to Jacob and repeated the request made by his father. Simon and Levi answered Hamor and Shechem deceitfully, saying: "All you have spoken unto us we will do. And, behold, our sister is in your house, but keep away from her until we send to our father Isaac concerning this matter, for we can do nothing without his counsel. He knows the ways of our father Abraham, and whatever he saith unto us we will tell you, we will conceal nothing from you."

Shechem and his father went home thereafter, satisfied with the result achieved, and when they had gone, the sons of Jacob asked him to seek counsel and pretext in order to kill all the inhabitants of the city, who had deserved this punishment on account of their wickedness. Then Simon said to them: "I have good counsel to give you. Bid them be circumcised. If they consent not, we shall take our daughter from them, and go away. And if they consent to do this, then, when they are in pain, we shall attack them and slay them." The next morning Shechem and his father came again to Jacob, to speak concerning Dinah, and the sons of Jacob spoke deceitfully to them, saying: "We told our father Isaac all your words, and your words pleased him, but he said, that thus did Abraham his father command [398] him from God, that any man that is not of his descendants, who desireth to take one of his daughters to wife, shall cause every male belonging to him to be circumcised."

Shechem and his father hastened to do the wishes of the sons of Jacob, and they persuaded also the men of the city to do likewise, for they were greatly esteemed by them, being the princes of the land.

On the next day, Shechem and his father rose up early in the morning, and they assembled all the men of the city, and they called for the sons of Jacob, and they circumcised Shechem, his father, his five brothers, and all the males in the city, six hundred and forty-five men and two hundred and seventy-six lads. Haddakum, the grandfather of Shechem, and his six brothers would not be circumcised, and they were greatly incensed against the people of the city for submitting to the wishes of the sons of Jacob.

In the evening of the second day, Shechem and his father sent to have eight little children whom their mothers had concealed brought to them to be circumcised. Haddakum and his six brothers sprang at the messengers, and sought to slay them, and sought to slay also Shechem, Hamor, and Dinah. They chided Shechem and his father for doing a thing that their fathers had never done, which would raise the ire of the inhabitants of the land of Canaan against them, as well as the ire of the children of Ham, and that on account of a Hebrew woman. Haddakum and his brothers finished by saying: "Behold, to-morrow we will go and assemble our Canaanitish brethren, and we will come and smite you and all in whom you trust, that there shall not be a remnant left of you or them."

[399] When Hamor and his son Shechem and all the people of the city heard this, they were sore afraid, and they repented what they had done, and Shechem and his father answered Haddakum and his brothers: "Because we saw that the Hebrews would not accede to our wishes concerning their daughter, we did this thing, but when we shall have obtained our request from them, we will then do unto them that which is in your hearts and in ours, as soon as we shalt become strong."

Dinah, who heard their words, hastened and dispatched one of her maidens whom her father had sent to take care of her in Shechem's house, and informed Jacob and his sons of the conspiracy plotted against them. When the sons of Jacob heard this, they were filled with wrath, and Simon and Levi swore, and said, "As the Lord liveth, by to-merrow there shall not be a remnant left in the whole city."

They began the extermination by killing eighteen of the twenty young men who had concealed themselves and were not circumcised, and two of them fled and escaped to some lime pits that were in the city. Then Simon and Levi slew all the city, not leaving a male over, and while they were looking for spoils outside of the city, three hundred women rose against them and threw stones and dust upon them, but Simon singlehanded slew them all, and returned to the city, where he joined Levi. Then they took away from the people outside of the city their sheep, their oxen, their cattle, and also the women and the little children, and they led all these away, and took them to the city to their father Jacob. The number of women whom they did not slay, but only took captive, was eighty-five virgins, among them a young damsel of [400] great beauty by the name of Bunah, whom Simon took to wife. The number of the males which they took captive and did not slay was forty-seven, and all these men and women were servants to the sons of Jacob, and to their children after them, until the day they left Egypt.

When Simon and Levi had gone from the city, the two young men who had concealed themselves in the lime pits, and were not slain amongst the people of the city, rose up, and they found the city desolate, without a man, only weeping women, and they cried out, saying "Behold, this is the evil which the sons of Jacob did who destroyed one of the Canaanite cities, and were not afraid of all the land of Canaan."

They left the city and went to Tappuah, and told the inhabitants all that the sons of Jacob had done to the city of Shechem. Jashub, the king of Tappuah, sent to Shechem to see whether these young men told the truth, for he did not believe them, saying, "How could two men destroy a large city like Shechem?" The messengers of Jashub returned, and they reported, "The city is destroyed, not a man is left there, only weeping women, neither are there flocks and cattle there, for all that was in the city was taken away by the sons of Jacob."

Jashub wondered thereat, for the like had not been heard from the days of Nimrod, and not even from the remotest times, that two men should be able to destroy so large a city, and he decided to go to war against the Hebrews, and avenge the cause of the people of Shechem. His counsellors [401] said to him, "If two of them laid waste a whole city, surely if thou goest against them, they all will rise up against us, and destroy us. Therefore, send to the kings round about, that we all together fight against the sons of Jacob and prevail against them."

The seven kings of the Amorites, when they heard the evil that the sons of Jacob had done to the city of Shechem, assembled together, with all their armies, ten thousand men, with drawn swords, and they came to fight against the sons of Jacob. And Jacob was greatly afraid, and he said to Simon and Levi, "Why have you brought such evil upon me? I was at rest, and you provoked the inhabitants of the land against me by your acts."

Then Judah spoke to his father: "Was it for naught that Simon and Levi killed the inhabitants of Shechem? Verily, it was because Shechem dishonored our sister, and transgressed the command of our God to Noah and his children, and not one of the inhabitants of the city interfered in the matter, Now, why art thou afraid, and why art thou displeased at my brethren? Surely, our God, who delivered the city of Shechem and its people into their hand, He will also deliver into our hands all the Canaanitish kings who are coming against us. Now cast away thy fears, and pray to God to assist us and deliver us."

Judah then addressed his brethren, saying: "The Lord our God is with us! Fear naught, then! Stand ye forth, each man girt with his weapons of war, his bow and his sword, and we will go and fight against the uncircumcised. The Lord is our God, He will save us."

Jacob, his eleven sons, and one hundred servants belong-[402] ing to Isaac, who had come to their assistance, marched forward to meet the Amorites, a people exceedingly numerous, like unto the sand upon the sea-shore. The sons of Jacob sent unto their grandfather Isaac, at Hebron, requesting him to pray unto the Lord to protect them from the hand of the Canaanites, and he prayed as follows: "O Lord God, Thou didst promise my father, saying, I will multiply thy seed as the stars of heaven, and also me Thou didst promise that Thou wouldst establish Thy word to my father.

Now O Lord, God of the whole world, pervert, I pray Thee, the counsel of these kings, that they may not fight against my sons, and impress the hearts of their kings and their people with the terror of my sons, and bring down their pride that they turn away from my sons. Deliver my sons and their servants from them with Thy strong hand and outstretched arm, for power and might are in Thy hands to do all this."

Jacob also prayed unto God, and said, "O Lord God, powerful and exalted God, who hast reigned from days of old, from then until now and forever! Thou art He who stirreth up wars and causeth them to cease. In thy hand are power and might to exalt and to bring low. O may my prayer be acceptable unto Thee, that Thou mayest turn to me with Thy mercies, to impress the hearts of these kings and their people with the terror of my sons, and terrify them and their camps, and with Thy great kindness deliver all those that trust in Thee, for Thou art He who subdues the peoples under us, and the nations under our feet."

God heard the prayers of Isaac and Jacob, and He filled the hearts of all the advisors of the Canaanite kings with great fear and terror, and when the kings who were unde-[403]cided whether to undertake a campaign against the sons of Jacob, consulted them, they said: "Are you silly, or is there no understanding in you, that you propose to fight with the Hebrews? Why do you take delight in your own destruction this day? Behold, two of them came to the city of Shechem without fear or terror, and they put all the inhabitants of the city to the sword, no man stood up against them, and how will you be able to fight with them all?"

The royal counselors then proceeded to enumerate all the mighty things God had done for Abraham, Jacob, and the sons of Jacob, such as had not been done from days of old and by any of the gods of the nations. When the kings heard all the words of their advisers, they were afraid of the sons of Jacob, and they would not fight against them. They turned back with their armies on that day, each to his own city. But the sons of Jacob kept their station that day till evening, and seeing that the kings did not advance to do battle with them in order to avenge the inhabitants of Shechem whom they had killed, they returned home.

The wrath of the Lord descended upon the inhabitants of Shechem to the uttermost on account of their wickedness. For they had sought to do unto Sarah and Rebekah as they did unto Dinah, but the Lord had prevented them. Also they had persecuted Abraham when he was a stranger, and they had vexed his flocks when they were big with young, and Eblaen, one born in house, they had handled most shamefully. And thus they did to all strangers, taking away their wives by force.[5]

The analysis of the above narrative will commence by noting the verbs which are used in relation to Dinah. The following overview allows the reader to see the various ways in which Dinah is used as subject and object.[6]

Will go abroad (395)
And shall be humbled (395)
Went abroad to see the dancing and singing women (395)

DINAH IN *THE LEGENDS OF THE JEWS* | 7

To entice her forth (395)
Had she remained at home (395)
Nothing would have happened to her (395)
She was a woman (395)
All women like to show themselves in the street (395)
Shechem caught sight of her (395)
He seized her by main force (395)
Young though she was (395)
And (he) violated her in a beastly fashion (395)

He concealed his daughter Dinah in a chest (396)
lest Esau desire to have her for wife (396)
and he be obliged to give her to him (396)
Dinah will have to marry Job (396)
Thou didst refuse to give her (396)
One that is uncircumcised will take her (396)
Thou didst refuse to give her to Esau (396)
She will fall a victim (396)
Jacob heard that Shechem had defiled his daughter (396)
He sent twelve servants to fetch Dinah from Shechem's house (396)
But Shechem … would not suffer them to come unto Dinah (396)
And he kissed and embraced her before their eyes (396)
Jacob … sent two maidens … to remain with Dinah (396)
Shechem bade … his friends … "Get me this damsel to wife." (396)
Hamor tried … to persuade his son not to take a Hebrew woman to wife (396)

"… Shechem has ravaged and committed fornication with our sister" (397)
Hamor came to speak to Jacob the words of his son concerning Dinah (397)
Our sister is in your house (397)
Keep away from her (397)
"… we shall take our daughter from them …" (397)
Shechem and his father came … to Jacob, to speak concerning Dinah (397)
any man … who desireth to take one of his daughters to wife (398)
Haddakum and his six brothers … sought to slay … Shechem, Hamor, and Dinah (398)
And that on account of a Hebrew woman (398)

Hebrews would not accede to our wishes concerning their daughter … (399)
Dinah, who heard their words (399)
hastened and dispatched one of her maidens (399)
and informed Jacob and his sons of the conspiracy plotted against them (399)

Shechem dishonored our sister (401)

For they had sought to do unto Sarah and Rebekah as they did unto Dinah (403)

Dinah is most often portrayed as the object of the preceding verbs; in only a handful of instances is she the subject. She is presented as the subject of only twelve verbs: will go abroad (395), went abroad to see (395), had she remained at home (395), was (a woman) (395), was (young) (395), will have to marry Job (396), she will fall victim (396), is in your house (397), heard their words (399), hastened and dispatched (399), and informed (399).

Two of the above verbs are stative (was a woman, was young). The phrase "is in your house" is both locative and stative. Three active verbs, "will go abroad," "will have to marry Job," and "will fall victim" are used in the context of Divine foreknowledge/curse of what will transpire in the lives of Jacob and Dinah. Obviously, although the verbs are technically active, Dinah lacks agency. The phrase "had she remained at home" is obviously subjunctive, that is, it expresses both a past contrary to condition, and offers the completion of that thought—what might not have happened had she stayed home.

Moving beyond the aforementioned verbs, one will notice that Dinah is fairly rarely truly an active subject. She went abroad to see, heard their words, hastened and dispatched, and informed. One could, of course, question how active the act of "hearing" is.[7] There is a level of passivity in that activity.

When comparing/contrasting the collective portrayal of Dinah here in *The Legends of Jews*, one can conclude that she is indeed presented as more of an active character in Ginzberg's rendering than she is in the biblical account. In Genesis 34, she is the subject of only one verb: went out (in v. 1). In some passages of *Legends*, Dinah truly has agency. For example, once she hastened and dispatched the maiden whom Jacob had sent to be with her. Genesis contains neither mention of this event nor of the servants/maidens sent by Jacob to Dinah.

The reader may also analyze the nouns and adjectives used in the above depiction of Dinah; the nouns are in bold print. Dinah is referred to in the following ways:

> on the merrow **thy daughter** will go abroad, and she shall be humbled." (395)
> she was a **woman**, and all women like to show themselves in the street. (395)

> he concealed **his daughter** Dinah in a chest (396)
> lest Esau desire to have her for **wife** (396)
> now she will fall a **victim** to the ravisher's illicit passion. (396)
> When Jacob heard that Shechem had defiled **his daughter** (396)
> "Get me this **damsel** to wife." (396)
> Hamor tried ... to persuade his son not to take **a Hebrew woman** to wife ... (396)

> Shechem has ravaged and committed fornication with **our sister** (397)
> And, behold, **our sister** is in your house (397)
> If they consent not, we shall take **our daughter** from them, and go away. (397)

> any man ... who desireth to take **one of his daughters** to wife (398)
> ... and that on account of **a Hebrew woman**. (398)

> the Hebrews would not accede to our wishes concerning **their daughter** ..." (399)

> It was because Shechem dishonored **our sister** (401)

In *Legends* I:394–403, Dinah is referred to as daughter (of Jacob: 395, 395, 396); woman (395); (potential) wife (of Esau, 396); victim (396); damsel (396); Hebrew woman (396, 398); our sister (with the referent once being the sons of Jacob and the other time being Simon and Levi) (397 twice); our sister (with reference to Judah, Simon and Levi (401); our daughter (Simon, 397); his daughter (in reference to Abraham (398); and their daughter (referent being the Hebrews (399). The only two adjectives used to refer to Dinah are "young" (395) and "Hebrew" (396 and 398). Some readers may gain sympathy for Dinah when she has been referred to as "victim" and young.

Never in this particular passage is Dinah referred to as Leah's daughter; that is different from the HB. Here in *Legends*, Dinah is primarily connected to Jacob, possibly because of all the references which speak of her as the means of Divine chastisement of Jacob. The father and daughter are more closely affiliated with one another in this text. As previously mentioned, Jacob tried to wrest Dinah from Shechem; when he was unable to do so, he sent maidens to be with her. The biblical account neither develops any sort of relationship beyond the biological father-daughter bond shared between these two characters, nor does the narrator refer to Dinah as a potential wife of Esau or a victim. Those are elements that one may consider new, especially if the reader has only encountered Genesis 34's portrayal of Dinah.

Temporarily moving away from Dinah, one can see the various ways in which the narrator portrays Jacob. At the beginning of this passage, on I:394, Jacob is said to have entered Shechem on a Friday, with his first concerns being about proper observation of the Sabbath, even before the *mitzvah*/commandment to remember Sabbath had been given. He is presented in ways that create a reader's affinity for him; he acts in accordance with proprieties of the time,[8] not only properly observing Sabbath, but also acknowledging both the notables and the commoners of Shechem. He is a righteous man, honoring both the rich and the poor. Furthermore, as was incumbent upon "men of substance" of that era, he purchased a parcel of land; Jacob's signature, which made official the land deal, bore the first two letters of the Divine Name, *Yod He*. On many levels, the link between Jacob and the Divine was strong. This is reflected in Jacob's behavior; his observation of Sabbath law, his purchase of a portion of land, and his signature all demonstrate his connection with the Divine. He is also portrayed as being in proper relationship with the indigenous people. His uprightness is not to endure without fault; the narrator soon introduces a snag—Jacob is too haughty before the Lord. Immediately, the Divine announces that Dinah, Jacob's daughter, will be "humbled" because of Jacob's hubris. Her "humbling" will allegedly serve to humble Jacob.[9]

Narrators use various details in the settings of their writings to draw contrasts between male and female characters. For example, even after presenting the above snag in the relationship between Jacob and the Divine, the narrator continues to paint a positive image of Jacob and his sons. Jacob's sons are presented as righteous or upright men in I:395; they, together with Jacob, were "sitting in the house of learning, occupied with the study of Torah."

The portrayal of Dinah is juxtaposed to this. Please remember that she had been earlier introduced as a ploy in the Divine's chastisement of Jacob; the reader soon learns more details about that event. As Jacob and his sons were sitting in the house of learning, studying the Torah, Dinah went abroad to see the dancing and singing women. Please note carefully how differently the males and the female are portrayed: men are sitting in the house, occupied with the study or Torah. The woman went abroad. Given all the connotations of "going abroad," especially in contrast to sitting in the house (temple/synagogue) studying Torah, the reader may negatively construe Dinah and her actions.

A similar tradition juxtaposing Dinah to her father and brothers may be found in *Ecclesiastes (Eccl.) Rabbah* X. 8.1:

> … And whoso breaketh through a fence, a serpent shall bite him: i.e. Dinah. While her father and brothers were sitting in the House of Study, she went out to see the daughters of the land (Gen XXXIV, 1). She brought upon herself her violation by Shechem the son of Hamor the Hivite, who is called a serpent, and he bit her; as it is written, And Shechem the son of Hamor the Hivite, the prince of the land, saw her, and he took her, etc. (ib. 2).[10]

Legends I:395 makes it clear that Shechem had hired singing and dancing women to entice Dinah forth, away from her land and people.[11] Shechem had premeditated his actions; the dancing and singing women are part of his ploy to lure Dinah. For some readers, this interpretation may construe a much more negative impression of Shechem; Dinah may be viewed as a more innocent "victim," who simply went out to see these women. Unfortunately, a very knowing and calculating person had contrived the situation for what he thought was his own benefit. In today's terms, one might call Shechem a predator with a history of premeditated rape. One may also wonder if the dancing/singing/festivities also helped to set the narrative stage for sexual improprieties.[12] Such details are not given in Genesis.[13]

Shechem's actions are portrayed more clearly in *The Legends of the Jews*. In Genesis, there is ambiguity over whether or not Dinah was raped.[14] Here in *Legends*, the narrator's language is stronger and clearer; I:395 reads, "When Shechem caught sight of her, he seized her by main force, young though she was, and violated her in beastly fashion." To a modern reader, obviously, mention of "force" and beastly violation scream "rape."[15]

There are other differences between *Legends* and the Genesis narrative about Dinah as well. Genesis 34:5 had stated that the sons of Jacob were out with Jacob's cattle, not with Jacob involved in Torah study, when Shechem encountered Dinah. Also, *Legends* comments that Dinah was young when this happened. Genesis has no information about her age. Furthermore, the biblical account contains no mention of dancing singing women which Shechem had hired to entice Dinah. Genesis simply stated, "Dinah went out to see the women of the region" (v. 2).

As is true of some other texts encountered in this study, *Legends*, is quite frequently critical of Dinah. The criticism against Dinah is lodged in the above quote from *Eccl. Rabbah*—"she brought upon herself her violation ..." Along similar lines, on I:395, the narrator states that nothing would have happened to her had she remained at home. And the narrator on I:395 groups Dinah together with all womankind, stating that she, like all women, liked to "show themselves in the street."

Dinah is frequently associated with her mother, Leah, who often serves as the woman to whom Dinah is compared. Note 285 on V:313 refers to *Gen. Rab.* 80.1 and the parallels cited by Theodor, in which "the biblical saying 'as the mother so the daughter' (Ezek. 16.44) is applied to Dinah and Leah, both of whom allegedly liked to go out to be 'looked upon.'"[16] Note both the agency given to and the valuing done to Leah and Dinah. There is also an intriguing mixture of action, intent, and passivity—they liked to go out to be looked upon. While painting both mother and daughter negatively in this passage, the ancient rabbis struggled to determine what it meant to say or infer that Leah, their ancestral mother was a harlot![17]

It was not so problematic to dub Dinah negatively; the concept related to the above, that Dinah was a gadabout, is scattered throughout *The Legends of the Jews*. In many of these contexts, Dinah is linked with other matriarchs, Eve, and even with Miriam:

> ... The daughters of Zion were haughty and walked with stretched forth necks and wanton eyes; Sarah was an eavesdropper in her own tent. When the angel spoke with Abraham; Miriam was a talebearer, accusing Moses; Rachel was envious of her sister Leah; Eve put forth her hand to take the forbidden fruit, and Dinah was a gadabout.[18]

The above sounds very close to *Gen. Rab.* 18.2:

> R. Joshua of Siknin said in R. Levi's name: Wayyiben is written, signifying that He considered well (*hithbonnen*) from what part to create her. Said He: 'I will not create her from [Adam's] head, lest she be swelled-headed; nor from the eye, lest she be a coquette; nor from the ear, lest she be an eavesdropper; nor from the mouth, lest she be a gossip; nor from the hand, lest she be light-fingered; nor from the foot, lest she be a gadabout; but from the modest part of man, for even when he stands naked, that part is covered.' And as He created each limb He ordered her, 'Be a modest woman.'

Yet in spite of all this, *But ye have set at nought all My counsel, and would none of My reproof* (Prov. I, 25). I did not create her from the head, yet she is swelled-headed, as it is written, *They walk with stretched-forth necks* (Isa. III, 16); nor from the eye, yet she is a coquette: *And wanton eyes* (ib.); nor from the ear, yet she is an eavesdropper: *Now Sarah listed in the tent door* (Gen. XVIII, 10); nor from the heart, yet she is prone to jealousy: *Rachel envied her sister* (ib. XXX, 1); nor from the hand, yet she is light-fingered: *And Rachel stole the teraphim* (ib. XXXI, 19); nor from the foot, yet she is a gadabout: *And Dinah went out*, etc. (ib. XXXIV, 1).[19]

Here the rabbis trace what they considered to be negative characteristics of the matriarchs, directly connecting them with Divine disappointment. The very traits which the Divine had attempted to eschew in creating Eve were visited upon Sarah, Rachel, and Dinah. Note the narrator's clear conclusions that these characteristics, especially when found in females, are marks of immodesty which disappoint the Creator and err from the Creator's will for women. One may certainly note the misogyny inherent in such passages.

To speak of the alleged errant women *Legends* I:66 uses language which is highly reminiscent of the Bible; they walked about with "outstretched necks." Such rhetoric may be found in Isa. 3:16; Neh. 9:16–17; and Jer. 7:26, 17:23, and 19:15. As can be seen from *Gen. Rab.* 18.2, the rabbis interpreted Dinah's going out as indicative of her being a gadabout.

One may critique the blame that these ancient and some modern commentaries deposit on women dubbed as licentious. This viewpoint unfortunately is in keeping with problematic modern views that blame the survivor/victim for the crime committed against her. Forms of this blame can focus on the woman's appearance (including how she was dressed/her beauty), where she was (location/if alone), and her attitude (she liked to be looked at/she was haughty). A classic example is the rape of Trisha Meili that occurred in Central Park in 1989. Some were quick to ask, "What on earth was she doing jogging there by herself? Didn't she know how dangerous the Park is for a woman alone?" The inference evidently suggests that by jogging alone in Central Park, a woman is "asking for" rape/mugging/trouble. Unfortunately, one may find this reaction in many cases—both modern and ancient. Does a sense of agency, specifically going or being somewhere, necessarily make one responsible for what happens to her in that location? How and why is blame placed upon the woman?

One of the addditional elements of shame in the sexual union of Dinah and Shechem was that he was not circumcised. Ginzberg's text draws a sharp distinction between those who were circumcised and those who were not. Jacob could/should have given his daughter to one who was circumcised (Esau); because he refused to do so, she was first taken illicitly by Shechem, who was not circumcised. Even after that outrage, she was taken in marriage by Job; neither Shechem nor Job was circumcised.[20] If one reads from the perspective of the narrator, this aspect entails another level of shame for both Jacob and Dinah.[21]

As one considers the situation involving Dinah and Shechem, some ancient writers accused Dinah of not wanting to leave Shechem, once she had had sexual intercourse with him. For example, *Gen. Rab.* 80.11 alleges that Dinah had to be dragged away from the uncircumcised man Shechem! That passage reads:

> AND TOOK DINAH OUT OF SHECHEM'S HOUSE AND WENT FORTH: R. Judah said: They dragged her out and departed [n. 6 alleging that she did not want to go]. R. Hunia observed: When a woman is intimate with an uncircumcised person, she finds it hard to tear herself away. R. Huna [also] said: She pleaded, "*And I, whither shall I carry my shame?*" (II Sam. XIII, 13), until Simeon swore that he would marry her.[22]

It is interesting to see how Dinah is portrayed by some of the ancient rabbis, as a woman who found it hard to "tear herself away" from a man with a foreskin! This is one of the few texts which attribute any thought, feeling, or will to Dinah. It is intriguing that Dinah and/or her union with Shechem is so highly sexualized in this passage. It is also quite ironic that supposedly a marriage promise from a full-brother could move Dinah beyond her attraction to/desire not to "tear herself away" from the uncircumcised Shechem.

One must also pause at this point to consider the various details with which the rabbis struggled. One, of course, was whether or not Dinah wanted to be separated from Shechem. Obviously, this would indicate that the prince was still alive at the time Dinah was taken/dragged away. Second, Rabbi Huna's comment indicates that he ascribed a sense of shame or disgrace to Dinah; that is, accordingly, Dinah felt shame. Here too one may wonder about Simeon's "adopting" her as his wife as an antidote to her having been humbled/shamed by her encounter with Shechem. The parallelism between her and Tamar, of 2 Samuel 13, is that neither of the women wanted severance from the men who had violated them. Tamar had begged Amnon not to send or cast her away; apparently the rabbis construed Dinah as someone who did not wish to be taken from Shechem.

Even though the reader is provided here with detail about Dinah's mindset, i.e., her not wanting to leave, overall the text portrays her as an object. The passage began "and took Dinah …," and it concludes, "Simeon swore that he would marry her." Dinah's alleged refusal to leave the person Shechem is enveloped between those two phrases, both of which present Dinah as the object.

These texts are indeed concerned with how various people reacted to the sexual violation of Dinah. The character of Jacob is differently developed in *Legends* than in Genesis on the matter of his wanting to "fetch Dinah from Shechem's house" (as is found on I:396).[23] First of all, please note how she is here presented as the object of the verb "fetch." This is one of few times when Jacob is portrayed as wanting to retrieve his daughter from Shechem's house. Nothing comparable may be found in Genesis; in fact, one of the baffling elements of the Genesis narrative is the narrator's lack of developing Jacob's character. As some scholars have done, the reader of Genesis 34 may conclude that Jacob was comfortable with the intermarriage of Dinah to Shechem.[24] That is not the case in *Legends*.

According to *Legends*, Jacob wanted to extricate Dinah from Shechem; he sent twelve servants to get her and bring her back to him. When these twelve arrive in Shechem, the reader gains an even more negative view of the man Shechem; Shechem is said to have kissed and embraced Dinah in front of the twelve servants. He seemed to have been overly comfortable displaying, in fact, flaunting his power and hold over Dinah.[25] As a second means of "getting through" to Dinah, after the failed attempt at fetching her from Shechem, Jacob sent two maidens to stay with Dinah in Shechem's house; I:399 further clarifies that Jacob had sent these two maidens to take care of Dinah. No such information appears in Genesis.

In *Legends*, Dinah is presented as being more active than she is in Genesis. One might notice the number of verbs of which she is the subject. In Genesis 34, Dinah is the subject only of one verb—"she went out" (Gen 34:1). In comparison, in this passage in *Legends*, she executes a fairly similar action on I:395, she "went abroad to see the dancing and singing women." She is also here the subject of four verbs which come in rapid succession. She heard the words (regarding the scheme of Shechem and Hamor on I:399), hastened, and dispatched one of her maidens, and informed Jacob and his sons of the conspiracy. The reader is also given the impression that one of the maidens, presumably one of the two sent by Jacob, did get into Dinah's presence and was at Dinah's dispatch. Indeed, one may conclude that Jacob's attempt to "take care of her" was extremely successful. Ironically, that attempt to care for her saved himself and his entire household/clan. The maiden and Dinah proved to be vital links in the chain of people who saved Jacob and his household, by informing Jacob and his sons of the conspiracy against them. In short, here in *Legends*, Dinah plays an active role in diverting the plot against her people.[26] She may be thought of as an Esther-type of woman, who saved her people from destruction.

One place where *Legends* and Genesis agree is that they both reflect an understanding that the entire city of Shechem bore responsibility for Shechem's act; the men of Shechem were held liable for Shechem's deed. They paid with their lives. There is one instance, Gen 34:27, where the verb "violate" is plural—they violated her. This pluralized or democratized violation is used within the narrative as the justification for the actions of the sons of Jacob. According to *Legends*, the men of Shechem were all held responsible because no one spoke a word to Shechem, confronting him about his ravaging and committing fornication with Dinah (I:397).

One may wonder what the attitude of the Shechemites was toward Hebrew women. In the account found in *Legends*, there are a few comments which address the issue of exogamy and related social standing. For example, on I:396, it is said that Hamor tried to persuade Shechem "not to take a Hebrew woman to wife." One may conclude that exogamy was not most acceptable; however, Hamor was quick to relent. In the passage on I:398, where Shechem and Hamor were chided by Hadakkum and his six brothers for their having risked raising the ire of the indigenous people all "on account of a Hebrew woman," one may deduce that a Hebrew woman was of lower or at least a significantly different status. When one considers these comments in *Legends*, it must be noted that Genesis belies a different slant. One can find no comparable material in Genesis coming from the perspective of the Shechemites. Any concern over exogamous marriage in Genesis 34 comes from the point of view of the narrator and the sons of Jacob, most specifically, but not exclusively, Simeon and Levi. One may also note the introduction in *Legends* of the new character, Hadakkum. *Legends* adds the piece of information that Dinah, along with Shechem and Hamor, were in jeopardy of being killed by Haddakum and his six brothers (I:398). To our knowledge, Dinah was under no such peril according to Genesis 34. Nor were the Hebrews endangered by Shechem and Hamor, as they are according to this same passage, I:399, where it is said that the Hivite father and son had planned to attack and annihilate the Hebrews as soon as they became strong, after recuperating from their circumcision.

In light of the disdain for intermarriage, it is intriguing that according to *Legends* Simeon took the Canaanite Bunah as a wife (I:399–400); readers are told that Bunah was a very beautiful young woman, one among the eighty-five virgin captives taken from Shechem. *Legends* makes no derogatory or evaluative comment about Simeon's intermarriage with a Canaanite woman.[27] It seems to have one of the two marriages Simeon had; that is, he was married both to Dinah (as he had convinced her to leave Shechem and marry him) and to Bunah. Genesis 34 has no parallel explicit comment about Simeon's intermarriage, although one may conclude that there was intermixing when one reads Genesis 35, with its sharp Divine concern about and emphasis on foreign gods. Foreign gods and foreign women were often linked together in Jewish Scripture. One may indeed conclude that Simeon, Levi, and the other sons of Jacob had sexually intermixed with the women whom they had taken captive from the city of Shechem.

There is a passing remark in Genesis which speaks of Simeon's intermixing with a Canaanite woman. Genesis 46:10 comments that he had had a son with a Canaanite. In an effort to maintain the purity of Simeon's bloodline, some have suggested that the record "the son of a Canaanite woman" (Gen. 46:10) refers to Dinah.[28] If one interprets this to be a reference to Dinah, it is one of the three adjectives used of her.²⁹ According to Genesis 38, Judah had intermarried as well. Certainly, the traditions about exogamy/endogamy in Genesis are multivalent.³⁰

In Genesis, readers are left with ambiguity about Jacob's views on what had transpired at Shechem; this is true regarding his stance on intermarriage and it is true concerning his role in or knowledge of his sons' ruse at Shechem. While he is physically present at the marriage negotiations between him and his sons on the one side and Hamor and Shechem on the other side, his sons spoke and took the lead in setting the parameters for the nuptials. Jacob very much falls into the background of the narrative until the very end, when he confronts Simeon and Levi with his fear about the possible ramifications of what they had done. In *Legends*, Jacob plays a much more active and knowing part in what transpired at Shechem. There is even consultation with the former generation of Hebrew patriarchs. On I:397 Simeon and Levi claim that it was necessary to consult with Isaac before proceeding any further—they asked that in that interlude Shechem "stay away" from Dinah. Later in the narrative, in I:402, both Jacob and Isaac pray about the impending warfare.

The element of spirituality—any the mention of the Divine—whether as God, Lord God, or Lord, is also markedly different from Genesis 34. To see this very clearly, one may simply count the number of references to God and Lord in *Legends*.³¹ The Divine Being is presented as a primary active character in the narrative. In Genesis 34, the Divine is never mentioned; that is, God is an absent character.³²

In *Legends*, Judah argues on I:401 that God had "delivered the city of Shechem into their (Simon and Levi's) hand." This fourth-born son of Jacob and Leah³³ proceded to deliver a pep-talk to Jacob, replete with theological underpinnings, "The Lord our God is with us! Fear naught, then! ... The Lord is our God, He will save us." As the younger two generations march off to war, Jacob and Isaac fervently pray. They reiterate to the Divine the covenantal promises. Indeed, the attackers hear what the God of the Hebrews has done on behalf of God's people and they turn back.

The reader will note, in other chapters of the book, how God was often portrayed as an active participant in the slayings at Shechem; for example, in *The Testament of Levi* 5:3 and in Judith 9:2–3, God or an angel is said to have armed Simeon with a sword, enabling and empowering the revenge.³⁴ Simeon and/or Levi are deemed to have been carrying out "the judgment of God" (*Legends* II:195) or are portrayed as slaying the city because "Shechem had ... transgressed the command of our God."³⁵

In *Legends* I:394–403, Simeon and Levi exclusively bear full responsibility for the slaying at Shechem; Genesis 34:27 speaks about the actions of the (other) sons of Jacob. Many scholars, including myself, have concluded that Simeon and Levi went into Shechem first and did the actual slaying; the rest of the sons of Jacob then followed Simeon and Levi's initial onslaught and plundered the city. *Legends* attests to only the actions of Simeon and Levi; the text frequently speaks of how the two of them alone slaughtered an entire city[36] or entire cities, plural. Not only did they annihilate Shechem, according to *Legends*, but all the cities of the Amorites. For example, in a letter addressed to the viceroy of Egypt, Jacob asks, in II:93:

> … Or hast thou not heard what my two sons Simon and Levi did to the eight cities of the Amorites, which they destroyed on account of their sister Dinah?[37]

Please also note that the following passage (II:194–96) presents the situation differently; it is more in accordance with the details of Genesis. In Genesis 34, there is no mention of an Amorite reprisal for what the sons of Jacob had done at Shechem. In Gen 34:30 Jacob voiced a fear that the native peoples might assemble themselves and annihilate him and his household. In some places in *Legends* that fear materialized; the narrative includes the seven kings of Amorites assembling to fight against the sons of Jacob (I:401–3 and II:138). In some passages a battle/fight actually occurred; in other texts, such as I:403, once the Amorites heard of the reputation of both the sons of Jacob and their God, they turned back and did not pursue Jacob's clan. Regardless of whether or not militaristic engagement actually was said to have occurred, in *Legends* Simon and Levi are paired together. Their destruction of the eight cities is said to have taken place "on account of their sister Dinah." Their vengeance or violence is linked to Dinah, their sister. She and what had been done to her serve as narrative justification for the action(s) of her brothers.

Legends II:84–85, in which Joseph and his brothers were conversing, contains a very similar sentiment; this is one of the instances where the actions of Simeon and Levi was confined to Shechem. Joseph said to them, "Report hath told us that two of you did massacre the people of Shechem on account of the wrong done to your sister, and now have ye come down into Egypt (85) to kill the Egyptians for the sake of your brother."[38] The two events of retribution for wrong done to Dinah and wrong done to Joseph are also connected in III:199. "Just as Reuben interceded to save his brother Joseph's life so did Simeon rise up for his sister Dinah when he took vengeance upon the inhabitants of Shechem for the wrong they had done her."[39] The wrong done to Dinah and the massacre at Shechem are consistently connected. See for example, IV:259, where the fates of the various later kings of Judah are recounted. The pertinent passage reads: "At first Joash sought to turn Amaziah aside from his purpose by a parable reminding him of the fate of Shechem, which the sons of Jacob had visited upon him for having done violence to their sister Dinah. Amaziah refused to be warned."[40]

All throughout the series of quotes in the above paragraph, note that Dinah is consistently referred to as "sister." It was this sibling relationship which invariably came to the foreground of the narrators' minds when seeking justification for the revenge which took place either in Shechem alone or subsequently against the Amorite cities.

The passage presented first in this chapter, namely *Legends* I:394–403, closes with a new datum: a reference indicating that Sarah and Rebekah had also been endangered by the Shechemites. There is no such biblical parallel to this idea; however, one may be found in *T. Levi* 6:8. In fact, this entire section bears close resemblance to *T. Levi*.[41] The ending of *Legends* I:403[42] may indicate that the Hivites were one of the ancient peoples who married by abduction. This may also fit with the wife-sister motif in Genesis, that the matriarchs were often exposed to sexual jeopardy when met by a foreign ruler.[43]

The astute reader may also wonder about the number of women within Jacob's household. One may also conclude that there must have been a fair number of unattached/available women in Jacob's clan to make intermarriage an attractive option for the men of Shechem. There are passages in *Legends* which pose the question whether Dinah was Jacob's only daughter. *Legends* V:319 n. 309[44] asserts that there is a discrepancy among ancient texts regarding whether Dinah was Jacob's only daughter.

One may choose to follow the lead which *Baba Batra* provides. *Baba Batra* is a tractate of the Babylonian Talmud. The Talmud is described as:

> The authoritative body of Jewish law and lore accumulated over a period of seven centuries (c. 200 BCE–c. 500 BCE) in Erets Israel and Babylonia. The word Talmud derives from the Hebrew root *l-m-d* ("study" or teach").[45]

At this particular point, *Baba Batra* 123a, readers are privy to a discussion about the enumeration of Jacob's clan as they left for Egypt:

> Abba Halifa of Keruya enquired of R. Hiyya b. Abba: [With regard to those weho entered Egypt with Jacob] ... A twin [sister] was [born] with Dinah; for it is written, *With[eth] his daughter Dinah*. But if so, was there also a twin sister with Benjamin, for it is written With[eth] Benjamin, his brother, his mother's son?[46]

Many texts refer to Dinah when they list or name the people who accompanied Jacob to Egypt. It is in this context that one may find the sole other biblical reference to Dinah beyond Genesis 34. Genesis 46:15 makes the allegation that Dinah was a part of Jacob's clan who went to Egypt.

While I:394–403 is the longest passage relating to the events at Shechem, a similar, but highly condensed story, may be found in II:194–96. At this juncture of the narrative, Levi was about to die, and he had gathered his children around him. He recounts:

> (194) I entered the first heaven, and I saw a great sea hanging there, and farther on I saw a second heaven, brighter and more resplendent than the first. I said to the angel, "Why is this so?" And the angel said to me, "Marvel not at this, for thou shalt see another heaven, brilliant beyond compare, (195) and when thou hast ascended thither, thou shalt stand near the Lord, and thou shalt be His minister, and declare His mysteries to men; and of the Lord's portion shall be thy life, and He shall be thy field and vineyard and fruits and gold and silver."

> "Then the angel explained the uses of the different heavens to me, and all that happens in each, and he proclaimed the judgment day. He opened the gates of the third heaven, where I beheld the holy Temple, and God seated upon the Throne of Glory. The Lord spake to me: 'Levi, upon thee have I bestowed the blessing of the priesthood, until I come and dwell in the midst of Israel.' Then the angel carried me back to earth, and give me a shield and a sword, saying, 'Execute vengeance upon Shechem for Dinah, and I will be with thee, for the Lord hath sent me.' I asked the angel what his name was, and he replied: 'I am the angel that intercedes for the people of Israel, that it may not be destroyed utterly, for every evil spirit attacks it.'

> "When I awoke, I betook myself to my father, and on the way, near Gebal, I found a brass shield, such as I had seen in my dream. Then I advised my father and my brother Reuben to bid the sons of Hamor circumcise themselves, for I was quivering with rage on account of the abominable deed they had done. I slew Shechem first of all, and then Simon slew Hamor, and all my other brothers came out and destroyed the whole city. Our father took this in ill part, and in his blessing he remembered our conduct. Although we did a wrong thing in acting thus against his wishes, yet I recognized it to be the judgment of God upon the people of Shechem on account of their sins, and I said to my father: (196) 'Be not wroth, my lord, for God will exterminate the Canaanites through this, and he will give the land to thee and thy seed after thee. Henceforth Shechem will be called the city of imbeciles, for as a fool is mocked at, so have we made a mockery of them.'"[47]

In this passage it is clear that Levi perceived that God/the Lord was behind his own actions, speaking of an angel equipping him with a shield and a sword, exhorting him to execute vengeance for Dinah. Once again, Dinah and vengeance/violence are linked. The angel allegedly vowed to further accompany Levi, announcing that the angel was to intercede for Israel, especially when Israel was attacked by an evil spirit. The above passage bears a striking similarity to *T. Levi*.

The HB makes no unequivocal statement about God's stance in this matter at Shechem; *Legends* does. According to *Legends*, not only does the Divine arm Levi via an angel, Levi purports that he was exacting God's judgment upon Shechem. He presents himself as the vehicle by which God executes righteous vengeance. He is clear that Jacob did not perceive the situation in the same way. Please notice the extent to which the narrator's rhetoric uses the Divine. The Divine and Levi are reported to have been on the same side.

The two above parties are clearly against the city of Shechem. Here in *Legends*, the said city receives more of a negative portrayal; it is dubbed "the city of imbeciles."[48] Levi proceeds to recount, in accordance with Genesis, how "they" (the Shechemites) had committed an abominable deed meriting death.[49] This reference may also add another piece of evidence to support the claim that Shechem's transgression and guilt was democratized to his entire city. It could be the case, as it was in *Legends* I:397, that no one in Shechem had spoken out against their leader's misdeed with Dinah.

Here in the above passage, unlike the HB parallel, Levi clarifies that it was he himself who killed Shechem, that Simon slew Hamor, and then all the "other brothers came out and destroyed the whole city." Some other details found in *Legends* vary from those in Genesis; the HB account does not differentiate between the actions of Simeon and Levi; the two together are said to have slain Hamor and Shechem in Gen 34:26. The datum that the other sons plundered/destroyed the city is consistent between the two accounts. Jacob's negative judgment upon his sons is also similar in Genesis and *Legends*; in both cases, he reprimanded them, remembered their deed at/against Shechem upon his deathbed (in Genesis 49), and expressed his not being a part of their violent action. Unlike the HB account, in *Legends* it is clear that the sons of Jacob (Simon, Levi, and/or the others) had first consulted with Jacob and then acted against their father's wishes.[50] In Genesis 34, Jacob seemed easily duped by his sons; one may conclude after reading the biblical version that he was not in the circle of those "in the know" of what was transpiring at Shechem. In the HB Jacob's severance from his sons can be seen most clearly in Genesis 49. Similar sentiments to Genesis 49 may be found in *Legends* II:142–43:

> (142) After Reuben had had his "ears pulled" thus, he retired, and Jacob called his sons Simon and Levi to his side, and he addressed them in these words: "Brethren ye were of Dinah, but not of Joseph, whom you sold into slavery. The weapons of violence wherewith ye smote Shechem were stolen weapons, for it was not seemly for you to draw the sword. That was Esau's portion. To him was it said, By thy sword shalt they live. Into the council of the tribe of Simon my soul will not come when they foregather at Shittim to do vicious deeds, and my glory will not be united unto the assembly of Korah, the descendants of Levi. In their anger Simon and Levi slew the prince of Shechem, and in their self-will they sold Joseph the bull into slavery. Accursed was the city of Shechem when they entered to destroy it. If they remain

united, no ruler will be able to stand up before them, no war will prosper against them. Therefore will I divide and scatter their possession among the possessions of the other tribes. The descendants of Simon will many of them be poor men, who will wander from tribe to tribe and beg for bread, and also Levi's tribe will gather its tithes and gifts from all the others."

The words of Jacob, "I will divide them in Jacob", spoken of Simon and Levi, were fulfilled on Simon in particular. When twenty-four thousand of Simon fell at Shittim, the widows they left behind married husbands of all the other tribes. Nevertheless Jacob did not dismiss Simon and Levi without blessing them; the tribe of Simon was to bring forth the teachers and the beadles needed by all Israel, and Levi, (143) the scholars that would expound the Torah and render decisions according to its teachings.[51]

Here, as in Genesis, the emphasis is on what Jacob thought of his two sons, Simeon and Levi. First of all, notice that they are referred to as "brethren of Dinah." Their actions may be construed as signs of loyalty for her.[52] Furthermore, this incident at Shechem, as I had pointed out in *Sexual Violation in the Hebrew Bible*, is used by the Genesis narrator as an explanation for why Simeon and Levi fell out of honor/favor with their father.

Very frequently in my teaching these texts, my students and I invariably struggle with the HB's silence about what happened to Dinah after that fateful event at Shechem.[53] The only other information given about her may be found in Gen 46:15, where it is said that she was among those who migrated to Egypt.[54] That tradition is indeed reflected here in *Legends of the Jews*.

The context of the following quote is that the clan of Jacob is preparing for their journey to Egypt. Dinah is mentioned along with Joseph's other family members as having received gifts of clothing and various accessories from Joseph. *Legends* II:114–15 reads:

For each of his brothers' children, he sent raiments, and also one hundred pieces of silver for each, but for each of the children of Benjamin he sent ten changes of raiment. And for the wives of his brethren he gave them rich garments of state, such as were worn by the wives of the Pharaohs, and also ointments and aromatic spices. To his sister Dinah he sent silver and gold embroidered clothes, and myrrh, aloes, and other perfumes, and such presents he gave also to the (115) wife and the daughters-in-law of Benjamin. For themselves and for their wives the brethren received all sorts of precious stones and jeweled ornaments, like those that are worn by the Egyptian nobility.[55]

Dinah is portrayed here simply as the recipient of Joseph's generosity; grammatically speaking, she is the indirect object of the sentence/phrase which bears her name. This reference may indicate the close relationship between Joseph and Dinah. Some quotes yet to be investigated will claim that Joseph had married Dinah's daughter Asenath. That marriage may have been a factor in their closeness. *Legends* may also provide evidence of their loyalty/intimacy by connecting the timing of their deaths. *Legends* II:27, which has some parallelism with *Jub.* 34:15–16, maintains:

> They arranged a great memorial service, and they wept and mourned over Joseph's death and their father's sorrow. But Jacob refused to be comforted. The tidings of his son's death caused the loss of two members of Jacob's family. Bilhah and Dinah could not survive their grief. Bilhah passed away the very day whereon the report reached Jacob, and Dinah died soon, and so he had three losses to mourn in one month. He received the tidings of Joseph's death in the seventh month, Tishri, and on the tenth day of the month, and therefore the children of Israel are bidden to weep and afflict their souls on this day.[56]

Another midrashic reference linking Dinah and Joseph is *Gen. Rab.* 90.4; it deals with Pharaoh's renaming of Joseph. It is the accompanying footnote which refers to Dinah.

> AND PHARAOH CALLED JOSEPH'S NAME ZAPHENATH-PANEAH (XLI, 45) … R. Aha said: The name connotes: The one that was hidden here, though hast come to reveal her.[57]

The corresponding footnote reads:

> Possibly this is an allusion to an old legend that Dinah had a daughter by Shechem (v. Gen. XXXIV, 2), whom Jacob drove out of his home after having tied a disc round her neck to indicate that she was of his family. She was the Asenath whom Joseph married, but he saw the disc and hid it, so that her identity might not be known.[58]

Whereas Genesis is silent about Dinah's fate beyond her relocating to Egypt, more personal information about Dinah's marriages and children may be found in *Legends*. According to some the tradition reflected in some texts, Dinah had become pregnant with a daughter as a result of the sexual encounter with Shechem. The most complete narratives about Dinah and her daughter Asenath may be found in *Legends* II:37–38 and II:76–77. The first of these two claims that Dinah refused to leave the city of Shechem. In *Legends* II:37, the narrator attributes direct discourse to Dinah. This is one of the few times that she speaks. Incidentally, this text portrays her using the same language found in the HB on the lips of King David's daughter Tamar. When Dinah expressed her reluctance to leave the city of Shechem, her brother Simeon promised to marry her; he later acted in accordance with that vow. The rabbis sought to portray Simeon in a positive light; i.e., he fulfilled the vow he had made with his sister. First of all, this would distinguish him from his father Jacob; please recall the earlier discussion about how Dinah was dishonored as punishment for Jacob's neglecting a vow he had made. Second, Simeon is certainly contrasted with Amnon, who according to 2 Samuel 13 had refused to marry Tamar, even after he had raped her. In sharp contrast to Amnon, Simeon may be perceived to be a faithful, loyal, "good" brother of a wronged sister:

> Simon married his sister Dinah first, and then a second wife. (38) When Simon and Levi massacred the men of Shechem,[59] Dinah refused to leave the city and follow her brethren, saying, "Whither shall I carry my shame?" But Simon swore he would marry her, as he did later, and when she died in Egypt, he took her body to the Holy Land and buried it there. Dinah bore her brother a son …[60]

Some commentators allege that the tradition that Simeon and Dinah married was created somewhat haphardardly or "uncritically" (to use Ginzerg's language)[61] to protect Simeon from the shame of intermarriage with a Canaanite. One may note the tendency reflected in the rabbinic tradition seen in *Gen. Rab.* 80.11 which claims that it was Dinah who was Simeon's "Canaanite" wife. According to 80.11, she was referred to in this way either because she had acted like a Canaanite, had sexual relations with one (Shechem), or because she had been buried in the land of the Canaan.[62] The text continues:

> But Simon swore he would marry her, as he did later, and when she died in Egypt, he took her body to the Holy Land and buried it there. Dinah bore her brother a son, and from her union with Shechem, the son of Hamor, sprang a daughter, Asenath, by name, afterward the wife of Joseph. When this daughter was born to Dinah, her brethren, the sons of Jacob, wanted to kill her, that the finger of men might not point at the fruit of sin in their father's house. But Jacob took a piece of tin, inscribed the Holy Name upon it, and bound it about the neck of the girl, and he put her under a thornbush, and abandoned her there. An angel carried the babe down to Egypt, where Potiphar adopted her as his child, for his wife was barren, Years thereafter, when Joseph traveled through the land as viceroy, the maidens threw gifts at him, to make him turn his eyes in their direction and give them the opportunity of gazing upon his beauty. Asenath possessed nothing that would do as a present, therefore she took off the amulet suspended from her neck, and gave it to him. Thus Joseph became acquainted with her lineage, and he married her, seeing that she was not an Egyptian, but one connected with the house of Jacob through her mother …
>
> Beside the son of Dinah, Simon had another son, whose name was Saul, by Bunah, the damsel he had taken captive in the campaign against Shechem.[63]

One may note the extent to which Asenath's story is reminiscent of Moses'. Both were born under threatening or jeopardizing situations. They were found and adopted by Eygptian royalty; both were reunited with their people. Asenath is one of the means of reconnection/reconciliation between Dinah and her family. In the above quote it was Joseph who realized who Asenath was; in the next passage, notice that it is Potiphar who first made that discovery, based upon the plate on Asenath's neck.

In a number of passages, Dinah is depicted as a mother. In various texts she is said to have given birth to: the aforementioned Asenath, a son with Simeon, and ten children with Job.

> The name of Joseph's wife pointed to her history in the same way. Asenath was the daughter of Dinah and Hamor,[64] but she was abandoned at the borders of Egypt, only, that people might know who she was, Jacob engraved the story of her parentage and her birth upon a gold plate fastened around her neck. The day on which Asenath was exposed, Potiphar went walking with his servants near the city wall, and they heard the voice of a child. At the captain's bidding they brought the baby to him, and when he read her history from the gold plate, he determined to adopt her. He took her home with him, and raised her as his daughter. The Alef in Asenath stands for On, where Potiphar was priest; the Samek for Setirah, Hidden, for she was kept concealed on account of her extraordinary beauty; the Nun for Nohemet, for she wept and entreated that she might be delivered from the house of the heathen Potiphar; and the Taw for Tammah, the perfect one, on account of her pious, perfect deeds.
>
> Asenath had saved Joseph's life while she was still an infant in arms. When Joseph was accused of immoral conduct by Potiphar's wife and the other women, and his master was on the point of having him hanged, Asenath approached her foster-father, and she assured him under oath that the charge against Joseph was false. Then spake God, "As thou livest, because thou didst try to defend Joseph, thou (77) shalt be the woman to bear the tribes that he is appointed to beget."
>
> Asenath bore him two sons, Manasseh and Ephraim, during the seven years of plenty, for in the time of famine Joseph refrained from all indulgence in the pleasures of life. They were bred in chastity and fear of God by their father, and they were wise, and well-instructed in all knowledge and in the affairs of the state, so that they became the favorites of the court, and were educated with the royal princes.[65]

In a section speaking about the blessings which Jacob bestowed on his sons and grandchildren, *Legends* II:138–39 reads:

> Joseph received two gifts from his father. The first was (139) Shechem, the city that Jacob had defended, with sword and bow, against the depredations of the Amorite kings when they tried to take revenge upon his sons for the outrage committed there. And the second gift was the garments made by God for Adam and passed from hand to hand, until they came into the possession of Jacob. Shechem was his reward, because, with his chastity, he stemmed the tide of immorality that burst loose in Shechem first of all. Besides, he had a prior claim upon the city. Shechem, son of Hamor, the master of the city, had given it to Dinah as a present, and the wife of Joseph, Asenath, being the daughter of Dinah, the city belonged to him by right.[66]

The above passages refer to the marriage between Aseneth/Asenath,[67] Dinah's daughter, and Joseph. One can note how the possession of the city Shechem passed through the hands of two women—Dinah and Asenath—as it went from Shechem to Joseph. This may indicate that women were able to inherit/possess properties/territories. The idea of other sorts of inheritance passed on to daughters will shortly be investigated. In the end, at least according to this tradition, the city of Shechem had become Joseph's via his marriage to Asenath, Dinah's daughter.[68]

One may also notice here the contrast between Joseph, with his chastity, and "the tide of immorality … in Shechem!" There are other passages, specifically in *Joseph and Aseneth*, where Joseph is portrayed as pure to the core. If one were to examine closely the portrayal of the city of Shechem, this passage could be placed alongside previous ones which spoke of the ill-repute of the city.

When considering how the city of Shechem had come into the hands of the Hebrews, this passage reveals the tradition that Jacob had defended Shechem against the Amorites with sword and bow; a discussion could ensure over how this may fit with Gen. 48:22.[69] Other passages stated that Jacob was not aware of what his sons were doing, nor was he involved in battle, nor did any battle ensure. Here it is clear that Shechem, the man, had given the city to Dinah as a present. It had passed from Dinah to Asenath and then to Joseph.

When one wonders, furthermore, about what became of Dinah after the incident with Shechem, some sections of *Legends* refer to a marriage between Job and Dinah.[70] For example, II:225 comments:

> Job, the most pious Gentile that ever lived, one of the few to bear the title of honor 'the servant of God,' was of double kin to Jacob. He was the grandson of Jacob's brother Esau, and at the same time the son-in-law of Jacob himself, for he had married Dinah as his second wife.[71]

The same tradition may be found in *Legends* II:241:

> The Lord blessed Job, and in a few days his wealth had increased to double the substance he had owned before misfortune overtook him. Zitidos having died during the years of his trials, he married a second wife, Dinah, the daughter of Jacob, and she bore him seven sons and three daughters …

Thereupon he divided his possessions among his sons, and to his daughters he gave what is more precious than all earthly goods, to each of them one riband of the celestial girdle he had received from God. The magic virtue of these ribands was such that no sooner did their possessors tie them around their waists than they were transformed into higher beings, and with seraphic voices they broke out into hymns after the manner of the angels."[72]

Here it is alleged that Dinah had ten children with Job.[73] The text goes on to say how three named daughters of Job and Dinah witnessed the departure of their father on the "great chariot."[74] These texts certainly reflect an understanding that daughters could and did inherit gifts from their fathers. The daughters of Dinah and Job are said to have taken on a new form when they received the special gift from their father. One may note the parallelism between *Legends* and *Testament of Job* 46–52 pertaining to the inheritance of Job's and Dinah's daughters.

Twice in *Legends* Dinah is presented as one of two wives: Simeon had two wives (Dinah and Bunah); Job is also said to have had two (Zitidos and Dinah). At least in the latter case, the text clarifies that Job's first wife had died before he married Dinah.

The final sort of reference to Dinah regards her burial site. The notes of *The Legends of the Jews* provide information about Dinah's final resting place. *Legends* V:336 n. 96 asserts that "Dinah's body was brought from Egypt to Palestine, the medieval authors maintain that her grave is at Arbel."[75]

Genesis Rabbah 80.11 credits Simeon as being the one who took Dinah's body to *Eretz Israel*, "… Simeon took and buried her in the land of Canaan."[76] This is very similar to one of the lines found in *Legends* II:37, "When she died in Egypt, he [Simon] took her body to the Holy Land and buried it there."[77]

Ginzberg reminds readers in n. 436 on V:375 that "Jub. 34.16 states that she, [Bilhah] as well as Dinah, died in Palestine many years before Jacob, and was buried "over against the tomb of Rachel"; the Testaments followed Jub. …"[78] An exploration of *T. Levi* and *Jubilee*s is forthcoming.

CONCLUSIONS

The idea that Dinah was dishonored as a form of punishment upon Jacob is a recurrent theme in *Legends*; it is on I:395 and I:411–12.[79] The dishonoring of Dinah is presented as an element of the Divine's "curse" upon Jacob on I:395. Similarly I:411–12 reads, "If a man voweth a vow, and he does not fulfill it in good time, he will stumble through three grave sins, idolatry, unchastity, and bloodshed. Jacob had been guilty of not accomplishing promptly the vow he had taken upon himself at Beth-el, and therefore punishment overtook him—his (412) daughter was dishonored, his sons slew men, and they kept the idols found among the spoils at Shechem."[80] On I:411 Dinah is portrayed entirely passively, underscoring her lack of agency. *Legends* 1:395 portrays the divine announcing to Jacob that Dinah "will go abroad" and that she "will be humbled." In both instances, Dinah is presented as Jacob's daughter. The Divine "uses" the daughter to punish her father.

Other reasons for God's curse upon Jacob include Jacob's pride and his concealing Dinah in a chest, not wanting to give her to Esau in marriage (see *Genesis Rabbah* 76.9, as found in ch. 2 of this book). While this "misfortune" affected and involved Dinah in a very real, personal, and physical way, it was aimed primarily at Jacob.

A number of *Legends* texts mention that Jacob had erred; the details vary. One explanation is the haughtiness he exemplified before the Divine, asserting himself as the Divine's terrestrial counterpart. *Legends* I:395–96 offers another reason for God's disappointment in Jacob. Here it is said that the patriarch should have given Dinah to Esau in marriage. However, he refused to do this, keeping Dinah hidden away in a chest, safe from Esau's sight; God chastised Jacob for this by having Dinah "fall a victim to the ravisher's illicit passion." This same tradition of Jacob withholding Dinah from Esau may also be found in *Gen. Rab.* 76.9.[81] Apparently a man's viewing/seeing a woman could indeed lead swiftly to sexual activity.[82] This is the impression given by Gen 34:2 as well. *Legends*, however, makes it clear that because Jacob had kept Dinah from Esau, she was allowed by the Divine to fall prey to Shechem. No such tradition can be found in Genesis. Once again, readers may note Dinah's lack of agency.

Modern readers, especially those concerned with feminist interpretations and women's roles in these stories, may question legitimately the characterization of the Divine at this and other junctures of the story. One may criticize a G/god who "uses" sexual crimes against women as a punishment against a man. Something very similar may be seen in 2 Samuel 12:11, where the Divine threatens that David's wives/women were to be given to other men as a punishment for David's transgression with Bathsheba. Some see the rape of Tamar, David's daughter, by David's son, Amnon, as a direct working out of this Divine curse/punishment. If one truly entertains that as a possibility, one may conclude that women are not safe "in the hands of" this divine being. Women's predicaments were too precariously dependent upon the actions of their men and Divine response to those male actions.[83]

The Legends of the Jews offers readers much more information about Dinah and develops her character than did the narrator of Genesis. *Legends* claims that Dinah was dishonored as a punishment for Jacob. It relays traditions surrounding her birth, her marriages, her children, and her death. From this source, though there are variant traditions interwoven, one has a much different, and in fact, a much richer impression of Dinah and her life after the fateful events at Shechem.

CHAPTER TWO

Dinah IN Midrashic Texts FROM THE Ninth Century C.E. AND Earlier

INTRODUCTION TO MIDRASH

Within the last fifty years, there has been a resurgence of scholarly interest in and academic engagement of midrashic texts.[1] The point of intrigue for this project is the various ways in which midrashic materials portray the characters involved in the incident at Shechem, particularly Dinah. There was a fluidity of the biblical tradition during the midrashic period(s). The writers/editors of these texts used the scriptural tradition as a starting point. They added, changed, and deleted various elements of the biblical text to address their own concerns. As Gary G. Porton explains:

> In rabbinic literature, the terms [*drs* and *mdrs*] are intimately connected with the Hebrew Bible and designate the process by which one interprets, explains, corrects, or expounds the text as well as the interpretation, explanation, correction, or exposition itself.[2]

Some have maintained that the goal of this process was to link the historical/biblical text with the present; *midrash* was a process, a way of engaging biblical texts to make them relevant to the current situation.[3] For example, Mishael Caspi states, that homiletic literature, such as *Tanhuma*, "does not bridge the gaps in the story by offering interpretations but rather by offering current social values as explanation."[4] Thus, one can map the interaction or dialectic between the interpreter and the scriptural basis. There will be points throughout the ensuing commentary when this will be noted.

The various types/kinds of *midrashim* have been classified. Porton's work may be considered a starting point:

> An expositional *midrash* follows the text of a given biblical book. It is a running commentary on the book or a major section of the book. While individual sections may

have been created in settings different from the present contexts and may in fact have no real relationship to the comments which surround them, a relationship has been imposed upon them by the order of the biblical text. The homiletical *midrashim* are collections of independent units which do not form a running commentary on the biblical books. Each pericope has its own coherence, and that coherence is based on a given topic or the relationship of non-consecutive biblical verses. ... Genesis Rabbah and the midrash on Lamentation are the major expositional midrashim.[5]

When comparing or contrasting midsrashic texts, it will be easier to understand what Porton has written. Consider, for example, *Genesis Rabbah* 79.1–80.12, found within the next few pages. From even a cursory reading of the text, notice its overall outline; one can see that it generally follows Genesis 34 and serves as a "running commentary," to use Porton's words.[6]

Midrashic texts offer a host of traditions about Dinah; they include but are not limited to: explanations of why she was violated or defiled by Shechem; that she did not wish to leave Shechem, that she became pregnant with him, and that she subsequently married Simeon or Job. These fairly early midrashic texts[7] have many references to Dinah.

GENESIS RABBAH

Genesis Rabbah is regarded as an exegetical *midrash* on Genesis.[8] It interprets the story from Genesis, moving verse by verse through the text, providing comment and intertextual links between the verse under consideration and other biblical passages using word threads.[9] H. L. Strack and G. Stemberger write: "It offers partly simple explanations of words and sentences, partly short or elaborate haggadic interpretations and expositions, often only loosely tied to the text, which are frequently interlaced with maxims and parables."[10] To be sure, the text expounds upon the details given in the HB.[11]

Turning to issues of dating the piece, it is certain, due to a number of internal clues, such as references to Babylonian and Palestinian rabbis, and the ruler Diocletian that the text must have been written/compiled after 400 C.E.[12] It is most feasible to believe that "the final redaction of this midrash will have been … in the fifth century, and probably in its first half."[13] *Genesis Rabbah* is also important in that it is "the first complete and systematic Judaic commentary to the book of Genesis."[14]

It makes sense that the provenance of *Genesis Rabbah* was Palestine. As Strack and Stemberger note, "the prevalence of Palestinian rabbis"[15] and the language of the text ("primarily Hebrew with many Greek loan words, but some parts also in Galilean Aramaic"[16]) support this conclusion.[17]

Strack and Stemberger, as well as Moshe David Herr, note that *Genesis Rabbah* shares similar traditions with other contemporary writings/writers, e.g., Philo, Josephus, the Pseudepigrapha, and Deuterocanonical texts.[18] They conclude that common oral traditions prevalent in Palestine probably account for much of this overlap.[19]

With that brief introduction, *Gen. Rab.* 72.6 claims that the birth of Dinah was surrounded with female prophecy and miracles; it asserts that Dinah had been originally created/conceived male. Her gender was changed as a result of Rachel's prayer:

> AND AFTERWARDS SHE BORE A DAUGHTER (XXX, 21). We learned: If, for instance, one's wife is pregnant and he prays, 'May it be Thy will that my wife bears a son,' it is a vain prayer. The School of R. Jannai said: This was taught of one who is actually about to give birth. R. Judah b. Pazzi said: Even when she is actually about to give birth [the sex] can be changed. As it is written, *O house of Israel, cannot I do with you as this potter? saith the Lord. Behold, as the clay in the potter's hand, so are ye in My hand, O house of Israel* (Jer. XVIII, 6): (just as a potter can break a cruse after he has made it and make something else, so can I do likewise even at the hour of birth). An objection was raised: But it is written, AND AFTERWARDS SHE BORE A DAUGHTER? R. Abba replied: Actually she was created a male, but she was turned into a female through Rachel's prayers when she said, *The Lord add to me another son* (Gen. XXX, 24). Said R. Hanina b. Pazzai: The matriarchs were prophetesses, and Rachel was of the matriarchs. It is not written, '*The Lord add to me* others sons,' but '*another son*': she said: 'He is yet destined to beget one more; may it be from me!' All the matriarchs assembled and prayed: 'We have sufficient (*dayyenu*) males; let her [Rachel] be remembered.[20]

First of all, the footnote corresponding to the word *dayyenu* in this passage indicates that "Rashi conjectures that this may be based on the name Dinah, which is connected with *dayyenu*, 'we have enough.'"[21] In other words, the matriarchs had decided that they had enough boys; they and their prayers deemed it time for a baby girl to be born. And so it was. This is the only reference in *Genesis Rabbah* containing the tradition that Dinah had been conceived male.[22] A very similar tradition, that is, that Dinah was first conceived male may be found in *Tanhuma* 8.18. The references show rabbinic discussion over how long during pregnancy the gender of the fetus was considered malleable.

Genesis Rabbah 72.6 is also important in that it is one of the few passages that speak about the powerful spiritual/magical influences of the matriarchs. The reader is here given a positive impression of the early women. They had the abilities to survey the situations in which they stood, to pray for change, and to affect the status quo. Although it is possible that these qualities were not always accepted or understood, one may note that other midrashic passages portray the matriarchs much more negatively.

As mentioned earlier, these two data sets exemplify the way in which the writers/editors of *Genesis Rabbah* expounded upon the material found in the HB, quite possibly revealing something about the times in which they lived and the questions over which people struggled.

One of the struggles was with whom to initially associate Dinah. Some references speak of or introduce Dinah specifically as Leah's daughter, often drawing out parallels between Leah and Dinah.[23] One may even reconsider the above passage's reference not only to Leah, but the other matriarchs. A number of passages shift the focus onto the biological link between Jacob and Dinah. That is, Dinah is referred to as "Jacob's daughter." Please note that Genesis 34 refers to Dinah both as Leah's daughter and as Jacob's daughter. Whereas the Genesis narrative may leave the contemporary reader stumped to decide for herself/himself who might have been at fault at Shechem, numerous midrashic texts are fairly quick not only to indict the women of the texts, but Jacob as well. Numerous texts allege that Jacob had committed a transgression which led directly to Dinah's defilement. For example, *Gen. Rab.* 73.9 connects Jacob's righteousness,[24] or specifically his lack thereof, to Dinah's misfortune:

> SO SHALL MY RIGHTEOUSNESS WITNESS AGAINST ME TO-MORROW (XXX, 33). R. Judah b. Simon said: It is written, *Boast not thyself of to-morrow* (Prov. XXVII, 1), yet thou sayest, SO SHALL MY RIGHTEOUSNESS WITNESS AGAINST ME TO-MORROW—to-morrow thy daughter will go out and be violated, as it says, *And Dinah the daughter of Leah went out*, etc. (Gen. XXXIV, 1)[25]

There were apparently a number of wrongs that may have gotten Jacob into trouble with the Divine. The above passage references his boasting. *Genesis Rabbah* 79.8, in similar fashion but with greater detail, indicates that Jacob had become too haughty, asserting himself as a "god in the terrestrial sphere." It is alleged that because of Jacob's misdeed, Dinah was dishonored. A similar thought, also connected with Jacob's assertion that he was "a god in the terrestrial sphere," may be seen in 80.4.[26]

Still other passages refer to Jacob concealing Dinah in a chest. *Genesis Rabbah* 76.9 alleges that Jacob had hidden Dinah from Esau[27];

> AND HE ROSE UP THAT NIGHT AND TOOK HIS TWO WIVES, AND HIS TWO HANDMAIDS AND HIS ELEVEN CHILDREN (XXXII, 23). Where then was Dinah? He put her in a chest and locked her in, saying, 'This wicked man has an aspiring eye; let him not take her away from me.' R. Huna said in the name of R. Abba Bardela the Priest: The Holy One, blessed be He, said to him: '*To him that is ready to faint kindness is due from his neighbor* (Job VI, 14): thou hast withheld kindness from thy neighbor; when thou gavest her in marriage to Job, didst thou

not convert him? Thou wouldst not give her in marriage to a circumcised person [Esau]; lo! She is now married to an uncircumcised one! Thou wouldst not give her in legitimate wedlock; lo! She is now taken in illegitimate fashion'; thus it is written, *And Dinah the daughter of Leah ... went out*, etc. (Gen. XXXIV, 1).[28]

In a number of these passages, Dinah's predicament resulted from something Jacob had neglected to do. In the above passage, it is said that he would not give her in marriage to Esau in legitimate or lawful wedlock. Thus she was taken illegitimately by one who was not circumcised. Fairly similar traditions may be found throughout the *midrashim*; e.g., *Gen. Rab.* 80.4 speaks of Jacob as withholding kindness from his brother/Esau and that because he had done so, she was taken illegitimately. *Tanhuma* 8.19[29] contains very similar elements: it states that it was because of Jacob's sin that "the uncircumcised one" came upon Dinah. It also has reference to Jacob's putting Dinah in a chest so that Esau would not be able to see her. This is one of the very few passages in which Jacob shows any concern for Dinah. He seemed to fear Esau's taking Dinah, when he exclaimed "Let him not take her away from me." This is one of the places where the bond between father and daughter is mentioned.[30]

Genesis Rabbah 76.9 also chides Jacob for having missed an opportunity to convert Esau. It cites Dinah's marriage to Job, claiming that through Dinah, Jacob had converted Job. One of Jacob's faults, or at least an accusation against him, was that he had withheld kindness from his neighbor/brother Esau by withholding Dinah from him. *Genesis Rabbah* 80.4 similarly presents the patriarch as someone who could have converted Esau. *Tanhuma* 8.19, however, makes reference to Dinah, not Jacob, as the agent of conversion.[31]

Even though Dinah is given or had a reputation of having been a positive influence on Job, there are times when these same texts refer to her marriage to Job. There he is said to have spoken of her as "vile" or "foolish." What a strange and interesting irony that this so-called foolish vile woman converted the pious Job! In *Gen. Rab.* 19.12 and 57.4, Job referred to Dinah, his wife, as "one of the vile women" (*nebaloth*). In *Gen. Rab.* 19.12, she is "vile" because Job had to resist her exhortations (he alleges that unlike Adam, he had resisted his wife). *Genesis Rabbah* 57.4 clarifies that Job considered her "vile" because she had been violated by Shechem.

Genesis Rabbah 19.12 reads, "R. Abba b. Kahana said: Job's wife was Dinah, for he said to her: *Thou speakest as one of the vile women* (nebaloth) *speaketh* (ib.10)."[32] The accompanying footnote reads: "While of Dinah it is written: *Because he had wrought a vile deed (nebalah) in Israel in lying with Jacob's daughter.*"[33] Very similar expressions to *Gen. Rab.* 19.12 may be found in *Gen. Rab.* 57.4: "R. Abba b. Kahana said: Dinah was Job's wife (for in the case of Job's wife it is written, '*Thou speakest as one of the foolish women* (nebaloth) *speaketh* (ib. II,10), while with respect to Dinah, it says, *Because he had wrought a vile deed* (nebalah) *in Israel* (Gen. XXXIV,7).'"[34]

One could inherit or attain disgrace (or the condition or status of being "vile") as a result of something done to her; I have explored such Hebraic reasoning in ch. 1 of *Sexual Violation in the Hebrew Bible*.[35] In these two cases from *Genesis Rabbah*, Dinah is considered "vile" or "foolish" because of Shechem's misdeed against/with her.

On multiple occasions, Jacob's and Dinah's actions were used to warn people against unrighteousness or unrighteous deeds. If a woman could inherit disgrace because of or as a result of another's actions against her, women must be incredibly careful. Some midrashic references were didactic, aimed at teaching men and women how they should live/behave.[36] One aspect of such teaching was that people were to know/learn/be taught their "proper place" in society. Men were admonished to "master their wives"; women were encouraged to stay out of the market place. Women and women's behavior(s) were to be controlled by men. Dinah's misfortune was used to scare women into staying "at home" or within their proper spheres or domains; Dinah becomes representative of "every woman." For example, in *Gen. Rab.* 8.12, the following statement is made: "every woman who goes out into the market place will eventually come to grief." What happened to Dinah became generalized or applied to "every woman." Her misfortune was used as a warning to both women and men, in the case of *Gen. Rab.* 8.12, illustrating the horror of what could happen if one dared to—or was allowed to—go out:

> '*We-kibshah*' (and subdue her) is written: the man must master his wife, that she go not out into the market place, for every woman who goes out into the market place will eventually come to grief. Whence do we know it? From Dinah, as it is written, *And Dinah … went out*, etc. (Gen. XXXIV, 1)[37]

In the above passage, as noted in the previous chapter, the rabbis asserted that Dinah's act of going out brought upon herself the grief/trouble she encountered. One can compare the line of thought found here with the proverbial "If you smile at or dare to be so bold as to talk with a man, you could get pregnant." The illogical yet proverbial "one thing leads to another" thinking overrides. Many significant, and in fact, critical steps are omitted! A similar thought pattern may be detected in *Tanhuma* 8.12, which will be explored later in this chapter. There it is made clear that "All the time that she was sitting at home she was not corrupted by transgression; but, as soon as she went out into the marketplace, she caused herself to come to the point of corruption."

Another related argument could be made about the way in the rabbis here portray the danger inherent in a woman's being seen. Although Genesis 34 and some of these midrashic texts move very quickly through the series of verbs: he saw, took, lay with, and violated her, such a clear and direct line is drawn between seeing or being seen and being violated. Much of the above paragraph comes into play in this instance as well. Significant steps are omitted! What about the man's taking and lying with a woman? Many of these texts and traditions focus undue attention and blame on the woman.

A number of passages from the Torah reveal the danger inherent in being seen. One needs only to consider the three wife-sister motifs of Genesis 12, 20, and 26. The Dinah incident is another such case. Judah of Genesis 38 is very quick to approach Tamar: "When Judah saw her, he thought her to be a prostitute, for she had covered her face. He went over to her at the road side, and said, '"Come, let me come in to you,' for he did not know that she was his daughter-in-law" (vv. 15–16).

One can indeed note the setting of these different passages. Judah met Tamar on the roadside. In the above passage one can note that Dinah is said to have gone out into the marketplace. I am not necessarily insinuating/stating that Dinah was sexually violated there. The rabbis add this marketplace setting or it had been present in oral tradition affiliated with Genesis 34. Note that the biblical account never mentioned a marketplace: Dinah had gone out to see the women of the land/region. This element is introduced here and may also be found in *Tanhuma*. If one chooses to follow the HB legal material, even regarding rape laws, one could note that if transgressions occurred in a public place (in the city), the woman was held more accountable, as it is presumed that she did not protest the man's sexual advances. See, for example, Deut. 22:23–24.[38]

A modern reader may, of course, challenge the above advice to men and to women. One may see the scare tactics in the philosophy that "every woman who goes out into the marketplace will eventually come to grief." How many women went out and returned home safely every day? How many women were involved in "marketplace behaviors" (commerce, etc.) and never had anything horrific happen to them? How many stayed home and met fates similar to those of Dinah? In today's world, of course, we must acknowledge how many women are violated in their own homes. In all too many situations involving domestic abuse, the home is anything but a safe refuge from the outside world. For biblical ancient support of this later point, one can cite the story of King David's daughter Tamar, in 2 Samuel 13, who was raped by her own half-brother in his chamber. Aside from the errancy of presumed safety within one's own house/household, we can also challenge the inherent problems of the archaic language of "mastery" of one person over another. These texts exhort men to control or master their wives/daughters.

One may also, of course, question the presumptions regarding "sitting at home" women and women who "go out." In regards to this issue, one of my students wrote, "this phrase implies a lot of social norms for women in this period. Would she really have been 'sitting' at home? The woman's job throughout the household would rarely have allowed her to sit."[39] It would be interesting to know who, that is, what groups of women, were targeted by these messages. Was it the woman with the small business, selling goods at the marketplace? Certainly the rabbis were not advocating that women passively sit around the house! How was a woman to "win" during this time period? It was alleged, on the one hand, that idleness led to certain trouble; going out, on the other hand, led to different kinds of troubles.

In this discussion, one can see how Dinah was "typed" or labeled throughout these texts. The most complete passage regarding Dinah, *Gen. Rab.* 79.1–80.12, follows:

CHAPTER LXXIX (VAYYISHLACH)

1. 'AND JACOB CAME SHALEM (E.V. 'IN PEACE'), etc (XXXIII, 18) *He will deliver thee in six troubles, yea, in seven there shall no evil touch thee* (Job V, 19). Whether there are six or seven, [said Jacob], I will withstand them. *In famine He will redeem thee from death (ib.* 20)*—For these two years hath the famine been in the land* (Gen. XLV, 6); *And in war from the power of the sword* (Job loc. cit.)*—It is in the power of my hand to do you hurt* (Gen. XXXI, 29) *Thou shalt be hid from the scourge of the tongue* (Job V, 21): R. Aha said: Slander is so cruel a thing that having created It [the tongue] He [God] made a place for it where it may be hidden. *Neither shalt thou be afraid of destruction when it cometh (ib.)*—that alludes, Laban who hungered for his [Jacob's] wealth to rob him. *For thou shalt be in league with the stones of the field (ib.* 23)*—And he took of the stones of the place* (Gen. XXVIII, 11). *And thou shalt know that thy tent is in peace* (Job V, 24): that is an allusion to the incidents of Reuben and Bilhah, and Judah and Tamar. *And thou shalt visit thy habitation, and not sin (ib.):* Jacob was eighty-four years old, yet had never experienced any nocturnal discharge. *Thou shalt know also that thy seed shall be great,* etc. *(ib.* 25): R. Judan said: Jacob did not depart from the [728] world until he saw thirty myriads of his descendants. *Thou shalt come to thy grave in ripe age—be-kelah (ib.* 26); R. Isaac and the Rabbis disagree. R. Isaac rendered: Thou shalt come with full vigour *(laklukith)* to the grave. The Rabbis interpreted: Thou shalt come with everything *(kulah)* to the grave, full and lacking nought, even as it says, AND JACOB CAME SHALEM (WHOLE).

2. *A Song of Ascents. Much have they afflicted me from my youth up, let Israel now say* (Ps. CXXIX, 1). Said the Holy One, blessed be He, to him: 'Yet have they prevailed against thee?' *They have indeed not prevailed against me (ib.* 2); thus, AND JACOB CAME SHALEM (WHOLE). *Many are the ills of the righteous,* etc. (Ps. XXXIV, 20). *'Many are the ills'* alludes to Esau and his chiefs; *'the righteous,'* to Jacob; *But the Lord delivereth him out of them all (ib.)*—AND JACOB CAME SHALEM (WHOLE). *The Lord shall guard thy going out and thy coming in, from this time forth and for ever* (Ps. CXXI, 8). *'Thy going out'—And Jacob went out* (Gen. XXVIII, 10); *'And thy coming in'—*AND JACOB CAME IN PEACE.

3. R. Hiyya b. Ba commenced thus: *If thou art pure and upright,* etc. (Job VII, 6). Not, *'If thou* wast *pure and upright'* is written, but *'If thou* art,' etc., implying, even if one had not been righteous in the past. *Surely now He will awake for thee, and make the*

habitation of (newath) *thy righteousness prosperous* (*ib.*). He will rouse Himself on thy account and reward thee for the benefit [to others] [729] of the righteous deeds which thou hast performed. Thus, since it is written, *And Jacob was a whole-hearted man* (Gen. XXV, 27), therefore, AND JACOB CAME IN PEACE.

R. Berekiah commenced thus: *Thou shalt also decree a thing, and it shall be established unto thee, and light shall shine upon thy ways* (Job XXII, 28). *'Thou shalt also decree a thing, and it shall be established unto thee'* alludes to Jacob; *'And light shall shine upon thy ways':* upon thy two ways light shall shine. Forasmuch. as it is written, *If God will be with me* (Gen. XXVIII, 20), [God assured him]: *And, behold, I am with thee: And will keep me—and will keep thee* (*ib.* 15); *So that I come back to my father's house in peace* (*ib.* 20)—AND JACOB CAME IN PEACE.

4. *They that sow in tears shall reap in joy* (Ps. CXXVI, 5). *'They that sow in tears'* applies to Jacob, who sowed the blessings in tears—*My father will peradventure feel me* (Gen. XXVII, 12); *'Shall reap in joy'*—*So God give thee,* etc. (*ib.* 28). Though he goeth on his way (Ps. *ob. cit.*)—*Then Jacob went on his journey* (Gen. XXIX, 1); *weeping—And he lifted up his voice, and wept* (Gen. XXIX, 11); *That beareth the drawing* [E.V. *'measure'*] *of seed* (Ps. *ob. cit.*)—he drew his seed and went on. *He shall come home with joy, bearing his sheaves*—*alumothaw* (*ib.*)—behold him returning bearing his young men and young women.

5. AND JACOB CAME WHOLE. Bodily whole: forasmuch as it is written, *And he limped upon his thigh* (Gen. XXXII, 32), [it tells us that] here in truth he was bodily [730] whole. Whole in respect of his children. For it is written, *And he said: If Esau come to the one camp, and smite it,* (Gen. XXXII, 9); in truth, however, he returned whole with [all] his children. 'Whole' in his wealth. For though R. Abin said in R. Aha's name: For nine years he honoured Esau, with that gift, yet in truth he was now whole in his wealth. R, Johanan said.: Whole in his learning; but Joseph forgot his, as it says, *For God hath made me forget all my toil* (*ib.* XLI, 51). (While elsewhere it says, *The soul that toileth, toileth for himself* (Prov. XVI, 26).

6. AND ENCAMPED (WAYYIHAN) BEFORE (ETH PENE) THE CITY (XXXIII, 18). He showed his regard (*hanan*) for the important men (*panim*) of the city by sending them gifts. Another interpretation of AND ENCAMPED BEFORE THE CITY; he began to set up bazaars and sell cheaply. This teaches that a man must be grateful to a place whence he derives benefit.

R. Simeon b. Yohai and his son were hidden in a cave for thirteen years. Their food consisted of withered carobs, until their bodies broke out in sores. At the end of this period he [R. Simeon] emerged and sat at the entrance of the cave and saw a hunter engaged in catching birds. Now whenever R. Simeon heard a heavenly voice exclaim from heaven, 'Mercy!' it escaped; if it exclaimed, 'Death!' it was caught. 'Even a bird is not caught without the assent of Providence,' he remarked; 'how much more then the life of a human being!' Thereupon he went forth and found that the trouble had subsided. Then they went and [731] bathed in cold baths. Said his son to him: 'Father, Tiberias has done us so much good; shall we then not purify it from the dead?' What did he do? He took lupines, cut them up, and threw down the pieces, whereupon the corpse would come up, and they carried it without the city, until they thus purified it from the dead. At night a certain peasant arose—some say, from the corn market, while others say, from the sack market—took a corpse and hid it. In the morning he said: 'Do you not maintain that the son of Yohai has purified Tiberias? Come and see a corpse there!' He then went and stood over it: 'I decree that he who is standing should lie down [dead] and that he who is lying [the corpse] should stand up [alive],' and so it happened. He then departed to spend the Sabbath at home. Passing Magdala of the Dyers he heard the voice of Nakai the Scribe saying: 'Have you not said that the son of Yohai has purified Tiberias? Yet it is now said that a corpse has been found there! May I be struck down if I am not in possession of as many laws as the hairs of my head to prove that Tiberias is clean apart from such-and-such a place.' 'Were you not with us when a vote was taken [whereby it was declared clean]? You have broken the fence set up by the Sages, *And whoso breaketh through a fence, a serpent shall bite him*' (Eccl. X, 8). Straightway he went out and this happened to him.

He then passed through the valley of Beth Tofah, when he saw a man standing and gathering the aftergrowth of [732] the Sabbatical year. 'Is this not the aftergrowth of the Sabbatical year?' he demanded. 'But you yourself have permitted it,' he retorted. (For did we not learn thus: R. Simeon said: All aftergrowths are permitted, except, the aftergrowth of the cabbage, because there is none like it among the vegetables of the field.) 'But my colleagues dispute this,' he retorted. Forthwith he lifted his two eyebrows and looked at him, whereupon he became a heap of bones.

Another interpretation of AND ENCAMPED BEFORE THE CITY: he entered on the eve of the Sabbath] at sunset and appointed his boundaries while it was yet day. This proves that Jacob kept the Sabbath before it was given.

7. AND HE BOUGHT THE PARCEL OF GROUND, etc. (XXXIII, 19). R. Judan b. R. Simon said: This is one of the three places regarding which the nations of the world cannot taunt Israel and say, 'Ye have stolen them.' These are they: The cave of Machpelah, the [site of the] Temple, and the sepulchre of Joseph. The cave of Machpelah: *And Abraham weighed to Ephron the silver* (Gen. XXII, 16). The Temple: *So David gave to Ornan for the place six hundred shekels of gold* (1 Chron. XXI, 25). And Joseph's sepulchre: AND HE BOUGHT THE PARCEL OF GROUND ... [733]

[FOR A HUNDRED KESITAH]. R. Abba b. Kahana said: That means for a hundred precious stones, a hundred [734] sheep, and a hundred *selas*. R. Simon said: The *kuf* stands for *hamilyah* (jewels), the *teth* for *Titrion*, the *samek* for *sela 'im*. What then is the purpose of the *yod heh?* R. Joshua of Siknin said in R. Levi's name: [The word KESITAH denotes the ornaments and hyacinths which are set in ear-rings. Who writes the deed [of purchase]? Said R. Berekiah: Jah writes the deed. And who attests the deed? Jah attests the deed. Thus it is written, *Whither the tribes went up, even the tribes of Jah* [the Lord], *as a testimony unto Israel, to give thanks unto the name of the Lord* (Ps. CXXII, 4), which means, Jah [the Lord] testifies that they are the children of their parents.

8. AND HE ERECTED THERE AN ALTAR, AND CALLED IT EL-ELOHE-ISRAEL (XXXIII, 20). He [Jacob] declared to Him: 'Thou art God in the celestial spheres and I am a god in the terrestrial sphere.' R. Huna commented in the name of R. Simeon b. Lakish: [God reproved him]: 'Even the synagogue superintendent

cannot assume authority of himself, yet thou didst take authority to thyself.' To-morrow thy daughter will go out and be dishonoured!" Hence it is written, *And Dinah the daughter of Leah went out*, etc. (Gen. XXXIV, 1). [735]

CHAPTER LXXX (VAYYISHLACH)

1. AND DINAH THE DAUGHTER OF LEAH WENT OUT (XXXIV, 1) … 'What is meant by the verse, [736] "*Behold, everyone that useth proverbs shall use this proverb against thee, saying: As the mother, so her daughter?* Said he:'Like the daughter so is the mother, like the generation so is its leader (*nasi*), like the altar so are its priests.' Kahana says: According to the garden so is its gardener. 'You have not yet completely appeased him for the first,' Resh Lakish exclaimed, 'and you are already bringing him another! What is really the meaning of this verse?' 'A cow does not gore unless her calf kicks; a woman is not immoral until her daughter is immoral,' he replied. 'If so,' said he, 'then our mother Leah was a harlot!' 'Even so,' he replied 'because it says, *And Leah went out to meet him* (Gen. XXX, 16), which means that she went out to meet him adorned like a harlot'; therefore AND DINAH THE DAUGHTER OF LEAH WENT OUT.

2. *And as troops of robbers wait for a man,* etc. (Hosea VI, 9): as robbers sit in the road, slay people and seize their wealth—did Simeon and Levi act thus in Shechem? Therefore Scripture continues: *The company of priests:* as a company of priests assemble, at a threshing floor to receive their portion [the priestly dues], so did Simeon and Levi act in Shechem: *They murder in the way toward Shechem, because they have committed whoredom (ib.).* Simeon and Levi acted in Shechem with a reason, *And they said: Should one deal with our sister as with a harlot* (Gen. XXXIV, 31). Said they: What mean they by treating us as public property? And what caused this? The fact that DINAH THE DAUGHTER OF LEAH WENT OUT, etc. [737]

3. *The thistle that was in Lebanon sent to the cedar* (II Kings XIC, 9). '*The thistle that was in Lebanon*' alludes to Hamor the father of Shechem; '*Sent to the cedar*' alludes to Jacob, [to whom he said,] *Give thy daughter to my son to wife' (ib.)*—*The soul of my son Shechem longeth for your daughter* (Gen. XXXIV, 8). *And there passed by the wild beasts that were in Lebanon, and trod down the thistle* (II Kings *loc. cit.*)—*And they slew Hamor and Shechem his son* (Gen. XXXIV, 26). What was responsible for this? The fact that DINAH THE DAUGHTER OF LEAH WENT OUT.

4. R. Judah b. Simon commenced: *Boast not thyself of to-morrow* (Prov. XXVII, 1), yet you [Jacob] have said, *So shall my righteousness witness for me to-morrow* (Gen. XXX, 33) To-morrow your daughter will go out and be violated. Thus it is written, AND DINAH THE DAUGHTER OF LEAH WENT OUT.

R. Huna commenced in the name of R. Abba Bardela the priest: *To him that is ready to faint kindness is due from his friend* (Job VI, 14). The Holy One, blessed be He, reproved him: 'Thou hast withheld kindness from thy brother; when she married Job, didst thou not convert him? Thou wouldst not give her in marriage to one who is circumcised [Esau]; lo! she is married to one who is uncircumcised. Thou wouldst not give her in legitimate wedlock; lo! she is taken in an illegitimate fashion'; thus it is written, AND DINAH WENT OUT. R. Simeon b. Lakish commenced: *And he erected there an altar, and called it El-elohe-Israel* (Gen. XXXIII, 20). He [Jacob] declared to Him: 'Thou art God in the celestial spheres and I am a god in the terrestrial sphere.' R. Huna commented in the name of R. Simeon b. Lakish: [God reproved him]: 'Even the synagogue superintendent cannot assume authority of himself, yet thou didst take authority to thyself!' To-morrow thy daughter will go out and be dishonoured,' as it is written, AND DINAH WENT OUT, etc. [738]

5. R. Joshua of Siknin commenced in R. Levi's name: *But ye have set at nought all My counsel* (Prov. I, 25). Thus it is written, *And the Lord built the rib* (Gen. II, 22). This is written *wayyiben*, signifying that He considered well *(hithbonnen)* from what part to create her. Said he: 'I will not. create her from [Adam's] head, lest she be light-headed [frivolous]; nor from the eye, lest she be a coquette; nor from the ear, lest she be an eavesdropper; nor from the mouth, lest she be a gossip; nor from the heart, lest she be prone to jealousy; nor from the hand, lest she be light-fingered; nor from the foot, lest she be a gadabout. But [I will create her] from the modest part of man, for even when he stands naked, that part is covered.' And as He created each limb, He ordered her, 'Be a modest woman, be a modest woman.' Yet in spite of all this, *"But ye have set at nought all My counsel,' and would none of My reproof.* I did not create her from the head, yet she is frivolous: *They walk with stretched-forth necks* (Isa. III. 16); nor from the eye, yet she is a coquette: *And wanton eyes (Ib.);* nor from the ear, yet she is an eavesdropper: *Now Sarah listened in the tent door* (Gen. XVIII, 10); nor from the heart, yet she is prone to jealousy: *Rachel envied her sister (ib.* XXXI, 19); nor from the hand, yet she is light-fingered: *And Rachel stole the teraphim (ib.* XXXI, 19); nor from the foot, yet she is a gadabout: AND DINAH WENT OUT.

AND DINAH THE DAUGHTER OF LEAH WENT OUT. R. Berekiah said in R. Levi's name: This may be compared to one who was holding a pound of meat in his hand, and as soon as he exposed it a bird swooped down and snatched it away. Similarly, AND DINAH THE DAUGHTER OF LEAH WENT OUT, and forthwith, AND SHECHEM THE SON OF HAMOR SAW HER. R. Samuel b. Nahman said: Her arm became exposed. [739]

AND HE TOOK HER AND LAY WITH HER—in a natural way; AND HUMBLED [i.e. VIOLATED] HER—unnaturally.

6. NOW JACOB HEARD THAT HE HAD DEFILED DINAH HIS DAUGHTER ... AND JACOB HELD HIS PEACE *(*XXXIV, 5). Thus it is written, *But a man of discernment holdeth his peace* (Prov. XI, 12).

AND THE SONS OF JACOB CAME IN FROM THE FIELD WHEN THEY HEARD IT (XXXIV, 7). Issi the son of Judah said: In five Scriptural texts there is a word which may be taken either way; viz. *se'eth*—bearing (Gen. IV, 7), *arur*—cursed *(Ib.* XLIX, 7), mahar—to-morrow (Ex. XVII, 9); *meshukadim*—almond-shaped *(ib.* XXV, 34); *wekam*—and will rise up (Deut. XXXI, 16). R. Tanhuma added the present verse [which may read either], AND THE SONS OF JACOB CAME IN FROM THE FIELD WHEN THEY HEARD IT, or, When they heard it the men were grieved. But in fact Scripture says nought else but, AND THE SONS OF JACOB CAME IN FROM THE FIELD WHEN THEY HEARD IT.[2]

WHICH THING OUGHT NOT TO BE DONE—even among the nations, because after the world had been smitten in the generation of the Flood they arose and eschewed immorality.

7. AND HAMOR SPOKE WITH THEM, SAYING (XXXIV, 8). R. Simeon b. Lakish said: The Holy One, blessed be He, manifested His love to Israel with three expressions of love, *debikah* (cleaving), *hashikah* (love), and *hafizah* (delighting in). *Debikah: But ye that did cleave* (hadebekim) *unto the Lord your God* (Deut. IV, 4). *Hashikah: The Lord did not set His love* (hashak) *upon* [740] *you ... because ye were more in number than any people* (ib. VII, 7). *Hafizah: And all nations shall call you happy; for ye shall be a delightsome* (hefez) *land* (Mal. III, 12). Here we learn them from the passage dealing with this wretch [Shechem]. *Debikah: And his soul did cleave* (Gen. XXXIV, 3); *hashikah: The soul of my son Shechem longeth* (hashekah) *for your daughter* (ib. 8); *hafizah: Because he had delight (hafez) in Jacob's daughter* (ib. 19). R. Abba b. Eliashib added another two: *ahabah* (love) and *dibbur* (speech). *Ahabah: I have loved you*—ahabti (Mal. I, 2); *dibbur: Speak* (dabberu) *to the heart of Jerusalem* (Isa. XL, 2). And we learn them from the passage dealing with this wretch: *Ahabah: And he loved* (wayye'ehab) *the damsel* (Gen. XXXIV, 3); *dibbur: And spoke* (wayyedabber) *to the heart of the damsel (ib.)* Can then a man speak to the heart? But it means with words that comfort the heart. He said to her: 'See how much money your father expended for a single field how much more will I, who can give you ever so many fields for planting and sowing!'

AND MAKE YE MARRIAGES WITH US, etc. (XXXIV, 9). R. Eleazar said: The Israelite never puts his finger into the heathen's mouth first unless the heathen first puts his finger into the mouth of the Israelite. [Thus they proposed], MAKE YE MARRIAGES WITH US, [though it is written], *Neither shalt thou make marriages with them* (Deut. VII, 3).

ASK ME NEVER SO MUCH DOWRY (MOHAR) AND GIFT—MATTAN (XXXIV, 12). MOHAR is dowry; MATTAN is the addition.

8. AND THE SONS OF JACOB ANSWERED SHECHEM ... WITH GUILE, etc. (XXXIV, 13). R. Samuel b. [741] Nahman said: What think you: that we have a case of deceit here? [No, for] the Holy Spirit states, BECAUSE HE HAD DEFILED DINAH THEIR SISTER (*ib.*)

AND SAID UNTO THEM: WE CANNOT DO THIS THING, TO GIVE OUR SISTER TO ONE THAT IS UNCIRCUMCISED, FOR THAT WERE A REPROACH UNTO US (*ib.* 14). R. Hunia said in the name of R. Justi b. Tabath: Where do we find that uncircumcision is called a reproach [shame]? From this text: FOR THAT WERE A REPROACH [SHAME] UNTO US.

SHALL NOT THEIR CATTLE AND THEIR SUBSTANCE AND ALL THEIR BEASTS BE OURS (*ib.* 23)? They thought to despoil them [sc. Jacob and his sons] and were themselves despoiled.

AND UNTO HAMOR AND UNTO SHECHEM HIS SON HEARKENED ALL THAT WENT OUT OF THE GATE OF HIS CITY (XXXIV, 24). When any one of them entered the city laden with his wares they said to him, 'Come and be circumcised,' while he would reply, 'Shechem is marrying her and Magbai must be circumcised!' ... [742][40]

9. THAT THE TWO SONS OF JACOB, SIMEON AND LEVI, TOOK EACH MAN HIS SWORD. Since it says, SIMEON AND LEVI, do we not know that they were Jacob's sons? But SONS OF JACOB teaches that they did not take counsel with Jacob. SIMEON AND LEVI—they did not take counsel with each other.

DINAH'S BRETHREN. Was she then the sister of these two [only] and not the sister of all the tribal ancestors? She is called by their name, however, because they risked their lives for her sake. Similarly we read: *And Miriam the prophetess, the sister of Aaron, took a timbrel in her hand* (Ex. XV, 20): *Aaron's sister and not Moses' sister?* But because Aaron showed special devotion to her, she [743] was called after him ...

... EACH MAN HIS SWORD. R. Simeon b. Eleazar said: They were then thirteen years old.

AND CAME UPON THE CITY CONFIDENTLY. Samuel asked Levi b. Sissi: What is the meaning of AND CAME UPON THE CITY CONFIDENTLY? They felt confident in the strength of the patriarch, he replied. Now Jacob had not desired that his sons should act so, but when his sons did perpetrate that deed he said: 'Shall I let my sons fall into the hands of the heathens?' What did he do? He took his sword and bow and stood at the entrance to Shechem and exclaimed, 'If the heathens come to attack my sons, I will fight them.' It was to this that he alluded, when he said to Joseph, *Which I took out of the hand of the Amorite with my sword and with my bow* (Gen. XLVIII, 22). And where do we find that our father Jacob took up his sword and bow?—In Shechem.

10. AND TOOK DINAH OUT OF SHECHEM'S HOUSE, AND WENT FORTH. R. Judah said: They dragged her out and departed. R. Hunia observed: When a woman is intimate with an uncircumcised person, she finds it hard to tear herself away. R. Huna [also] said: She pleaded, *'And I, whither shall I carry my shame?'* (II Sam. XIII, 13), until Simeon swore that he would marry her. Hence it is written, *And the sons of Simeon ... and Shaul the son of a Canaanitish woman* (Gen. XLVI, 10): (this means, the son of [744] Dinah who was intimate with a Canaanite). R. Judah said: It means that she acted in the manner of the Canaanites. R. Nehemiah said: It means that she was intimate with a Hivite [Shechem] who is included in the Canaanites. The Rabbis said: [She was so called because] Simeon took and buried her in the land of Canaan.

11. AND JACOB SAID TO SIMEON AND LEVI: YE HAVE TROUBLED ME (XXXIV, 30). The Rabbis commented: The vat was clear, and ye have muddied it. The Canaanites have a tradition that they will one day fall by my hand, but the Holy One, blessed be He, has stated: *Until thou be increased, and inherit the land* (Ex. XXIII, 30)— to sixty myriads. R. Judah b. Simon said: [They answered]: 'The vat was muddied,

and we have purified it. AND THEY SAID: SHOULD ONE DEAL WITH OUR SISTER AS WITH A HARLOT (XXXIV, 31)? 'Will they treat us as common property,' they exclaimed. What caused all this? The fact that *Dinah went out'* (*ib.* 1).[41]

In *Gen. Rab.* 79.2 there is reference to the "ills of the righteous." One can see the parallelism between this and the traditions which portray Jacob bemoaning his travails; for example, in *Gen. Rab.* 84.3, Jacob speaks of the sorrows/difficulties that befell him through Dinah:

> *I was not at ease, neither was I quiet* (*ib.* III, 26). *'I was not at ease'*—from Esau; *'Neither was I quiet'*—from Laban; *Neither had I quiet* (*ib.*)—through Dinah; *And trouble came* (*ib.*)—through Joseph ...[42]

Through Jacob's first-person perspective, the reader is told that he did not feel himself to be "in peace" or whole, as he had when he had first entered Shechem as reported in Gen 33:18. He is given the voice/role of focalizor, i.e., the reader learns from him firsthand. "He" (i.e., his character) forthrightly tells the reader/hearer of his unrest. In fact, there is another passage, *Gen. Rab.* 84.21, which asserts that Jacob's suffering with Dinah was said to be so intense that his knowing her was portrayed as regrettable:

> AND ALL HIS SONS AND ALL HIS DAUGHTERS ROSE UP TO COMFORT HIM (XXXVII, 35) ... ALL HIS DAUGHTERS? How many daughters then did he have? One, and would that he had not known her.[43]

Whereas some of these quotes speak of Jacob's sufferings over the incident involving Dinah, Genesis was silent about his emotional state. Instead, according to the biblical account, it was his sons who were deeply grieved when they had heard what Shechem had done to their sister. Shechem's transgression deeply affected the wholeness of the family.

Genesis Rabbah 79.5 above speaks of the wholeness/well-being/peace (*šlm*) of Jacob and his family upon their entrance into the land. One may note the "before—after" difference in their arrival at and departure from Shechem. At the beginning of this episode Jacob and his children were whole/safe/at peace. An element of the ancient rabbis' positive portrayal of Jacob was his setting up bazaars, at which he would sell goods at reasonable/low prices.[44] This practice was hailed as a mark of his gratitude to the city. It was not too long before things went awry for Jacob, his daughter, and the rest of his family. As I had stated earlier, things changed very quickly in the narrative. This particular passage from *Genesis Rabbah* indicates that Jacob became too haughty, asserting himself as god of the land. Because of Jacob's misdeed, Dinah was dishonored.[45] This represents one thread throughout the midrashic material.[46]

One may pause to note how different things were at this point. Dinah was defiled; she was no longer "whole." As the narrative progresses the rabbis debate the ramifications of Dinah's going out. For example, in *Gen. Rab.* 80.1, they read into the text of Genesis 30:16, that Leah had gone out to meet Jacob adorned like a prostitute. The likening of her to a prostitute is not at all present in the biblical narrative. By introducing it at this point, the rabbis align Leah's going out with Dinah's going out. Note that the women are painted increasingly negatively. Both mother and daughter were associated with immorality and harlotry.[47] The claim was made that each generation of women had a negative impact on the other. Here specifically, it is stated that "a woman is not immoral until her daughter is immoral." Dinah's actions negatively reflected upon her mother, in fact, causing Leah to become immoral.[48]

When considering how Dinah was portrayed, it is important to note the refrains of numerous midrashic passages. *Genesis Rabbah* 80.2, 3, and 12 asked and answered, "And what caused this? The fact the DINAH ... WENT OUT." In both *Gen. Rab.* 80.2 and 80.12, her going out was said to be the cause of their (the clan of Jacob's) being treated as common/public property, AKA "a harlot." Not only Dinah, but her family, is treated in this way by Shechem and his group. *Genesis Rabbah* establishes a causal relationship between Dinah's going out and her people's "being treated as a whore."[49] Furthermore it claims a causal relationship between her going out and Shechem and Hamor's death; for this, please see *Gen. Rab.* 80.3.

Her act, her going out, not Shechem's act of defiling her, becomes part of the refrain of this passage and is alleged to be the proverbial ball which got this debacle or debauchery rolling. This is problematic on many different levels. Foremost is the issue of placing the blame on a victim/survivor; this is true even within the context of *Genesis Rabbah*. How interesting that in *Gen. Rab.* 80.6 the rabbis succinctly state that even among the nations, Shechem's action was morally deplorable. One must ask why the refrain was not written in such a way that would point a finger repeatedly at Shechem for his heinous offense. The perpetrator's guilt was compromised by the consistent refrain which asserted that Dinah had erred.

In all fairness to the ancient commentators, one can see the rabbis' negative evaluation of Shechem. It is stated in *Gen. Rab.* 80.2 that they had committed "whoredom;" presumably this refers to Shechem and the men of his city. The guilt of the man Shechem was democratized to his whole city. His offense is so bad that in *Gen. Rab.* 80.7, Shechem is characterized as a "wretch." However, Shechem's words of alleged or professed love for Dinah (found in Gen. 34:3) are used by the rabbis in an attempt to demonstrate how loving he was toward Dinah. These professions of love are then used to speak of how loving the Divine is towards Israel.[50] The Divine and Shechem are compared in a manner that needs to be challenged! It is highly problematic to have the Divine compared to a sexual violator, unless the rabbis were identifying with Dinah, feeling violated. There may have been elements in the fourth/fifth century which might suggest that this is plausible. Dinah was portrayed frequently as comparatively passive and silent. She was consistently the object of Shechem's longing, love, and obsession.[51] She was never given a speaking voice; she never served as focalizer. She was, however, consistently blamed for going out.

When considering ancient rabbinic works, one obvious trend was to assign blame to Dinah. Naomi Graetz's work, "Dinah the Daughter," articulately places *Genesis Rabbah* within a longer line of tradition, which includes Ben Sirach; an aspect of this inheritance is a negative view of daughters and a tendency to blame the woman.[52] Graetz maintains that another stream of interpretation is reflected in these very same texts; this alternate view portrays Dinah more positively, oftentimes presenting her as the victim. These passages are inclined to focus on Dinah as Asenath's mother, Job's wife, or Simeon's wife.[53] It is as though either a good marriage (be that to Job or Simeon) or birthing a good daughter "redeems" what had happened to Dinah.[54] To use Graetz's language, these passages "glorified the mother-wife role, and denigrated any signs of female initiative or other deviations from the norms of the period."[55] For example, Dinah played the role of Asenath's mother; Asenath was said to have later married Joseph. Via this connection through Dinah, Joseph's marriage was proper, i.e., endogamous. One line of thinking was that Dinah's trials at least resulted in a baby girl who played an important role in Israel's story. Even within one midrashic text, *Genesis Rabbah*, these seemingly diverse portrayals of Dinah may be found.

One may pause to consider this vacillation and, especially in the case of *Genesis Rabbah*, note the historical importance of the time during which this text was compiled. Neusner wrote:

> Genesis Rabbah came to closure, all scholars generally concur, sometime after the end of the fourth century. The document in its final form therefore emerges from that momentous century in which the Roman Empire passed from pagan to Christian rule, and in which, in the aftermath of Juliam's abortive reversion to paganism. Christianity adopted the politics of repressing paganism that rapidly engulfed Judaism as well. The issue confronting Israel in the Land of Israel therefore proved immediate—the meaning of the new and ominous torun of history, the implications of Christ's worldly triumph for the otherworldly and supernatural people, Israel, whom God chooses and loves.[56]

This may be connected with the character Dinah. Dinah, whether complicit with Shechem or raped, found herself pronounced defiled, violated, and unclean. Many Jewish traditions found themselves in a similar situation; they were pronounced "illegitimate" by the Roman Empire which now allied itself with Christianity. For the editors of *Genesis Rabbah* to struggle with the character of Dinah was profound. In some regards like Dinah, they had been deemed "unacceptable."

There may have been some efforts to review the recent past and to determine what and where things went awry. Some may have asked themselves if there was anything they may have done, or not done, which may have brought on the situation. Did they possibly do anything to call unwanted attention to themselves? Certainly, the question, "Where to go from here?" rang true for many. The traditions of Dinah, especially where Job or Asenath were concerned, may have offered great hope at this particular historical time. Through someone who was considered or deemed "defiled" new life sprang up—even conversions happened! New Jewish life could still be a reality.

That may have been the angle from which the rabbis engaged this text. It is intriguing to see the various references to the reactions of Simeon and Levi. Much has been written regarding the historical implications of taking the side of Simeon and Levi, on the one hand, or of Jacob, on the other.[57] In *Gen. Rab.* 80.2, the rabbis pose the question whether the two sons of Leah and Jacob stalked their prey as troops of robbers. However, they quickly conclude that Simeon and Levi acted with reason—they murdered, but only because they (the men of Shechem) had committed whoredom. Furthermore, because their sister had been dealt with as a harlot, treating the whole Hebrew people as "public property," the actions of Simeon and Levi were justified. Here the two maternal brothers of Dinah are compared to priests.

The rabbis uphold them and Jacob furthermore in *Gen. Rab.* 80.7, where it is said that since they did not initiate the intermarriage, it was acceptable. They were deemed justified in speaking with deceit in *Gen. Rab.* 80.8. Also in that same passage, the rabbis found affirmation for their concern about giving Dinah to a man who had not been circumcised. In *Gen. Rab.* 80.10, the rabbis spoke of how "Dinah's brothers" risked their lives for her; her brothers are portrayed heroically, coming to Dinah's defense. The brothers do all this without Jacob's knowledge. Thus the patriarch is omitted from responsibility in his two sons' ruse at Shechem.

This passage, 80.10, also contains one of the few midrashic references to the age(s) of any of these characters, stating that Simeon and Levi were thirteen years old. Here the two sons of Leah and Jacob are considered to be the same age. Does this insinuate that they were twins? That does not line up with the biblical account. Lastly, if one imagines that they were thirteen, this would make Dinah eleven or so (allowing for the birth of Judah in between the two aforementioned and Dinah). These barely teens are portrayed coming swiftly and independently to their young sister's defense. Each, allegedly on his own, armed himself with his sword and came confidently upon the city of Shechem.

At that point, when his two sons had begun fighting "the heathens," Jacob took his sword and joined in. The enemy/heathen is here referred to as the Amorites.[58] The passage from *Genesis Rabbah* links this Amorite reference to Gen. 48:22. What is presented in Genesis as two separate events is telescoped or blended together in *Genesis Rabbah. Gen. Rab.* 80.10 conflicts with other passages; it was more typical for the rabbinic traditions to keep Jacob at bay from militant action. Many midrashic texts, following Genesis 34, had forthrightly asserted that no war broke out because the terror of God had descended upon the Canaanites. This passage veers from that trend.

When one pauses at the point in the story of *Genesis Rabbah* where the sons of Jacob were leaving the city Shechem after annihilating it, one may notice that some rabbinic traditions offer various explanations for biblical characters. For example, *Gen. Rab.* 80.11 claims that Dinah did not want to leave Shechem; the reason given is that women find it hard to tear themselves away from an uncircumcised man! Dinah is definitely "sexualized" by this text.[59] This may be an attempt to portray her in a negative light, as a "bad" woman who wanted more sex with this uncircumcised man. Ironically, it is presumed that the vow of her full-blood brother Simeon to marry her quickly moved Dinah beyond her obsession with the uncircumcised Shechem.

This same reference (80.11) from *Genesis Rabbah* further besmirches Dinah's reputation by speaking of her as a Canaanite. She is referred to as such, as the text says, either because she had acted as one, had had sexual relations with one, or because she was buried in Canaan by Simeon.

It is possible to note the predispositions of the rabbis' attitudes toward people who were defined as "others." According to one of my student's papers, "Societal differences play a large role in this interpretive text. The constructs of xenophobia in the period of these stories, and the period in which the text is written affect the comments that these rabbis make. Rabbi Judah says that Dinah acted like a Canannite (*Gen. Rab.* 80.11). Although she might have been forced into intercourse with a Hivite, Dinah is still considered to have joined that cultural sphere. This seems to mark her as a Canaanite for the rest of her life."[60] Indeed it did, for the "rest of her life" and beyond. There are many modern interpreters who see Dinah as one who was "open to the other."[61]

Furthermore, this passage collapses Dinah's character with that of Tamar, King David's daughter, who was concerned about where she would/could carry her shame related to Amnon's rape. It does, at least, give a speaking voice to Dinah. Her character informs the reader/hearer that she had acquitted shame as a result of what Shechem had done to her. Dinah's character was worried about how she would carry/deal with that shame. In response to this shame, *Genesis Rabbah* introduced the idea of a marriage between Dinah and Simeon. Here again, the midrashic text parts way with the biblical account. Not only do Dinah and Simeon marry, *Gen. Rab.* 80.11 speaks of their producing a son together. It also protects Simeon from an exogamous marriage with a Canaanite woman, by claiming Dinah was the Canaanite with whom he had a son.

As this passage from *Genesis Rabbah* closes, it rejoins the stream of tradition found in Genesis 34; Jacob's household was in danger of being annihilated, and Jacob feared for his and his household's very existence. His sons had exterminated the men of Shechem, thus jeopardizing Jacob and all who belonged to his clan.

Amidst this threat, his two sons maintained their stance. They and Jacob stood divided. The rabbis entered into the debate, dividing along the lines of Jacob on the one side and his two sons on the other. Some held, as did Jacob, in *Gen. Rab.* 80.12, that "the vat was clear and Simeon and Levi muddied it." Others maintained, as did the two brothers of Dinah, that "the vat was muddied, and we have purified it." This section comes to a close raising two questions, "Should one deal with our sister as with a harlot? Will they treat us as common property?" And the refrain—"What caused all this? 'Dinah went out.'" Once again, she is said to have started this. Her brothers, in some passages fare fairly well. In the most positive reference, *Gen. Rab.* 80.2, both Simeon and Levi were likened unto priests.

In one pericope, *Gen. Rab.* 92.9, Judah and his brothers firmly maintained their righteousness and sought to clear their collective name:

> AND JUDAH AND HIS BRETHREN CAME ... AND JUDAH SAID: WHAT SHALL WE SAY UNTO MY LORD in respect of the first money; WHAT SHALL WE SPEAK in respect of the second money; HOW SHALL WE CLEAR OURSELVES in the matter of the cup. [Again] WHAT SHALL WE SAY unto the Lord in the matter of Tamar; WHAT SHALL WE SPEAK in the matter of Bilhah; HOW SHALL WE CLEAR OURSELVES in the matter of Dinah. WHAT SHALL WE SAY to our father in Canaan in respect of Joseph; WHAT SHALL WE SPEAK in respect of Simeon; HOW SHALL WE CLEAR OURSELVES in respect of Benjamin. Shall we say that we have sinned? Yet indeed it is known and manifest that we have not sinned.[62]

Judah and his brethren speak up and wonder how they were to clear themselves in the matter involving Dinah. The sons are the focalizers, pondering aloud how they needed to be cleared before the Lord. This is one of the few places where God is brought into the dialogue, although the Divine has no speaking voice. They maintain however, at the end, that they had not sinned!

In the above passage, please notice that reference is made to "Judah and his brethren/brothers." I have written about the tendency of some traditions to limit responsibility for the Shechem massacre to only Simeon and Levi. That trend may be seen, not only in Gen 34:25, 26, and 30 and Genesis 49, but also *Gen. Rab.* 98.5 and 99.7:

98.5: SIMEON AND LEVI ARE BRETHREN (XLIX, 5)—brothers of Dinah, but not of Joseph[63] ... FOR IN THEIR ANGER THEY SLEW A MAN—this alludes to Hamor the father of Shechem.[64]

99.7. SIMEON AND LEVI ARE BRETHREN (XLIX, 5)—brethren in degredation. Ye were brothers in the case of Dinah, said he to them as it is written, *And two of the sons of Jacob, Simeon and Levi, Dinah's brethren, took each man his sword* (*ib.* XXXIV, 25) ...[65]

LEVITICUS RABBAH

Simeon and Levi, the two brothers of Dinah are paired together in many traditions including Genesis 34 and 49; in some instances they are portrayed as acting too swiftly, without concern for the ramifications of their actions. There is a great deal of variety in how these two brothers were portrayed. In some instances they are depicted as heroes of the narrative; for example, *Gen. Rab.* 92.9 had maintained their innocence and *Gen. Rab.* 80.2 compared the two to priests. On a very different note, *Leviticus Rabbah* presents them as "bloodshedders" who "slew all the males." This particular *midrash* is homiletical.[66] Jacob Neusner classified *Leviticus Rabbah* as topical, organized by "independent principles."[67] It is commonly dated to the fifth or sixth century CE[68] and is thought to have originated from within Palestine.[69]

In this text's only reference to Dinah, *Lev. Rab.* 37.1, one can hear the redactor exhorting people toward righteousness/morality:

> R. Huna said: An incident is related of a person who made a vow and did not pay. He went on a voyage on the Great Sea and his ship sank and he died at sea. R. Samuel b. Nahman said: If any one makes a vow and delays to fulfill it, he will ultimately be involved in the worship of idols, in sexual immorality, in bloodshed, in slander. From whom can you infer all this? From Jacob, who because he made a vow and delayed to fulfill it, came to be involved in all these. Whence do we know this of idol worship? *Then Jacob said unto his household ... Put away the strange gods* (Gen. XXXV, 2). Whence of sexual immorality? From Dinah, of whom it says, *And Dinah ... went out*, etc. (*ib.* XXXIV,1). Whence of bloodshed? From the fact that it says, *And it came to pass on the third day, when they were in pain, that the two sons of Jacob ... slew all the males* (*ib.* 25) ...[70]

Note the list of all the things that came upon Jacob as a result of him not fulfilling a vow.[71] Incidentally, this may be added to the list started earlier, enumerating Jacob's possible transgressions. The reader is given no details about that vow. It is maintained that his failure to fulfill it, however, led to a number of family trespasses. Jacob's transgression paved the way to his children's misfortunes, including

Dinah's so-called "sexual immorality."[72] In a fairly similar way, *Lev. Rab.* 37.1 and *Tanh.* 8.20 list tripartite transgressions. In both *Tanhuma* and *Leviticus Rabbah*, Dinah is cited for her alleged sexual immorality and/or unchastity.

PIRQE RABBI ELIEZER

Pirqe Rabbi Eliezer (*Pirqe R. El.*) is a continuous narrative or "rewritten Bible,"[73] which seems to have taken shape during the eighth or ninth centuries.[74] Most conclude that it had its origin in Palestine[75] and has points of contact with Deuterocanonical and Pseudepigraphical books.[76]

Please note the flowing narrative style of the passage, *Pirqe R. El.* 36, where one finds reference to the birth and naming of Dinah:

> Rabbi Eliezer said: Leah bare her sons after seven months, and in seven years there were born unto Jacob eleven sons and one daughter. And all of them were born, each with his partner with him, except Joseph, whose partner was not born with him, for Asenath, the daughter of Dinah, was destined to be his wife, and (also) except Dinah, whose partner was not born with her. She said: This child is (according to) justice and judgment, therefore she called her name Dinah.[77]

This is one of the aforementioned texts that contain the tradition that Dinah's daughter, Asenath, had married Joseph.[78] The births of Joseph and Dinah were made analogous or comparable in that each was born without a partner. One could connect this reference to the earlier discussion, in ch. 1, as to whether Dinah's birth was singular or multiple. One might also note that although Joseph was born without a partner, he married Asenath; no comparable datum is given regarding later Dinah's marriage. Already at the point of telling about Dinah's birth, the narrator connected her character with justice and judgment.

When Dinah's "partner" was referred to above, the idea of a marriage partner emerges. It is surprising how *Pirqe R. El.* 32 characterizes Shechem, upholding him as a prototype of an honorable man whose soul clung to his loved one. The similarity among *Pirqe R. El.* 32, *Gen. Rab.* 80.7, and *Tanh.* 8.20 is evident. The following is *Pirqe R. El.* 32:

> Rabbi José said: Isaac observed mourning during three years for his mother. After three years he married Rebecca, and forgot the mourning for his mother. Hence thou mayest learn that until a man marries a wife his love centres in his parents ... Does a man then *leave* his father and mother with reference to the precept, "Honour"? But the love of his soul cleaves unto his wife, as it is said, "And his soul clave (unto Dinah)" (*ibid.* XXXIV.3); and it says, "And he shall cleave unto his wife" (*ibid.* II.24).[79]

The text clearly portrays Dinah as Shechem's wife. As was the case with the text of Genesis 34, one can certainly note that *Pirqe Rabbi Eliezer* focused solely on

Shechem's point-of-view and did not give any narrative attention to Dinah's perspective. Once again, Dinah is the object/indirect object of Shechem's being/soul. It was to her that his soul clung. Readers are given no insight into her feeling or thought world. She is the silent partner.

While it might be said that *Pirqe R. El.* 32 put a positive spin on Shechem's attraction/clinging to Dinah, notice how differently *Pirqe R. El.* 38 speaks of the prince:

> "Or went into the house and leaned his hand on the wall, and the serpent bit him" (Amos V. 19). When Jacob went into his house in the land of Canaan the serpent bit him. And who was the serpent? This was Shechem, the son of Chamor. Because the daughter of Jacob was abiding in the tents, and she did not go into the street; what did Shechem, the son of Chamor do? He brought dancing girls who were (also) playing on pipes in the streets. Dinah went forth to see those girls who were making merry; and he seized her, and he slept with her, and she conceived and bare Asenath. The sons of Israel said that she should be killed, for they said that now people would say in all the land that there was an immoral daughter in the tents of Jacob.
>
> What did Jacob do? He wrote the Holy Name upon a golden plate, and suspended it about her neck and sent her away. She went her way. Everything is revealed before the Holy One, blessed be He, and Michael the angel descended and took her, and brought her down to Egypt to the house of Potiphera; because Asenath was destined to become the wife of Joseph. Now the wife of Potiphera was barren and (Asenath) grew up with her as a daughter. When Joseph came down to Egypt he married her, as it is said "And he gave him to wife Asenath, the daughter of Potiphera priest of On" (Gen. XLI. 45).
>
> Simeon and Levi were moved by a great zeal on account of the immorality, as it is said, "And they said, Should he deal with our sister as with an harlot?" (*ibid.* XXXIV. 31) And each man took his sword and slew all the men of Shechem. When Jacob heard thereof, he became sorely afraid. For he said: Now all the people of the land will hear, and they will gather together against me and smite me. He began to curse the wrath of his sons, as it is said, "Cursed by their anger, for it is fierce" (*ibid.* XLIX. 7); and he also cursed their sword in the Greek language, for he said: "Weapons of violence are their *swords*" (*ibid.* 5). All the kings of the earth heard (thereof) and feared very much, saying: If two sons of Jacob have done all these great things, if they all band themselves together, they will be able to destroy the world. And the dread of the Holy One, blessed be He, fell upon them, as it is said, "And the terror of God was upon the cities ... and they did not pursue after the sons of Jacob" (*ibid.* XXXV. 5).[80]

Shechem is likened to a snake which/who bit Jacob. The above reference, speaking of biting snakes, can be compared to *Gen. Rab.* 79.6, in which Jacob is also said to have been the one who transgressed and who was bitten.[81] This passage infers that Jacob had either transgressed a boundary or he had come too close to the one separating himself and his clan from the Hivites. Thus he is held at least partially responsible for what happened to Dinah.

One may notice the additional layers of tradition put forward in *Pirqe R. El.* 38. While some of *Genesis Rabbah* had portayed both Jacob and Dinah negatively (as having erred, etc.), *Pirqe R. El.* portrays them positively. The patriarch is said to have intervened to save Dinah's life. *Pirqe Rabbi Eliezer* contains some very interesting elements pertaining to both Dinah and her father Jacob.

Dinah "was abiding in tents, and she did not go into the street." At the risk of sounding pedantic, at first (in the "before shot") Dinah is presented as the proverbial "good girl." In other texts, she was introduced as a gadabout who liked to show herself in the streets.[82] In *Pirqe R. El.* 38, her innocence is maintained and her reputation strictly upheld. However, things seemed to changed very quickly. From reading/hearing the third and closing sentences of the first paragraph in the above quote, one can see the narrator coming full circle: Dinah began as "the daughter of Jacob ... abiding in tents," was lured out, and the situation pauses at a place where her life was endangered. Her father's sons concluded that she had become "an immoral daughter in the tents of Jacob." Notice that because of something done to her, she moves from being the daughter abiding in tents to the immoral daughter in the tents.

One could connect this to the earlier reference investigated, *Pirqe R. El.* 36, when Dinah's name was linked to justice/judgement. Little fault is assigned here to Dinah; Shechem is said to have brought out dancing girls to entice Dinah out of the tent. When she went forth to see the merry-making, Shechem is said to have "seized her," a verb which obviously connotes force against/upon its object. *Pirqe Rabbi Eliezer* is one of the few texts asserting that after Shechem had seized her and slept with her, Dinah conceived and bore Asenath.

One now moves to the "after" shot—the once "good girl" who did not go out of the tents is now pregnant—with a Hivite. Jacob's sons are the ones who serve as the moral police, announcing that Dinah should be killed. The good daughter who once resided in the tents has become "the immoral daughter in the tents of Jacob." Jacob intervened to spare his daughter's life. One must note internal issues with the text. It obviously makes sense that Dinah is the so-called "immoral daughter." Given ages, and so on, it would also appear logical to conclude that Dinah was the one sent away who eventually "went her way." The infant Asenath could not "be sent away" or "go her way." It was at that point that Michael, the angel, descended and took her to Egypt, to the house of Potiphera. For Asenath who was destined to be Joseph's wife. One can note a Mosaic theme here; a person, here a pregnant woman, is whisked away from danger, only to later turn up within the Egyptian royal courts.[83]

One may note the arrangement of the details of this narrative. Once Dinah is spirited away from Jacob's tents, Simeon and Levi attack Shechem. First of all, in contrast to Genesis 34, *Pirqe R. El.* 38 has Dinah long gone from Shechem by the time her brothers had descended on the city. In the biblical account, they had taken her out of Shechem's house when they attacked the city. In both places, Genesis 34 and here, they are portrayed as acting with zeal on account of the immorality Shechem had committed. Jacob's reaction is contrasted to that of his two sons, paralleling Genesis. Here the narrator makes it clear that Jacob heard what his sons had done and he "became sorely afraid." *Pirqe R. El.* 38 presents Jacob as a much more active character than does Genesis 34. *Pirqe Rabbi Eliezer* 38 concludes by saying that the terror of God fell upon the cities; this too is very close to the details found in the Genesis account.[84]

The closing reference to Dinah in *Pirqe Rabbi Eliezer*, *Pirqe R. El.* 39, deals with Jacob's migration to Egypt, claiming that the Divine descended with Jacob and his clan down into Egypt. Dinah was one of the people who made that trip:

> The fourth descent was (when) He descended into Egypt, (as it is said), "I will go down with thee into Egypt" ... The Holy One, blessed be He, said to him: Jacob do not fear: "I will go down with thee into Egypt, and I will also surely bring thee up again.
>
> Jacob heard this word, and he took his wives, and his sons, and his daughters, and the daughters of his sons. Another Scripture says, "With his daughter Dinah" (*ibid.* 15). And all that he had, and he brought them to Egypt, as it is said, "His sons, and his sons' sons with him," etc. (*ibid.* 7). Another Scripture says, "With his daughter Dinah" (*ibid.* 15). Whereas another text says, "His daughters" (*ibid.* 7) to teach thee that the daughters of Jacob were the wives of his sons ...[85]

This is the final reference to Dinah; in many ways, the detail here parallels the biblical account in Gen. 46:15, which states that Dinah went down to Egypt with the rest of Jacob's household. One may note here a recurrence of a thread which was explored in chapter 1—the question of whether Dinah was Jacob's only daughter. Note here the rabbinic debate between "his daughter" and "his daughters." The conversation about Dinah in *Pirkei de Rabbi Eliezer* ends on that point. Dinah and the rest of Jacob's family find themselves in Egypt. There is a variance of details within *Pirqe Rabbi Eliezer*. According ch. 38, Michael, the angel, has whisked Dinah off to Egypt. This last passage reports that the Divine had promised to go down to Egypt with Jacob. Jacob obediently followed the divine exhortation and went down, with his entire household. Obviously, the modern reader can reconcile these two passages, concluding that Dinah had made multiple trips to Egypt.

ECCLESIASTES RABBAH

Ecclesiastes Rabbah is most likely an eighth-century[86] C.E. Palestinian text[87] which is exegetical in nature.[88] Whereas *Pirqe R. El.* 38 and *Gen. Rab.* 79.6 spoke of the snake, Shechem, biting Jacob, in *Eccl. Rab.*, it is Dinah who erred and therefore was bitten. *Ecclesiastes Rabbah* X. 8.1 reads:

> And whoso breaketh through a fence, a serpent shall bite him: i.e. Dinah. While her father and brothers were sitting in the House of Study, she went out to see the daughters of the land (Gen XXXIV, 1). She brought upon herself her violation by Shechem the son of Hamor the Hivite, who is called a serpent, and he bit her; as it is written, And Shechem the son of Hamor the Hivite, the prince of the land, saw her, and he took her, etc. (ib. 2). 'He took her'—he spoke seductively to her, as the words is used in Take with you words (Hosea XIV, 3); And lay with her—in natural intercourse; and humbled her—in unnatural intercourse.[89]

This passage claims that while Jacob and his sons were sitting in the House of Study, Dinah went out.[90] Here, it is said, "she broke through a fence." One may conclude that Dinah transgressed a boundary. Referring back to this same analogy found in *Gen. Rab.* 79.9, the sages had reinforced this fence; in both passages, the transgressor is immediately bitten. This, unlike the passage just explored, places the blame on an errant Dinah. First, her behavior is contrasted to that of her father and brothers. While they sit and study in the *bet hamidrash*, she goes off awandering. The text clearly said, "She brought upon herself her violation." A rabbinical discussion found in *Tanhuma* claims that Dinah willfully "put herself out there" to be seen. As such, she was "fair game."

Even so, Shechem is called a serpent. In keeping with the behavior one might expect of a serpent, Shechem "takes" Dinah by speaking seductively to her. His words seduce her.[91] To garner further attestation of Shechem's character, a note corresponding to the passage calls to our attention that "Hivite" is connected with the Aramaic word for "serpent."

One must note that the order of the verbs in this passage from *Ecclesiastes Rabbah* is different from the sequence of Genesis. As noted above, Shechem's taking Dinah here is done through his seductive speech. In the case of Genesis, the reader is told that Shechem saw, took, lay (with), and violated Dinah (v. 2). It is only in the next verse where the reader is informed that he spoke tenderly to her. The speaking and humbling/violating is presented in reverse order in *Ecclesiastes Rabbah* versus Genesis 34.

TANHUMA

Tanhuma is yet another homiletical text[92] which originated in Palestine,[93] and received its final form by the ninth century.[94] This text, like *Genesis Rabbah*, is very lengthy and is believed to contain some very old material.[95] *Tanhuma* is another example of a midrashic text which has a long section dealing with Dinah and her character. Like *Ecclesiastes Rabbah* and other texts, it has a tendency to place a lot of blame upon Dinah, as it speaks negatively about her and her initial action of going out. It also contains the most references to the character of Leah. *Tanhuma* claims that Dinah, as her mother before her, was comfortable going out to meet men. To further underscore this, the text contextualizes her "going out" as having taken place on the *Shabbat* and asserts that she was "flaunting" herself decked out with jewelry. Dinah is directly linked with the concept of harlotry in 8.12. It is the only early midrashic text that alleges that Dinah went out not only to see but to be seen. Thus, even more doubt is cast upon Dinah's intentions and hence on her character.

The following text is *Tanhuma* 8.12–8.22:

8.12 Genesis 34:1ff., Part I

(Gen. 34:1:) NOW LEAH'S DAUGHTER DINAH <WHOM SHE HAD BORNE TO JACOB> WENT OUT. Let our master instruct us: Is it legitimate for a woman to go out with her jewelry on the Sabbath into a public place? Thus have our masters taught (according to *Shab*. 6:1): A WOMAN SHALL NOT GO OUT into a public place on the Sabbath with her jewelry, NOR WITH A HAIR NET … NOR WITH A GOLDEN TIARA, NOR WITH A CATELLA {i.e., a type of jewelry} <…> NOR WITH A NEEDLE HAVING NO EYE. BUT, IF SHE SHOULD GO OUT, SHE IS NOT LIABLE FOR [A SIN OFFERING], <i.e.,> when she goes out <of her rooms> with them <but remains> within the house. Let her not, however, go out into a public place with a single piece of jewelry. Now our masters say: Even on a weekday she must not go out into a public place. Why? Because people will stare at her. Thus the Holy One gave jewelry to a woman only for her to adorn herself with them inside of the house; for one does not give an opening to the trustworthy person, let alone to the thief. And so Job has said (in Job 31:1): I HAVE MADE A COVENANT WITH MY EYES. HOW THEN SHALL I GAZE ON A MAIDEN? Come and see Job's righteousness. If in the case of a maiden, at whom any man has a right to look, perhaps to marry her or perhaps to marry her to his son or to one of his kin, Job did not look at her, how much the less in the case of someone's wife, at whom he has no right to look. It is therefore written (in Ps. 45:14 [13]): ALL GLORIOUS IS THE KING'S DAUGHTER WITHIN. So, if she acts to conceal herself and is worthy, (ibid., cont.:) HER CLOTHING IS OF GOLD BROCADE. R. Levi said: She was worthy to raise up priests to put on the high priestly garments. Now there is no BROCADE except priestly garments. Thus it is stated (regarding Aaron's vestments in Exod. 28:13): AND YOU SHALL MAKE GOLD BROCADE. There is already an allusion in the Torah about this thing, that a woman should not go about a lot in a marketplace. Where? Where it is so written (in Gen. 1:28): THEN GOD BLESSED THEM, AND GOD SAID TO THEM: <BE FRUITFUL AND MULTIPLY, FILL THE EARTH> AND SUBDUE HER. [AND SUBDUE HER is written <here>]. The man subdues the woman, and the woman does not subdue the man. But if she walks about a lot and goes out into the marketplace, she finally comes to a state of corruption, to a state of harlotry. And so you find in the case of Jacob's daughter Dinah. All the time that she was sitting at home, she was not corrupted by transgression; but, as soon as she went out into the marketplace, she caused herself to come to the point of corruption.

8.13 Genesis 34:1ff., Part II

(Gen. 34:1:) NOW LEAH'S DAUGHTER DINAH … WENT OUT. This text is related (to Prov. 11:12): ONE WHO DESPISES HIS NEIGHBOR IS LACKING IN SENSE. Whoever scorns his neighbor is called LACKING IN SENSE. But, if that same person who was despised was a person of knowledge and understanding, he would put his hand over his mouth and be silent. Thus it is stated (*ibid.*, cont.): BUT A PERSON OF UNDERSTANDING WILL KEEP SILENT. (Prov. 11:12:) ONE WHO DESPISES HIS NEIGHBOR IS LACKING IN SENSE. This is Hamor, the father of Shechem, who said (in Gen. 34:8): THE SOUL OF MY SON, SHECHEM, LONGS FOR YOUR DAUGHTER. (Prov. 11:12, cont.:) BUT A PERSON OF UNDERSTANDING WILL KEEP SILENT. This is Jacob of whom it is stated (in Gen. 34:5): SO JACOB KEPT SILENCE UNTIL THEY CAME. For what reason? On account of this corruption (in Gen. 34:1–2): NOW LEAH'S DAUGHTER DINAH, <WHOM SHE HAD BORNE TO JACOB> WENT OUT … <THEN SHECHEM BEN HAMOR THE HIVITE, THE PRINCE OF THE LAND, SAW HER. SO HE TOOK HER, LAY WITH HER, AND VIOLATED HER>.

8.14 Genesis 34:1ff., Part III

[(Gen. 34:1:) NOW LEAH'S DAUGHTER DINAH … WENT OUT.] This text is related (to Ezek. 16:44): BEHOLD, EVERYONE WHO USES PROVERBS WILL USE A PROVERB ABOUT YOU AND SAY: LIKE MOTHER, LIKE DAUGHTER. Our master asked R. Hiyya: In what sense do you say: LIKE MOTHER, LIKE DAUGHTER? He said to him: Just as the altar, so are its priests. Rabbi (in his day) had taken a lot of pains with <this text>. He said to him: Tell <me> the truth; in what sense do you say it? He said to him: Just as the prince, so is the generation.

Another interpretation (of Ezek. 16:44): LIKE MOTHER, LIKE DAUGHTER. This refers to Dinah. What is written of Leah (in Gen. 30:16)? LEAH WENT OUT TO MEET HIM. So also (in Gen. 34:1): NOW <LEAH'S DAUGHTER> DINAH … WENT OUT.

8.15 Genesis 34:1ff., Part IV

(Gen. 34:1:) NOW LEAH'S DAUGHTER DINAH … WENT OUT. This text is related (to II Kings 14:9): THE THISTLE THAT WAS IN LEBANON.

This thistle was Shechem's father, Hamor. (Ibid., cont.:) SENT TO THE CEDAR THAT WAS IN LEBANON. That is Jacob, as stated (in Ps. 92:13 [12]): THE RIGHTEOUS ONE SHALL FLOURISH LIKE THE PALM, LIKE A CEDAR IN LEBANON SHALL HE GROW. (II Kings 14:9, cont.:) GIVE YOUR DAUGHTER TO MY SON FOR A WIFE. Thus it says (in Gen. 34:8): PLEASE GIVE HER TO HIM FOR A WIFE. (II Kings 14:9, cont.:) BUT A WILD BEAST PASSED BY. These are the tribes, who have been compared to wild beasts. Thus it is stated (in Gen. 49:9): JUDAH IS A LION'S WHELP, (in vs. 27:) BENJAMIN IS A RAVENOUS WOLF, (in vs. 21:) NAPHTHALI IS A HIND LET LOOSE, (and in vs. 14:) ISSACHAR IS A STRONG-BONED ASS. (II Kings 14:9 cont.:) AND TRAMPLED DOWN THE THISTLE. This is Hamor and his son Shechem, whom <the tribes> killed with the edge of the sword because of Dinah, as stated (in Gen. 34:1): NOW LEAH'S DAUGHTER DINAH ... WENT OUT. In every place the female child is accompanied by males, but here she is accompanied by her mother. Thus, the corruption had begun with her mother.

8.16 Genesis 34:1ff., Part V

Another interpretation (of Gen. 34:1:) NOW <LEAH'S DAUGHTER> DINAH ... WENT OUT. But <had she gone out> from sin? After all, Jacob had said (in Gen. 32:11 [10]): I AM UNWORTHY OF ALL THE KINDNESSES. R. Aha said: <The Holy One said>: I have nourished your ancestors from their <good> deeds, but you say: I AM UNWORTHY! The Holy One said to him: Jacob, <it is> through your righteousness <that> I have done all these miracles of which you say that you are unworthy. But look, she is going out; yet your merit shall remain for you. (Gen. 34:1:) NOW <LEAH'S DAUGHTER> DINAH ... WENT OUT.

8.17 Genesis 34:1ff., Part VI

[(Gen. 34:1:) NOW <LEAH'S DAUGHTER> DINAH ... WENT OUT.] This text is related (to Prov. 1:25): BUT YOU HAVE SPURNED ALL MY COUNSEL AND WOULD NOT ACCEPT MY REBUKE. <The verse> speaks about Eve. When the Holy One wanted to create her, the Holy One said: If I create her from Adam's head, her spirit will be haughtily above her; <if> from his eyes, <she will be> flirtatious; <if> from his mouth, she will be loquacious; <if> from his hands, she will be a thief; <if> from his feet, she will be a gadabout. The Holy One said: All this counsel I took before I created her, and I did not depart from it. I said: If I create her from his head, her spirit will be haughtily above her; <yet>, as stated (in Is. 3:16): MOREOVER, THE LORD SAID: BECAUSE THE DAUGHTERS OF ZION ARE HAUGHTY.... <If> from his eyes; <yet>, (*ibid.*, cont.:) <HER> EYES ARE ROVING ABOUT. <If> from <the> ears; <yet>, (in Gen. 18:10:) SARAH WAS LISTENING <AT THE ENTRANCE OF THE TENT>. <If> from his mouth; <yet>, (in Numb. 12:1:) THEN MIRIAM ... SPOKE <AGAINST MOSES>. <If> from his hands; <yet>, (in Gen. 31:19) RACHEL STOLE. <If> from his feet, she will be going in and out; <yet>, (in Gen. 34:1) DINAH ... WENT OUT. Ergo (in Prov. 1:25): BUT YOU HAVE SPURNED ALL MY COUNSEL. ...

8.18 Genesis 34:1ff., Part VII

(Gen. 34:1:) NOW LEAH'S DAUGHTER DINAH ... WENT OUT. R. Hiyya bar Abba said: The male is always attributed to the wife, and the female, to the husband. Then why is this <daughter> attributed to her mother? Because her pregnancy was originally male. However, when Leah had borne six <sons>, Billah, two, and Zilpah, two, for a total of ten; then she prayed on behalf of <the barren> Rachel, and <the child> in her womb became female. For that reason, she was attributed to her mother. (Gen. 34:1:) NOW LEAH'S DAUGHTER DINAH ... WENT OUT.

8.19 Genesis 34:1ff., Part VIII

(Gen. 34:1:) <NOW LEAH'S DAUGHTER DINAH, WHOM SHE HAD BORNE TO JACOB, WENT OUT> TO SEE THE DAUGHTER OF THE LAND. TO SEE <implies> TO BE SEEN. To what is the matter comparable? To one who was walking in the marketplace with a piece <of meat> in his hand. A dog, having seen it, went after it, and snatched it from him. Thus did Dinah go out TO SEE (and TO BE SEEN) when Shechem saw her and seized her. Another interpretation (of Gen. 34:1): TO SEE THE DAUGHTERS OF THE LAND. When the children of Jacob came into the land of Israel, they began to exhibit their strength, their wealth, and their beauty. They exhibited their strength (according to Gen. 34:25): THAT TWO OF JACOB'S SONS, <SIMEON AND LEVI, BROTHERS OF DINAH>, [EACH TOOK HIS SWORD ... AND KILLED EVERY MALE]. They exhibited their wealth (according to Gen. 33:17): BUT JACOB JOURNEYED TO SUCCOTH, BUILT A HOUSE FOR HIMSELF, AND MADE STALLS (*sukkot*) FOR HIS CATTLE. He began opening <cattle> bazaars. And where is it shown concerning their beauty? (In Gen. 34:1:) NOW LEAH'S DAUGHTER DINAH, WHOM SHE HAD BORNE TO JACOB, WENT OUT TO SEE AND TO BE SEEN. (Gen. 34:2:) THEN SHECHEM BEN HAMOR THE HIVITE, THE PRINCE OF THE LAND, SAW HER. <It is> the wicked <who> "see." (Thus in Esth. 3:5:) WHEN HAMAN SAW. (Similarly in Gen. 28:6:) WHEN ESAU SAW. THEN SHECHEM BEN HAMOR ... SAW. David said (in Ps. 69:24:) LET THEIR EYES BE DARKENED SO THAT THEY DO NOT SEE.

Gen. 34:2, cont.:) SO HE TOOK HER, LAY WITH HER, AND VIOLATED HER. Because of what sin did the uncircumcised one come upon her? It is written (in Job 6:14) TO ONE WHO IS DESPONDENT LOYALTY IS DUE FROM HIS NEIGHBOR EVEN THOUGH HE SHOULD ABANDON THE FEAR OF THE ALMIGHTY. However, when our father Jacob came along with the tribes, Dinah was with him <as well>. As soon as the messengers came and said to him (according to Gen. 32:7 [6]): WE CAME UNTO YOUR BROTHER ESAU,

Jacob took Dinah and put her in a chest so that Esau would not see her and take her for a wife. The Holy One said to him: You have withheld her from him. By your life, she is ready for an uncircumcised man, i.e., the one about whom it is written (in Job 6:14): TO ONE WHO IS DESPONDENT LOYALTY IS DUE FROM HIS NEIGHBOR. If she had been married to Esau, perhaps she would have converted him. When Job took her, did she not convert him? He therefore withheld her. See, <now> the son of a cursed (rt.: *'RH*) one has come across her. Ergo (in Gen. 34:2): THEN SHECHEM BEN HAMOR … SAW (rt.: *R'H*) HER.

8.20 Genesis 34:1ff., Part IX

What is written above on the matter (in Gen. 33:18)? NOW JACOB CAME WHOLE. <When> he had come from Paddan-Aram under conditions that the Holy One had set with him, he did not lessen him in any respect. What did Jacob do? He began opening bazaars. The Holy One said to him: Have you forgotten what you vowed to me? And did you not say this (in Gen. 28:20): IF GOD IS WITH ME, so that I do not commit idolatry, (ibid., cont.:) AND PROTECTS ME, from bloodshed (*ibid.*, cont.:) ON THE WAY, from unchastity, as stated (in Prov. 30:20): SUCH IS THE WAY OF AN ADULTERESS, SHE EATS, WIPES HER MOUTH, AND SAYS: I HAVE DONE NO WRONG. The Holy One did protect him, for it so states (in Gen. 28:15): AND I WILL PROTECT YOU WHEREVER YOU GO. Jacob said (in Gen. 28:22): [AND] OF ALL THAT YOU GIVE ME, I WILL SURELY SET ASIDE A TITHE FOR YOU. As soon as he came to the land of Israel, he forgot this vow. The Holy One said: By your life, through the very things which you said you would observe, through them you shall come to grief. Where is it shown in regard to idolatry? Where it is stated (in Gen. 35:4): THEY THEY GAVE UNTO JACOB ALL THE ALIEN GODS THAT THEY HAD. … Where is it shown in regard to bloodshed? Where it is stated (in Gen. 34:25): THAT TWO OF JACOB'S SONS, SIMEON AND LEVI, BROTHERS OF DINAH, EACH TOOK HIS SWORD … [AND KILLED EVERY MALE]. Where is it shown in regard to unchastity? From Dinah, of whom it is stated (in Gen. 34:2–3): THEN SHECHEM BEN HAMOR THE HIVITE, THE PRINCE OF THE LAND, SAW HER. <…> AND HIS SOUL CLUNG TO JACOB'S DAUGHTER DINAH. R. Abbahu said: We have learned things from putrid secretions (i.e., mere mortals): (Gen. 41:44:) PHARAOH SAID TO JOSEPH: I AM PHARAOH. I have said that you shall be king. The Holy One said to Israel concerning each and every commandment which they do: I AM THE LORD (e.g., in Lev. 19:3, 4, 10, 12, 14, 16, etc.). I am the one who is going to repay each and everyone with his reward. Now, just as in the case of flesh and blood, when it said: I AM PHARAOH, it raised him to great dignity; so much the more so with me when I say something. And just as you said (in Gen. 41:40): ONLY WITH RESPECT TO THE THRONE SHALL I BE GREATER THAN YOU, <so> has the Holy One said to Israel (in Deut. 28:13): AND YOU ONLY SHALL BE AT THE TOP. Just as an "only" from flesh and blood (i.e., from Pharaoh) magnified Joseph, so much the more so in the case of an "only" from the Holy One.

It is written of Israel (in Deut. 7:7): THE LORD HAS DELIGHTED IN YOU AND CHOSEN YOU. It is also written (in Gen. 34:3): AND HE (Shechem) LOVED THE MAIDEN (Dinah). Now you would not know what that love was; [however, from the fact that he set his soul upon her, you do know what love was]. How much the more so in the case of the Holy One, when he said to Israel (in Mal. 1:2): I HAVE LOVED YOU! (According to Deut. 7:7:) THE LORD HAS DELIGHTED IN YOU; you do not know how. We do, however, learn from Shechem, as stated (in Gen. 34:8): THE SOUL OF MY SON, SHECHEM, LONGS FOR YOUR DAUGHTER. R. Abbahu said: We have learned from putrid secretion (i.e., mere mortals). It is written about Shechem (in Gen. 34:3): AND HIS SOUL CLUNG TO JACOB'S DAUGHTER DINAH; and it is written about Israel (in Deut. 4:4): BUT YOU WHO CLUNG TO THE LORD YOUR GOD ARE ALL ALIVE TODAY. ...

8.22 Genesis 35:1ff., Part II

It is written (in Ps. 50:14): SACRIFICE A THANK OFFERING TO GOD. When Jacob left his father's house, he left with nothing but his staff, as stated (in Gen. 32:11 [10]): WITH ONLY MY STAFF I CROSSED THIS JORDAN. Immediately Jacob had made a vow before the Holy One, as stated (in Gen. 28:20): THEN JACOB VOWED A VOW: What is written at the end of the passage (in vs. 22)? AND OF ALL THAT YOU GIVE ME. But, when he enriched him, as stated (in Gen. 30:43): SO THE MAN (Jacob) BECAME VERY VERY PROSPEROUS, he forgot his vow ... Immediately the angel blessed him, as stated (in Gen. 32:30 [29]): AND HE BLESSED HIM THERE. (Hos. 12:5 [4]:) SO HE STROVE WITH AN ANGEL AND PREVAILED. What did he say to him? Go, fulfill your vow. (Eccl. 5:4 [5]:) IT IS BETTER NOT TO VOW <THAN TO VOW AND NOT FULFILL>. What did Simeon and Levi do immediately? TWO OF JACOB'S SONS, [SIMEON AND LEVI, BROTHERS OF DINAH, EACH TOOK HIS SWORD] ... <AND KILLED EVERY MALE>. <Jacob> immediately fell on his face and did not get up until <the Holy One> gave him permission ... He immediately journeyed with his whole house; and the Holy One put his fear upon all about him, as stated (in Gen. 35:5): AND, AS THEY JOURNEYED, A TERROR FROM GOD CAME <UPON THE CITIES THAT WERE ROUND ABOUT THEM>. ...[96]

A number of the parallels have been identified for us within the Buber rescension of the text, via footnotes that Buber and/or his editors/translator made. The majority of texts mentioned, especially those from *Genesis Rabbah*, are included within this chapter and are discussed above. The first parallel may be seen in *Tanh.* 8.12. Toward the end, with the discussion on "subdue," the Buber rescension includes a footnote, citing *Gen. Rab.* 8.12.[97] Both passages claim that a woman should be mastered/subdued, lest she either "come to grief" (*Genesis*

Rabbah) or "come to a state of corruption, a state of harlotry" (*Tanhuma*). Incidentally, both texts cite the marketplace (not an open field) as the place where Dinah met her ill fortune. Note that she is held at least partially liable or responsible for what happened to her.[98] It is however implied strongly in both passages that someone had not subdued or controlled Dinah; hence she met this horrible fate. Much of that negative attention (blame or liability) falls upon Leah here.

One may note a parallelism between *Tanh.* 8.13 and *Gen. Rab.* 80.6. Both portray Jacob's silence positively. In *Genesis Rabbah*, he is called a "man of discernment"; *Tanhuma* referes to him as a "person of knowledge and understanding." Very positive conclusions are drawn about Jacob's silence; it is contrasted with Hamor's willingness to speak and ask for his sons' desires.

In *Tanh.* 8.14, a footnote calls our attention to the fact that *Gen. Rab.* 80.1 also deals with the likeness between Leah and Dinah. It alleges, incorrectly, that *Tanhuma*, does not conclude that Dinah, like her mother, had "played the harlot."[99] I certainly read *Tanhuma* differently; it claims that Dinah, as her mother before her, was comfortable going out to meet men. In fact, Dinah is directly linked with the concept of harlotry in *Tanhuma* 8.12. One of my student's papers contains the following: "Another implication of *Tanhuma* 8.14 is that Leah is the source of some of Dinah's sinful acts … Women are sinful and pass it on to their daughters."[100]

A note corresponding to *Tanh.* 8.15 cites *Gen. Rab.* 80.3 as having comparable material dealing with Hamor as a thistle sent to Jacob, the cedar. Note that so much of the troubling or irritance is presented as male-to-male. Hamor is the thistle to irritate Jacob. Jacob is the recipient of the trouble. Dinah is the silent sufferer whose sexual violation is aimed at troubling Jacob. Her brothers are the ones who "take on" the offense and seek revenge. Thus the thistle was uprooted by the tribal action. One may focus temporarily on the word "tribal." Some commentators have noted that Genesis 34 sounded tribal; i.e., the tribes of Simeon and Levi attacked Shechem.[101] This might fit into that sort of an understanding or reading.

One may interpret *Tanh.* 8.15 as forwarding the idea that an intermarriage between Dinah and Shechem may have been the source of "flourishing" for Jacob and his clan. One may wonder about the financial/resource base of this tradition. It may have been advantageous for Jacob to consider and allow the intermarriage. Another reason, using only evidence found within these midrashic texts, is that possibly via Dinah's marriage, the Hivites may have been converted.

It is disturbing that rabbinic interpreters did not consider Shechem/Hamor to be the wild beast, who violated Dinah. Especially when "Hamor" means "ass," it would be sensible to view him as "a wild ass" that made an assault upon the family of Jacob (Israel) by lying with Dinah.

Dinah is again used as a type. She, not what Shechem did to her, is put forward as narrative justification for the tribes' killing Hamor and Shechem. This can be connected to other discussions, concluding that the rabbis used "Dinah" as a shorthand reference to the event at Shechem. One must presume that the reader/hearer of these midrashic passages was aware of what Shechem had done to/with her and what, in short, had happened to Dinah.

Tanhuma 8.16 presents an intriguing image of Jacob and the Divine. The two appear to be watching as the errant Dinah goes her way.[102] This is the only time in these midrashic texts where the verb is imperfect or present; i.e., "she is going out" not perfect or past, "she went out." The Divine speaks with the patriarch, as they watch Dinah go out; the Divine reassures the man "your merit will remain for you." What a collusion! Is any responsibility to be lain at the feet of the Divine, especially as this writer portrays that character? Can female characters be held responsible— and even blamed—when the Divine shows such an affinity for male characters? Could Divine intervention have prevented this incident at Shechem? Could, or would, the Divine have ever reassured Dinah, Eve, Sarah, Rachel, or Miriam[103] that their merit would remain with them?

What was the relationship beteen the matriarchs and the Divine? A note corresponding to *Tanh.* 8.17 cites the parallelism between *Gen. Rab.* 18.2 and 80.5,[104] which cast aspersions on all the matriarchs. *Genesis Rabbah* 18.2 reads as follows:

> R. Joshua of Siknin said in R. Levi's name: Wayyiben is written, signifying that He considered well (*hithbonnen*) from what part to create her. Said He: 'I will not create her from [Adam's] head, lest she be swelled-headed; nor from the eye, lest she be a coquette; nor from the ear, lest she be an eavesdropper; nor from the mouth, lest she be a gossip; nor from the heart, lest she be rpone to jealousy; nor from the hand, lest she be light-fingered; nor from the foot, lest she be a gadabout; but from the modest part of man, for even when he stands naked, that part is covered.' And as He created each limb He ordered her, 'Be a modest woman.' Yet in spite of all this, *But ye have set at nought all My counsel, and would none of My reproof* (Prov. I, 25). I did not create her from the head, yet she is swelled-headed, as it is written, *They walk with stretched-forth necks* (Isa. III, 16); nor from the eye, yet she is a coquette: *And wanton eyes* (*ib.*); nor from the ear, yet she is an eavesdropper: *Now Sarah listened in the tent door* (Gen. XVIII, 10); nor from the heart, yet she is prone to jealousy: *Rachel envied her sister* (*ib.* XXX, 1); nor from the hand, yet she is light-fingered: *And Rachel stole the teraphim* (*ib.* XXXI, 19); nor from the foot, yet she is a gadabout: *And Dinah went out*, etc. (ib. XXXIV, 1).[105]

Above is discussed a passage (*Gen. Rab.* 72.6, the very first pericope in this chapter), which spoke of the wonderful prophetic gifts/powers of the matriarchs. Here in these three parallels it is alleged that, from the onset, women had disappointed the Divine, consistently interfering with and veering away from the Divine plan.[106] In many regards, the women of this passage are portrayed as being anti-creational; that is, they countered the Divine will since the time of Creation. Whereas the divine had allegedly intended women to be modest, the writers contend that women were immodest. One can certainly note the misogyny expressed in passages like this. There is also a certain religious/political power involved in rhetoric expressing that the divine had/has intentions that counter so many of women's tendencies. It is indeed a powerful ploy to allege that the Divine had certain intentions and that women countered them from the beginning of time.

A modern reader may get the impression that "the mere fact that Dinah is female contributes to her guilt in the eyes of the midrashic authors."[107] One could conclude that an inherent sinfulness or tendency toward transgression was a trait particularly associated with women. "Because women were apparently so immoral, it is necessary for men to 'master' or 'subdue' them."[108]

One's gender mattered greatly. Perhaps that is why the rabbis struggled with the tradition that Dinah had been conceived male. A note corresponding to *Tanh.* 8.18 cites *Gen. Rab.* 72.6 as a parallel, which also refers to Dinah's having been conceived originally male.[109] The details vary between these two texts. In *Genesis Rabbah*, Rachel had made the prayer; in *Tanh.* 8.18, it was Leah who had offered the prayer. In both cases, the child (Dinah) with whom Leah was pregnant switched genders from male to female. *Tanhuma* alleges that this is why Dinah is so closely affiliated with her mother, Leah.

Tanhuma 8.19, first of all, may be paralleled to *Gen. Rab.* 80.6 as both contain word plays on the words "see" and "cursed" or "accursed." On the one hand, *Tanhuma* makes Dinah comfortable being seen by men. On the other hand, *Tanhuma* 8.19 stated, "It is the wicked who 'see.'" Shechem is cited as having transgressed. This is one of the very few midrashic passages which hold him responsible for his action(s). Interestingly, his "seeing" Dinah is problematic here. Please remember earlier points about this; his seeing is presumed to have led directly to his lying with her. "Seeing" is more emphasized than inappropriate sexual relationships. This may have been part of that era's ways of speaking "more delicately" about his offense. This way of speaking/writing favored men; in fact, Dinah is likened to "a piece of meat."

Although the ancient rabbis had no foreknowledge of the way in which idioms might be used currently, note their comment in *Tanhuma* 8.19 that compares Dinah's going out with one walking about carelessly dangling a piece of meat which can be seen and snatched by a dog. Read in today's context, this sexualized Dinah. Thus when Dinah went out to see and to be seen, it was only reasonable that Shechem saw her and seized her. Notice the tendency later in that same passage of the rabbis to envision women's beauty as a powerful danger; this can be connected back to the idea of a "sexualized gaze."[116] She was beautiful and her brothers were strong.

A note corresponding to *Tanh.* 8.19 refers the reader back to *Gen. Rab.* 80.5. Whereas, *Tanhuma* likened Dinah to a "piece of meat" snatched by a dog, *Genesis Rabbah* had used the analogy of "pound of meat" which a bird swooped down to snatch.[110] Another footnote in the same section references *Ecc. Rab.* X.8.1, as it speaks about how Shechem "took" Dinah.[111]

At *Tanh.* 8.19 one can find another note linking the tradition found in *Tanhuma* with that of *Gen. Rab.* 79.6 when it comes to Jacob's setting up bazaars.[112] That tradition was also encountered in *Legends of the Jews*. Another familiar tradition found in *Tanhuma* which parallels *Gen. Rab.* 57.4 and 80.4, is that Jacob had hidden Dinah away from Esau by putting her/concealing her inside a chest. To that list, I would add *Gen. Rab.* 74.9.

In *Tanh.* 8.19, one may note the way in which the narrator expressed Jacob's actions toward Dinah. "Jacob took Dinah and put her in a chest so that Esau would not see her and take her for a wife." Notice that Dinah "was taken" and "put in a chest" by her father lest Esau see and take her. All four times Dinah is the object. Note also the two verbs used in reference to Esau—see and take. Indeed, according to Genesis 34:2, Shechem "saw, took, lay with, and violated" Dinah was the object. In *Tanhuma*, Jacob shares the blame/responsibility for what happened to Dinah. Because Jacob prevented her from being seen by Esau, now the son of a cursed one had seen and had taken her. Jacob shares the blame/responsibility for what happened to Dinah.

Some of the information found in *Tanh.* 8.20 is reminiscent of *Lev. Rab.* 37.1 and 79.8 which also speak of threefold transgressions. In *Tanhuma*, the tripartite trespasses are: idolatry, bloodshed, and unchastity. *Leviticus Rabbah* delineates the three: idol worship/idolatry, sexual immorality, and bloodshed. In both *Tanhuma* and *Leviticus Rabbah* Dinah is cited for her alleged sexual immorality and her unchastity. This offense was allowed to happen because of Jacob's transgression.

Like other midrashic texts, *Tanhuma* vacillates between portraying Jacob as the righteous man, characterized by silence, versus the errant one, whose behavior of withholding his daughter from a legitimate marriage, characterized how he had withheld loyalty from his neighbor. *Tanhuma* 8.19 credits Dinah with the conversion of Job, her husband. First Job and Dinah are presented as husband and wife. Second, Jacob is held responsible for Dinah's not having the opportunity to convert Esau via marriage. Jacob had erred. Dinah was an agent of conversion. The final paragraph of 8.19 begins, "Because of what sin did the uncircumcised come upon her?" The text proceeds to speak about how Jacob was remiss in withholding Dinah from Esau. Because of this, the cursed one/uncircumcised one "came across" her. The text concludes that "by" or because of Jacob's life, Dinah was "ready for an uncircumcised man." Once again, one can note the way in which one person's behavior was said to have a direct bearing on what happened to another.

Specifically, in this case, Jacob's transgression was interpreted as the reason why his daughter was sexually violated.

As mentioned before, there are a few midrashic passages that refer to the love Shechem had allegedly felt toward Dinah. Toward the very end of *Tanh.* 8.20, one can see the writer/redactor of the text comparing Shechem's love for Dinah with Divine love for Israel. This was also the case in *Gen. Rab.* 80.7; *Pirqe R. El.* 32 uses a very similar tradition as well.

In *Tanhuma* 8.21 Jacob is also said to have forgotten a vow he made with the Divine. As soon as he began opening up bazaars, and so on, he apparently neglected to tithe proceeds. Because of this offense, idolatry, bloodshed, and unchastity, befell his household via his children. Again, Jacob's trangressions were seen as the cause of his children's going astray or suffering ills.

Some modern readers might conclude that the writers/editors of *Tanhuma* showed a particularly intense animosity toward Dinah. The text made Dinah responsible for a number of transgressions: she may have gone out on the Sabbath, she may have been adorned (with jewelry, e.g.), she may also have gone out in order to be seen. *Tanhuma* is one of the few texts which made this latter assertion. It claims that Dinah, bedecked in jewelry, drew people's attention to her. Unfortunately, Shechem saw her; the act of his seeing quickly led to his other trespasses with/against her. There was something incredibly powerful about the "sexualized gaze."[113]

The writer(s) of *Tanhuma* negatively portrayed Dinah in 8.12 by contrasting Job's modesty with Dinah's lack thereof. Whereas she went out to see and to be seen, Job had refused to gaze upon a maiden. Dinah is clearly said to have "caused herself to come to the point of corruption" by going out into the marketplace. One must note that *Tanh.* 8.12 deposits part of the blame for what happened to Dinah on Jacob, who "should have subdued" or controlled his daughter and/or her behavior. According to that passage, it was considered inappropriate for a woman "to go about a lot in the marketplace." Any female desire to do so, the texts allege, should have been subdued by a man (be that the woman's father or husband). One must note the rabbinic line of reasoning here; they drew a parallel between subduing the earth and subduing women. When commenting on Gen. 1:28, "Fill the earth and subdue her," they noted that "the earth" (הָאָרֶץ) is a feminine noun. They maintained that the alleged Divine imperative to subdue should was intended to be extended to include men subduing women, specifically Dinah, in this instance. Once again, one may note the attempt to use the Divine as a means to achieving a certain social role for men and women.

Consider the rhetoric of *Tanhuma* 8.12; when speaking of Job, the rabbis comment, "If in the case of a maiden, at whom any man has a right to look. Perhaps to marry her or perhaps to marry her to his son or to one of his kin, Job did not look at her …" One can wonder why it was so egregious then for Dinah to be seen. Was it Shechem's identity as a Hivite? Did "any man" have a right to look, while women were to be entirely modest? There is indeed a way in which the text itself sexualizes women and female bodies. One of my students has written, "The simple act of walking out in a marketplace is enough for a woman to become corrupt and enter a 'state of harlotry.' The reference to people 'staring at her' implies that the female body is something to be objectified and is naturally sexualized by the gaze upon it."[114]

Tanhuma, especially 8.13–14, often linked Dinah with her mother Leah,[115] as noted above. While mother and daughter are paired because of their alleged questionable tendencies "to go out," Jacob's righteousness is centered in the spotlight. *Tanh* 8.13 calls him "a person of understanding" because he kept silent. A very similar tradition may be found in *Gen. Rab.* 80.6, which calls Jacob "a man of discernment" because he "held his peace." In *Tanhuma,* the very talkative Hamor, on the other hand, is deemed "lacking in sense." *Tanhuma* 8.13 alleges that the reason for his silence was the corruption of his daughter. The honor of Jacob, Dinah's father, is maintained, while mother and daughter fare badly in the estimation of the early rabbis. *Tanhuma* 8.15 indeed closes with a sentence clearly stating "the corruption [of Dinah] had begun with her mother. *Tanhuma* 8.17 carries this thought further, calling Dinah a gadabout.

Tanhuma 8.21 is the passage which, similarly to Genesis 34, portrays Dinah as the object/indirect object of Shechem's love, longing, and the person to whom his soul clung/longed for. He is said to have: loved the maiden, he set his soul upon her, his soul longed for Dinah and clung to her. Once again, one may notice how centered this is on Shechem's affect and behavior. With the exception of her intial "going out," she apparently took no other action. She is portrayed as being very passive throughout *Tanhuma* and throughout Genesis 34. The reader certainly knows more about Shechem's thought, feeling, and "soul" worlds than one does of Dinah's. One must note the problematic of making this analogous to the Divine's love for Israel. That is especially true when sexual violation is a factor in the Shechem-Dinah relationship.

CONCLUSIONS

There are two references to the tradition that Dinah had been conceived male: *Tanh.* 8.18 and *Gen. Rab.* 72.6. The details surrounding her change of gender vary: according to *Tanhuma,* Leah, after delivering six sons had prayed for the change in gender; for this reason, the text alleges, Dinah was closely associated with her mother. According to *Genesis Rabbah,* it was Rachel who had prayed.

It was also important during this era that these texts were written or edited to present Dinah as Jacob's only daughter. That tradition may be found in *Gen. Rab.*

84.21 and in *Pirqe R. El.* 36 and 39. When comparing and contrasting these passages, one notes that *Pirqe R. El.* 36 is unique in that it alone alleges that Dinah was born without a partner. These references alternate between calling Dinah Jacob's or Leah's daughter. Incidentally, while making concluding comments about each of these texts, one may note that only *Pirqe R. El.* (36 and 38) makes reference to Asenath, Dinah's daughter.

As mentioned in both these first two chapters, the sexual violation of Dinah was clearly linked to a transgression on Jacob's part. The texts present the patriarch's misdeed(s) differently; in summary, Jacob either had become too proud, had neglected or forgotten a vow, or he had hidden in a chest, lest she be seen and taken by Esau. His hubris is the focus of *Gen. Rab.* 73.9, 79.8, and 80.4 (twice). *Genesis Rabbah* 76.9 and *Tanh.* 8.19 allude to Jacob's concealing Dinah in a chest, away from Esau. The issue of the patriarch not fulfilling a vow he had made comes to the forefront in *Lev. Rab.* 37.1 and *Tanh.* 8.20 and 8.22. In the last reference, Jacob's reputation vis-à-vis the Divine is upheld or maintained.

In order to maintain this balance or diverse range of opinion or conclusion about what happened at Shechem, some texts, such as those mentioned above, stress that the patriarch had erred. One more, *Pirqe R. El.* 38, speaks of him "leaning his hand against the wall," quite possibly alleging that he had come too close to the Hivites with his family. Although Jacob may have settled his clan close to the Hivite settlement, the vast majority of midrashic texts focused attention on Dinah "going out." That was such a constant refrain throughout these passages, that I did not track every attestation of the phrase. Some passages squarely and unequivocally place the blame on Dinah.

The passage from *Ecclesiastes Rabbah* (X.8.1) clearly claims that she "brought upon herself the violation." It is the text which begins presenting Dinah as the one who had "broken through a fence" and was thus bitten by a snake. One could conclude that the ancient rabbis held Dinah responsible for what happened to her by claiming that she had transgressed a socially proscribed boundary. *Tanhuma* 8.12 may be construed as a close parallel to this line of thinking. It puts forward the idea that Dinah "caused herself to come to corruption." It alleges that because Dinah went out into the marketplace and because she did not "act to conceal herself," she "gave an opening" to Shechem. In short, she, using our language "put herself out there." This action, according to these rabbis, paved the way for Shechem to do what he did. Significant blame is placed on survivor/victim.

A refrain that occurs three times throughout *Genesis Rabbah* is that Dinah's going out caused a number of events to happen: see *Gen. Rab.* 80.2, 80.3, and 80.12. In 80.2 and 80.12 she, or most properly, her going out, caused Jacob's clan to be treated as public property. According to 80.3, her going out led direcly to the slaughter of Hamor and Shechem. This is another instance in which the behaviors of one person had direct impact on others. The same may be said of the passages that claim that Dinah was punished for something Jacob did or neglected to do. These texts portray people's actions as having direct results on the fate of others. In both *Gen. Rab.* 84.3 and 84.21, Dinah is presented as a source of disquiet, trouble, or sorrow for her father, Jacob.

When the texts speak of Dinah as one who "went out," very frequently the writers/redactors connote a negative value either to her or to her action. Dinah is referred to frequently as a gadabout. This may be seen in *Gen. Rab.* 80.5 and 18.2 (where she is also said to have been "immodest"); *Lev. Rab.* 37.1 and *Tanh.* 8.17 use similar language. Three of these[117] are very close parallels, saying that not only Dinah, but many of the well known women in the HB disappointed the Divine, spurning God's reproof and creational advice.

Dinah fared especially badly. She was said to have been immoral in a number of references: *Gen. Rab.* 80.1, *Pirqe R. El.* 38, *Lev. Rab.* 37.1, and *Tanh.* 8.14 and 8.15. She is associated with unchastity in *Tanh.* 8.20. In some of these situations she is paralleled with her mother Leah; that is the case in *Gen. Rab.* 80.1 and in *Tanh.* 8.14 and 8.15.

As was also the situation in Genesis 34, Simeon and Levi come to the forefront of the *midrashim*, in terms of connecting them directly with Dinah. The following texts do so explicitly: *Gen. Rab.* 80.10, 98.5, and 99.7; *Pirqe R. El.* 38; and *Tanh.* 8.19 and 22.

There is midrashic evidence of three different marriages of Dinah; she is called the wife of Shechem (in *Gen. Rab.* 76.9 and 80.8), Job (*Gen. Rab.* 19.12, 57.4, 80.4 and *Tanh.* 8.19), and Simeon (*Gen. Rab.* 80.11).

These texts conclude their references to Dinah in a way that is similar to the HB. There is an understanding that she went to Egypt with Jacob and his family (*Pirqe R. El.* 39). Unlike the HB, *Gen. Rab.* 80.11 refers to her death and burial, preserving the tradtion that she was buried in Canaan by Simeon, her brother and husband.

CHAPTER THREE

Dinah IN THE *Targumim*

INTRODUCTION TO THE *TARGUMIM*

The word "targum" derives from the Hebrew root *trgm* (תרגם) meaning "to translate" or "to render into another language." Some have concluded that at least since the time of Ezra, the Torah occupied a central place within Judaism.[1] As one of the "basics" of Jewish life, the Torah was read or recited in synagogue worship/ liturgical life. As language shifts occurred, specifically, as people no longer spoke Hebrew, the need arose to translate or render the Torah into a new language; two generally well-known examples of this are the Greek Septuagint and Aramaic *Targumim*. It is clear that these were used in the context of Jewish worship. A reference from *b. Berakot*, in the *Mishnah*, indicates a precedent that translations or versions of the Torah were read together or side-by-side in (Jewish) worship: "twice from the Biblical/Hebrew text and once from the Targum."[2] Worship leaders read from these texts. Schools and synagogues used the Torah as one of the bases upon which they taught people about a life of faith.[3] Many struggled with these texts, getting them to suit the needs of particular contexts; this is one of the reasons for the numerous textual traditions of the *targumim*.

Not only the basic meaning of the root *trgm* (תרגם), but also the witnesses of the *targumim* themselves, makes it evident that these "versions" of the biblical texts are more than just translations of the Hebrew. The *Targumim* contain significant blocks of additional material which give witness to various traditions about Dinah. This may be haggadic (narrative/story) and/or exegetical/interpretive in nature. In a few cases, it even expresses the writer's/redactor's/narrator's hope or intent as to how the story will be used in future generations. Dinah is mentioned in the following *Targumim*: *Neofiti I*, *Onqelos*, *Pseudo-Jonathan*, and *Job*.

INTRODUCTION TO *TARGUM NEOFITI I*

It is generally agreed that *Targum Neofiti* is of Palestinian origin.[4] Its language is "a form of Palestinan Jewish Aramaic close to the Galilean dialect of the Jerusalem

Talmud."[5] As is the case with the vast number of the *targumim*, this text shows telltale signs of redaction.[6] While some have argued for an extremely late dating of *Neofiti*'s final redaction, even up into the time of the Renaissance,[7] there appears to be evidence in support of very early material within *Neofiti*.[8] As Philip S. Alexander has written, "it is a text which has evolved over a very long period of time. Analysis suggests that underlying *Neof.* is a base text which applies certain standard exegetical procedures and employs certain standard equivalents for the original Hebrew, but that this text has been glossed and reworked over a considerable period of time."[9] He concluded that "there are no good grounds for dating anything in *Neof.* later than the 3d/4th cent. C. E."[10]

The first reference deals directly with Dinah at Shechem. As is frequently the case with the HB, multiple extant manuscript traditions allow readers the opportunity to deal with the textual issues pertinent to the Dinah stories. The following is *Neofiti: Genesis*, Chapter 34[11]:

> 1. And Dinah, the daughter of Leah, whom she had borne[12] to Jacob, went out *to let herself be seen* with the daughters *of the people* of the land.[13] 2. And Shechem, the son of Hamor[14] the Hivite, the master of the land, saw her and took her and abused[15] her[16] and disgraced her. 3. And his soul found delight in Dinah, Jacob's daughter; and he was enamored of the maiden[17] and he spoke *words of peace* with the heart of the maiden,[18] 4. And Shechem said to Hamor, his father, saying: "Take this maiden[19] (for me" as wife." 5. And Jacob heard that he had defiled Dinah, his daughter; and his sons were with the cattle[20] in the field, and Jacob remained silent[21] until the time they came. 6. And Hamor, the father of Shechem, went out to Jacob to speak with him. 7. And the sons of Jacob entered from the field when they heard (of it); and the men were very angry and they were very much offended because he had done[22] an abomination in Israel in having intercourse with[23] the daughter of Jacob, for it was *not proper*[24] that such a thing be done. 8. And Hamor spoke with them saying: "The soul of Shechem, my son, found delight in your daughter. I pray give her in marriage to him as wife,[25] 9. and mingle[26] with us; give us[27] your daughter and take our daughters for yourselves. 10. And you shall dwell with us and the land will be before you. Dwell[28] and *trade in it* and take possession of it." 11. And Shechem said to his father and brothers: "I have found[29] grace *and favor* in your sight, and what you will say to me I will give. 12. Make very great for me the *dowry* and the *marriage contract*[30] and I will give just[31] as you say to me, but give me the maiden as wife." 13. And the sons of Jacob answered Shechem and Hamor his father in the *vastness of their wisdom*,[32] and they spoke[33] (thus), because he had violated[34] Dinah their sister. 14. And they said to them: "We cannot do this thing—to give[35] in marriage our sister to a man who has <a foreskin>[36] because he is a disgrace[37] to us. 15. But we will *become mingled*[38] with you if you become like us, circumcising every male of you. 16. And we will give our daughter to you, and your daughters we will take to ourselves, and we will dwell with you and *all of us* will become one people. 17. And if you will not listen to us by becoming circumcised, we will take our daughter and go." 18. And their words were

pleasing[39] in the sight of Hamor and in the sight of Shechem, the son of Hamor. 19. And the young man[40] did not delay to do the deed because his soul found delight in the daughter of Jacob; and he was the most honored of all *the men of* the house of his father. 20. And Hamor came, and Shechem and his son, to the gate of their city and spoke with the men of their city,[41] saying: 21. "These men are perfect *in good work*[42] with us, and let them dwell the land and trade in it; and the land—behold, it is broad *in its territory*—lies before them. We will take their daughters to us as wives and we will give our daughters to them. 22. But only on this condition will the men *mingle* with us, to dwell with us, to become one nation: that we circumcise[43] every male as they are circumcised. 23. Their possessions and their wealth[44] and all their cattle, are they not ours? Only *let us mingle* with them and they will dwell with us." 24. And every one going out the gate of his city listened to Hamor and Shechem, his son; and they circumcised every male, everyone going out the gate of his city. 25. And it happened that on the third day, when they were sore *from their circumcision*,[45] two sons of Jacob, Simeon and Levi, brothers of Dinah, took each man his sword, and entered the city in all safety and killed every male. 26. And they killed Hamor and Shechem, his son, with the edge of the sword and took Dinah from the house of Shechem and went out. 27. The sons of Jacob went in upon the slain and plundered the city because they had defiled their sister.[46] 28. They took their sheep and their oxen, <and their he-asses>,[47] and what was in the city and what was in the field; 29. and all their *wealth*[48] and all their little ones and their wives and all that was in the houses they took captive and made (their) spoil. 30. And Jacob said to Simeon and Levi: "You have done evil to me, *making my name*[49] *evil* before the inhabitants of the land, among the Canaanites and the Perizzites. I am a people few in number and they will be gathered <against me and will kill me>[50] and *will blot out (both) me* and *the men of* my house."[51] 31. And *the two sons*[52] *of Jacob*,[53] *Simeon and Levi, answered*[54] and said *to Jacob, their father: "It is not fitting that they should say*[55] *in their congregations and in their schools.*[56] <*Uncircumcised*>[57] *have defiled virgins*[58] *and servers* <*of idols*>[59] *the daughter of Jacob.*[60] *But it is fitting that they should say in the congregations*[61] *of Israel and in their schoolhouse:*[62] *'Uncircumcised were slain on account of a virgin* <*and servers of idols*>[63] *because they defiled*[64] *Dinah, the daughter of Jacob; so that after all this Shechem,*[65] *the son of Hamor, might not become proud in his soul and exalted in his heart and say: 'Like a woman who has not a son of man, avenging humiliation,* thus was it done to *Dinah* our sister: like a lost woman, *a prostitute.*'"[66]

There are numerous textual variants or glosses. Quite a few of these were derived from the marginal glosses of *Neofiti* (*Nfmg*). McNamara wrote:

> A notable feature of Codex Neofiti 1 is the numerous marginal glosses (in this edition noted as Nfmg) and the occasional interlinear glosses (Nfi) it contains. The indications are that all these are drawn from genuine Targum texts (whether complete or fragmentary) available to the annotators in the early sixteen century, some of which are apparently now lost. These glosses were written by ten different hands or so, some of them identical with the chief scribes. ...[67]

Textual variants abound, allowing the reader to see the multiplicity of traditions and the tendencies that various strands had to make the language of the text more palatable and less offensive. Some of the traditions sought to uphold the reputation of the patriarch Jacob and his sons, presenting the younger generation, for example, as speaking with wisdom instead of with deceit. Much more analysis could be done in this regard. However, the primary goal of this exploration is to focus on the portrayal of Dinah in the *targumim*.

In *Targum Neofiti* Dinah is introduced very similarly to how she is presented in the MT. The narrator delineated her biological relations, naming both of Dinah's parents. *Targum Neofiti* reads with the MT, "the daughter of Leah, whom she had borne to Jacob."

As the text states Dinah's intent for going out, *Tg. Neof.*'s statement that Dinah went out "to let herself be seen" resembles the midrashic traditions which alleged that Dinah was willing to take some risks, possibly even wanting to be associated and seen with the daughters of the people of the land. In that regard *Tg. Neof.* is especially similar to *Tanh.*, which had portrayed Dinah as one who went out to be seen. It may come as less than a surprise to the reader, than is the case with the HB account, that Shechem saw her.

One can note a similarity between this text and the HB or MT: this first sentence of the text (v. 1) is the only place where Dinah is portrayed as the subject of any verbs; in every other instance, she is the object. However, although *Tg. Neof.* begins by saying "she went out" (an active verb), unlike the HB, it soon combines Dinah's activity with passivity—she went out to let herself be seen. The verb "let herself be seen" is grammatically in a reflexive passive voice.

The text continues in v. 2: "Shechem ... saw her and took her and abused her and disgraced her."[68] While she may have gone out to let herself be seen with the daughters of the people of the land, the rhetoric of "abuse" may lead a modern reader to conclude that the sexual intercourse between Shechem and Dinah was not consensual. This is especially underscored by McNamara's footnote indicating that this particular Aramaic verb literally means "use." These two points lead modern readers to the impression that this instance of sexual violation was a rape. Even at this early point in the text, *Tg. Neof.* presented Dinah as a vulnerable victim.

In these early verses, this *Targum* consistently refers to Dinah as a "maiden;" that word occurs twice in v. 3 and once each in vv. 4 and 12. For the modern reader, "maiden" may be a young woman of marriageable age; in some instances, it may imply virginity.

Her innocence might also be read into the text of v. 3, which alleges that Shechem spoke words of peace to her. This may insinuate that there was a need to "calm her down" or reassure her after intercourse. The same may be said of a man's need to "speak to the heart of" a woman, as is in the HB.

Also, closely in line with the HB, in v. 7, when the sons of Jacob heard, "they were very angry and they were very much offended because he had done an abomination in Israel in having intercourse with the daughter of Jacob, for it was not proper that such a thing be done." According to this verse, Shechem's offense was grave. "Abomination" connotes a serious affront; it is loaded with theological import. One can connect it to numerous HB passages which speak specifically of the "abominations of Canaan." Thus the text portrays Shechem acting in a manner consistent with or expected of a foreigner, a Hivite. There is a particularly negative characterization of him in this text. As he is developed more negatively, Dinah is shown in a more innocent light.

The sons of Jacob certainly hold a different perspective than Shechem. This was also true in the HB[69]; whereas Shechem loved or was enamored with Dinah, the sons consider the offense to be heinous. The perspectives of the narrator and Jacob's sons coalesce; it had been the narrator who first defined the intercourse, Shechem's deed, as having "abused" and "disgraced" Dinah. The sons of Jacob view the situation similarly.

On the other hand, Shechem, and his father, Hamor, were in another thought world—their primary intent was to "take Dinah" as a wife for Shechem. One can note a few issues with the *Tg. Neof.* text: it is more unclear than the HB; one could indeed interpret v. 8 as being Hamor's words spoken only to the sons of Jacob. That is, it is possible that Jacob was not in their midst. This reading could be reinforced by what seems like an error in v. 11: "And Shechem said to *his* father and brothers." In the HB, this verse reads, "And Shechem spoke to *her* father and brothers." They propose an invitation "mingle" or intermarry; their offer is clearly understood by Jacob's sons as the "becoming one people" (v. 16). This is especially possible, they allege after the rite of circumcision.

Consider more closely the words of the sons of Jacob in v. 14. *Targum Neofiti* is one of the few texts which allege that he (i.e. Shechem) himself was a disgrace. It is worth noting that it was not necessarily "just" his state of being uncircumcised which was considered disgraceful; he himself was a disgrace. Many traditions, including the HB and other *targumim*, claim that "it," i.e., the sons' giving their sister to one with a foreskin, was or would be a disgrace. When one changes that focus from the act of giving to the very man Shechem as a disgrace, again, Dinah's reputation fares well.

Throughout this section, the reader is aware (v. 13) that the sons of Jacob answered Shechem and Hamor "in the vastness of their wisdom." Note that this rendering of "wisdom" conflicts with the MT/HB tradition which has them speaking with deceit (or as McNamara says, "with guile"[70]). This particular use of "wisdom" may take on the connotation of "cunning." One can note the way in which the text furthers their characterization as "wise"; in the closing paragraph,

Simeon and Levi speak with an air of wisdom and authority, as one might expect of sages, passing along their own tradition and interpretation of the event. Indeed, quite possibily setting their own tradition and interpretation of how they wanted their sister and this event at Shechem remembered.

The sons of Jacob certainly were persuasive; this is underscored by Shechem's desire to act as quickly as possible in order to secure Dinah as his wife. As a reader encounters v. 20, once again, he or she may wonder about an error in the text: it reads, "And Hamor came, and Shechem *and* his son ..." Were three generations of men present? This seems unlikely given that v. 19 referred to Shechem as a "young man." McNamara had even noted that one of the glosses used the word "boy" in reference to Shechem. However the textual error is intriguing. If the reader even entertains the possibility that there were three generations present, i.e., that Shechem had a son, this may indicate that Shechem was significantly older than Dinah. When considering the possibility that he had a son, certain questions arise: Was his wife deceased—what was the relationship between Shechem and the mother of Shechem's son? Was the "relationship" or incident with Dinah an instance of adultery or polygamy/polyamory? There are indeed many gaps in this narrative.

As the Hivite father and son (and grandson?) return to their home, and present the terms of the negotiations to their fellow men, v. 21 puts forward a new perspective of Jacob's clan. Hamor and Shechem conclude that they are "perfect in good work." Again, this is an ironic statement, showing how easily duped and gullible the Hivites were.[71] For very soon afterwards (at least in narrative time), "Simeon and Levi, entered the city in all safety and killed every male."

As the two generations of Hebrew men respond to the mass slaughter of the Hivite men, Jacob expressed his fear about the implications of his sons' actions. In v. 30, the patriarch accuses his two sons, "You have done evil to me, making my name evil before the inhabitants of the land ..." Note that according to the HB, Jacob had alleged that they had "made him odious." *Targum Neofiti* may at this point be protecting the reputation of the patriarch by not including the "odious" phrase. However, Jacob fears that his name, or honor, has suffered damage. As was the case with the HB, the older ancestor focuses on himself and his "house" or lineage, while the younger generations hone in on what this meant for Dinah and her reputation and honor.

The closing paragraph clearly demonstrates the concern of Simeon and Levi over how their sister Dinah might be remembered by the generations; it is an attempt to "set the record straight." It attests to there already being a multiplicity of traditions at that point in history. Some of these traditions side with Jacob the patriarch; others side with Simeon and Levi.

The closing paragraph, all one verse, begins, "It is not fitting that they should say in their congregations and in the schools uncircumcised have defiled virgins."

Obviously some were making the allegations encountered. There was a strong tradition, as evidenced by the *midrashim*, that the Hivite Shechem had indeed done this to Dinah.

One may pause here to note that this paragraph puts forth the claim that Dinah was a virgin. That had not been clearly stated in the MT of Genesis 34. Note too the various traditions, in the form of textual variants, which sought to clarify her virginal status, claiming that she was a "virgin with regard to virginity" versus a "virgin with regard to menstruation." It was important that she was nubile (i.e., a menstruating woman, one capable of conceiving). That may indeed fit in well with the aforementioned understanding of "maiden."

There is an intriguing use of the expression "son of man" to parallel one who avenges humiliation. "Son of man" may just mean a person, as Céline Mangan has asserted.[72] When interpreting the meaning of this verse, one can conclude resolutely that Dinah was humiliated, in the sense of suffering an affront against her status or state, i.e., she was "humbled" or made lower as a result of the intercourse with Shechem. A number of the textual variants make this claim.[73]

It was not only the fact that she had been a virgin before her encounter with Shechem. His identity as a Hivite made a significant impression on the sons of Jacob, who clearly referred to the Shechemites as "uncircumcised" "idol worshippers." First of all, one may note that the Shechemites had become circumcised. This tradition, while noting the circumcision in the narrative, overlooks it at the end. The focus remains on what they had done to Dinah—they had defiled her; the word "defile" is used twice in this verse. The two sons guaranteed by murder that Shechem would never boast about what he had done to Dinah. Note here the preposition "to." A modern reader, who might discern between something sexually being done "to" versus "with" a woman may note that this preposition alone buttresses the interpretation that this offense was heinous and that Dinah had not consented to the intercourse.

The variants of this verse may reveal a cultural understanding or assumption with which Simeon and Levi were acting. One can note the categories of "lost women, "prostitutes," "those without an avenger (of blood) (of humiliation)," and "whoring women" mentioned. Apparently these were women who neither had the right nor the connections to be protected. It was proposed that Shechem or the Shechemites had treated Dinah like a woman from one of these categories when they acted in a way that assumed no one would take action against them, avenging the wrong done to Dinah.

The tone of the closing section of *Tg. Neof.* clearly seeks to safeguard Dinah's reputation. This interpretation, it is hoped, will be passed along via congregations and schools/school houses.[74] One may wonder about the interface between the *targumim* and *midrashim*. The *targumim* certainly offer a counter-interpretation to what was seen in the *midrashim*. In many of the midrashic passages, Dinah was portrayed as a "whore" or "prostitute," one who had erred. In many ways, *Targum Neofiti* demonstrates that some had hopes that the tradition reflected in that text would either help to define or make its way into developing Judaism(s). According to *Targum Neofiti*, Simeon and Levi themselves had established this tradition. Dinah, an innocent virgin, was the victim of a horrible crime. The dastardly perpetrator, Shechem, was rightly punished by death.

INTRODUCTION TO *TARGUM ONQELOS*

Like many of the other *Targumim* and writings, *Targum Onqelos* (*Tg. Onq.*) is comprised of layers of traditions. To use Bernard Grossfeld's language, one may choose to distinguish between relative dates of the Targum's "original composition" and its "final redaction."[75] Many scholars speak of Proto-Onqelos, a Palestinian tradition which was reworked or edited at least once.[76] Most conclude that *Targum Onqelos* received its final form in Babylonia in the third or fourth century C.E.[77] Philip S. Alexander argued for a fourth or fifth century final Babylonian editing or redaction of *Tg. Onq.*[78] Others opt for a Palestinian provenance.[79]

Targum Onqelos was "widely accepted by Jews as the most authoritative Targum to the Pentateuch."[80] Even within centuries of its final redaction, it was quoted; the first reference to *Tg. Onq.* comes from the 8th or 9th century text *Pirqe R. El.*[81] *Targum Onqelos* is also referred to throughout the Babylonian Talmud (BT).[82] Although there are significant historical issues with the BT legend, a tradition credits Onqelos, the proselyte, with having written the Targum along with R. Eliezer and R. Joshua,[83] thus the Targum's name, Onqelos. It will become evident, as others have noted, *Tg. Onq.* follows the MT version of Genesis 34 very closely.[84] The following is *Targum Onqelos: Genesis*, Chapter 34.[85]

> 1. Now Dinah, the daughter of Leah to whom she had given birth for Jacob, went out to look at the women of the land. 2. And Shekhem, son of Hamor the Hivite, the chief of the land, saw her; whereupon he took her and lay with her, and thus abused her. 3. And *he*[86] *was delighted with*[87] Dinah, the daughter of Jacob, and he loved the girl and *spoke*[88] to the heart of the girl. 4. Then Shekhem said to his father Hamor, as follows, "Get this girl for me as a wife," 5. Now Jacob had heard that he had defiled his daughter Dinah, while his sons were in the field with his cattle; but Jacob kept silent until they came <home>. 6. Then Hamor, Shekhem's father went out to Jacob to speak with him. 7. When Jacob's sons heard <this> as they were coming <home> from the field, the men were distressed and very angry; for he had committed a disgraceful act in Israel by lying *with*[89] Jacob's daughter, since it was not *proper*[90] <for such a thing> to be done. 8. And Hamor spoke with them, as follows, "My son Shekhem his soul is delighted with your daughter. Give her now to him as a wife. 9. And intermarry with

us {by} giving us your daughters for yourselves. 10. And you shall dwell with us, and the land shall be <open> before you; dwell *and trade in it*,[91] and acquire possessions in it." 11. Then Shekhem said to her father and her brothers, "Let me find *mercy in your sight*,[92] and whatever you say to me I will grant. 12. Demand of me an abundance in dowry and presents, and I will grant whatever you tell me; but give me the girl for a wife." 13. Then Jacob's sons answered Shekhem and his father Hamor *with wisdom*,[93] and they spoke up, because he had defiled their sister. 14. And they said, "We are unable to do this thing, to give our sister to a man who is uncircumcised, for that would be a disgrace to us. 15. Nevertheless, on this <condition> will we agree to you; if you become like us by circumcising every male among you. 16. Then we will give our daughters to you and take your daughters for ourselves; and we will live with you and become one nation, 17. But if you will not *listen* to us to become circumcised, then we will take our daughter and go." 18. Now their words appealed to Hamor, and to Shekhem, son of Hamor. 19. So the youth did not delay to do *the*[94] thing, for he was delighted with Jacob's daughter. Now he was the most honored one in his father's house. 20. Then Hamor and his son Shekhem came to the gate of their city and spoke with the men of the city, as follows, 21. "These men are *friendly*[95] with us; let them, therefore, dwell in the land *and trade in it*, for, here, the land is *large enough*[96] for them. We will take their daughters for ourselves as wives, and our daughters we will give to them. 22. Nevertheless, on this <condition> will the men agree to dwell with us, to become one people: That every male among us be circumcised as they are circumcised. 23. Would not their flocks, their possessions, and all their cattle {then} be ours? Only let us agree with them, so that they will dwell with us." 24. So all who went out of the gate of the city *listened* to Hamor and his son Shekhem, and all who went out of the gate of the city circumcised all the males. 25. Then it happened on the third day, *when their pain had grown severe on them*,[97] that the two sons of Jacob—Simeon and Levi, brothers of Dinah—each took his sword, and came upon the city *which dwelt*[98] in security, and slew all the males. 26. And they put Hamor and his son Shekhem to the sword, and they took Dinah out of Shekhem's house and departed. 27. The sons of Jacob *came to strip the slain*[99] and plundered the city, because they had defiled their sister. 28. They *plundered*[100] their sheep, their oxen, and their donkeys, as well as that which was in the city, and that which was in the field. 29. And all their property, and all their children and their wives, and all that was in the house, they captured and plundered. 30. Then Jacob said to Simeon and Levi, "You have brought trouble on me *by placing enmity between me and the natives of the land*[101]—the Canaanites and the Perizzites; and I have a host of numbered people, so that if they gathered themselves against me and attacked me, I and *the members of* my household would be destroyed." 31. But they said, "*Should our sister be made a harlot?*"[102]

Dinah is introduced in the text very similarly to how she is presented elsewhere, with the naming of both of her parents. *Targum Onqelos* renders this verse slightly differently either from the MT or *Tg. Neof.* with its expression "whom she had given birth for Jacob."

In this same verse, as the text states Dinah's intent for going out, *Tg. Onq.*'s statement that Dinah went out "to look at the women of the land" is very reminiscent of the HB's, "went out to see the daughters of the land." Also paralleling the HB, this first sentence of the text (v. 1) is the only place where Dinah is portrayed as the subject of any verbs; in every other instance, she is the object. Unlike *Tg. Neof.*, which had alleged that "she went out to let herself be seen with the daughters of the people of the land," this text makes no comment on her comfort/intent with being seen with or by anyone. It portrays more actively—she went out to see.

The text continues in v. 2: "Shechem ... saw her, whereupon he took her and lay with her and thus abused her." Here too Dinah is the object of these four verbs. This narrative, however, while it uses the same language of "abuse" found in *Tg. Neof.*, makes it clear that Shechem's taking and lying with Dinah is what had "abused" her; this is accomplished by the word "thus." Even though the word "abused" is in the text, a reader may not feel the same level of antipathy toward Shechem as one had with Tg. *Neof.* Still there is a sense in which Dinah was a vulnerable victim.

This impression may be underscored as this *Targum* consistently refers to Dinah as a "girl"; that word occurs twice in v. 3 and once each in vv. 4 and 12. For the modern reader, "girl" may conjure up ideas of a younger more innocent female than a "maiden."

In the next verse, *Tg. Onq.* lines up extremely well the HB, when it asserts that Shechem "spoke to the heart of the girl." One may note that some interpreters have concluded that this means that Shechem had to calm or reassure Dinah after they had been together sexually.

Also, closely in line with the HB, in v. 7, when the sons of Jacob heard, "the men were distressed and very angry, for he had committed a disgraceful act in Israel by lying with Jacob's daughter, since it was not proper for such a thing be done." This text's language of "disgraceful act" is reminiscent of the HB's "heinous offense." Both *Tg. Neof* and *Tg. Onq* are closely aligned in translation and in interpretation.

This is also true when one considers the initial ambiguity of the addressees of Hamor's words in vv. 8–10. However *Tg. Onq.* clarifies that Jacob was present as Shechem said his piece (vv. 11–12). There the narrator alleges that Shechem spoke to "her father and her brothers."

Targum Onqelos also is in closer agreement with the HB than with *Tg. Neof.* in v. 14's allegation that it would have been a disgrace for the sons of Jacob to have given their sister to an uncircumcised man; remember that *Neofiti* had claimed that Shechem himself was a disgrace.

As had been the case with *Tg. Neof.*, the sons of Jacob answered Shechem and Hamor "with wisdom." This is different from the HB's assertion that they spoke with deceit. *Targum Onqelos* is different from *Tg. Neof.*, in that the lengthy elaboration of Simeon's and Levi's motivation is missing from v. 31.

Hamor and Shechem are presented as being gullible; that has been true consistently in other texts. Here they deem Jacob and his sons to be "friendly." When the readers are aware of the outcome of this episode, they can note how ironically sad their "read" of this clan was.

Targum Onqelos is more in agreement with the HB than is *Tg. Neof.*, in its careful identification of only two Hivite men, father and son, Hamor and Shechem returning to the gate of their city. In *Neofiti*, there had been some cause to conclude that Shechem had a son who was with them at this point.

The conclusion of *Tg. Onq.* is closer to the HB's account than is *Tg. Neof.* Jacob was frightened by the implications of his sons' actions. In v. 30, the patriarch upbraids his two sons, alleging that they and their actions had placed enmity between him and the natives of the land. This language is slightly different from the HB, where Jacob had alleged that they had "made him odious." Once again this *Targum* may be an attempt to protect the patriarch and his reputation by not including the "odious" phrase.

However, Jacob fears that his name, or honor, has suffered damage. As was the case with the HB, the older ancestor focuses on himself and his "house" or lineage, while the younger generations hone in on what Shechem's actions meant for Dinah's reputation and honor, and quite potentially their own standing.

Generally speaking, although there have been a number of minor shifts in language between the HB and *Tg. Onq.*, this text is a "more faithful" translation of HB, in terms of a closer correspondence to the MT. There are fewer embellishments in *Onqelos* than there were in *Neofiti*. The third Targumic text which mentions Dinah is *Targum Pseudo-Jonathan*.

INTRODUCTION TO *TARGUM PSEUDO-JONATHAN*

Targum Pseudo-Jonathan (Tg. Ps.-J.) is generally regarded as one of the Palestinian *targumim*.[103] It has received its name because of a common, albeit problematic, legend attributing its authorship to Jonathan ben Uzziel.[104] It has been noted that "Pseudo-Jonathan (Ps.-J.) provides us with a translation of almost every verse of the Pentatuech."[105] Its close relationship to *Tg. Onq.* has also been noted.[106] Michael Maher has written that "its hybrid language is a mixture of Palestinian forms with linguistic elements that are characteristic of Eastern Aramaic."[107] While a number of scholars have commented on *Tg. Ps.-J.*'s tendency to be fairly "indelicate" or even "coarse" (to use Maher's language)[108] in matters relating to sexuality,[109] there does not seem to be such a tendency relative to the Dinah incident. In fact, at least in the passage below, the opposite is true. Maher maintains that "this Targum in its final form cannot be dated before the seventh or eighth century."[110] Some have concluded that there was a Babylonian rescension of a Palestinian text which led to the Babylonian Jewish community giving acceptance and authority to this Targum.[111] The passage relating to Dinah is *Targum Pseudo–Jonathan: Genesis*, Chapter 34[112]

> 1. Dinah, the daughter of Leah, whom she had borne to Jacob, went out to see *the customs of*[113] the daughters of *the people of* the land. 2. Shechem, son of Hamor the Hivite, the chief of the land, saw her and took her *by force*[114] and lay with her and afflicted her. 3. And he took delight in Dinah, the daughter of Jacob, and he loved the maiden and spoke *soothing words*[115] to the maiden's heart. 4. Shechem said to his father Hamor, saying, "Take this girl for me as wife." 5. And Jacob heard that he had defiled his daughter Dinah; his sons were with his livestock in the field, and Jacob was silent until they came. 6. Hamor, Shechem's father, went out to Jacob to speak to him. 7. Jacob's sons came in from the field when they heard of (it); and the men were distressed and very angry because *Shechem* had done a disgraceful deed in Israel in lying with Jacob's daughter, since it was not *proper*[116] that such a thing be done. 8. And Hamor spoke with them, saying, "The soul of Shechem my son takes delight in your daughter; give her to him, I pray, as wife. 9. *Intermingle* with us *through marriage*; give your daughters to us, and take our daughters for yourselves, 10. And you shall dwell with us, and the land shall be before you; dwell *where you will be at ease, and do business there*, and take possession of it." 11. Shechem said to her father and to her brothers, "Let me find mercy in your eyes, and whatever you say to me I will give. 12. Demand of me a great bride price and a present, and I will give according as you say to me; but give me the maiden as wife." 13. The sons of Jacob answered Shechem and his father Hamor *with wisdom*,[117] and they spoke (thus), because he had defiled their sister Dinah. 14. And they said to them, "We cannot do this thing, to give our sister to a man who is uncircumcised, for that is a shame for us. 15. Only on this (condition) will we agree with you; if you become like us by circumcising every male among you. 16. Then we will give our daughters to you, and we will take your daughter for ourselves; and we will dwell with you, and we will become one people. 17. But if you will not listen to us and be circumcised, we will take our daughter *by force* and go." 18 Their words were pleasing to Hamor and to Shechem, Hamor's son. 19. The young man did not delay in doing the thing, for he delighted in Jacob's daughter. Now he was the most honored in all his father's house. 20. Hamor and his son Shechem came to the gate of their city and spoke with the men of *the gate of* their city, saying, 21. "These men are peaceful toward us; let them dwell in the land and *do business*[118] in it, for, behold, the land is broad in its boundaries before them. Let us take their daughters to us as wives, and let us give them our daughters. 22. But (only) on this (condition) will the men agree with us to dwell among us so that we may become one people; that we circumcise every male among us, just as they are circumcised. 23. Will not their livestock and their possessions and all the cattle be ours? Only let us agree with them, so that they may dwell with us." 24. All who went out of the gate of his city listened to Hamor and to his son Shechem; and they circumcised every male, all who went out of the gate of his city. 25. And on the third day, when they were *weakened by* the pain *of their circumcision*, two *of the* sons of Jacob, Simeon and Levi, Dinah's brothers, took each man his sword, entered the city which *was dwelling* in

security,[119] and killed every male. 26. And they killed Hamor and his son Shechem with the edge of the sword, took Dinah out of Shechem's house, and went away. 27. *The rest of* the sons of Jacob went in *to strip*[120] the slain, and they plundered the city because they had defiled their sister *within it*. 28. They *plundered* their sheep, their oxen, and their asses, whatever was in the city and whatever was in the field. 29. All their possessions, all their little ones, <their wives>,[121] and all that was in the house they took captive and plundered. 30. And Jacob said to Simeon and Levi, "You have brought trouble upon me, *spreading a bad reputation*[122] *about me* among the inhabitants of the land, among the Canaanites and among the Perizzites. I have few men, and (if) they unite against me and smite me, I will be wiped out, I and *the members of* my house." 31. *Simeon and Levi answered, "It is not fitting that it should be said in the congregation of the children of Israel:*[123] *'(The) uncircumcised defiled the virgin, and the worshipers of idols polluted the daughter of Jacob.' But this is what it is fitting to say: '(The) uncircumcised were killed on account of the virgin, and the worshipers of idols on account of the daughters of Jacob.' And Shechem, Hamor's son, will not boast against us with his words;* he would have treated our sister like a prostitute, *a harlot who has no avenger,*[124] *if we had not done this thing."*[125]

There is a very consistent way of initially presenting Dinah as "the daughter of Leah" with a following statement that Leah had borne this daughter to Jacob. There is just a slight variation among our three *targumim* when it comes to the wording of the verse which re-introduces Dinah to the reader.

The reader finds in *Tg. Ps.–J.* a new piece of data in v. 1's statement that Dinah had gone "out to see the customs of the daughters of the people of the land." This is the only Targum which makes reference to her wanting to see "customs." Although for most modern readers, it simply refers to Dinah's curiosity about the ways of women surrounding her, in some contexts it was interpreted as a less than desirable trait, a proverbial "playing with fire."[126] This may have been especially true for women.

However, although the modern reader may be aware of these various interpretations and different meanings or senses that might be relevant, *Tg. Ps.–J.* makes no comment or implication that Dinah was at fault. The following investigation will make that even more evident.

This text, like all *targumim* so far and like the HB, presents Dinah as an active character (i.e., the subject of verbs) only here in v. 1. As has been elsewhere, *Tg. Ps.–J.* portrays Dinah in the next verse as the object of four consecutive verbs. Here it is said that Shechem, "saw her and took her by force and lay with her and afflicted her."

Unlike the other two *targumim* explored, Maher's translation of *Tg. Ps.–J.* does not use the word "abused;" instead, he uses the verb "afflicted." A modern reader may struggle to interpret the word "afflicted" in this context. It may be taken as the emotional/spiritual damage done to Dinah. It may also refer to the lowering of her status. For example, later on in the text (in v. 31) she is referred to as having been a virgin when she had first encountered Shechem. He is said to have "defiled" her. That defilement, the loss of her virginity, and the accompanying sense of shame or disgrace could indeed be considered an affliction. As previously mentioned, Dinah's experience with Shechem would have "lowered" her and her status. This text is different from others in that it makes clear that Shechem took Dinah by force. This verse sets *Tg. Ps.-J.* apart from the other *targumim*; it is the only one which claims that Shechem took Dinah by force. To a modern reader, this verse defines the intercourse as "rape" or at least/best abduction. It is possible to conclude that by using force, Shechem had hurt Dinah; affliction therefore may refer to a physical harm.

Targum Pseudo-Jonathan is the only Targum which says "he spoke soothing words" to Dinah (v. 3). This may infer that Dinah needed to be "soothed" after Shechem had afflicted her. It sounds like Dinah was upset. Of course, that is eisegesis, or reading into the text.

This *Targum* also differs from the previous two in that it is inconsistent in how it refers to Dinah; it vacillates between calling her a "maiden" and a "girl."[127] Looking closely at vv. 3, 4, and 12, one will note that in v. 3, the word "maiden" is used. In v. 4, Shechem uses the word "girl" when he speaks to his own father. And in v. 12 Shechem refers to Dinah as a "maiden" when speaking with her father and brothers.

At the point in the narrative of v. 4, one may conclude that Shechem was referring rather innocently or most delicately to Dinah when addressing his own father. This may have had implications for himself, as well. Obviously, he spared his father the detail that he had just "taken" the girl by force. This may be construed as a piece of evidence which portrays Shechem negatively.

Most modern readers may be inclined to think of a "maiden" as a young woman of marriageable age. This may be why Shechem switched his rhetoric when speaking with Dinah's brothers and father.[128] He may have wanted to emphasize her readiness for marriage, the very thing he and his father was proposing to her clan.

This text, *Tg. Ps.-J.*, is very closely related to the other *targumim* and the HB in its handling of v. 7. Readers get a clear idea that Jacob's sons perceived the situation very differently than Hamor and Shechem. This lays the groundwork for the conflict which ensues.

Some modern readers interpret this *Targum* to have more of a business or commercial nature than other texts; this may be due to the word "business" in vv. 10 and 21. It speaks to the importance of commerce in this era and how marriage was often a factor in business–relations. One could connect this with the traditions found in *Legends of the Jews* and in the *midrashim* which presented Jacob as a business person who had set up stalls/*succot* in the area and who had treated the people fairly.

All three *targumim* allege (v. 13) that the sons of Jacob answered Shechem and Hamor "with wisdom." As had been the case with *Tg. Neof.*, *Tg. Ps.–J.* includes the longer justification of Simeon and Levi's actions in v. 31.

As is the case with *Tg. Onq.*, *Tg. Ps.–J.* asserts that the brothers of Dinah maintained that giving their sister to one with a foreskin, was or would be a disgrace to them. *Targum Neofiti* does not fit this pattern, as it had claimed in v. 14 that he (i.e., Shechem) himself was a disgrace.

There are ways in which *Tg. Ps.–J.* coalesces with and differs from the other two *targumim* which deal with this event involving Dinah and Shechem. One minor way in which it differs is that only *Tg. Ps.–J.* presents the sons of Jacob saying in v. 17, "if you will not listen to us … we will take our daughter by force." This is the second time "by force" is used by only *Tg. Ps.–J.* This second use of the expression (in v. 17) parallels Shechem's first taking Dinah by force (in v. 2). Both imply taking Dinah against her will.

A significant contribution of *Tg. Ps.–J.* comes in v. 27, where it is said that Dinah had been defiled in the city. On some occasions,[129] it has been important to analyze various HB passages which deal with rape and other forms of sexual violation. In some of the case laws, in particular, the setting of the offense makes a great deal of difference. A woman had a greater chance of being heard protesting if she happened to be within the city. As has been noted before, the setting of Dinah's violation, both in relation to Genesis 34 and in some of midrashic texts, becomes crucial for interpretation.

Tracking some of the patterns noted before, like *Tg. Onq.*, *Tg. Ps.–J.* asserts that only Shechem and Hamor had returned to the gate of their city to speak with the men of Shechem (v. 20). In this regard, *Tg. Neof.* does not fit the overall pattern, as it alone comments that Shechem's son had been with his father and grandfather.

It has been noted how tragically wrong Hamor and Shechem were in their appraisal of Jacob and his clan. In v. 21, *Tg. Ps.–J.* asserts that the Hivite father and son had deemed the Jacobites "peaceful." That corresponding adjective has been rendered "friendly" in *Tg. Onq.* and "perfect in good work" in *Tg. Neof.*

There have also been a few slight variations of v. 30 from *Targum* to *Targum*. *Tg. Ps.–J.* differs when Jacob accuses his sons of "spreading a bad reputation about me among the inhabitants of the land." Other texts had read "You have done evil to me, making my name evil before the inhabitants of the land …" (*Tg. Neof.*) and "You have brought trouble on me by placing enmity between me and the natives of the land …" (*Tg. Onq.*).

Once again, Jacob is concerned with his own honor and the potential threat to his entire clan. His sons are more concerned with their sister, her reputation, honor, and name. The closing paragraph of *Tg. Ps.–J.* is very similar to that of *Tg. Neof.* It clearly demonstrates how Simeon and Levi want their sister Dinah to be remembered by the generations; like *Tg. Neof.* it is an attempt to "set the record straight." This is accomplished by its assertion that Dinah had been a virgin and they had been in the right to avenge her defamation, thus restoring her and their own honor. The focus in both of these endings upon her initial virginity may in and of itself serve as the first step in her maternal brothers' "clearing" or redeeming her name.

When considering the textual variants to v. 31 of *Tg. Ps.–J.*, one can note how relatively simple and straightforward it is compared to *Tg. Neof.* One may be reminded of the characteristic or trait of *Neofiti*; it has multiple textual attestations.

In closing, I will return to a comment made by Maher in the introduction; he had alleged that *Tg. Ps.–J.* could be rather coarse at times. However, even compared to other *targumim*, I would claim that the narrator is relatively delicate, at least here in regards to a sexual violation of a woman. The language and rhetoric deals very respectfully with her, with Shechem, and with the sexual congress. Let me illustrate this by a few points. *Targum Pseudo-Jonathan* does not mention the word "foreskin" (in v. 14) as does the HB. Instead, *Tg. Ps.–J.* uses the circumlocution, "We cannot do this thing, to give our sister to (a) man who is uncircumcised …". The actual mentioning of "foreskin" had been omitted from *Neofiti* in many of its glosses; *Onqelos* too uses the circumlocution above. Both *Tgs. Ps.–Jon. and Onq.* have included or added the preposition "with" to v. 2's "lay with." Even the HB had not included that nicety. One of the points that Maher made was that "since the Targums were intended to be read in the synagogue in the presence of a devout congregation which included women and children, the targumists were careful to avoid coarse and vulgar language, especially in matters related to sex."[130] One can see that trend, even in comparison to the HB.

INTRODUCTION TO *TARGUM JOB*

The texts/manuscripts of *Targum Job* (*Tg. Job*) are intriguing in that at least fourteen of them exist.[131] Some have pointed out the particular literary patterns which distinguish it from other *targumim*.[132] Since those features are not apparent in the passage below, which is directly related to Dinah, no further details are necessary. Suffice it to say that a number of *targumim* scholars have concluded that this *Targum*, as others, underwent significant revision/redaction. It is maintained that the final redaction may have taken place as late as the 8th or 9th centuries C.E.[133] It is entirely plausible that some of the traditions behind the final edition may have their origins in 4th or 5th century Palestine.[134]

Job, Chapter 2[135]

1. Now on the day *of the great Judgment, the day of the remission of offences, bands of angels* came to stand *in judgment* before the Lord. {*Satan also came in their midst to stand in judgment* before the Lord.} 2. The Lord said to Satan" "where are you coming from?" Satan answered the Lord: "From roaming the earth *to investigate the works of human beings* and from walking about on it." 3. Then the Lord said to Satan: "Have you considered my servant Job that there is no one like him in *all* the land *of the gentiles*—a blameless and upright man, who fears *from before* the Lord and turns aside from evil? He is still steadfast in his integrity, so you have incited *my Memra* against him to destroy him without cause." 4. Satan answered the Lord; "*Limb* for *limb*; indeed everything a person has he will give up for the sake of his life. 5. But stretch forth, then, *the plague* of your hand and *draw near to* his bone and flesh, and he will surely *blaspheme* you to the face of your *Memra*." 6. And the Lord said to Satan: "See, he is *handed over* into your hand; only spare his life." 7. Satan went out from *before* the Lord *with authority* and struck Job with severe inflammation from the sole of his foot to the crown of his head. 8. And he took a potsherd to scrape himself as he sat among the ashes. 9. His wife, *Dinah*[136] said to him: "Are you still hold fast to your integrity? Bless *the Memra of* the Lord and die."[137] 10. And he said to her" You talk as any woman *who acts shamefully from*[138] the house of her father[139] talks. Since we accept good from *before* the Lord should we not accept evil?" In all this Job did not sin with his lips, *but in his mind he thought on words.*[140]

This is the only *Targum* text which ascribes direct discourse to Dinah; the narrator gives her voice. It is also the only *Targum* text which connects Job and Dinah in marriage. That had been one of the traditions found in *Legends of the Jews* and in *Gen. Rab.* 19.12, 57.4, and 76.9.

Whereas both *Tg. Neof.* and *Tg. Ps.–J.* sought to clear Dinah's reputation, *Tg. Job* has Job himself "badmouthing" Dinah. He refers to her as a woman "who acts shamefully from/in the house of her father." He is quick to cut to the core of her worst experience in the HB. The rhetoric he uses places blame/responsibility on Dinah. He claimed that she had acted shamefully. Job clearly connected Dinah with the "Shechem event," or so one may assume. He also acts in a way that counters the kind of preaching/teaching that is found at the end of both *Tg. Neof.* and *Tg. Ps.–J.* His comment here in Tg. Job reminds us of the midrashic traditions found in *Gen. Rab.* 19.12 and 57.4, which also portrayed Job speaking in a fairly similar negative way about his wife, Dinah.

Targum Job also has some strange ways of linking evil, Satan, and Dinah. Dinah uses almost the same language (in v. 9) that the Divine had used in v. 3; both verses speak of him "being steadfast in/or holding to his integrity." Job connects her advice to her alleged misdeed. The narrator closes by asserting that "Job did not sin with his lips." He did not follow Dinah's advice to bless/curse the Divine. She and "sin" become linked. One may also note the air of misogyny in Job's comment to Dinah; he links her way of talking with women. He makes a very gendered negative generalization about her. "You speak as any woman who has acted shamefully from the house of her father." Dinah is inextricably bound to womankind and shame. Note that according to Job, Shechem played no role in this. Did Dinah act shamefully? Was it not Shechem who did? Again, the reader comes full circle to the line of questioning at the end of *Tg. Neof.* and *Tg. Ps.–J.*

In this text Dinah attempted to persuade Job to "Bless the Memra of the Lord and die!" One could conclude that Dinah had some issues with the Divine! Or she had issues with the ideology of such suffering. Much of the rhetoric of *Tg. Job* deals with integrity and wholeness. Obviously, if one were to read with some other texts which assert that Dinah had been defiled, she would have suffered a loss to her integrity. She may have been someone who, like the writer of Ecclesiastes, questions whether integrity matters. Although she serves as a foil for Job, making him look more pious and righteous, she certainly asks the questions of and has the attitude of a wise one. That is, she speaks within the tradition of wisdom literature. Additionally, one may wonder how this text may also be brought into the conversation about the misrashic tradition that Dinah had converted Job. The two depictions of her seem not to fit together well or smoothly.

CONCLUSIONS

Targums Neofiti, *Onqelos*, and *Pseudo–Jonathan* are quite faithful retellings of the Genesis 34 narrative. Many of the differences examined have dealt with the reason given for why Dinah went out, what Shechem did to her, the statements that her brothers (the sons of Jacob) spoke with wisdom,[141] whether or not Dinah was said to have been a virgin, and how Simeon and Levi wanted Dinah and this event at Shechem to be remembered.

Targum Job does not fit with the three *targumim* mentioned above. First of all, it is a Targum on the book of Job, not on Genesis, as are the other three. Second, it paints Dinah in a more negative way than the others. *Targum Job* reflects a portrayal of Dinah which is closer to that of the *midrashim*, Dinah is held liable for her action of "going out." These early texts attest to the multiplicity of traditions about Dinah and about what happened at Shechem.

When considering the ways in which Dinah is presented to the reader in *Targums Neofiti*, *Onqelos*, and *Pseudo–Jonathan*, one may note that they consistently use the following nouns to refer to her: daughter (of Leah; of Jacob), sister (of Simeon and Levi; and of the "sons of Jacob"), girl/maiden. *Targum Job*, on the other hand, refers to her only as Job's wife and as "one who acted shamefully from the house of her father."

On the point of assigned blamed, not one of these *targumim* pointed fingers at Leah. Nothing negative is said of her; she is in no way held responsible for Dinah's actions. The only time when she is mentioned is in the opening verse, which simply identifies her as the biological mother of Dinah. It imputes no character flaw to Leah.

In *Tgs. Neof.*, *Onq.*, and *Ps.–J.*, the blame is consistently placed upon Shechem. Although the actual nouns used to speak about his offense vary (abomination, disgraceful act/deed), reference is made to the fact that Shechem had severely erred. *Targum Job* stands apart from the three because it alleges that Dinah "acted disgracefully."

Once again, one can note how engaging the story and the character of Dinah is and was. This event at Shechem held significant meaning on a number of levels for people of the targumic era. They sought to wrestle with the characters of this passage and to import to and extract meaning from them.

CHAPTER FOUR

Dinah IN THE Pseudepigrapha

AN INTRODUCTION TO THE PSEUDEPIGRAPHA

"Pseudepigrapha" refers to a relatively recently collected body of ancient literature, most of which was written between 250 BCE and 200 CE. These writings are crucial to the understanding of early Judaisms and Christianities, the plurals intentionally underscoring the diversity of both movements during these eras. The Pseudepigrapha affirm that developing Judaism and Christianity were not monolithic. Those who composed the writings felt free to ask their own questions of and to expound very differently upon biblical texts. Various conclusions and portrayals were made about biblical events and characters. In some cases, for example, the *Testament of Levi* and the book of *Jubilees*, authors felt comfortable attributing the writings themselves, visions, and testaments to biblical figures, even though these "people" or characters would have been long deceased, had they existed at all.

During this time, people were also comfortable reworking or adapting the texts. In some cases tremendous liberties were taken as they came close to rewriting the accounts or episodes found within the Jewish Scripture. At times they added material, greatly expanding upon the original texts; at other times, significant portions of biblical texts or particular portrayals of characters were omitted or reworked. One of the hallmarks of this era was a fluidity of the biblical traditions. The biblical basis of the text was reworked to address the current situation most appropriately.

Scholarship has been concerned with the historical events and situations in which these texts were born. People have considered how the times dictated or at least informed how various biblical characters themselves were reframed to "speak to" the current circumstances of the day. This has led to debates about the origins of these texts in terms of dates, provenance, and the authors' locations within Judaism. All the books considered within this chapter clearly had their origins within Judaism.

While many have been interested in questions of apocalyptic and/or messianism, this study focuses on the character of Dinah and the incident at Shechem. The writers expanded on and altered the biblical narrative found in Genesis 34. In his book *Old Testament Pseudepigrapha* (*OTP*) and his article in the *Anchor Bible Dictionary* (*ABD*),[1] James H. Charlesworth divided the Pseudepigrapha into six genres: Apocalyptic Literature and Related Works; Testaments; Expansions of the OT and Legends; Wisdom and Philosophical Literature; Prayers, Psalms, and Odes; and Fragments of Judeo-Hellenistic Works.[2] The literature encountered in this chapter, all referring to Dinah, will come from five of the six categories; she is not mentioned in Apocalyptic Literature. This study will begin with the Testaments.

THE *TESTAMENTS OF THE TWELVE PATRIARCHS*

The *Testaments of the Twelve Patriarchs* (*T. 12 Patr.*) is a document comprised of twelve testaments; each is pseudepigraphical, i.e., it is (fictitiously) attributed to one of the twelve sons of Jacob.[3] The twelve are arranged in their birth order according to their birth mothers. That is, all six sons of Leah and Jacob appear first together, although according to Genesis 29–30, Bilhah and Zilpah each had two sons with Jacob (Dan, Naphtali, Gad, and Asher) who were born between the times that Leah and Jacob had Judah (their fourth son) and Issachar (their fifth son).

Reminiscent of Jacob's parting words to his sons in Genesis 49 and of Moses' farewell speech in Deuteronomy 33, *T. 12 Patr.* purports to contain the final words of blessing/warning that the twelve sons of Jacob said to their offspring as they gathered their descendants around them before they passed away. A focus of scholarship has been the genre of testaments in the Second Temple period.[4]

Fairly evocative of Torah/Pentateuch scholarship, a source critical approach has been used in an attempt to reconstruct the hypothetical stages of development through which this document might have passed. Many have detected what might be referred to as Christian expressions throughout *T. 12 Patr.*; various conclusions have been reached. For example, R. H. Charles argued that these expressions were, as mentioned in the previous introduction to the Pseudepigrapha, simply Christian interpolations.[5] Marinus DeJonge dissented, concluding that the entire document was of Christian origin from around 200 CE.[6] Regardless of the origin, most would date the document to the beginning or the mid-second century CE.[7]

Scholars have debated about the original language of the document. Charles argued that the document was originally written in Hebrew; when fragments of an Aramaic version of *T. Levi* were found both in the Cairo Genizah and at Qumran, many presumed that the Greek version/edition was based on an earlier

Aramaic or Hebrew model. In part due to the plethora of Hellenisms in *T. 12 Patr.*, which have no exact Aramaic/Hebrew parallels, H. C. Kee and De Jonge were convinced that the original text was Greek.[8]

Some have asserted that the document, as a whole, has a pro-Levi/levitical and Hasmonean *tendenz*.[9] Levi is indeed presented in a very favorable light. According to the testaments, it is from Levi that the dyarchic messianic anointed priest was to descend; he and Judah come to the foreground in this regard.[10]

Testament of Levi, the third son of Jacob and Leah

One part of the *Testaments of the Twelve Patriarchs* is *Testament of Levi (T. Levi)*; it is the only testament of the twelve which refers to Dinah. The following is from *T. Levi* 2:

> (1) Levi, was born in Haran, and I came with my father to Shechem. (2) I was a youth, about twenty years old. It was then, that together with Simeon, I performed vengeance against Hamor because of our sister, Dinah. (3) As I was feeding the flocks in Abel-Maoul a spirit of understanding from the Lord came upon me, and I observed all human beings making their way in life deceitfully. Sin was erecting walls and injustice was ensconced in towers. (4) I kept grieving over the race of the sons of men, and I prayed to the Lord that I might be delivered.[11]

The first reference to Dinah is found in 2:2. She, or her character, is used here too as narrative justification for the vengeance which Levi and Simeon performed against Hamor. This can be paralleled to Genesis 34, which often used Shechem's actions against/with Dinah as narrative justification for the reactions of Jacob's sons. For examples, in Gen 34:13 the sons of Jacob spoke with deceit because he had defiled their sister Dinah; in Gen 34:27 the sons of Jacob plundered the city because they, the inhabitants of the city, had defiled their sister Dinah.

A passage very similar to 2:2 may be seen in 5:3, which may be found later in this chapter. In both passages, Levi was either commanded to (5:3) or reported to have performed vengeance either for the sake of or because of Dinah. In these instances from *T. Levi*, Levi comes to the foreground of the narrative, allegedly receiving a message of purpose and support from an angel/the Divine.

In this source, Levi is portrayed as a priest. The *Testament of Levi* 2:4 depicts Levi as one who was affected deeply and emotionally by the error of people's ways. Because of the depth of that feeling, Levi sought relief and aid from the Divine. He prayed. The *Testament of Levi* established a clear relationship between the Divine and Levi. In fact the concerns of the third-born son of Jacob and Leah parallel those of the Divine. As one continues to read *T. Levi* 3, that thought is developed further. Throughout *T. Levi* 3 and 4, there is abundant rhetoric about injustice, sin, and trespass. These will be met by God's righteous judgment (3:2), as well as Divine and human punishment. An aspect of this reckoning is vengeance, as is evidenced in 3:3. The reader may note that this sort of vengeance was said to have been performed by Levi because of Dinah (*T. Levi* 2:2).

Throughout this section in particular, a clear distinction is made between the unrighteous (who keep sinning, etc.) and the righteous; Levi is clearly on the side of God. In fact, in 4:2 Levi is referred to as a son of the Most High, one of God's priests and ministers. Levi was also portrayed as a sun, a source of light and guidance, for Israel. According to *T. Levi* 5, Levi was to be a priest of God, preserving the purity/cleanliness of Israel until the Divine was to come and dwell in Israel. In fact, according to *T. Levi* 5:3, an angel literally gave Levi a sword and exhorting him, "Perform vengeance on Shechem for the sake of Dinah, your sister, and I shall be with you, for the Lord sent me."[12] Levi's priesthood is confirmed at this point. Levi's prayers were heard. God acted on behalf of Israel, ridding the Israelites/Hebrews of the sons of Hamor. In close partnership with the Divine, Levi acted on behalf of God, cleansing Israel.

Levi's actions, according to *T. Levi*, were sanctioned and empowered by the Divine. This is also the case in *Jubilees* 30:18; the idea of Divine backing of Simeon is also found in Jdt 9:2.[13] Post-Hebrew Bible traditions differently develop the characters of Simeon and/or Levi, particularly with respect to their acting as agents of God. That trend is also evidenced in more subtle or indirect ways. For example, in *T. Levi* 6:3, where further details are given about the actual attack on Shechem, Levi states, "I was filled with zeal on account of the abominable thing they had done to my sister."[14]

When an infraction was committed against one of his people, he dealt with the offense zealously. He is consistently portrayed as someone concerned with ensuring his people's cleanliness. In the aforementioned passage from *T. Levi* 6:3, with the reference to Shechem's offense as "an abominable thing," one may note that "abominable" is a theologically loaded word. In a number of places in the HB, one of the ways of protecting people from the spread of abomination was to kill/slaughter the offender(s). Priests often did the slaying.[15] In fact, by this very action of doing away with the offensive party, the person was often considered set apart or consecrated for the priesthood. This is precisely the depiction given of Levi in *T. Levi*.

One of the unique aspects of *T. Levi* is that is the sole attestation of the tradition that Levi had advised Jacob not to have the Shechemites/sons of Hamor circumcised. Kee concluded, "Levi's opposition to circumcising the Shechemites was based on his determination to kill them in revenge."[16] Levi played both the counselor role as well as that of priest.[17] For example, according to *T. Levi* 6:6, one of the reasons Jacob was distraught was that the Shechemites had been circumcised before they were killed. In the face of his father's criticism, Levi firmly maintained his own righteousness. Levi even alleged that he and the Divine saw and evaluated this situation similarly, in a way differently than his own father did. He went on to exhort his father to have faith in the Divine, reminding the patriarch of the Divine's covenantal promises.

As one considers how *T. Levi* depicted the incident involving Dinah, one may note that it veers away from the details found in Genesis. In the above paragraph mention was made that *T. Levi* alleges that Levi had strongly suggested that the Shechemites not be circumcised; in Genesis 34, the sons of Jacob insist that it be done, saying that they could not give their sister to one with foreskin.[18] The MT offers details about Shechem and Hamor speaking with the men of their city about the necessity of becoming circumcised. It is then reported that the men were all circumcised. The account of the actual circumcision of Shechem and his men is not mentioned in *T. Levi*.[19] Because of the comments regarding Jacob's regret, he reader knows that the Shechemites had been circumcised. However the reader does not know when or under what circumstances this occurred.

While in some ways, *T. Levi* and Genesis differ, there are other ways in which the two accounts coalesce, at least in tone. When one considers the reference above, *T. Levi* 6:3, which alleged that the Shechemites had done an "abominable thing" to Dinah, the depiction of Shechem's horrific offense is certainly in harmony with Genesis, where Shechem was said to have committed a heinous offense. Here in *T. Levi* this phrase is used to explain the zeal of Levi. According to Genesis 34, all the sons of Jacob felt indignation and anger. Here, the focus is on Levi. The narrator of *T. Levi* also differently puts Levi in the spotlight by saying that Levi first killed Shechem and that Simeon attacked Hamor; then Levi's brothers came and destroyed the city. In Genesis, Simeon and Levi were said to have killed Shechem and Hamor and all the men of the city.

The information found in *T. Levi* 6:6, that Jacob was angry and sorrowful because the Shechemites had received circumcision and then died, is also new to the reader, when compared to other texts examined. It certainly appears that Jacob was willing to give Dinah to Shechem as long as he was circumcised. *T. Levi* makes it clear that Jacob was not part of the ruse at Shechem. The sons of Jacob, according to v. 7, had acted in ways that were contrary to the opinion of their father.

The reader may also be struck by the new datum (found in *T. Levi* 6:8) that the Shechemites had also wanted to do the same thing to Sarah and Rebecca as they had done to Dinah. Although the HB makes no such comment about the Hivites endangering the other matriarchs, it may be found in *Legends of the Jews* 1:403. Some commentators have linked this comment to the wife-sister incidents in Genesis 12, 20, and 26.[20] Certainly in *T. Levi*, especially 6:8, all the men of Shechem are portrayed negatively. This might be regarded as another example of democratization of the guilt/responsibility of Shechem himself, or *T. Levi* may put forward the impression that literally every man of the city of Shechem was horrible and deserving of annihilation. Indeed, when speaking specifically about *T. Levi*, Collins wrote, "The rape of Dinah becomes a kind of original sin for the people of Shechem … The folly of the Shechemites was a common Jewish taunt."[21] This negative depiction of the Shechemites is reinforced by *T. Levi* 3:10 and 4:1. Furthermore *T. Levi* 6:11 claims that the Shechemites regularly captured the wives of nomadic people and killed them. In *T. Levi*, the Shechemites were depicted as a heinous people, who deserved divine and human retribution. *T. Levi* 6:8 clearly states that Levi had seen that God's sentence upon the Shechemites was "Guilty." God's anger was made manifest through Levi (6:11), and Jacob and his sons are seen as Divine agents bringing the Canaanites to an end, resulting in Jacob and his clan/household receiving their land. Throughout this section, the impiety of the Shechemites is stressed. The city of Shechem was dubbed senseless/heinous because of the heinous offense they committed with Dinah.[22] This tradition was also evident in *Legends* II:196. The communal nature of Shechem's crime is apparent. This issue has been addressed sufficiently, as it has occurred in a number of texts. Suffice it to say that all the inhabitants of Shechem bore responsibility for Shechem's offense.

The Shechemites are portrayed as being so horrific that they merited the "scoffing" of the Israelites/Hebrews. One may note in *T. Levi* 7 that "scoffing" is synonymous with utter annihilation. What was the explanation given for why this was done? It is said, that "by defiling Dinah, they [the Shechemites] committed folly in Israel."[23] As I wrote in *Sexual Violation in the Hebrew Bible*, "folly" might better be translated as "a heinous offense"; frequently meriting the death penalty/revenge killing.[24] Levi, the priest, was the one who primarily carried out this vengeance.

There is only one other indirect reference to the incident involving Dinah in the *Testament of Levi*. In *T. Levi* 12:5, Levi lists his various ages when important events occurred in his life: according to this passage, he was eight years old when he entered Canaan and eighteen when he killed Shechem.[25] One may figure out that he and his family had spent ten years in Canaan when the "Dinah incident" occurred. A reader may compare/contrast the information found in this passage with that from other sources. There are a few issues with the datum above regarding Levi's age. First, there is a slight internal disagreement within the same writing: according to *T. Levi 2:2*, Levi claimed he "was a youth, about twenty years old"[26] when he both came with Jacob to Shechem and that it was then that he and Simeon killed Hamor/Shechem. It does not appear that the reference *T. Levi* (2:2) allows for the ten year passage of time, found in 12:5. The material found in *T. Levi* 12:5 does not fully agree with the material found in Demetrius. Both Demetrius and 12:5 report that ten years passed between when Jacob and his family entered Canaan and when Shechem was killed.[27] However, Demetrius claims that Levi had been over 20 when he attacked Hamor and Shechem. Demetrius and *T. Levi* 2:2 are more in harmony in that regard. Neither reference to the passage of ten years nor the ages of any of the characters is found in the MT version of Genesis 34.

In conclusion, *T. Levi* offers readers information that is not included in the MT. This mid-second century text claims that Levi was either eighteen or twenty years old when he and Simeon took vengeance upon Shechem because of Dinah. The writer/editor of *T. Levi* assumes that the reader is well aware of what Shechem had done to Dinah.

Only once in the text can a reader find Dinah to be the object of a verb in the semantic domain of defile, pollute, rape, or sexually violate. In *T. Levi* 7:3, it is alleged, "they (the men of Shechem) had done an abominable thing" to Dinah, Levi's sister. As might be expected, since *T. Levi* purports to be the last will and testament of Levi, the only noun used of Dinah is "sister." The brother-sister relationship (i.e., sibling relationship) is stressed in this text.

Allegedly, through Levi's recounting of this episode at Shechem, it becomes clear that he was acting on behalf of his sister, on behalf of the Divine, and on behalf of Israel. Because of the affront done to Dinah and Israel, Levi was ordered by the Divine to seek redress or justice against not only a person, but a people. He was equipped to do so by an angel. In short, according to *T. Levi*, the Shechemites had wronged Dinah, her brothers, and their God.

TESTAMENT OF JOB

The *Testament of Job* is yet another example of a testamentary writing. As was the case with the *Testaments of the Twelve Patriarchs*, in the *Testament of Job* (*T. Job*), the patriarch gathers his ten children around him as he offers his farewell address to them, recounts the highlights of his life, and divides his material and spiritual inheritance among his descendants. Of particular interest to our ongoing conversation is the fact that the ten children gathered about Job allegedly belonged to him and Dinah. According to this testament, Dinah was Job's current wife; Sitis, Job's first wife died, along with their ten children.

As Job spoke with his and Dinah's ten children, narrating his life, he presented himself as being of the seed of Esau, of his having formerly been named Jobab, and of his being a ruler/king.[28] Throughout the document, there are many references to the fact that Job and both his families had at one time enjoyed a royal status. Scholars have attempted to reconcile this datum with the HB reference to Jobab, who, according to Gen 36:33–34 was one of the kings of Edom. The LXX additions to Job identify Job/Jobab as the second king of Edom. Some citations within the testament specify that Job was the king of Egypt.[29] Due in part to the numerous references to Egypt within the document, many have concluded that the *Testament of Job* might have an Egyptian provenance.[30]

There is general consensus that *T. Job* was originally a Jewish document. Most have concluded that it came from Egypt and thus reflected the concerns of a Hellenistic Jewish community. As scholars have sought to trace how and by whom the *Testament of Job* was used, it is apparent that most references to the document come from Christian sources.[31] Some of these help to date the testament; most would conclude that it was written no later than 200 CE.[32] R. P. Spittler dates the testament to the first centuries either BCE or CE.[33]

Most contemporary scholars have concluded that the *Testament of Job* was originally composed in Greek; this is due, in part, to its close relationship with the LXX version of Job.[34] Scholars differ in their conclusions about dependence of these two on one another. George W. E. Nickelsburg and Spittler, for example, asserted that the *Testament of Job* relied on the LXX.[35]

It is important to keep this information in mind as references to Dinah as Job's wife are explored.[36] Russell noted that a number of writings from 200 BCE to 200 CE expounded upon the biblical character Job.[37] This can also be said regarding the character Dinah and/or the incident at Shechem. Possibly because of the tradition which claimed that Dinah was married to Job, many of these writings about Job also mention Dinah. The writings all seek to portray Job as a man of great integrity, endurance, and piety; Dinah's marriage to such a man reflects well upon her and her character.

With that having been said, relatively little information is given about Dinah in *T. Job*; she is only referred to as the mother of Job's living ten children—seven boys and three girls. Although she is not well developed as a character, one may juxtapose her to Job's first wife, Sitis. Dinah is the mother of ten; she is the mother of three daughters who inherit profound spiritual abilities immediately prior to the time their father passed away.[38] They lost all concern about earthly matters and were given the language of angels to sing and compose praises of the Divine. Because of the emphasis on women's roles in society (such as inheritance rights) and their share in the ecstatic prophetic realm, many have conjectured that this document's origins may lie with the Jewish group the *Therapeutae*.[39] One can cite the brazenness and respect with which the three approached Job and asked for their inheritance.[40] He promised his daughters that their inheritance was better than that of their seven brothers (46:4). With the numerous references to women and the way in which the females are portrayed, some scholars have proposed that the document was edited, composed, or adopted by the Montanist movement as women within that tradition enjoyed relatively elevated status.[41]

The context of *T. Job*'s reference to Dinah is that Job had fallen ill and gathered his seven sons and three daughters to him, as he prepared to die. In *T. Job* 1:5–6, Job said, "I am your father Job, fully engaged in endurance. But you are a chosen and honored race from the seed of Jacob, the father of your mother. (6) For I am from the sons of Esau, the brother of Jacob, of whom is your mother Dinah, from whom I begot you. (My former wife died with the other ten children in a bitter death.)"[42]

Dinah is referred to as Job's current wife in *T. Job*. *L.A.B.* 8:8 also refers to her as Job's wife. There are some marked differences between the two passages. The end of the *Testament of Job* parallels Ginzberg's account in its description of how Dinah's and Job's three daughters, Kasia, Hemera, and Amaltheia's Horn inherited gifts of tremendous spiritual power.[43] Dinah is here portrayed as an important part of Job's family. She bore the three daughters who inherited Job's powers.

LIBER ANTIQUITATUM BIBLICARUM

This work, known by its Latin name, *Liber Antiquitatum Biblicarum* (*L.A.B.*), and by the English equivalent, *Biblical Antiquities*, was first ascribed to Philo in a manuscript dating from the 14th century CE.[44] *L.A.B.* appears to have been circulated with Philo's works[45] and has often been referred to as Pseudo-Philo. Many scholars have noted its similarity to the Book of *Jubilees*; both might be called "rewritings of the Bible" including stories from Adam through David.[46] It also bears similarities to Josephus' *Antiquities*; this may explain the origin of its title.[47] Most have concluded that *L.A.B.* has a Palestinian synagogue provenance and might attest to the sort of biblical interpretation which was conducted in the early- to mid-1st century CE.[48] There are some scholars who date the work to this general time period because of the perceived parallels with 4 Ezra and 2 Baruch.[49] *L.A.B.* was most probably written in Hebrew originally, although it was subsequently translated into and transmitted in both Greek and Latin.[50]

As Daniel Harrington has pointed out, in the passage found below, one finds the earliest reference to Dinah as Job's wife.[51] That tradition is also attested in the *Testament of Job* and in *Legends of the Jews*. One of the themes found throughout *L.A.B.* is that intermarriage between Jews and Gentiles is/was distasteful to the Divine and an abrogation of the covenant.[52] That way of thinking, quite possibly reflecting a strand of Palestinian synagogue mindset at the time, may have given birth to the tradition that Dinah and Job were wife and husband. The purity of both would be renewed and maintained. It is curious to note that any defilement/disgrace incumbent upon Dinah due to the rape/sexual violation done to her by Shechem did not serve to defile Job. This might be the case because of what

Nickelsburg, citing a number of scholars' works, noted: *L.A.B.* has an "unusually positive attitude toward women."⁵³ The following is *L.A.B.* 8:6–8 and 11:

> (6) Now Jacob took for himself as wives the daughters of Laban the Syrian, Leah and Rachel, and two concubines, Bilhah and Zilphah. And Leah bore to him Reuben, Simeon, Levi, Judah, Issachar, Zebulun, and Dinah their sister ... These are the twelve sons of Jacob and one daughter. (7) And Jacob dwelt in the land of Canaan, and Shechem the son of Hamor the Hurrite raped Dinah his daughter and humiliated her. And the sons of Jacob, Simeon and Levi, went in and killed the whole city of them by the sword; and they took their sister Dinah and went away from there. (8) And afterward Job took her as a wife and fathered from her fourteen sons and six daughters; that is, seven sons and three daughters before he was struck down with suffering, and afterward seven sons and three daughters when he was healed. And these are their names: Elifac, Ermoe, Diasat, Filias, Diffar, Zelud, Thelon; and his daughters: Meru, Litz, Zeli. And such as had been the names of the former, so were those of the latter.
>
> (11) And these are the names of the sons of Israel who went down to Egypt with Jacob, each with his own household ... And Dinah their sister bore fourteen sons and six daughters. And these are the generations of the sons that Leah bore to Jacob, all the sons and daughters being 72.⁵³

Like many biblical and extra-biblical texts, this passage begins by listing the names of the children of Leah and Jacob. When various interconnections of these texts are noted, in its reference to Hamor and Shechem as Hurrite people, *L.A.B.* agrees with the LXX version of Gen 34:2.⁵⁵ Notice that here no details are given about Dinah's going out to the city of Shechem, etc. Dinah is simply introduced as one of Leah's and Jacob's children. Jacob was said to have dwelt in the land of Canaan. The story quickly reverts back to Dinah. However, she is not the subject of any verbs. Rather, she is the object of two successive verbs of which Shechem is the subject. She is taken as an object both by her two maternal brothers and by Job. The text reads, "Shechem ... raped Dinah ... and humiliated her. And the sons of Jacob, Simeon and Levi, went in and killed the whole city of them by the sword; and they took their sister Dinah and went away from there. And afterward Job took her as a wife."⁵⁶ The account found in *L.A.B.* ascribes no agency, no action, to Dinah.

On numerous occasions, I have noted that Dinah or what Shechem did to her is used as narrative justification for what the sons of Jacob did to Shechem. *L.A.B.* provides yet another attestation of that pattern. Reinhard Pummer wrote, "The deed of Simeon and Levi is neither condemned nor specifically commended, although it is depicted as revenge for the rape of Dinah and thus at least implicitly justified."⁵⁷

L.A.B. also provides another piece of the evidence of the tradition that Dinah had married Job. In this passage, as opposed to *T. Job*, it is here said that Dinah was Job's only wife. She bore him twenty children—two sets of seven boys and three girls. The situation before and after his and his family's suffering was mirrored. That is according to *L.A.B.* Dinah survived and had borne both sets of ten children. All ten before/after children had the same names. That is presented differently in *T. Job*, where Dinah was said to have been Job's second wife, after Sitis, Job's first wife, and their ten children had passed away (as part of his suffering). In *T. Job*, Dinah was said to be the mother of Job's ten (not twenty) children, seven boys and three girls. Such are the sort of variations one finds in this exploration.

According to *L.A.B.* Dinah was the mother of both sets of Job's ten children. That is, she had mothered twenty children: two analogous sets of seven sons and three daughters. In fact, both sets had the same names! This interpretation is supported by *L.A.B* 8:8 and 11, which state that Dinah bore fourteen sons and six daughters.

When the reader adds the *targumim* to this discussion, specifically *Tg. Job*, *L.A.B.* is different from *Tg. Job* in that it makes no derogatory comment about Dinah. It had been in *Tg. Job* where Job had accused Dinah of speaking as one who had acted shamefully from the house of her father. Nothing like that is said in *L.A.B.*; Dinah is not alleged to have transgressed any boundary. Furthermore, *Tg. Job* alleged that Dinah had spoken as one who had acted shamefully. *Tg. Job*, *Gen. Rab.* 19.12 and 57.4 all claimed that Job spoke in a fairly similar negative way about his wife, Dinah. Such allegation may be contrasted with *L.A.B.*, which attributes no transgression to Dinah, whether it be physical or in speech. In fact, it assigns her no direct discourse.

How Dinah is portrayed in these texts? Grammatically speaking, in *L.A.B.*, Dinah is most frequently presented as the object of verbs. The following statements are made: Leah bore Dinah (8:6); Shechem raped and humiliated Dinah (8:7); Simeon and Levi took Dinah and went away (8:7); and Job took her as a wife (8:8). Never once does *L.A.B.* assert or insinuate that Dinah had erred in any way. The only verb of which Dinah is the subject in *L.A.B.* is "bore."

In summation, *L.A.B.* seems to present Dinah as a blessing to Job. Through her, he bore numerous daughters and sons. This text matter-of-factly speaks of her as the mother of twenty of his children. At the end of the text, Dinah's and Job's fourteen children are reckoned as belonging to the line of Leah.

JOSEPH AND ASENETH

Most scholars conclude that *Joseph and Aseneth* (*Jos. Asen.*) was originally written in Greek.[58] As C. Burchard has reported, the primary one who dissented from this consensus has been P. Riessler, who was convinced of the existence at least one Hebrew antecedent text.[59] No such text is extant. Most scholars date the text as having been written prior to 200 CE.; "some have placed it as early as the second century BCE."⁶⁰ Randall D. Chesnutt has concluded, for various reasons, that the range of dates should be narrowed to 100 BCE–115/117 CE.⁶¹

As was the case with the *Testament of Job*, *Joseph and Aseneth* may be classified as Hellenistic Jewish literature.⁶² Those who proposed a Christian re-editing of the text have detected Christian interpolations.⁶³ Like *T. Job*, *Jos. Asen.* may hail from Egypt.⁶⁴ The document also belies knowledge of the LXX tradition.⁶⁵ When it comes to style, it differs from *T. Job* in that it is not testamentary, but is more of a romance.⁶⁶ Chesnutt described the story as "a midrashic elaboration of Gen 41:45, 50–52; and 46:20, which briefly mention Joseph's marriage to Asenath (LXX Aseneth), daughter of Potiphera (LXX Pentephres). Priest of On (Heliopolis)."⁶⁷ As is the case with Jubilees, a concern throughout *Jos. Asen.* is intermarriage with pagans. This was true of Joseph's adamant insistence that he would never so much as kiss a woman who did not worship his G-d.⁶⁸ As was the case with *T. Job*, women are portrayed as strong and pious characters.⁶⁹ This is especially true for Aseneth after her conversion.

The reference to Dinah in *Jos. Asen.* is found in the context when pharaoh's firstborn son discovered that Joseph had married Aseneth. Allegedly, the prince himself had been promised Aseneth in marriage; in his own words according to *Jos. Asen.* 23:4, Aseneth was his "envisaged wife who was betrothed to me from the beginning."⁷⁰ Much affronted by Joseph's marriage to Aseneth, the pharaoh's son decided to kill Joseph and take Aseneth as his own. Seeking to rule Egypt himself, he tried unsuccessfully to enlist the help of Simeon and Levi in murdering Joseph. The two maternal brothers of Dinah refuse to take part, and, in 23:14, warn the Egyptian prince:

> (14) And Simeon and Levi drew their swords from their sheaths and said, "Behold, have you seen these swords? With these two swords the Lord God punished the insult of the Shechemites (by) which they insulted the sons of Israel, because of our sister Dinah who Shechem the son of Hamor had defiled." ⁷⁰

Simeon and Levi are paired together in 23:6 and 14; that coupling has been fairly common in many of the texts, biblical and extra-biblical, that have been investigated thus far. The narrator of *Joseph and Aseneth* described Simeon as "a daring and bold man"⁷¹ (23:7); this portrayal was shown to be true when he was ready to draw his sword at the prince's provocation. C. Burchard connects this characterization of Simeon back to Gen 34: 25–31 and 49:5–7.⁷² The two are, in the words of Nickelsburg, "introduced as Aseneth's friends and protectors."⁷³ One may indeed link this back to the incident at Shechem, where one might interpret them as Dinah's friends and protectors, reacting against Shechem with calculated celerity. Nickelsburg maintains that in this passage, Simeon and Levi play similar roles to those they assumed in Genesis 34; they are the protectors of an endangered woman.⁷⁴

This text differs from the HB account in that it differently develops the character of Levi. Whereas Simeon is here presented as the hot-headed one, this text portrays Levi as a prophet (23:8), one able to see the intentions of the heart.[75] Knowing what his brother had intended to do, Levi stopped him from acting wrathfully. The narrator further developed Levi's positive attributes in vv. 10 and following: "his face (was) cheerful, there was not the least bit of anger in him, but in meekness of heart he said …"[76] Levi proceeded to enumerate the various ways in which the men of his family are connected with the Divine; it was this relationship which precluded them from drawing their swords against pharaoh's son. However, if the prince persisted in speaking ill of Joseph, they were ready to fight. Levi's speech is theocentric, using their relationship with the Divine as justification for the behavior.

The next section continues that theocentrism. It is ironic how quick Levi and Simeon were to threaten pharaoh's son. Although they talk about their relationship with the Divine, and how unfitting it was for a worshipper to injure another, they were quick to draw their swords and threateningly tell the prince in 23:14 that, with those same two swords, "the Lord God punished the insult of the Shechemites"[77] because Shechem had defiled Dinah. The Divine was portrayed as the primary actor; Simeon and Levi, or more accurately, their swords, were instruments of Divine justice, because Shechem had defiled Dinah. Notice, too, that the affront is here referred to as an "insult."

As two of Dinah's brothers are shown standing with their drawn swords, confronting the prince of Egypt, speaking about the way in which God had used those swords once before, one can indeed see the parallelism between pharaoh's son and Shechem, the son of Hamor, the ruler of the land. Pharaoh's son plays a role analogous to Shechem; both threatened a woman of the Israelites/Hebrews. Both were smitten by so-called "love" for a woman.[78] Each had requested his father to "get the woman as his wife."[79]

Not only do the antagonists parallel one another. Aseneth becomes a woman in danger of being "taken" by a man, thus paralleling Dinah. Some scholars have concluded that Dinah had been abducted from her family.[80] Aseneth is "made in Dinah's image" in a number of passages in *Jos. Asen.*

One may still wonder about Jacob's role in this text. In v. 14 it is clear that Shechem's defiling Dinah had "insulted the sons of Israel."[81] The text goes on to offer details that it was the sons of Israel/Jacob who suffered injury because of what had been done to their sister. While the plot of Genesis 34 revealed the same thing, the biblical narrator did not make such an overt comment. In both cases, the reader may be somewhat surprised that it was not Jacob who was insulted or offended by Shechem's actions. Shechem's behavior sent waves of reactions; the shame/insult went from an action Shechem took against/toward Dinah (defiling her) to affecting the sons of Israel. Shechem's action also had catastrophic ripple effects for the men of the city.

Dinah is fairly consistently used as narrative justification for Simeon's and Levi's actions against Shechem. Their wrath is presented as a vehicle of Divine judgment. As the text clearly says, "With these two swords the Lord God punished the insult of the Shechemites (by) which they insulted the sons of the Israel, because of our sister Dinah who Shechem the son of Hamor had defiled." After Dinah's defilement, God intervened on behalf of Israel. The Divine is portrayed as having acted through Simeon and Levi.

THEODOTUS

Only fragments of Theodotus' work exist. There is scholarly debate as to whether Theodotus was a Samaritan or a Jewish author.[82] He lived during the second or early first centuries BCE; his work was preserved by Alexander Polyhistor, the Greek historian of the mid-first century BCE.[83] Fairly recent archeological excavation at Shechem has helped to establish that the author/poet's description of the city site of Shechem fits the period prior to the mid-second century BCE.[84]

F. Fallon has noted the similarities between the traditions preserved in Theodotus and those contained in Judith, *Jubilees*, and *T. Levi*[85]; these will be noted throughout the commentary.

Theodotus provides a significant amount of detail about Dinah and Jacob's sons. In comparison with the MT and other texts examined, adjectives abound! Theodotus goes to great lengths to describe the city setting of Shechem. One of the points of interest is that in Fragment 1, the city is described as a sacred town.[86] There is an element of religiosity; i.e., Shechem stands for, or represents, a sacred tradition which obviously differs from that of Levi and his family. Theodotus spent a good deal of narrative attention describing the sacred city. This is the primary focus of the first fragment.

In Fragment 2, Theodotus historically situates Jacob's clan in Shechem. He then moves on to focus on Hamor and Sychem/Shechem, describing them as "a very stubborn pair."[87] Theodotus' details do not end there. In Fragment 3, he notes that Jacob's eleven sons "were exceedingly wise in mind."[88] When it comes to introducing Dinah, Theodotus is one of the few writers to describe her physically, writing that she "had a beautiful form, an admirable frame, and a noble spirit."[89] All such depictions of her, whether physical, spiritual, or emotional are unique.

In Fragment 4, Theodotus wrote of the incident involving Dinah:

> … from the Euphrates Jacob came into Shechem to Hamor. He welcomed him and gave him a portion of the land. Jacob himself tilled the land; his sons, eleven in

number, herded sheep; and his daughter, Dinah, and his wives worked with wool. And Dinah, still a virgin, came into Shechem when there was a festival, since she wished to see the city. But when Sychem the son of Hamor saw her, he loved her; and after seizing her as his own, he carried her off and ravished her.[90]

Fallon has pointed out that one of the ways in which this account differs from Genesis is that in Theodotus, Hamor gave Jacob a portion of the land; according to Gen 33:19, Jacob purchased the land from Hamor for one hundred *qesitah*.[91] Theodotus, unlike other writers, also described some of the day-to-day activities in which Jacob's family was involved. From this source, the reader has a better idea of what daily life was like for the ancestral family. Jacob tilled; his eleven sons herded sheep. Dinah and Jacob's wives worked with wool.[92] In some regards, it was Jacob who was not a direct part of the cycle of life. He is depicted more as a settled agrarian; his sons were nomadic herders. Obviously the women and Jacob's sons were interdependent. The women needed the wool from the sheep. One would safely presume that the woolen articles, in part, went to clothe the shepherds and provide temporary shelters. Jacob's tilling seems to be "out of this loop." This may forebode that his relationships with his family where also "out of sync."

Theodotus transitioned quickly from his descriptions of what the ancestral family did to Dinah's virginal status. Only a few other pseudepigraphical texts refer to Dinah as a virgin. One may certainly wonder why Dinah was so intrigued with the festival city of Shechem; was there a link between her wool-based activities and the festival or the city? Was she interested in seeing the festival attire, from a business-sense, to see what she and the matriarchs might be able to sell in the "new land?" Theodotus provides no clear or overt link between her working with wool and the festivities at the city Shechem; he simply wrote of her trip to the city immediately after describing her work.

The reader is simply told "she wished to see the city."[93] Compared to and contrasted with the various passages considered, this is the first time that Dinah was said to have wanted to see "the city." Other texts have said that she wanted to see the women of the land or the customs of the women of the land. Unlike any of the other pseudepigraphical texts, Theodotus retells the part of the Genesis story in which Dinah went out or "came into Shechem."[94] No other pseudepigraphical source mentions that specific act. The emphasis of the vast majority of other texts is upon Shechem's having defiled or raped Dinah.

Theodotus' rhetoric about the meeting/encounter between Shechem and Dinah is engaging. One may focus on the five verbs of which Dinah is the object: Shechem/Sychem saw her, loved her, seized her as his own, carried her off, and ravished her.[95] A modern reader may question how the verb "love" fits in with the other four verbs. Shechem's final three actions in the above sentence may strike the modern reader as very aggressive. In all cases, Dinah is acted upon; she has little agency. She is objectified. It appeared that he did with her as he pleased. To find "love" mentioned in that context is surprising. One may note that is come fairly early in the list of verbs. That is, he apparently loved her and then seized her as his own, etc. The word order found in Theodotus may be contrasted to that in the HB account, where Shechem's alleged love came after he had lay with and violated Dinah.

A reader may also conclude, influenced by Theodotus' rhetoric, that Shechem had abducted Dinah. Much more detail is found in Theodotus than in many other texts. It is my interpretation that "seizing and carrying off" a woman means that Shechem took Dinah away from the site where he had first seen her. The language may lead one to conclude that Shechem's actions were done against Dinah's will. This is yet a point of ambiguity. As was the case in the HB, Dinah does not serve as a focalizer here; neither her thoughts nor feelings about the man Shechem are included in the text. All the reader knows is that she had wished, at one time, to see the city.

After Shechem "ravished" Dinah, the Hivite/Hurrite father and son approached Jacob, with the intention of asking for Dinah in marriage. In the negotiations, Theodotus' account differs from the MT in that Jacob is central. According to Theodotus, Jacob spoke; it was he who insisted that all the inhabitants of Shechem become circumcised and thus become Jews. Note that in Genesis, it was the sons of Jacob who had made the proposal of circumcision. The actual rite is presently differently in Theodotus, as well. Here it is clearly a rite which makes foreign men "Jewish."[96] Fragment 5 continues Jacob's monologue about circumcision, adding much of the theology behind the rite.[97]

Fallon highlighted an important set of differences between Theodotus and Genesis:

> In contrast to Gen 34 it is noticeable that there is no elaboration in the paraphrase of Shechem's love for Dinah or of his offer to give or do anything in order to obtain her as his wife. Absent also is the motif of the anger of the sons of Jacob when they heard of the deed and their decision to deal deceitfully with the Shechemites. The discussion between Hamor and the sons of Jacob about the merging of their respective peoples in terms of marriage, sharing of the land, and trade is also omitted.[98]

Fallon also discussed at length the omission of the actual account of the circumcision.[99] In part because of these differences, the reader is less apt to have sympathy for Shechem. He is presented more coldly here; he and his father were some of the first characters described by Theodotus (as stubborn). In contrast, Dinah is presented more innocently and naïvely. First, she is identified as a virgin. That had not been overtly stated in Genesis 34. Here one may conclude that she had an element of either curiosity (wishing to see the city) or even business savvy. The setting of her "coming into Shechem" at time of a festival may also add to the impression that possibly a fairly innocent "wool-working woman" may not know the dangers or perils that might lie in a more urban area at the time of a festival. Because none of these details appears in Genesis, a modern reader gets a different impression of Dinah from Theodotus. One might note the parallelism between Theodotus' account and Josephus' *Antiquities*, as both include the festival setting.[100] This point will be revisited later.

Fragment 6 introduces the idea that it was Simeon who came up with the idea of killing Hamor and Sychem. Simeon allegedly used theological rationale for the attack.[101] That sentiment will be developed further below.

Another significant difference between the rhetoric of Fragment 6 and Genesis 34 is that Theodotus refers to "the violent attack upon his (Simeon's) sister."[102] Such language helps the reader come to the conclusion that Shechem had raped Dinah. It allows one to return to Fragment 4, and to read "and after seizing her as his own, he carried her off and ravished her"[103] as an abduction and a rape.

Fragment 7 develops the characterization of the Shechemites; Fallon notes that Genesis "has no mention of the impiety of the Shechemites."[104] While that is true, literally; that is, the Genesis narrator never used the word "impious," one must recollect the very strong statements made within the biblical text. Both the sons of Jacob and the narrator claimed that Shechem had committed a heinous offense in Israel. It is also said that he did "something that ought not to be done." Certainly, such strong HB accusations allege that Shechem, had severely transgressed codified norms. At the beginning of Genesis 34, twice it was said that he had defiled Dinah (vv. 5 and 13); in v. 27, that verb is plural. In the latter instance, they, the people of Shechem, had defiled Dinah. One may conclude that they shared in Shechem's impiety. In regards to language like "impiety," etc., modern readers may note how language has changed. The court system and the general public might use rhetoric of "sexual perpetrator" or "rapist" to describe Shechem, as depicted by Theodotus. "Impious" has lost much of its meaning or "zing." An aspect of that accusation is theological.

Fragments 5–7 highly theologize the circumcision of and the attack on Shechem. Clearly, according to this text, God used the sons of Jacob as an instrument through which the Divine carried out judgment and justice.[105] For example, Fragment 7 claims that God smote the Shechemites because of their consistent and persistent evil nature.[106] The final statement of Fragment 7 reads, "deadly works were their care"[107] thus villainizing the entire people of Shechem. The Schemites had grievously erred. Collins wrote, "The condemnation of the Shechemites for general wickedness is more pronounced here than in any of the other accounts."[108] That point has received sufficient attention elsewhere in this book.

The details found in Fragment 8, which describe in detail the attack upon Shechem, align with *T. Levi* 6:4 in that both texts allege that Simeon killed

Hamor and Levi fatally attacked Shechem.[109] Fallon has noted that Simeon takes the initiative and comes to the foreground both here and in Judith.[110]

As Theodotus concludes his account about Dinah, the reader is left with a different impression of Dinah. Fragment 8 reads, "after rescuing their sister, they carried her off with the prisoners to their father's quarters."[111] First of all, to propose that this was "a rescue" obviously insinuates that Dinah was at risk in or with Shechem. Genesis 34 had not given the reader that impression. In contrast, the midrashic tradition had alleged that Dinah found it difficult to "tear herself away from the uncircumcised man Shechem." Theodotus leaves the modern reader with a sense that Dinah needed to be "rescued" from the evil impious man/men. As was the case with Genesis 34, both narrators re-use the same verb regarding Dinah's brothers' action and Shechem's. Here it is said that they "carried her off"; Fragment 4 had first used that verb in relation to Shechem's having carried Dinah off. In a very parallel manner, both Genesis 34:2 and 26 use the verb "took" in relation to Dinah. Shechem first took Dinah; her brothers/the sons of Jacob later took her from Shechem's house. Theodotus clarifies that the sons of Jacob (here referred to as "other brothers") returned Dinah, along with the prisoners, to their father's quarters. That is presumed in Genesis 34, although never stated. Both accounts end there, with an ambiguity about how, or if, Jacob ever dealt directly with Dinah or not.

To recap some of Theodotus' contributions, recall his extensive descriptions—of the once-sacred city of Shechem, of Dinah herself, and of a number of the other characters included in this episode at Shechem. One character who Theodotus added to this account was God.[112] This historian was not the only writer of this general time period to do so. God's presence in this event, as related by Theodotus, makes it clear that Levi and Simeon had been rightly inspired to act in the way they did.

JUBILEES

Jubilees is an interesting book in that while it uses the material from the HB book of Genesis as its starting point, it provides halakic teaching for the people of its time, aiming to instruct people, setting out moral ways in which they should go/walk.[113] *Jubilees* contains some of the strongest invectives against intermarriage. *Jubilees* 30:7, reads, "If there is any man in Israel who wishes to give his daughter or his sister to any man who is from the seed of the gentiles, let him surely die, and let him be stoned because he has caused shame in Israel. And also the woman will be burned with fire because she has defiled the name of her father's house and so she will be uprooted from Israel."[114] Verse 11 is allegedly addressed to Moses, "Command the children of Israel and exhort them not to give any of their daughters to the gentiles and not to take for their sons any of the daughters of the gentiles because that is contemptible before the Lord."[115] Verse 13 of that same chapter reads, "And it is a reproach to Israel, and to those who give and those who take any of the daughters of the gentile nations because it is a defilement and it is contemptible to Israel."[116]

Passages from the HB legal material sound very similar to the above directives. A number of scholars, myself included, have used this legal material to question the portrayal of Jacob in the MT. In Genesis, he seemed willing to "go along" with Shechem/Hamor's proposals of intermarriage. Passages like Deuteronomy 7 would clearly outlaw such exogamy, particularly with Hivites.[117]

In fact, speaking of the Mosaic Law, the book of *Jubilees* purports to be a divine revelation to Moses, mediated through an angel of the presence.[118] Some have thought that this document may have been a Testament of Moses.[119] Moses exhorts his people and their descendants to live a life in strict harmony with the covenant. Two of the primary marks of this covenant are circumcision and endogamous marriage.[120] Those who support such lifestyles are heralded as heroes. It is in this context that Levi and Simeon are extolled for their slaying of Shechem.[121] Shechem had committed an abomination; as *Jubilees* 30 clearly attests, the death penalty was upheld for those who transgress the Divine Law.

Many have concluded that *Jubilees* was written by a priest, as there are special foci both on the person of Levi and on priestly matters.[122] There has been much debate about the party affiliations of this writer.[123] It is typically thought to have been written in the mid-second century BCE.[124] Many have concluded that the "author belonged to the religious movement at least some of whose members later withdrew from Jewish society and produced the Dead Sea Scrolls."[125] This would make sense as the first known reference to the book comes from Qumran CD (The Cairo Genizah copy of the Damascus Document), where it is referred to as "the book of the divisions of the times according to the *Jubilees* and their weeks."[126]

It is believed that the document's provenance was Palestine.[127] Many have asserted that the book was "composed in Hebrew … translated into Greek and from Greek into Ethiopic, in which language alone it is extant in its entirety."[128] O. S. Wintermute, following James C. VanderKam, would add two stages in between Greek and Ethiopic: Syriac and Latin.[129]

The first reference to Dinah found within the book of *Jubilees* is 28:23, which refers to Dinah's birth to Leah and Jacob:

> And Jacob went into her again and she conceived and she bore twins, a boy and a girl, and she called the boy Zebulun and the girl's name was Dinah, in the seventh day of the seventh month in the sixth year of the fourth week.[130]

This is different from other texts in its claim that Dinah and Zebulun were twins. *Jubilees* is consistent in that allegation; when it later lists Dinah as one born to

Jacob and Leah (44:17–18), her name appears after the accounting of Zebulun and his sons. While according to 28:23, Dinah was part of a multiple birth, *Jubilees* presents her as Jacob's only daughter (33:22 and 44:18). These two pieces of information do not necessarily contradict each other.

Dinah is mentioned in *Jub.* 44:18, where the writer enumerates the children of Jacob. It is said that Leah and Jacob had given birth to Reuben, Simeon, Levi, Judah, Issachar, and Zebulun. After each of their sons is mentioned by name, the text continues:

> And these are the sons of Jacob and their sons, whom Leah bore to Jacob in Mesopotamia, six, plus one girl, Dinah, their sister. And all of the persons who (were) sons of Leah and their sons, who entered Egypt with Jacob, their father, were twenty-nine. And Jacob, their father, was with them. And they totaled thirty.[131]

This is one of the references to Dinah being a member of Jacob's clan who went to Egypt. This exploration has detected that this datum was important to post-HB writers. Dinah's inclusion in this southern migration may be considered a parallel to Gen 46:15.

Other portions of *Jubilees* contain more detailed and developed accounts regarding Dinah. A lengthy parallel to Genesis 34 may be found in *Jubilees* 30–31. The context surrounding this passage deals with intermarriage, which according to *Jubilees*, is a serious infraction of the covenant.[132] Much of the rhetoric of this passage belies the understanding that intermarriage is considered an "abomination," to use HB terminology. Nickelsburg states, "The vengeance of Simeon and Levi on Shechem and their refusal to allow him to marry Dinah show that marriage to a foreign spouse is categorically prohibited."[133]

One may also conclude that Simeon and Levi were full of righteous rage because as *Jub.* 30.2 asserts, Dinah was twelve years old when Shechem had snatched her and lay with her.[134] Her age will be considered again later in this chapter, when Demetrius' work is engaged. When the narrator presents her age here, "this detail reinforces the reader's sense of the heinous nature of the crime, and thus also justifies the revenge of the brothers."[135] The rhetoric of Shechem snatching a little twelve year old and laying with her supports the interpretation that this was an instance of rape. In this regard *Jubilees* parallels Theodotus.

In light of *Jub* 30:7 and 13, one would expect more culpability/blame to fall upon Jacob. According to v. 7, Jacob should have been stoned to death for his transgression. Yet once again, strangely, v. 12 maintains, in accordance with Genesis, that it was the sons of Jacob who were more indignant, considering it a transgression/reproach to give their sister to one with a foreskin.[136] That same verse clearly asserts that all the Shechemites affronted Dinah. This could be placed back into earlier discussions about the responsibility borne by the entire city of Shechem.

In the *Jubilees* account it is clear that the author/narrator positively evaluated the actions of Levi, in particular, and Simeon and Levi, generally. What is considered their vengeance in some texts is here reckoned as "righteousness." The narrator forthrightly asserts that the two had killed the Shechemites painfully. He goes on, in 30:17 to write, "And it was a righteousness for them and it was written down for them for righteousness."[137] Furthermore, vv. 18–19 read, "the seed of Levi was chosen for the priesthood and levitical (orders) to minister before the Lord always just as we do. And Levi and his sons will be blessed forever because he was zealous to do righteousness and judgment and vengeance against all who rose up against Israel. And thus a blessing and righteousness will be written (on high) as a testimony for him the in the heavenly tablets before the God of all."[138] Certainly it was decided that Levi, Simeon, and the sons/children of Jacob had done the right thing when they annihilated the men of Shechem. The language of vv. 17–18, depicting Shechem and all as having "risen up against Israel," is used to buttress the positive characterization of Levi.[139] Similar positive sentiments about "the children of Jacob" may be found in v. 24, where a clear dichotomy is drawn between the good and the bad. The Shechemites are referred to as "sinners."

According to v. 24, the children of Jacob "brought forth Dinah, their sister, from the house of Shechem."[140] This stands in partial agreement with Gen 34:26; in *Jubilees*, however, the children of Jacob bring these people/goods to Jacob. The picture that the reader gleans from *Jubilees* sounds reminiscent of Theodotus, who wrote that they had brought Dinah "with prisoners back to their father's quarters."[141] In Genesis, Jacob was removed from the narrative/happenings at this juncture.

In conclusion, *Jubilees* 30–31 shares a good deal of information in common with Genesis; Jacob's reprimand, the terror of the Lord, and the way in which the sons of Jacob were not pursued. This may be put alongside other accounts explored. For example *Legends* I:401–403 allege that a horrible battle ensued when the Amorites came out to meet Jacob and his clan. Other accounts are more in agreement with *Jubilees* and Genesis; for example *Pirqe R. El.* 38.[142]

The beginning of *Jubilees* 31 sounds reminiscent of Genesis 35:1–5. In the latter, Jacob bids his household to purify themselves and change their garments (vv. 1–5) Genesis 35:2 also refers to foreign gods that had become part of Jacob's household. In Gen 35:4, as in *Jubilees*, the reader is told that the people handed over the earrings that were in their ears ... and that Jacob hid those items under the oak at Shechem. One difference between the two accounts is that Rachel's theft of her household gods is not alluded to in Genesis 35. In Genesis, the reader may conclude that these foreign gods made their entrée via the loot collected from Shechem and/or via the women who were taken captive from Shechem.

The writer of *Jubilees* offers no other information about Dinah besides where she was buried. *Legends* II:27 had also given this data. Information about Dinah's burial place may be found in *Jub.* 34.15–17. Verse 15 infers that she died within a month of Joseph's death. The next verse identifies the place of her burial as being "opposite the tomb of Rachel."[143]

Jubilees, therefore, with its insistence against exogamy, glorifies Simeon and Levi, presenting them as heroes who came to Dinah's defense and upheld the purity of Israel. They did so to "save" Israel from affronts, such as the one presented by Shechem and the Shechemites. In *Jubilees*, Shechem is said to have done the following: the men of Shechem "polluted Dinah" (30:4);[144] it is insinuated that Shechem had defiled her (30:5–6); "the men of Shechem … caused a shame in Israel" (30:5);[145] and they had performed deeds against Dinah (30:12).[146] The verb "defile" is found in 30:2, 3, 5, and 6.[147] Obviously, the incident involving Dinah is used to show how bad Shechem and the Shechemites were. *Jubilees* offers proof that Dinah and her community were horrifically wronged by Shechem. Such wrongdoers, who transgress the Divine covenant or one of the Divine's covenanted people should and would be punished with swiftness and with severity.

DEMETRIUS THE CHRONOGRAPHER

As was the case with Theodotus' work, only fragments of Demetrius' chronological accounts exist; there are six extant fragments. In writing about the process by which these texts have been handed down, J. Hanson remarked, "Fragments 1–5 are preserved in Eusebius, *Praeparatio Evangelica*, Book 9, where he has excerpted the work of Alexander Polyhistor *On the Jews*; Polyhistor had, in turn, excerpted the work of Demetrius."[148]

Hanson has concluded that Demetrius used the LXX as a base from which to work.[149] This helps to date his writing no earlier than 250 BCE; the fact that Polyhistor excerpted his work helps establish the later end of the range to dates to before the first century BCE.[150] Hanson has argued for Egyptian provenance of the text.[151]

The work of Demetrius is unique with respect to the other pseudepigraphical material considered so far. The genre of his work is chronography, or recording/preserving traditions about the passing of time. Establishing any sort of dependence/knowledge of other traditions is difficult.[152] This is especially true because of Demetrius' penchant, as a chronographer, for information about character's/people's ages when various events happened to them. For example, in Fragment 2:3–5 Demetrius tells the years and months in which Jacob's children were born. Note that this sort of information is missing from the HB; obviously the two accounts have different aims or intentions. According to this passage from Demetrius, Dinah and Joseph are born in the same month of the same year, of different mothers. Also, according to Demetrius' chronology, Dinah and Levi were four years apart in age. Simeon and Dinah were five years apart in age. In both of these cases, Levi and Simeon, the males were older than Dinah. This point will be later revisited, vis-à-vis other pseudepigraphal references, in the conclusion. According to the chronology given by Demetrius, Jacob was ninety-one when Dinah was born.

The text continues the narrative of Jacob and his family, again offering their ages and comment on the time that has elapsed between various events. Verses 8–9 give many details about the relative ages of Jacob's children at various junctures/events within the story. First of all, according to Demetrius, ten years had elapsed between the time when Jacob and his clan entered Canaan and when Shechem violated Dinah.[153] This information agrees with other details Demetrius puts forth: Dinah was a little over six when Jacob came to Canaan, and it is said that she was sixteen years old when she was defiled by Shechem. Unfortunately, one of the gaps remaining in this account, as is also the case regarding Genesis, is that the reader is given any information about the relationship that did or did not exist between Jacob and his family and the Shechemites/Canaanites/Hivites. To the modern reader, knowing more about that detail might make a difference in how the congress of Dinah and Shechem is perceived. If some were to think that the two groups of people had had regular contact with one another, and that the relationship was good or healthy, they might "read" or interpret the situation differently and more positively. The details around the relationship remain vague.

Demetrius offered the detail that Dinah was sixteen when she encountered Shechem. This datum differs from that given in *Jubilees*. I am not the first to notice that according to *Jub.* 30:2 Dinah was twelve.[154] Also, it is said here that Levi was twenty when he killed Shechem; that information agrees with the datum given in *T. Levi* 2:2.

Demetrius wrote, "Israel's daughter Dinah was defiled by Shechem the son of Hamor."[155] Please note the verb "defile." Along parallel lines, later in that same verse (v. 9), the offense against Dinah is called "a defilement." Consistent with the way in which the Genesis narrator (and others) wrote of this event, Demetrius used the defilement of Dinah as the narrative justification for why Simeon and Levi "rushed out and slew both Hamor and his son Shechem."[156] As has frequently been the case, one again the two sons of Jacob, brothers of Dinah, are said to have committed the slaying. In past pages, authors/narrators attributed that action to either Simeon, Levi, or both of them.

One can conjecture about Jacob's age (107); it is not surprising to read that his sons, Simeon and Levi, at 21 and 20 years of age (i.e., men who were 86 or 87 years younger) were the ones who "rushed out" and slew the Shechemites. Especially because the focus of Demetrius' passages is chronology, very little detail about characters' traits, professions, emotions, etc. is included. Demetrius makes the HB look chock-full of descriptions. Theodotus might almost seem superfluous in the information he provided. It is important to note that Demetrius had very little concern with the theological implications of this material; he did nothing to develop the texts in ways that might garner a reader's sympathy/empathy for any of the characters. His sole emphasis was chronography: producing/preserving data about time and people's ages.[157]

Demetrius, like many other writers already considered, wrote of Jacob and his family descent into Egypt, claiming that Dinah was then thirty-nine years old. Demetrius did not include information about Dinah's death or burial. In that way it can be contrasted to some of the other references investigated.

Demetrius frequently focused on people's/characters' ages. That was obviously the historian's emphasis; it may be noted that not one adjective appears in this passage. The text lacks much of the details and the interpretation that are found elsewhere. Like Genesis, Demetrius never mentions the Divine. It offers no comment about peoples' affects—unlike Genesis, the reader is not told that the sons of Jacob were very angry over what Shechem had done to Dinah. Nor is anything said of Shechem's alleged love for Dinah. In some ways, what appears in Demetrius' work are the "cold hard facts," without interpretation or evaluation.

CONCLUSIONS ABOUT THE PSEUDEPIGRAPHA

In this conclusion, the focus will remain on the information given about Dinah and what was done to her. As might be expected, many texts introduce Dinah by giving information about her birth. That is the case in *L.A.B.*, Theodotus' Fragments 3 and 4, *Jub.* 28:23, and Demetrius' Fragment 2, v. 9; it is not the case in *T. Levi*, *T. Job* and *Jos. Asen.* The four texts which present Dinah this way[158] all mention that Dinah was born of Leah. The passage from *Jubilees* is unique in that it is the only reference to Dinah's being a twin of Zebulun.

The *Testament of Levi* introduces Dinah first in 2:2 as the sister of Levi and Simeon; she is referred to as "our sister" in 6:8 (with the referent being either Simeon and Levi, or all Levi's brothers); she is also referred to as the sister of Levi in 5:3, 6:3, and 7:3. Obviously, the emphasis is on Dinah's being Levi's sister, as "sister" is the only noun used of Dinah.

The *Testament of Job* introduces Dinah as a mother and as the implied wife of Job. There she is portrayed as the mother of ten children, the ten which Job and she had had following Job's suffering.

Only two of the pseudepigraphical texts refer to Dinah as a virgin: Theodotus' Fragment 4 and *Jub.* 30:6. The passage from *Jubilees* insinuates that Dinah was a virgin at the time Shechem polluted her.

This group of pseudepigraphical texts has very sparse references to Dinah's going out. This stands in stark contrast to the *midrashim*, where her action, interpreted as an infraction, seemed to be a primary focus. The only text which mentions her act is Theodotus, Fragment 4, where it is said, she "came into Shechem when there was a festival, since she wished to see the city."[159] No other pseudepigraphical source mentions that specific act. The focus of the vast majority of texts is upon Shechem's having defiled or raped Dinah. Because this one action is downplayed by these texts, there is no reference to Dinah as a whore, harlot, or a prostitute. In none of these texts did Simeon or Levi allege that Shechem had even treated her as one. That is completely missing from these writings.

Two of these texts give specific ages for Dinah at the time she met Shechem. *Jubilees* 30.2 claims that "she was little, only twelve years old."[160] This kind of rhetoric increases the reader's sympathy/empathy for Dinah. Demetrius records that Dinah was sixteen years and four months old when she was defiled by Shechem. According to Demetrius' chronology, Dinah and Levi were four years apart in age.

Other than noting Dinah's age at the time of defilement, Theodotus is the source which offers the most information about Dinah. It was he who, in Fragment 3, introduced Dinah, noting that she "had a beautiful form, and admirable frame, and a noble spirit."[161] The next Fragment gives the details noted earlier, that Dinah had worked with wool and that she was still a virgin when Shechem first encountered her.

Shechem was discredited with having affronted Dinah. According to *T. Levi* 6:3, Levi was "filled with zeal on account of the abominable thing they had done to (his) sister."[162] "They," in this case, refers to the Shechemites or the sons of Hamor. It is also in *T. Levi* 6:8, that it is alleged that "they had wanted to do the same thing to Sarah and Rebecca that they did to Dinah."[163] This is the text which develops the Shechemites as sinners. One other passage addresses their infraction; *T. Levi* 7:3 reads, "by defiling my sister they committed folly in Israel."[164]

The *Testament of Job* completely overlooks the incident between Shechem and Dinah. It focuses on Dinah as Job's wife and the mother of his children. Using fairly circuitous language, Jacob spoke of how he begot his children from Dinah. *Liber Antiquitatum Biblicarum* (*L.A.B.*), which also refers to Dinah as Job's wife and the mother of his children, presents Dinah as the subject of at least one active verb. Before doing so, however, it includes the Shechem episode: 8:7 says that Shechem "raped Dinah his (Jacob's) daughter and humiliated her."[165] It quickly goes on to record that Job took Dinah as his wife. The passage concludes its references to Dinah in 8:11, identifying her in reference to her brothers, "And Dinah their sister bore fourteen sons and six daughters."[166]

As Simeon and Levi drew their swords in *Joseph and Aseneth* 23:14, they make the claim, "With these two swords the Lord God punished the insult of the Shechemites (by) which they insulted the sons of Israel, because of our sister Dinah who Shechem the son of Hamor had defiled."[167] It is alleged that Shechem had defiled Dinah, thus insulting the sons of Israel. This passage also adds the character of God into the assault against Shechem.

In Fragment 4, Theodotus wrote, "But when Sychem the son of Hamor saw her, he loved her; and after seizing her as his own, he carried her off and ravished her."[168] Theodotus later (Fragment 6) referred to Shechem's assault on Dinah as "a violent attack."[169]

According to *Jub.* 30:2, "Dinah, the daughter of Jacob, was snatched away to the house of Shechem ... he lay with her and defiled her, but she was little, only twelve years old."[170] The same verb "defile" is used in *Jub.* 30:3, 5, and 6; v. 4 uses the verb "polluted."[171] Verses 17–18 insinuate that Shechem had "risen up against Israel."[172] *Jubilees* 30:24 states that the children of Israel "brought forth Dinah…from the house of Shechem ... to Jacob, their father."[173] The only other account of this "return/rescue" of Dinah is in Theodotus' Fragment 8.

The next to the last piece of information to be considered mentions Dinah as one of those who had gone to Egypt with Jacob and his clan. That may be found in *Jubilees* 44:18, as well as in Demetrius 2:17.

The closing datum provided by these texts pertains to her final resting place, i.e., her burial place. *Jubilees* 34:15–17 speaks about the timing of her death and identifies her burial place as "opposite the tomb of Rachel,"[174] where Bilhah was also buried. Thus, these texts come full circle, starting with her birth and concluding with her death.

CHAPTER FIVE

Dinah IN Apocryphal/Deuterocanonical Writings

JUDITH

Introduction to Judith

The Roman Catholic tradition considers the book of Judith a deuterocanonical text; Jewish and Protestant traditions regard it to be apocryphal.[1] Regardless of its classification, all commentators have noted the historical issues of the text. Two examples of such issues are directly relevant to our exploration. The first is the uncertain location of Bethulia.[2] Some have alleged that it might indeed be Shechem.[3] This may provide a geographical link between the events described in this apocryphal book and those of Genesis 34.

There is another connection between the two narratives, also with an affiliated historical issue. In Judith 9, Judith passionately beseeches the God of her ancestor Simeon. Simeon was obviously one of the leading characters in Genesis 34. However, the genealogy given for Judith in Judith 8:1 ironically does not include Simeon's name. It might be that Simeon's name is intended, to use David deSilva's language, "as the father of Sarsadai and grandfather of Salamiel, as is the case in Num 1:6.[4] Numerous such theories have arisen to address the alleged inconsistencies or incongruities within the book, some positing the existence of various traditions behind or prior to the current text.[5] It is surprising to note the extent to which Judith identified with her ancestor Simeon, regardless of how fictitious her genealogical line back to Simeon might have been.

Scholars have focused upon the literary structure of the book of Judith, coming to various conclusions about its genre. For an excellent and concise summary of the landscape of opinions, please see Carey Moore's work.[6] He concludes that "the book of Judith is best regarded as a folktale which offers an example story of a pious widow who, strengthened by her religious faith, courageously took matters into her own hands and defeated the enemy."[7] Along similar lines, Denise Dombkowski Hopkins wrote, "The book of Judith offers a popular example of the ancient Jewish novel in the Greco-Roman world in the period between 200 B.C.E. and 100 C.E., when increased literacy among the upper classes (including women), and the rise of a class of merchants and bureaucrats, created an audience that read for entertainment."[8]

Whether written for entertainment or spiritual edification, the book of Judith and the character Judith reveals the centrality of faith. Toni Craven wrote,

> Judith's success is grounded in her trust in Yahweh. On a theological level, her story challenges all who would imprison God in doctrines of their own making. She is faithful to her tradition and its regulations, but at the same time she is free to act as the circumstances of her particular situation dictate. She demands that her frightened community not put themselves in the place of God. She declared unequivocally that God must be free either to defend them or to witness their destruction. Her confidence is that God will provide, but only her faith assures her of this.[9]

Many have concluded that the sort of faith expressed above seems to be in congruence with that of a Palestinian Jew,[10] most likely of a Pharisaic background.[11] In terms of dating, Moore concluded that "the Judith story received its final form sometime after 107 BC[E].[12] The book of Judith is one of the texts not found among the Dead Sea Scroll cache.[13]

It is presumed by most that the text was originally written in Hebrew, although the "basic text is in Greek."[14] Many are of the opinion, as Moore wrote, that the "LXX gives every indication of being a translation of a Hebrew text."[15] This is true because much of the LXX appears to contain multiple Hebraic expressions, phrases, and idioms. With that introduction, the references to Dinah and the incident at Shechem will now be considered.

After Judith had confronted the magistrates or elders of Bethulia, encouraging them by recounting God's mighty acts, they besought her to pray on their behalf. Uzziah recognized Judith as a woman of great wisdom and referred to her as a "God-fearing woman" (8:28–31). Note the prophetic role Judith is portrayed as playing.[16] The city magistrates asked her to intervene on their behalf. Before commencing with her prayer, she informed them in vv. 32–34 that she and God were about to perform something that would be remembered for generations. She foreshadowed the miraculous imminent deliverance. She then addressed the Divine, doing so at time of evening incense offering at Jerusalem. It was at this point that she, Judith, offered the first and most obvious intertextual reference to the incident at Shechem. The following is her prayer, according to Jdt 9:1–6[17]; I have added the italics for emphasis:

> Then Judith prostrated herself, put ashes on her head, and uncovered the sackcloth she was wearing. At the very time when the evening incense was being offered in the house of God in Jerusalem, Judith cried out to the Lord with a loud voice, and said,

(2) "O Lord God of my ancestor Simeon, to whom *you* gave a sword to take revenge on those strangers who had torn off a virgin's clothing to defile her, and exposed her thighs to put her to shame, and polluted her womb to disgrace her; for *you* said 'It shall not be done'—yet they did it. (3) So *you* gave up their rulers to be killed, and their bed, which was ashamed of the deceit they had practiced, was stained with blood, and you struck down slaves along with princes, and princes on their thrones. (4) *You* gave up their wives for booty and their daughters to captivity, and all their booty to be divided among your beloved children who burned with zeal for you and abhorred the pollution of their blood and called on you for help—O God, my God, hear me also—a widow.

(5) For *you* have done these things and those that went before and those that followed. *You* have designed the things that are now, and those that are to come. What *you* had in mind has happened; (6) the things *you* decided on presented themselves and said, "Here we are!" For all your ways are prepared in advance, and your judgment is with foreknowledge."

Notice how Judith's prayer engages the Divine, who she believed had equipped Simeon with a sword. One may be reminded of the four pseudepigraphical texts, *T. Levi, Jos. Asen.*, Theod., and *Jub.*, which alleged that God was a primary actor in this incident or had motivated either Simeon and/or Levi's successful attack on Shechem. This must be seen as a diversion from Genesis 34; Judith added the Divine as a primary character to that episode. In doing so, the reader is led to the impression, as was John Collins, "Judith assumes that Simeon's deed was fully approved by God."[18] The rhetoric found in these verses from Judith 9 is very theocentric.

The themes of vengeance and revenge tie the two narratives together, whether or not it is actually named. Genesis 34 is very clear in making the point that the sons of Jacob did what they did because he/they had defiled Dinah, their sister. This is reiterated in vv. 5, 13, and 27. Judith also picks up that point in 9:2: (κύριε ὁ θεὸς τοῦ πατρός μου Συμεων ᾧ ἔδωκας ἐν χειρὶ ῥομφαίαν εἰς ἐκδίκησιν ἀλλογενῶν). She states that God was the one who had given the sword to Simeon for revenge (ἐκδίκησιν). That word is one of the threads running throughout the narrative of Judith.[19] A bit more than half of the time, it is God who executes vengeance, oftentimes through human hands, such as Simeon's or Judith's. There are also a fair number of references in Judith where Nebuchadnezzar/Holofernes spoke about taking vengeance. In fact, ch. 8 serves as a turning point; there Judith is blessed/empowered by Uzziah and the magistrates of Bethulia to do to their enemies what Simeon and God had done to the Shechemites.

Judith's argument or case before God is buttressed by her allegation in v. 2 that God had given the commandment, which the Shechemites (here, "those strangers") had transgressed. Judith painted a picture in which the Shechemites, as a group, were clearly acting out against God; this has an incredible rhetorical power. This may provide another verbal link back to Genesis 34. Judith used the phrase "For you said 'It shall not be done,' yet they did it." (εἶπας γάρ οὐχ οὕτως ἔσται καὶ ἐποίησαν). This expression is very close to that found in Gen 34:7 on the lips of the sons of Jacob, "he [Shechem] had committed an outrage in Israel by lying with Jacob's daughter, for such a thing ought not to be done (καὶ οὐχ οὕτως ἔσται). In both instances the commission of an outrage is used as the justification for revenge.

One of the ways in which Judith downplayed Shechem was that she refused to name him. She simply referred to him and his clan as "those strangers" (9:2). In much the same way that Judith never used Shechem's proper name, she also neglected to mention Dinah by name, some commentators have noticed. Hopkins wrote, "… she refuses to name Dinah in her prayer and refers to her simply by the generic 'virgin,' thus robbing Dinah of her personhood. She equates Dinah's rape with the siege of Bethulia [which is related to the Hebrew word for 'virgin']."[20] She goes on to write about how Judith had identified more with Simeon than with Dinah.[21]

Judith's strength and humility is highlighted when she prayed to the God of Simeon. Moore wrote in his *ABD* article, "Judith, covered with sackcloth and ashes, prayed to the Lord, begging him for the same support he had granted her ancestor Simeon when he avenged Hamor's rape of Dinah."[22] Note Moore's conclusion that Dinah had been raped and that it had been Hamor who did this. This datum may indeed be seen as conflicting with the HB tradition in which Shechem was said to have violated/defiled Dinah. In my opinion, deSilva handled this in a manner that is more faithful to the HB; he wrote, "She [Judith] prays …, invoking the zeal of her ancestor Simeon, who was empowered by God to kill and plunder those who had *defiled* his sister Dinah."[23]

Furthermore, according to Judith's prayer, it was God who had given up the Shechemite rulers to be killed; the Divine had "struck down slaves along with princes," and had given up their wives and daughters. Lest anyone miss her point in this series of crystal clear statements, Judith repeated to the Divine, "you have done these things."

With God as the primary actor/power, Simeon was seen as an agent of Divine justice. After seeing more of the text of Judith, it will be obvious that the same thing, Divine agency, can be said of Judith herself. Suffice it to say, Judith makes Simeon into a hero. Depending on one's interpretation of Genesis 34, this may stand in contrast to the HB tradition. For example, deSilva indicated that Bissell was highly critical of the book of Judith because, in Bissell's opinion, it contradicted the point of view found in Genesis 34.[24] For someone like Bissell, the text of the Torah/Pentateuch served as a ruler by which to measure or gauge other texts. Moore also commented that previous scholars, such as Deprez, had noted the way in which "Judith, like such pseudepigraphical works as Jubilees 30 and the Testament of Levi, tends to rehabilitate the tribe of Simeon."[25] There is a tendency of a number of post-HB Jewish texts to characterize the actions of Simeon and Levi as heroic, defending and protecting Dinah's honor and that of Israel.

Before addressing the character portrayal of Dinah in the book of Judith, it is imperative to comment on the overlapping semantic domains of the two narratives. There are numerous points of contact between the two narratives; some instances are overlapping vocabulary from the LXX account of Genesis 34 and others are thematic ties. The next section will focus on those overlapping places.

There were offenses committed against Dinah and her clan and Israel, which according to Judith, gave her, Judith, the right to ask the Divine for strength as she went about her business. Notice how much of the rhetoric deals with shame, pollution, and defilement; directly connected to the offense is Divine vengeance or justice. Keep in mind that, according to Judith, God was offended by what "those strangers" had done. Simeon was the vehicle by which God had addressed that affront.

In 9:2, Judith addressed the God of her father, Simeon. She alleged that the Divine had given into Simeon's hand a sword unto vengeance on the strangers (plural) who had loosed the clothing of a virgin unto pollution (εἰς μίασμα) and had exposed her thigh unto shame (εἰς αἰσχύνην). "Pollution" and "shame" appear together here as a word pair, describing what Shechem had done to Dinah. In 9:4, Judith continues that the Divine's "beloved children" (the sons of Jacob) had "burned with zeal for the Divine and abhorred the pollution of their blood" (μίασμα αἵματος αὐτῶν). Note here, as in many places, the pollution, which had once been more localized on Dinah is now also upon her family, particularly her brothers. She uses that same noun, pollution, later to claim that the sons of Jacob and she held the same point of view. As they had called on the Divine for help, so Judith beseeched God. A common or coalescing of point of view becomes evident: the narrator, the sons of Jacob, and Judith tend to view things in the same way. The reader clearly knows of Judith's outrage at what had happened at Shechem and her dependence on the God of her father. She sets out to act in a way that parallels both her ancestor and his and her God. The second noun of the above pair, αἰσχύνη, is also found on the lips of Bogoas, in 14:18, when discovered what Judith had done to Holofernes and exclaimed, "One Hebrew woman, had brought shame (ἐποίησεν αἰσχύνην) on the house of Nebuchadnezzar."

The two nouns which appeared in Judith for the first time as a word pair in 9:2, when describing Shechem's offense against Dinah, are also found together in 13:16. In this particular verse, neither offense had been committed; Judith had been neither polluted nor shamed. Judith becomes the anti-Dinah or the reverse of Dinah in this regard.²⁶ She exclaimed to all who had come out to meet her at the city gate, "he committed no sin with me to defile and shame me" (καὶ οὐκ ἐποίησεν ἁμάρτημα μετ' ἐμοῦ εἰς μίασμα καὶ αἰσχύνην). Note that the narrative returns to these two nouns, contrasting Judith's fate with that of Dinah. However, at the point of the narrative when Judith first prayed to God, she was still incredibly vulnerable. The reader realized that there was a possibility that Judith could be harmed as she went out. Instances like the ones involving Dinah and King David's daughter, Tamar, reinforce that the Divine did not always intervene to avert rape.

In commenting on the connections between Dinah and Judith, Thibodeau wrote

> First, since there was every possibility that she (Judith) may be raped by the uncircumcised foreigner Holofernes, Judith sees her own position as analogous to that of the hapless Dinah who was raped by Shechem. In calling herself a widow in verse 5 of this prayer, she obviously sees herself as even more vulnerable than Dinah who at least had two brothers to help her; Judith has no one.²⁷

Judith's widowhood and wealth both played a role in what she was able to accomplish in this story. At some junctures, her being a widow made her appear vulnerable and dependent on the divine; at other points in the story, it was her widowhood that allowed her to dress up the way she did, leave town, and come as close as she did to seducing Holofernes. Neither an unbetrothed virgin nor a married woman would have been able to have done that without suffering potential dishonor/disgrace.

Judith 9:2 shares a verbal link with the LXX's account of Genesis 34. One of the phrases describing Shechemites' offense against Dinah is that they had polluted her womb unto disgrace (ἐβεβήλωσαν μήτραν εἰς ὄνειδος).²⁸ The Greek noun used for "disgrace" may also be found in Gen 34:14, when the sons of Jacob alleged that it would be a disgrace for them to give their sister to one with a foreskin (γὰρ ὄνειδος ἡμῖν). This same noun was frequently used by the LXX to translate the Hebrew word חֶרְפָּה;²⁹ it appears throughout the beginning of the book of Judith.³⁰

Furthermore, the above verb ἐβεβήλωσαν, "polluted," is used as one of the verbal threads throughout the beginning of the book of Judith. This word, too, falls within the semantic domain of honor/shame. The word may be found in Jdt 4:3, 4:12, 8:21, and in 9:2 and 9:8. In those attestations, the following are objects: vessels, altar, and temple collectively in 4:3; the sanctuary, in 4:12, 8:21, and 9:8; and Dinah's womb in 9:2. The word "polluted" may also be found as part of a word pair with the noun ὄνειδος, "disgrace, reproach," in Jdt 8:22 and 9:2.

In 9:4, Judith had alleged that the Divine had given up the women of the Shechemites for booty or for plundering and their daughters for captivity. In

16:3–5, Judith praised God, recounting how the Divine intervened to block the plans of Holofernes. She rejoiced, "The Assyrian came down from the mountains of the north; he came with myriads of his warriors; their numbers blocked up the wadis, and the cavalry covered the hills. (4) He boasted that he world burn up my territory, and kill my young men with the sword, and dash my infants to the ground, and seize my children as booty, and take my virgins as spoil. (5) But the Lord Almighty has foiled them by the hand of a woman."

Some women served as aggressors; others were victims. This dichotomy is true when contrasting Judith and Dinah, it is also true for the women in the book of Judith. As Judith delineated the various ways in which the Divine exacted vengeance/revenge upon the Shechemites, she recalled, according to 9:4, "You gave up their wives for booty and their daughters to captivity …" Moore translated, "their wives for rape," referring to the same expression found in Jdt 4:12. As he pointed out,[31] there is high likelihood that both Israelite women (in the case of 4:12) and Shechemite women (in the context of 9:4) would have suffered rape as part of the military attack, as that is and was a stratagem of war. It is, however, fairly rare to have women/children (i.e. humans) be the object of this verb or modified by this noun—that is true whether the language is Hebrew (as in Gen 34) or Greek, in this case (εἰς προνομὴν).[32] Consider the other attestations of this expression or similar phrases found in the Judith narrative: 1:14; 2:23, 26; 7:26; 8:21; 15:6, 11; and 16:4. In ch. 1, Nebuchadnezzar was said to have "taken as booty" the markets/broad streets of Ecbatana. In the first instance of ch. 2, it is the Rassisites and the Ishmaelites who were thus taken; in v. 26 it is the sheepfolds of the Midianites. In ch. 7, although "the whole city" of Bethulia was to surrender to Holofernes for plundering; obviously it is the people who are the objects of this intent. In 8:21, the sanctuary of Bethulia was at risk of being captured and plundered. With the reversal of fate which Judith set in motion, in Jdt 15:6, the people of Bethulia plundered the Assyrian camp, taking their possessions as spoils of war; v. 11 specifies that they did so for thirty days. Lastly ch. 16, spoken by Judith, recounted the threat of the Assyrian Holofernes: he had threatened to take her children (Israel) and give them as spoils of war (v. 4). On quite a few occasions the book of Judith speaks about the plundering and despoiling of people, male and female. Whether rape was necessarily concomitant with attack on any city is uncertain.[33]

There are numerous thematic and vocabulary links between Genesis 34 and Judith. Some are most clear when the LXX account of Genesis 34 is considered next to Judith. For example, in Judith 9:3 and 10 there are numerous references to princes and rulers. Moore saw v. 10's reference to both "ruler and his servant" as a hearkening back to "the Shechem incident."[34] First of all, the word ἄρχων (prince) occurs both in Gen 34:2 and in Jdt 9:3 and 9:10 (twice). Speaking in general terms, both narratives deal with unexpected triumph over the wealthy/

noble. In both stories, victory is accomplished through deceit. The sons of Jacob were said to have spoken with deceit because Shechem had defiled Dinah (Gen 34:13). In 9:13, Judith prays that her deceitful words bring wound and bruise on those who have aimed to hurt God's covenant and God's covenant people.

As the Divine had struck down the slaves along with the princes, Judith, with God's backing, aimed to strike down those who rivaled Bethulia. In Jdt 9:3, Judith retold the Shechem incident, saying that it had been God who struck down both classes of people. The verb for "struck down" in 9:3 is ἐπάταξας. This verb and its objects are repeated in 9:10, when Judith prays that by her deceit God may strike down princes and servants. It appears in the narrative at the place where Judith struck Holofernes' neck twice, severing his head from his body (13:8). Again, when she triumphantly entered Bethulia with Holofernes' head, she exclaimed, "The Lord has struck him down by the hand of a female!" (13:15). Lastly, in her song, she sings, "... nor did the Titans strike him down ... but Judith daughter of Merari ..."[35] Indeed, like her father before her, Judith becomes the instrument through whom the Lord works vengeance, striking down those who challenge the beloved of the Lord.

The reader familiar with Genesis 34 knows of the deceit and the vengeance inflicted upon Shechem. This early prayer of Judith, combined with the narrator's portrayal of her, makes it clear that she set out on a path similar to her ancestor Simeon, using the Divine as justification. In the words of Reinhard Pummer:

> In the case of Judith, Genesis 34 has an additional function, namely, the legitimation of Judith's ruse. In the text of Judith one can discern allusion to several Old Testament stories about the use of stratagems, such as Rebekah ... Tamar ... Ehud ... and Simeon and Levi. It is as if the author wanted to show that in comparison with all those other figures, Judith did not commit an evil act but used a ruse against an unjust aggressor.[36]

Even early in the narrative, Judith referred to the Shechemites simply as "those strangers." By portraying them as negatively as she did, alleging that they had: "torn off a virgin's clothing to defile her, exposed her thighs to put her to shame, and polluted her womb to disgrace her." These strangers are clearly antagonists—against Dinah, Israel, and the Divine. This foreshadows the role into which Holofernes would be cast; he too proved to pose a threat to Judith, Israel, and the Divine.

What were the offenses against Dinah and how Dinah is portrayed? She is referred to as a virgin. She had been referred to as such previously, in a number of targumic and pseudepigraphal texts. Specifically, *Tgs. Neof.* and *Ps.–J.*, Theod. and *Jub.* 30:6[37] all refer to her as such. The text alleges that one of the offenses against her, stated in Jdt 9:2, was that "those strangers" had torn off her clothing. Judith paints a poignant picture of a rape victim—complete with torn clothes, exposed thighs, and a polluted womb. It is fairly typically said, in the post-HB texts explored thus far, that Dinah had been defiled. Never before have narrators included such details as: her thighs had been exposed, thus putting her to shame; or that her her womb had been polluted. *Jubilees* 30 contained the accusation that "they had polluted Dinah, their sister." Once again, it was typically said that she had been disgraced. Even these common expressions of defiling and disgracing are couched in new language in the book of Judith, with the result that, to modern readers, Dinah looks like a victim/survivor of an assault.

This opening section concluded, leaving the reader curious as to whether or not Judith will be successful in whatever her endeavor or plan might entail. Even in this early pairing of Judith and the Divine, there is a foreshadowing that Judith is the protagonist/heroine of the story. The pious, wise, God-fearing woman invites God to stand by her side and strengthen her for battle. As she prays, recounting significant chunks of the Genesis 34 story, the narrator artistically interweaves that with the mission she envisions for herself. It certainly would appear here that "Dinah's God" is a God of vengeance and violence, in keeping with the God-ordained response of her full-blood brothers. Judith sets out for similar vengeance.

Most often the male characters, Simeon and Levi, have expressed such vengeance and violence. One may pause to note what it is like for the modern reader to meet a woman with such qualities. The biblical scholar may be reminded of Jael, from the book of Judges. In her article on the book of Judith, Hopkins wrote, "The ambiguity of Judith forces us to confront the presuppositions about gender that we bring to her text."[38] Some might be appalled by Judith's characteristics; some may find it refreshing. "Judith, however, assumers the man's role of protector-avenger associated with her ancestor …"[39] Besides the alleged biological tie back to Simeon, this is one of the ways in which Judith identified with her ancestor.

The same full range of reactions—from hearty sympathetic embrace to disgust or antipathy—was also seen in scholars' responses to the characterization of Simeon and Levi. It was often those two, or one of the two brothers, who were portrayed as having zealous piety. In many cases, that was upheld as a virtue, in some cases, ordaining the descendents of Levi for priesthood. For example, recall the previous chapters' discussions regarding *T. Levi*, *Jos. Asen.*, Theod., and *Jubilees*.

One could also consider Judith's sentiments expressed in verse 11 as standing in polar opposition to Jacob's fear. She maintains that God's strength did not depend on numbers; Jacob feared that he and his household were few in number and that the Canaanites and Perizzites could too easily assemble themselves against him and win. In the aftermath of Jacob's leaving Shechem for Bethel (Gen 35:1–8), indeed, God does intervene and via a "terror from/of God" (v. 5), Jacob and his clan were enabled to exit the land unharmed. Thus, in the end, although Dinah had suffered sexual defilement/violation, the group, as a whole, was protected by the Divine.[40]

The next reference comes from Judith 9:

> (7) "Here now are the Assyrians, a greatly increased force, priding themselves in their horses and riders, boasting in the strength of their foot soldiers, and trusting in shield and spear, in bow and sling. They do not know that you are the Lord who crushes wars; the Lord is your name. (8) Break their strength by your might, and bring down their power in your anger; for they intend to defile your sanctuary, and to pollute the tabernacle where your glorious name resides, and to break off the horns of your altar with the sword. (9) Look at their pride, and send your wrath upon their heads. Give to me, a widow, the strong hand to do what I plan. (10) By the deceit of my lips strike down the slave with the prince and the prince with his servant; crush their arrogance by the hand of a woman.
>
> (11) "For your strength does not depend on numbers, nor your might on the powerful. But you are the God of the lowly, helper of the oppressed, upholder of the weak, protector of the forsaken, savior of those without hope. (12) Please, please, God of my father, God of the heritage of Israel, Lord of heaven and earth, Creator of the waters, King of all your creation, hear my prayer! (13) Make my deceitful words bring wound and bruise on those who have planned cruel things against your covenant, and against your sacred house, and against Mount Zion, and against the house your children possess. (14) Let your whole nation and every tribe know and understand that you are God, the God of all power and might, and that there is no other who protects the people of Israel but you alone!"

In Judith's prayer of 9:8, she beseeches the Divine: (8) Break their strength by your might, and bring down their power in your anger (ἐν τῷ θυμῷ σου); for they intend to defile (βεβηλῶσαι) your sanctuary, and to pollute (μιᾶναι) the tabernacle …" The second verb, here translated as "pollute" is the one which is used throughout the LXX version of Genesis 34 to describe three times what he (Shechem) and they (the Shechemites) had done to Dinah. It may be found in the LXX at Gen 34:5, 13, and 27, where it is consistently used to translate the Hebrew verb טָמֵא (defile).

Judith 9:11 claims that the Divine is a God of the lowly/humbled (ἀλλὰ ταπεινῶν εἶ θεός). This provides yet another linkage back to Genesis 34:2, where it is used in reference to Dinah. The LXX reads καὶ ἐταπείνωσεν αὐτήν; and he humbled/violated her. The word is used in many forms throughout the book of Judith. It is used to describe women and children in 7:32, not necessarily in the sexual sense. That is, it deals more with the morale of the women and children—in fact, the NRSV translates "they were in great misery." It is used fairly similarly in 13:20 as it was in 7:32, this time with "our nation" as the subject.

When it occurs in 16:11, the sense is an oppressed or weakened people. Lastly, in 5:8, its subject is the Divine and the object, Egypt. It is the Greek equivalent of the Hebrew ענה. For a full discussion of this verb, please see my earlier book.[41] As Judith demonstrates, historically the Lord has been faithful to the Lord's people. God is a "God of the oppressed,"[42] who is willing to oppress those who challenge and threaten God's beloved. In this instance, the Divine uses a female to accomplish that.

When one looks at the general tone and therefore the rhetoric of both Genesis 34 (and its working out in 49) and Judith, it is not surprising that the narratives share a number of vocabulary words. "Wrath" or "anger" appears numerous times throughout Judith; the narrator switched between two close synonyms. For example, consider two phrases from Jdt 9:8–9: καὶ κάταξον τὸ κράτος αὐτῶν ἐν τῷ θυμῷ σου and ἀπόστειλον τὴν ὀργήν σου εἰς κεφαλὰς αὐτῶν: ("bring down their power in your anger") and ("send your wrath upon their heads") respectively. One may note that as Jacob prepared to die, according to Gen 49:6–7, he "cursed" Simeon and Levi for their anger. In both instances the noun used by the LXX is θυμός.

Some readers of Genesis 34 are rather surprised at the action which occurs in v. 27: "And the other sons of Jacob came upon the slain, and plundered the city, because they had defiled their sister (οἱ δὲ υἱοὶ Ιακωβ εἰσῆλθον ἐπὶ τοὺς τραυματίας καὶ διήρπασαν τὴν πόλιν ἐν ᾗ ἐμίαναν Διναν τὴν ἀδελφὴν αὐτῶν)." The word used for "slain" or "wounded" also appears in Jdt 9:12, when she prays that God might make her words their wound. The reader stands poised to discover what Judith and God will do.

> **Judith 10**: (1) When Judith had stopped crying out to the God of Israel, and had ended all these words, (2) she rose from where she lay prostrate. She called her maid and went down into the house where she lived on sabbaths and on her festal days. (3) She removed the sackcloth she had been wearing, took off her widow's garments, bathed her body with water, and anointed herself with precious ointment. She combed her hair, put on a tiara, and dressed herself in the festive attire that she used to wear while her husband Manasseh was living. (4) She put sandals on her feet, and put on her anklets, bracelets, rings, earrings, and all her other jewelry. Thus she made herself very beautiful, to entice the eyes of all the men who might see her. (5) She gave her maid a skin of wine and a flask of oil, and filled a bag with roasted grain, dried fig cakes, and fine bread; then she wrapped up all her dishes and gave them to her to carry.
>
> (6) Then they went out to the town gate of Bethulia and found Uzziah standing there with the elders of the town, Chabris and Charmis. (7) When they saw her transformed in appearance and dressed differently, they were very greatly astounded at her beauty and said to her, (8) "May the God of our ancestors grant you favor and fulfill your plans, so that the people of Israel may glory and Jerusalem may be exalted." She bowed down to God.

(9) Then she said to them, "Order the gate of the town to be opened for me so that I may go out and accomplish the things you have just said to me." So they ordered the young men to open the gate for her, as she requested. (10) When they had done this, Judith went out, accompanied by her maid. The men of the town watched her until she had gone down the mountain and passed through the valley, where they lost sight of her.

(11) As the women were going straight on through the valley, an Assyrian patrol met her (12) and took her into custody. They asked her, "To what people do you belong, and where are you coming from, and where are you going?" She replied, "I am a daughter of the Hebrews, but I am fleeing from them, for they are about to be handed over to you to be devoured. (13) I am on my way to see Holofernes the commander of your army, to give him a true report; I will show him a way by which he can go and capture all the hill country without losing one of his men, captured or slain."

(14) When the men heard her words, and observed her face—she was in their eyes marvelously beautiful—they said to her, (15) "You have saved your life by hurrying down to see our lord. Go at once to his tent; some of us will escort you and hand you over to him. (16) When you stand before him, have no fear in your heart, but tell him what you have just said, and he will treat you well."

(17) They chose from their number a hundred men to accompany her and her maid, and they brought them to the tent of Holofernes. (18) There was great excitement in the whole camp, for her arrival was reported from tent to tent. They came and gathered around her as she stood outside the tent of Holofernes, waiting until they told him about her. (19) They marveled at her beauty and admired the Israelites, judging them by her. They said to one another, "Who can despise these people, who have women like this among them? It is not wise to leave one of their men alive, for if we let them go they will be able to beguile the whole world!"

(20) Then the guards of Holofernes and all his servants came out and led her into the tent. (21) Holofernes was resting on his bed under a canopy that was woven with purple and gold, emeralds and other precious stones. (22) When they told him of her, he came to the front of the tent, with silver lamps carried before him. (23) When Judith came into the presence of Holofernes and his servants, they all marveled at the beauty of her face. She prostrated herself and did obeisance to him, but his slaves raised her up.

Verse 4 speaks of her dressing up to "entice the eyes of all the men who might see her." Note how in Genesis, it was often very dangerous for a woman "to be seen" by a foreign ruler; he would immediately want her sexually.[43] That same thought is expressed in Judith 10:19. The women of the Israelites were so beautiful that they all said "It is not wise to leave one of the men alive!" Beauty threatened the safety of both women and men.

Notice Judith's comfort with her own beauty at this point in the narrative. She knew how to use her looks, and "played it to the max." She, like Jael in Judges, used her beauty to entice the foreign male enemy. Possibly because she was widowed, she had a freedom to act in this way.[44] Such action may not have been possible or "safe" for a virgin. To underscore that thought, one may recall the ways in which the rabbis and *Tg. Neof.* accused Dinah of going out with the intention of wanting to be seen.[45] Her actions, and she, as a character, are sometimes negatively interpreted. It has often been concluded that Dinah overstepped boundaries, acting with an agency that she "should not have" acted or that did not belong to her. Judith certainly is portrayed as having that agency and knowing how to use it. Surprisingly, she is painted as channeling that agency from the Divine and using to benefit her God and her people. That agency begins with two simple acts—praying and going out.

Here it is said that Judith, as had Dinah before her, "went out." Judith does so both in 10:6 and 10:10.[46] In both instances, Judith was accompanied by her companion and maid. Such detail is not given about Dinah in Genesis. Perhaps that is one of the reasons why some ancient and modern commentators lay some of the blame on her. Many have been quick to assert that Dinah's "going out" was a transgression of proscribed boundaries. Perhaps it is because the narrator of Genesis offered so little detail about Dinah's intention with "seeing the women of the land" that the reader does not know what Dinah thought, felt, etc. Notice how fully developed a character Judith is in contrast to Dinah. She speaks to the magistrates of her town, to Holofernes, and to the Divine. The direct discourse which the narrator provides for her helps the reader understand her actions.[47] For example, the reader may see the link between what she said in 11:6 and 11:16 to Holofernes and what she had told the magistrates in 9:33. The way in which the narrator developed Judith obviously helps the reader interpret her actions. Incidentally, both the magistrates and Holofernes deem her to be wise (9:29 and 11:23). The theme of Judith's wisdom and its repercussions runs throughout chs. 8–16.

> **Judith 11:** (1) Then Holofernes said to her, "Take courage, woman, and do not be afraid in your heart, for I have never hurt anyone who chose to serve Nebuchadnezzar, king of all the earth. (2) Even now, if your people who live in the hill country had not slighted me, I would never have lifted my spear against them. They have brought this on themselves. (3) But now tell me why you have fled from them and have come over to us. In any event, you have come to safety. Take courage! You will live tonight and ever after. (4) No one will hurt you. Rather, all will treat you well, as they do the servants of my lord King Nebuchadnezzar."
>
> (5) Judith answered him, "Accept the words of your slave, and let your servant speak in your presence. I will say nothing false to my lord this night. (6) If you follow out the words of your servant, God will accomplish something through you, and my lord will not fail to achieve his purposes. (7) By the life of Nebuchadnezzar, king of the whole earth, and by the power of him who has sent you to direct every living being!

Not only do human beings serve him because of you, but also the animals of the field and the cattle and the birds of the air will live, because of your power, under Nebuchadnezzar and all his house. (8) For we have heard of your wisdom and skill, and it is reported throughout the whole world that you alone are the best in the whole kingdom, the most informed and the most astounding in military strategy.

(9) "Now as for Achior's speech in your council, we have heard his words, for the people of Bethulia spared him and he told them all he had said to you. (10) Therefore, lord and master, do not disregard what he said, but keep it in your mind, for it is true. Indeed our nation cannot be punished, nor can the sword prevail against them, unless they sin against their God.

(11) "But now, in order that my lord may not be defeated and his purpose frustrated, death will fall upon them, for a sin has overtaken them by which they are about to provoke their God to anger when they do what is wrong. (12) Since their food supply is exhausted and their water has almost given out, they have planned to kill their livestock and have determined to use all that God by his laws has forbidden them to eat. (13) They have decided to consume the first fruits of the grain and the tithes of the wine and oil, which they had consecrated and set aside for the priests who minister in the presence of our God in Jerusalem—things it is not lawful for any of the people even to touch with their hands. (14) Since even the people in Jerusalem have been doing this, they have sent messengers there in order to bring back permission from the council of the elders. (15) When the response reaches them and they act upon it, on that very day they will be handed over to you to be destroyed.

(16) "So when I, your slave, learned all this, I fled from them. God has sent me to accomplish with you things that will astonish the whole world wherever people shall hear about them. (17) Your servant is indeed God-fearing and serves the God of heaven night and day. So, my lord, I will remain with you; but every night your servant will go out into the valley and pray to God. He will tell me when they have committed their sins. (18) Then I will come and tell you, so that you may go out with your whole army, and not one of them will be able to withstand you. (19) Then I will lead you through Judea, until you come to Jerusalem; there I will set your throne. You will drive them like sheep that have no shepherd, and no dog will so much as growl at you. For this was told me to give me foreknowledge; it was announced to me, and I was sent to tell you."

(20) Her words pleased Holofernes and all his servants. They marveled at her wisdom and said, (21) "No other woman from one end of the earth to the other looks so beautiful or speaks so wisely!" (22) Then Holofernes said to her, "God has done well to send you ahead of the people, to strengthen our hands and bring destruction on those who have despised my lord. (23) You are not only beautiful in appearance, but wise in speech. If you do as you have said, your God shall be my God, and you shall live in the palace of King Nebuchadnezzar and be renowned throughout the whole world."

Judith 12: (1) Then he commanded them to bring her in where his silver dinnerware was kept, and ordered them to set a table for her with some of his own delicacies, and with some of his own wine to drink. (2) But Judith said, "I cannot partake of them, or it will be an offense; but I will have enough with the things I brought with me." (3) Holofernes said to her, "If your supply runs out, where can we get you more of the same? For none of your people are here with us." (4) Judith replied, "As surely as you live, my lord, your servant will not use up the supplies I have with me before the Lord carries out by my hand what he has determined."

(5) Then the servants of Holofernes brought her into the tent, and she slept until midnight. Toward the morning watch she got up (6) and sent this message to Holofernes: "Let my lord now give orders to allow your servant to go out and pray." (7) So Holofernes commanded his guards not to hinder her. She remained in the camp three days. She went out each night to the valley of Bethulia, and bathed at the spring in the camp. (8) After bathing, she prayed the Lord God of Israel to direct her way for the triumph of his people. (9) Then she returned purified and stayed in the tent until she ate her food toward evening.

(10) On the fourth day Holofernes held a banquet for his personal attendants only, and did not invite any of his officers. (11) He said to Bagoas, the eunuch who had charge of his personal affairs, "Go and persuade the Hebrew woman who is in your care to join us and to eat and drink with us. (12) For it would be a disgrace if we let such a woman go without having intercourse with her. If we do not seduce her, she will laugh at us."

(13) So Bagoas left the presence of Holofernes, and approached her and said, "Let this pretty girl not hesitate to come to my lord to be honored in his presence, and to enjoy drinking wine with us, and to become today like one of the Assyrian women who serve in the palace of Nebuchadnezzar." (14) Judith replied, "Who am I to refuse my lord? Whatever pleases him I will do at once, and it will be a joy to me until the day of my death." (15) So she proceeded to dress herself in all her woman's finery. Her maid went ahead and spread for her on the ground before Holofernes the lambskins she had received from Bagoas for her daily use in reclining.

(16) Then Judith came in and lay down. Holofernes' heart was ravished with her and his passion was aroused, for he had been waiting for an opportunity to seduce her from the day he first saw her. (17) So Holofernes said to her, "Have a drink and be merry with us!" (18) Judith said, "I will gladly drink, my lord, because today is the greatest day in my whole life." (19) Then she took what her maid had prepared and ate and drank before him. (20) Holofernes was greatly pleased with her, and drank a great quantity of wine, much more than he had ever drunk in any one day since he was born.

Judith 13: (1) When evening came, his slaves quickly withdrew. Bagoas closed the tent from outside and shut out the attendants from his master's presence. They went to bed, for they all were weary because the banquet had lasted so long. (2) But Judith was left alone in the tent, with Holofernes stretched out on his bed, for he was dead drunk.

(3) Now Judith had told her maid to stand outside the bedchamber and to wait for her to come out, as she did on the other days; for she said she would be going out for her prayers. She had said the same thing to Bagoas. (4) So everyone went out, and no

one, either small or great, was left in the bedchamber. Then Judith, standing beside his bed, said in her heart, "O Lord God of all might, look in this hour on the work of my hands for the exaltation of Jerusalem. (5) Now indeed is the time to help your heritage and to carry out my design to destroy the enemies who have risen up against us."

(6) She went up to the bedpost near Holofernes' head, and took down his sword that hung there. (7) She came close to his bed, took hold of the hair of his head, and said, "Give me strength today, O Lord God of Israel!" (8) Then she struck his neck twice with all her might, and cut off his head. (9) Next she rolled his body off the bed and pulled down the canopy from the posts. Soon afterward she went out and gave Holofernes' head to her maid, (10) who placed it in her food bag.

Then the two of them went out together, as they were accustomed to do for prayer. They passed through the camp, circled around the valley, and went up the mountain to Bethulia, and came to its gates. (11) From a distance Judith called out to the sentries at the gates, "Open, open the gate! God, our God, is with us, still showing his power in Israel and his strength against our enemies, as he has done today!"

(12) When the people of her town heard her voice, they hurried down to the town gate and summoned the elders of the town. (13) They all ran together, both small and great, for it seemed unbelievable that she had returned. They opened the gate and welcomed them. Then they lit a fire to give light, and gathered around them. (14) Then she said to them with a loud voice, "Praise God, O praise him! Praise God, who has not withdrawn his mercy from the house of Israel, but has destroyed our enemies by my hand this very night!"

(15) Then she pulled the head out of the bag and showed it to them, and said, "See here, the head of Holofernes, the commander of the Assyrian army, and here is the canopy beneath which he lay in his drunken stupor. The Lord has struck him down by the hand of a woman. (16) As the Lord lives, who has protected me in the way I went, I swear that it was my face that seduced him to his destruction, and that he committed no sin with me, to defile and shame me."

(17) All the people were greatly astonished. They bowed down and worshiped God, and said with one accord, "Blessed are you our God, who have this day humiliated the enemies of your people."

(18) Then Uzziah said to her, "O daughter, you are blessed by the Most High God above all other women on earth; and blessed be the Lord God, who created the heavens and the earth, who has guided you to cut off the head of the leader of our enemies. (19) Your praise will never depart from the hearts of those who remember the power of God. (20) May God grant this to be a perpetual honor to you, and may he reward you with blessings, because you risked your own life when our nation was brought low, and you averted our ruin, walking in the straight path before our God." And all the people said, "Amen. Amen."

In the early verses of this passage, Judith attempts to stave off possible contamination from without through spiritual rituals. Judith was very adamant about her piety; she bathed, kept kosher, and prayed.⁴⁸ Judith 12:1–9 is full of elements describing Judith's purity. She had also purified herself before and after coming in social contact with Holofernes. After ritually bathing in 12:19, she returned to camp purified or clean (καὶ εἰσπορευομένη καθαρὰ). In 16:18, the entire people of Bethulia went to Jerusalem, purified themselves (προσεκύνησαν τῷ θεῷ καὶ ἡνίκα ἐκαθαρίσθη ὁ λαός), and worshipped God. This allowed them to offer the appropriate offerings, etc. One can note the recurrent thread, whether in verbal or adjectival form, of the people purifying themselves and thus doing what the Lord had commanded them to do. This too was an element in the aftermath of the incident at Shechem. When God entered the narrative as an active character in Gen 35:1, the Divine ordered Jacob and his clan to purify themselves, putting away the strange G/gods in their midst (τοὺς θεοὺς τοὺς ἀλλοτρίους τοὺς μεθ᾽ ὑμῶν). They did so and then made a journey, as had also been the case in Judith 16. In Genesis, after putting away the strange gods/paraphernalia, they moved from Shechem to Bethel. There were various methods to achieve purification from the "strange." The word "strange" (ἀλλογενῶν) was used, for example, in Jdt 9:2 to refer to how strangers had defiled Dinah. Judith helped purge or purify Israel of the impinging contamination/defilement that loomed on the horizon due to the threat of Nebuchadnezzar/Holofernes.

The use of important religious rituals links Judith and Genesis 34. As just stated, Judith often used prayer and keeping kosher as elements in her tricking Holofernes. The sons of Jacob used circumcision as part of their ruse against the Shechemites. What can be essential ritual displays of obedience to the Divine become ploys and guises leading to murder to these central offending characters. In both instances, these "offending characters" were outsiders; that is, they were not Hebrew/Israelite/Jewish men. Men wanted Judith.

The irony found within the book of Judith is so profound that even Holofernes' eunuch is portrayed as one who speaks as if he sexually wants Judith; his use of the plural is intriguing in Jdt 12:12, "For it would be a disgrace if we let such a woman go without having intercourse with her. If we do not seduce her, she will laugh at us." The reader soon discovers in 12:16 that Holofernes is the one who "had been waiting for an opportunity to seduce her from the day he first saw her." The act of the leader is made plural. Such democratization of the leader's sexuality has been common in these post-HB writings.

In Judith 12:13, Holofernes refers to Judith as a maiden or girl (παιδίσκη). This may be seen as hearkening back to the parallel way in which Shechem had requested his father to "get the girl" (Dinah) for him as a way. Both Gen 34:4 and Jdt 12:13 refer to the women, Dinah and Judith, in this way.⁴⁹ It may be a ploy to have either the women or themselves seem more innocent than they were.

There was indeed a significant amount of trickery in the book of Judith and in Genesis 34. In Jdt 11:20 Judith's words and beauty pleased Holofernes; he and his men were easily distracted by her. This, in some ways parallels Gen 34:18. As Hamor and Shechem negotiated with the sons of Jacob and heard their propositions, v. 18 told the reader that their (the sons of Jacob) words were good or pleasing in the eyes of Hamor and Shechem. The Greek phrasing of the two sentences is verbatim: καὶ ἤρεσαν οἱ λόγοι. This similarity may indeed be another link between the two. The person familiar with the two stories may indeed see that both sets of "outside men" are easily duped by the Hebrew/Jewish strategists at whose hands they quickly came to their demise.

A point of difference between the texts of Judith and Genesis is that Judith clearly portrays the Divine as her backing. In 13:15–16, she says to the people of her town, "The Lord has struck him down by the hand of a woman. As the Lord lives, who has protected me in the way I went, I swear that it was my face that seduced him to his destruction, and that he committed no sin with me, to defile and shame me." Judith 13:11–17 is one place where Judith was portrayed as an agent of the Divine. There are numerous references to God in the above section and God is used in ways that parallel Judith's opening prayer. Consistently, praise is given to the Divine for what has been done to those who would challenge Israel's honor. That is true in the book of Judith in both the incidents involving Holofernes and Shechem. Indeed, Judith has become like her ancestor Simeon: God has worked through yet another generation. As Moore had pointed out, multiple times in this narrative, "While all Israel, including Judith, gave the primary credit to God, they all simultaneously recognized Judith as the means."[50] Moore went on to cite 13:15, 13:20, and 16:5 as passages illustrating the above. One may recall Judith's prayer to see that she had done the same thing regarding crediting both Simeon and the Divine for the massacre at Shechem.

Judith uses "defile and shame" to speak of the intercourse that did not happen. Considering that hypothetical congress, one may see clearly that she had been deceitfully seducing him at the same time that Holofernes was indeed seducing her with the intent of having intercourse with her (12:12). Moore noted the way in which Judith was intent on sharing with her fellow Bethulians, that "her 'honor' was still intact."[51] Having intercourse with a "stranger," that is, a non-Israelite, would have defiled her (13:16). However, Holofernes did not defile Judith. This is obviously a point of contrast between Judith and Dinah.

Many have seen in the character of Judith a reversal of Dinah; Nickelsburg is one such scholar.[52] In Jdt 9:2 it is said that Shechem's being with Dinah had "had polluted her womb to disgrace her." Two significant points of contrast: Judith was the woman who had not sexually defiled/dishonored by a "stranger." According to Judith 13:16, Judith clearly stated that Holofernes had neither defiled nor shamed her, crediting her protection to God. Moreover, Bagoas cried out, "One Hebrew woman has brought disgrace on the house of Nebuchadnezzar" (14:18). Judith had brought disgrace on "others" without being disgraced herself. Moore noted that "Judith found herself in a position analogous to Dinah's, i.e. she herself might end up being raped by the uncircumcised Holofernes."[53] According to the words put on Judith's lips in 13:16, "As the Lord lives, who has protected me in the way I went, I swear that it was my face that seduced him to his destruction, and that he committed no sin with me, to defile and shame me."[54] Much of the rhetoric, once again, falls into the semantic domain of honor/shame.

The same is true of Genesis 34. The two men involved, Holofernes and Shechem, were both "outsiders;" a significant portion of the rhetoric in both narratives relates to the fact that Holofernes and Shechem were Gentile men. One aspect of this identity was that neither man was circumcised. Although that is presented and used very differently in the two narratives, it is a common link between Dinah and Judith, or Genesis 34 and Judith. For example, Collins noted, "its significance [that Simeon's deed had been fully approved by God] provides another case of a woman abused "by strangers."[55] Many commentators have noted that a crucial theme throughout Judith is personal and political Jewish: Gentile relations.[56] That is also the case with Genesis 34.

There is a cross-gender identification which takes place in Judith. She is clearly the reverse of Dinah. D. N. Freedman has rightly commented that "Judith is going to emulate Simeon, not Dinah … She was much more concerned about killing Holofernes. In other words, she identifies with the avenger, Simeon, rather than with the victim, Dinah."[57] She returned home a heroine. In Genesis, nothing is said about the way in which Dinah was received back into her family/clan after her time in Shechem's camp.

Moore, following others, said of the narrator of the book of Judith, "… the storyteller obviously subscribed, without any reservation, to two very popular but highly debatable aphorisms, namely, "All's fair in love and war" and "The end justifies the means."[58] The same can be said of Judith's ancestor, Simeon, whose God Judith besought for courage and strength!

There are a number of commonalities between Judith and her alleged ancestor, Simeon. Both exhibit a sense of heroism. Both act in ways that might be considered morally questionable. Like Judith, who could be considered a "bold-faced liar" and "ruthless … clever assassin,"[59] so too could Simeon, Levi, and the sons of Jacob.

This scenario becomes tragically comical in the book of Judith through the narrator's use of irony. Almost every commentator has remarked on how powerfully the narrator employed this device, irony.[60] A few of the most striking examples are that while the pious Judith dressed up most seductively with the intent of killing Holofernes, she was careful to remain kosher. In fact, after slaying

Holofernes, she carried his severed head, wrapped in his deathbed-canopy, back to her camp in that same food bag!

When the narrator spoke/wrote of her getting ready to meet Holofernes, it is said that she went out, dressed in all her finery (12:15), looking as great as she did when her husband Manasseh was alive and when together, they would celebrate the most joyous occasions (10:3–4). In speaking about this, many commentators use Moore's phrase: Judith went out to meet Holofernes "dressed to kill."[61] Readers know of her intent; Holofernes most certainly did not.

In many ways, readers know much more than the characters; this is also true in Genesis 34. In both cases, because of the information given by the narrator, particularly through the various speeches of the characters, the reader is privy to a lot of "inside information." For example, in Genesis 34, when the negotiations for Dinah's marriage were in process, the sons of Jacob spoke with deceit. Both stories belie a comfort with guise and deceit as a way of gaining the upper hand. DeSilva has written a very thoughtful section on the cultural implications of how deceit was an acceptable way to deal with challenges to honor. He warns against commentators taking too ethical a stance in criticizing these characters of ancient narratives or applying puritanical standards to their behavior.[62]

Another parallel that might be seen between the characters in Judith and those in Genesis 34 may be revealed through a comment that Harrington made. He wrote, "Judith, of course, is the main character. She is a pious widow whom God uses to save Israel through her piety, beauty, and cleverness (which includes flattery and lies, as well as the beheading of Holofernes ... Uzziah is the timid and ineffectual leader in Bethulia."[63] One may conclude that the way in which Uzziah's character was developed—his inefficacy and his being in the background—allowed Judith to come to the foreground. The same can be said of Jacob's timidity and ineffectiveness, which allowed Levi and Simeon to come to the foreground. As I wrote in *Sexual Violation in the Hebrew Bible,* Jacob, the father, responded with silence and passivity; his sons with violence and vengeance.[64]

There are a number of parallels between Genesis 34 and Judith. Not many scholars have noted these commonalities. While Harrington alluded to Genesis 34, he alleged that "the most obvious biblical source is the story of Jael."[65] Scholars have, for the most part, overlooked the literary parallels between Genesis 34 and Judith. deSilva is one who mentioned the ways in which the book of Judith uses Genesis 34. He wrote:

> Judith specifically invokes the episode of Simeon's and Levi's vengeance upon Shechem in Genesis 34 in her prayer (Jdt. 9:2–4) as models for active, and even violent, expressions of faith—a pattern that she intends to reenact. Bissell (1899: 163) criticizes the author for reversing Jacob's own judgment that Simeon and Levi's act of anger is to be "cursed" rather than emulated (Gen. 49:6–7); cf. 4 Macc. 2:18–20).

Judith is not alone in her exoneration of Simeon and Levi. *Testament of Levi* also overturns Jacob's verdict, in no less a court than God's own. God personally orders Levi to take vengeance on Shechem: while it costs Levi his father's blessing, God awards Levi with the honor of a perpetual priesthood for his zeal to keep Israel pure (*Testament of Levi* 5–8). Together, these texts evidence of reading of Genesis 34 in which it is Jacob, not Levi and Simeon, who is out of touch with God's values.[66]

Post-HB texts have put various spins on the incident of Genesis 34. deSilva summarizes these well, noting how the various writers/texts affiliated with either Simeon, Levi, or Jacob. This book is obviously a study in the characterization of Dinah throughout these texts.

While there is indeed a plethora of similarities between Genesis 34 and the book of Judith, significant differences remain. Judith's theocentric grounding distinguishes it from Genesis 34. I have frequently reviewed the many times when the narrator or Judith herself pointed to God's past, present, and future involvement. God's role in this story may predispose a reader to embrace Judith's story as it allegedly is an outworking of Divine will. Per the story, the Divine smiles upon her as she went out from Bethulia to meet Holofernes. She again beseeches the Divine, ironically with sword in hand, and the Divine is portrayed as even further empowering her as she lopped off Holofernes' head. It has been made clear that other narratives (*Jubilees* and the *Testament of Levi*) portray the Divine acting similarly with Simeon and/or Levi at Shechem. The narrator of Genesis 34 did not mention God. The reader is left to wonder about God as a character in that incident; one may become judgmental of the Divine's silence, as it does mimic Jacob's silence and passivity. One may also use the narrative in a rather pithy didactic/homilectic manner and conclude, "This is the kind of chaos that occurs when God is absent." Returning to the narrative at hand, Judith, God's involvement in this story has indeed troubled many commentators.

Judith, who was first introduced as "a God-fearing woman," acts in ways that many question. Her deceptive killing of Holofernes is the primary example. Simultaneously, she is referred to as wise. In fact, numerous times throughout the narrative, Judith is referred to as "wise" or described as acting with wisdom. This is the case in Jdt 11:20–21, 11:8, 23, and 28–31. The LXX Gen 34:13 described the sons of Jacob as speaking with "wisdom" instead of the MT "deceit." It could be the case that wisdom and deceit were flip sides of the same coin.

Coming back to the positive ways in which Judith is depicted, many scholars have noted that the book of Judith uses Deuteronomic ideas throughout.[67] This is true of Judith's dietary rectitude, her reliance on prayer and fasting, and the centrality of the covenant. She was first both described and portrayed as a very pious woman—prostrated, with ashes on her head, covered with sackcloth. She was bowed down, following the proscribed regulations of mourning. She was first introduced as a widow,[68] a woman in mourning, not only for her husband, who had died some three and a half years ago, but also as a pious woman lamenting her town's willingness to consider conceding to Holofernes and Nebuchadnezzar. At one point, Holofernes rhetorically asked Achior, "Who are you, Achior ... to prophesy among us as you have done today and tell us not to make war against the people of Israel because their god will defend them? What god is there except Nebuchadnezzar? He will send his forces and destroy them from the face of the earth. Their god will not save them ..." (6:2–3). In the context of Holofernes' discourse with Achior, note how Judith's prayer illustrates the polar opposite point, the "zinger" coming especially in Jdt 9:14, above. She is to show that there is only one God—the God whose people are Israel. That is entirely Deuteronomic, reminding modern readers of Deut 6:4's *Sh'ma*, "Hear, O Israel, The Lord is our God, the Lord alone."

The Deuteronomic trend is also evident in what the book omitted. For example, Parry noted, "There is no mention of the circumcision of the Hivites, nor of their desire to legitimise [sic.] the relationship of Shechem and Dinah, nor of Jacob's condemnation of the deed."[69] Each of these points could be informed by Deuteronomic legalities; the book of Judith, as is the case with some pseuedepigraphal or targumic references, might be considered an attempt to "clean up" the characters found in Genesis 34.

Also Deuteronomic in tone is the way in which Judith was portrayed as being reliant upon God to accomplish what she was sure was God could do. She is pictured as having sublime trust in the Divine (along with a great ability to wield a sword)!

She is indeed portrayed as prophetess/sage. There were a number of instances in the *targumim*, particularly in *Tgs. Neof.* and *Ps.–J.*, that Simeon and Levi played the role of sages, offering their own interpretation of what happened to Dinah and how they wanted her remembered. This is one of the few times when a woman plays that role. The character of Judith served to interpret the event at Shechem, de-emphasizing Shechem's role and highlighting that of God and Simeon. "There is no mention of Shechem the individual—rather, Simeon is said to avenge 'those strangers' who 'put her [Dinah] to shame.' The action of an individual is applied to his/her community. We see such applications all over the Hebrew Bible—e.g., Dinah's defilement is seen as a defilement of the House of Jacob."[70] The horrific nature of the defilement of Dinah justified the violence and vengeance.

Conclusions Regarding Judith

The way that Judith's character is portrayed in this deuterocanonical book makes it clear that her deceit helped accomplish God's intentions. Judith's prayer set the stage for the reader to expect that God was about to act in and through her.

God miraculously empowered her to "destroy the enemies who have risen up against us" (13:5). Through her, God "humiliated the enemies of your [God's] people" (13:17).

The previous thread found throughout Judith is reminiscent of *Jubilees* 30:18, "And Levi and his sons will be blessed forever because he was zealous to do righteousness and judgment and vengeance against all who rose up against Israel." It is possible to detect a theme claiming that God had intervened on behalf of Simeon and Levi because Shechem and Holofernes were perceived as enemies who had risen up against Israel. The book of Judith used the incident involving Dinah as one piece of evidence of how God came to the defense of God's people, arming Simeon.

Furthermore, as the narrative of the book of Judith progresses, the character of Judith becomes the opposite of Dinah. Judith was a woman who was able to "go out," crossing typical boundaries, into enemy and "other" camps. She dressed up with the intent of making it look like she was seducing Holofernes, but obviously used that "intimate moment" to strike him dead. Fortunately, for her, nothing sexual happened. She was not raped; nor was she "defiled." This contrasts her with Dinah. In our next and last deuterocanonical book, the reader will meet another female character; this one, the mother of seven, without naming Dinah, actually presents herself as Dinah's antithesis.

4 MACCABEES

By way of introductory remarks about 4 Maccabees, the book is included in several texts of the LXX.[71] It was also found among a number of manuscripts containing the works of Josephus; this had led some people to conclude (erroneously) that Josephus had authored the text.[72] The text has no internal clues to the actual identity of the author. However, a general consensus has been reached regarding what was important to the author of the text and the proficiency of the writer's Greek.

The author was a Greek-speaking Jew. One of the writer's aims was to show that following the Torah was exemplary of wisdom and philosophical prudence. The actual text of 4 Maccabees is well written, in terms of the Greek. H. Anderson, for example, describes the Greek as "free and idiomatic, indicating that he thinks in that language; it is his native tongue."[73] While it is philosophical in nature, its focus is to exhort people to follow the Torah.[74] In fact, the book aimed to marry Stoic/Platonic Hellenistic philosophy with Torah obedience.[75] Following the Torah was, in the writer's opinion, one of the ways of living a life filled with wisdom and prudence. The heroic characters of the story, Eleazar, the seven brothers, and the mother of seven, all exemplify this virtue.

Because of the references throughout the book, some have concluded that it comes from the time period in which the Jerusalem temple was still standing, i.e., prior to 70 C.E.[76] Most would date the book to somewhere between 63 B.C.E. and 70 C.E.,[77] specifically in the middle of the first century CE.[78] Furthermore, many conclude that its provenance was not Palestinian.[79] In narrowing down the options, the following suggestions have been offered: Alexandria, Egypt and Antioch, Syria.[80]

In terms of its style or genre, 4 Maccabees may be classified as a "philosophical tract,"[81] following the author's own introduction of his work as "a philosophical exposition" (1:1).[82] Yehoshua Amir said of the book,

> It is of special interest as the only surviving major piece of Greek rhetoric in Jewish literature. IV Maccabees is a philosophical sermon on the theme "pious reason masters passion."[83]

The entire first chapter of 4 Maccabees is a philosophical introduction to the inquiry as to whether "reason is sovereign over the emotions." The writer turns to Genesis 34 to illustrate the main theme. Some passages from 4 Maccabees name characters found in Genesis 34; others are much more indirect. The references to be considered are: 4 Maccabees 2:18–20, 17:1, and 18:7–8.[84] I have included the entire ch. 2, to give the reader a better idea of the background and context of the quote:

> **4 Maccabees 2: (1)** And why is it amazing that the desires of the mind for the enjoyment of beauty are rendered powerless? (2) It is for this reason, certainly, that the temperate Joseph is praised, because by mental effort he overcame sexual desire. (3) For when he was young and in his prime for intercourse, by his reason he nullified the frenzy of the passions. (4) Not only is reason proved to rule over the frenzied urge of sexual desire, but also over every desire. (5) Thus the law says, "You shall not covet your neighbor's wife or anything that is your neighbor's." (6) In fact, since the law has told us not to covet, I could prove to you all the more that reason is able to control desires.
>
> Just so it is with the emotions that hinder one from justice. (7) Otherwise how could it be that someone who is habitually a solitary gormandizer, a glutton, or even a drunkard can learn a better way, unless reason is clearly lord of the emotions? (8) Thus, as soon as one adopts a way of life in accordance with the law, even though a lover of money, one is forced to act contrary to natural ways and to lend without interest to the needy and to cancel the debt when the seventh year arrives. (9) If one is greedy, one is ruled by the law through reason so that one neither gleans the harvest nor gathers the last grapes from the vineyard.
>
> In all other matters we can recognize that reason rules the emotions. (10) For the law prevails even over affection for parents, so that virtue is not abandoned for their sakes. (11) It is superior to love for one's wife, so that one rebukes her when she breaks the law. (12) It takes precedence over love for children, so that one punishes them for misdeeds.

(13) It is sovereign over the relationship of friends, so that one rebukes friends when they act wickedly. (14) Do not consider it paradoxical when reason, through the law, can prevail even over enmity. The fruit trees of the enemy are not cut down, but one preserves the property of enemies from marauders and helps raise up what has fallen.

(15) It is evident that reason rules even the more violent emotions: lust for power, vainglory, boasting, arrogance, and malice. (16) For the temperate mind repels all these malicious emotions, just as it repels anger—for it is sovereign over even this. (17) When Moses was angry with Dathan and Abiram, he did nothing against them in anger, but controlled his anger by reason. (18) For, as I have said, the temperate mind is able to get the better of the emotions, to correct some, and to render others powerless. (19) Why else did Jacob, our most wise father, censure the households of Simeon and Levi for their irrational slaughter of the entire tribe of the Shechemites, saying, "Cursed be their anger"? (20) For if reason could not control anger, he would not have spoken thus. (21) Now when God fashioned human beings, he planted in them emotions and inclinations, (22) but at the same time he enthroned the mind among the senses as a sacred governor over them all. (23) To the mind he gave the law; and one who lives subject to this will rule a kingdom that is temperate, just, good, and courageous.

(24) How is it then, one might say, that if reason is master of the emotions, it does not control forgetfulness and ignorance?

Joseph is upheld as pious or virtuous for his ability to "nullify the frenzy of passions," particularly sexual desires. This portrayal of Joseph parallels that found in *Jos. Asen.* In both instances, Joseph is lauded for his ability to control his passions.

As the text considered other males of the ancestral era, it is clear that the books of Judith and 4 Maccabees used the "Dinah incident" in polar opposite manners.[85] Judith upholds Simeon as a hero and paragon of strength to whose God she appealed for like courage, while 4 Maccabees used the households of Simeon and Levi to illustrate non-temperance, an instance in which anger (emotion) overcome reason. Thus, they were unlike Joseph. First, note that in the text it is the "households" of Simeon and Levi, not necessarily two individual men. 4 Maccabees may be cited as evidencing a tradition that this was a tribal attack on Shechem. According to this text, the affront, the slaughter of the entire tribe of the Shechemites, was termed "irrational." 4 Maccabees unequivocally sides with Jacob, particularly because he rebuked or censured Simeon and Levi. The patriarch is here called "our most wise father" (4 Macc 2:19).[86] The text goes on to allege that Jacob would not have spoken in such a way if reason had not been able to exert control over anger (2:20). It would appear that the writer of 4 Maccabees had knowledge of Genesis 49, in which the tribes of Simeon and Levi are cursed for their anger; while Jacob certainly reprimands his two sons in Genesis 34:30, his rebuke of them and their descendents is stronger and of further consequence in Genesis 49. 4 Maccabees parallels Genesis 49 in its language, tone, and its affinity for Jacob. There have been very few texts in which Jacob's character is as lauded as it here. For example, one may recall that midrashic texts wavered in their depiction of Jacob, both within a particular text, i.e., individually, and as a whole. There were times when they accused him of having committed an offense against the Divine[87] and there were times when he was espoused as a man of great discernment, particularly for holding his peace until his sons returned from the fields.[88]

One of the main points of 4 Maccabees is that reason is sovereign over emotions.[89] Its writer/editor reinterprets HB stories to amass evidence of that point in a number of the above passages. It is said that "reason is clearly lord of the emotions" (2:7) and "reason rules the emotions" (2:9). Verse 2:16 reiterates that "the temperate mind repels all these malicious emotions, just as it repels anger—for it is sovereign over even this." Another verse (2:18) claims that "the temperate mind is able to get the better of the emotions …" Furthermore it is alleged that the Divine "enthroned the mind among the senses as a sacred governor over them all" (2:22). Lastly, 2:24 claimed that "reason is master of the emotions …" A point of the above passage is that Simeon and Levi can be considered exemplary of what happens when reason is not allowed to control the emotions—emotions can run amuck and an entire village can be annihilated.

One can note how differently 4 Maccabees spins this tale. A number of texts have upheld the zealous piety of Simeon and/or Levi. Judith, Theod., *T. Levi*, *Jubilees*, and *Jos. Asen.*, all fall into that category, expressing the opposite point of view of 4 Maccabees.[90]

Another possible indirect reference to Dinah may be found in 4 Macc 18:7–8. While the above passage glorifies Jacob, the next passage hails the mother of the seven sons. Neither the mother nor Dinah is explicitly named.[91] It is intriguing that 4 Maccabees concludes with a woman's testament to her children. She began this section upholding her own chastity and piety, saying in 18:7–8, "I was a pure virgin and did not go outside my father's house; but I guarded the rib from which woman was made. (8) No seducer corrupted me on a desert plain, nor did the destroyer, the deceitful serpent, defile the purity of my virginity."

One may, of course, wonder how a mother of seven could have considered herself virginal! For this to be at all plausible or credible, it would have to be a reference back to time before she met her husband, the father of her seven sons. One can then see that the mother of seven was proposing that she, unlike Dinah, was chaste and did not leave her father's house. Numerous post-HB texts and contemporary scholars have made inferences about Dinah's "going out."[92] Dinah was violated (Gen 34:2), and she had been defiled (Gen 34:5, 13, and 27). The above directly speaks of how the mother of seven had been neither defiled nor had she been corrupted. This contrasts her with Dinah. The mother of the seven was also very proud of herself, that she had maintained boundaries, such as not leaving her father's house. This pride could be connected to rabbinic sources which gave such advice to the women of their time.[93]

There are also rabbinic references to Shechem as a "snake" or "serpent." This way of referring to a particular type of person as a snake/serpent may have been fairly common during this time period. In some passages, deceit is a mark of such a person. This woman's rhetoric about the snake/serpent could be connected also the passages in Judith where Holofernes' attempts to seduce Judith were spoken as instances of "deceiving" her. Here the mother of seven is proud to say, as was Judith, that no one had been able to take advantage of her; that apparently was true sexually, as well.

One may also see another inference to Dinah, depending on the way in which one interprets the account of the mother's suicide. 4 Maccabees 17:1 recounts, "Some of the guards declared that when she also was about to be seized and put to death she threw herself into the flames so that no one would touch her body." Some commentators conclude that one of her ultimate concerns was that she not be sexually violated by one of the Gentile guards. deSilva's work illustrates my point; he wrote: "She dies by her own hand before her body can be violated by a Gentile's touch (15:29–17:6)."[94] This can be used as further support of her own parting words in 4 Maccabees 18:7. Writing along parallel lines as deSilva, Harrington stated, "Rather than be taken by the king's soldiers and run the risk of sexual abuse, the mother throws herself into the flames ..."[95] It remains clear that the mother of seven, like Judith and unlike Dinah, had never been defiled. Her experience is juxtaposed to Dinah's.

Conclusion to 4 Maccabees

The mother of seven fairly boldly contrasts her lot in life with that of Dinah. She asserts that she had acted properly, presumably as a young woman, "guarding the rib," i.e., not trespassing sexually. As an adult, after witnessing the torture and deaths of seven of her sons, she committed suicide rather than allow herself to be touched by a Gentile. In both respects, her situation was opposite Dinah's.

CONCLUSIONS

The books of Judith and 4 Maccabees both contain characters, Judith and the mother of seven, who stand for the opposite of Dinah. The mother of seven alleged in 18:7 that she was a pure virgin who did not go outside her father's house; she committed suicide rather than be touched by a Gentile man. One can see in that rhetoric a barb against Dinah. By contrast, in the book of Judith, Dinah is presented more as a victim/survivor of a heinous offense than as one who had transgressed.

CHAPTER SIX

Dinah IN Philo AND Josephus

The works of Philo and Josephus are important for students considering first-century B.C.E. and first-century C.E. Judaisms and nascent Christianities. Again, the plural "Judaisms" and "Christianities" underscores the fact that there were many strands of Jewish and Christian thought within first centuries B.C.E. and C.E; neither tradition was monolithic.[1] One reason why Philo's work is important is that it allows readers to see how one person of that era construed his thoughts, intermingling Greco-Roman philosophy with various tenets of Judaism. The writings of Philo and Josephus are some of the few extant manuscripts of this time.

In writing this chapter, I will depart from what had been the norm in most of previous chapters of this book. Obviously, Josephus' and Philo's work are different from the *midrashim* and from Pseudepigraphal and Deuterocanonical books in that not only are the actual identity of the authors known, but there is also additional information about their lives and the times in which they lived. There are several references within these texts that pertain to Dinah. As has been the previous practice, first will come a consideration of the references and second will be explored how the character of Dinah is developed and portrayed.

PHILO

Introduction to Philo

Philo is believed to have lived from ca. 20 B.C.E. to 50 C.E.[2] He was from a leading family in Alexandria, Egypt; that is obvious from his knowledge of Greek culture, including philosophy and rhetoric, the arts, and his reported lifestyle.[3] There are references in his writings and other historical references to his brother, Alexander, a prominent politician, with ties to both Herodian and Roman leadership; Philo himself also served a religio-political function in the state. For example, he was apparently part of an elected delegation sent by the Jews of Alexandria to Rome, specifically to Gaius Caligula, in ca. 40 C.E. to address the Jewish status quo in Alexandria.[4] The Jewish people in Alexandria had been facing increasing prejudice, resulting in a horrible reduction of their rights. Caligula had had his own image/statue erected in Alexandrian synagogues.[5] Philo was elected to appeal to Caligula, that this practice be discontinued and that Jews be allowed to worship and to live without threat. Not only in his political advocacy, but also in his writings, Philo sought to encourage and to further Torah knowledge and obedience. Like his contemporaries and predecessors, he sought to marry Greco-Roman philosophy with Jewish life and ideals.

Philo was steeped in the Hellenistic culture of his time. His knowledge not only with the Greek language, but also with Greek "literature, science, and philosophy ... was vast ..."[6] All his writings were originally in Greek. Scholars often conclude that he used the LXX; Philo may not have had knowledge of Aramaic or Hebrew.[7]

Oftentimes when Philo commented on or expounded upon biblical texts, he did so using allegory. He is well known for his allegorical interpretation and use of the Jewish Scriptures.[8] For example, in *On the Migration of Abraham (Migration)*, various biblical characters represent virtues, vices, or abstractions.[9] When the narratives of the ancestors and their families involved journeys, Philo tended to use this same rhetoric to speak of the "journeys"—spiritual, psychological, or emotional experiences—of every person.[10] He wrote, for example, of the "mind, going forth out of the places ... to have traveled through the land."[11] He encouraged his readers, "Do then, O my soul, travel through the land, and through man ... "[12] Similarly, the places the ancestors visited, such as Shechem ("Sichem" in Philo), are interpreted allegorically, and applied to what the enlightened person must encounter and learn on the journey called "life."

Robin Parry wrote regarding Philo's *Migration of Abraham*,

> Philo reads God's call to Abram in [Gen] 12:1-4 as the call to a person to leave their body (land), sense (kinsfolk) and speech (father's house) and head toward higher realities. The promise is that God will cause a "multitude of qualities" (great nation) to reach full maturity in that person. God will also give mastery of language (make your name great) as well as their inner person.[13]

The person was to embark on this call, with a sense of integrity and adventure. In many respects, Dinah was "every person." Her going forth to the unknown parts of Shechem (the city) represented the call of every man and every woman.

References to Dinah may be found in the following of Philo's works: *On the Migration of Abraham (Migration)*, *On the Change of Names (Names)*, and *Allegorical Interpretation* 3.[14] These three pieces are usually referred to as expansions of the biblical texts of Moses.[15] Some scholars, such as Peder Borgen, group them (along with others) together as "Allegorical Interpretations of Genesis."[16] The first reference to Dinah is found in Philo's *Migration:*

> XXXIX. (216) The mind, therefore, going forth out of the places which are in Charran, is said "to have travelled through the land until it came to the place of Sichem, to a lofty Oak." And let us now consider what this travelling through the land means. The disposition which is fond of learning is inquisitive and exceedingly curious by nature, going everywhere without fear or hesitation and prying into every place, and not choosing to leave anything in existence, whether person or thing, not thoroughly investigated; for it is by nature extraordinarily greedy of everything that can be seen or heard, so as not only not to be satisfied with the things of its own country, but even to desire foreign things which are established at a great distance. (217) At all events, they say that it is an absurd thing for merchants and dealers to cross the seas for the sake of gain, and to travel all round the habitable world, not allowing any considerations of summer, or winter, or violent gales, or contrary winds, or old age, or bodily sickness, or the society of friends, or the unspeakable pleasures arising from wife, or children, or one's other relations, or love of one's country, or the enjoyment of political connections, or the safe fruition of one's money and other possessions, or, in fact, anything whatever, whether great or small, to be any hindrance to them; (218) and yet for men, for the sake of that most beautiful and desirable of all possessions, the only one which is peculiar to the human race, namely, wisdom, to be unwilling to cross over every sea and to penetrate every recess of the earth, inquiring whenever they can find anything beautiful either to see or to hear, and tracing out such things with all imaginable zeal and earnestness, until they arrive at the enjoyment of the things which are thus sought for and desired. (219) Do thou then, O my soul, travel through the land, and through man, bringing if you think fit, each individual man to a judgment of things which concern him; as, for instance, what the body is, and under what influences, whether active or passive, it co-operates with the mind; what the external sense is, and in what manner that assists the dominant mind; what speech is, and of what it becomes the interpreter so as to contribute to virtue; what are pleasure and desire; what are pain and fear; and what art is capable of supplying a remedy for these things; by the aid of which a man when infected with these feelings may easily escape, or else perhaps may never be infected at all: what folly is, what intemperance, what commiting injustice, what the whole multitude of other discases, which it is the nature of all destructive vice to engender; and also what are the means by which they can be averted. And also, on the contrary, what justice is, what prudence is, and temperance, and manly courage, and deliberate wisdom, and in short what each virtue is, and what the mastery over the passions is, and in what way each of these virtues is usually produced. (220) Travel also through the greatest and most perfect being, namely this world, and consider all its parts, how they are separated in respect of place and united in respect of power; and also what is this invisible chain of harmony and unity, which connects all those parts; and if while considering these matters, thou canst not easily comprehend what thou seekest to know, persevere and be not wearied; for these matters are not attainable without a struggle, but they are only found out with difficulty and by means of great labour; (221) on which account the man fond of learning is taken up to

the field of Sichem; and the name Sichem, being interpreted means, "a shoulder," and intimates labour, since it is on the shoulders that men are accustomed to bear burdens. As Moses also mentions in another passage, when speaking of a certain athlete he proceeds in this manner, "He put his shoulder to the labour and became a husbandman." (222) So that never, O my mind, do thou become effeminate and yield; but even if any thing does appear difficult to be discovered by contemplation, still opening the seeing faculties that are in thyself, look inwards and investigate existing things more accurately, and never close the eyes whether intentionally or unintentionally; for sleep is a blind thing as wakefulness is a sharp-sighted thing. And it is well to be content if by assiduity in investigation it is granted to thee to arrive at a correct conception of the objects of thy search. (223) Do you not see that the scripture says that a lofty oak was planted in Sichem? meaning under this figurative expression to represent the labour of instruction which never gives in, and never bends through weariness, but is solid, firm, and invincible, which the man who wishes to be perfect must of necessity exert, in order that the tribunal of the soul, by name Dinah, for the interpretation of the name Dinah is "judgment" may not be seized by the exertions of that man who, being a plotter against prudence, is labouring in an opposite direction. (224) For he who bears the same name as this place, namely Sichem, the son of Hamor, that is, of irrational nature; for the name Hamor means "an ass;" giving himself up to folly and being bred up with shamelessness and audacity, infamous man that he was, attempted to pollute and to defile the judicial faculties of the mind; if the pupils and friends of wisdom, Sichem and Levi, had not speedily come up, having made the defences of their house safe, and destroyed those who were still involved in the labour devoted to pleasure and to the indulgence of the passions and uncircumcised. For though there was a sacred scripture that, "There should be no harlot among the daughters of the seer, Israel," these men, having ravished a virgin soul, hoped to escape notice; (225) for there is never a scarcity of avengers against those who violate treaties; but even though some persons fancy there may be, they will only fancy it, and will in the reality of the fact be proved to entertain a false opinion. For justice hates the wicked, and is implacable, and a relentless avenger of all unrighteous actions, overthrowing the ranks of those who defile virtue, and when they are overthrown, then again the soul, which before appeared to be defiled, changes and returns to its virgin state. I say, which appeared to be defiled, because, in fact, it never was defiled; for of involuntary accidents that which affects the patient is not in reality his suffering, just as what is done by a person who does wrong unintentionally, the wrong is not really his action.[17]

In the above passage, Dinah is presented positively. The quote begins by lauding the one who goes forth without concern or hesitation, beckoned by curiosity and learning. Philo's readers/hearers are encouraged to seek wisdom at all costs and risks. "Dinah" was representative of every person. In 39.221 Philo wrote, "… the man fond of learning is taken up to the field of Sichem …"[18] According to 39.216, even foreign elements might be explored for the sake of knowledge and wisdom.[19] Philo's writing may reflect his own openness to Hellenism. He was more open to Greek ideas and practices, compared to the writer of 4 Maccabees.

Philo wavers in his presentation of Sichem (Shechem). In 39.221, "Sichem," interpreted allegorically as hard work/labor, is presented as something one must be willing to encounter or, at least, endure. In this passage (221), Sichem is understood as a place, not a person. In 39.223, Philo encouraged people to persevere, writing, "in order that the tribunal of the soul, by name Dinah, for the interpretation of the name Dinah is 'judgment' may not be seized by the exertions of that man who, being a plotter against prudence, is labouring in an opposite direction. Here Sichem, although not named by Philo, is called a "plotter against prudence," one "labouring in an opposite direction." Thus "he" is against that for which humanity should strive. In short, Dinah and Shechem stand for opposites.[20]

In the next verse, 224, Philo presents Sichem negatively—he represents irrational nature, "an ass" inclined to "giving himself up to folly and being bred up with shamelessness and audacity, infamous man that he was, attempted to pollute and to defile the judicial faculties of the mind." He also wrote in that same verse, that they had "hoped to escape notice." Not only did Shechem (and his townsmen) err, they hoped to get away with their offense against Dinah, Israel, and the Divine.

Whereas Shechem et al. are the antagonists of Philo's narrative, Simeon and Levi are some of the protagonists of the story. Philo upholds the attributes and the actions of the two. In 39.224, "Sichem and Levi" are presented as friends of wisdom."[21] I assert that "Sichem" should read "Simeon." Judging from the way in which Philo wrote about them, it would make sense to conclude that it is a reference to Simeon and Levi. For example, "they speedily came up ... and destroyed those who ..." This verse is reminiscent of the way in which Genesis 34 speaks of Simeon and Levi, when it is said,

> (25) And it happened on the third day of their being in pain that two of the sons of Jacob, Simeon and Levi, brothers of Dinah, each took his sword and came upon the city unbeknown. And they killed every male. (26) They killed Hamor and Shechem, his son, with the mouth of the sword.[22]

Philo wrote positively of the two maternal brothers of Dinah; in 39.225, he said, "... there is never a scarcity of avengers against those who violate treaties ... For justice hates the wicked, and is implacable, and a relentless avenger of all unrighteous actions, overthrowing the ranks of those who defile virtue ..."[23] This tendency to support the actions of Simeon and Levi may derive from Philo's own identity; Mangey, who had written the original Preface to *The Works of Philo*, asserted that Philo was "a descendant of the sacerdotal tribe of Levi."[24] This affiliation may have predisposed his interpretation, leading him to favor the two, as opposed to Jacob. Other texts, such as Judith and the *Testament of Levi*, similarly portrayed the two brothers positively.

Philo put forward to the modern reader not only a new allegorical reading of the incident from Genesis 34, but one can also detect a severance or dichotomy between the body and the mind/soul. Such an understanding has not yet been witnessed in other texts examined. For example, in 39.224, he wrote how "these men ... ravished a 'virgin soul.'" First of all, note the plural (these men); this democratizing of guilt has been attested previously. Second, notice that the soul received Philo's focus. In 39.225 the soul, AKA "Dinah," which "appeared to be defiled" returned to a virginal state. Such a return to virginity was possible, Philo alleged, because the offense was not Dinah's. He called the incident, at least from her perspective, an "involuntary accident." He left room for interpreters to hold her liable to some degree by writing, "what is done by a person who does wrong unintentionally, the wrong is not really his action."[25]

It is problematic that Philo did not deal with the ramifications of sexual violation against the body. His writing "denies that she suffers at all!"[26] Such a sharp split between the body and mind may be troubling for today's reader; one realizes that the virginity of a rape victim is not restored or returned. The allegorizing and spiritualizing of this incident is problematic. It is, however, refreshing that Philo did not hold Dinah accountable for what had happened to her.

In his view, her innocence was maintained. She therefore reaped benefits or rewards of her journey, she was acquitted. She met with folly (AKA Shechem), remained steadfast, and, through the efforts of her maternal brothers, prevailed. Dinah was lauded for her quest for wisdom and her sense of right judgment, i.e., innocence.[27]

Although there is little/no reference to the Divine throughout the above passage, one may conclude that in accordance with the way in which Philo wrote of the Dinah incident, the Divine sided with Simeon and Levi and Dinah. Regarding the two brothers, one may wonder if "friends of wisdom" would infer that the two were also friends of Divine.[28] One of the main themes of Philo's work is that a person is to seek wisdom at all risk/cost.

That seeking may bring one into contact with folly. Throughout *Migration*, Sichem/Shechem was held responsible and liable for the wrong. He is certainly the antagonist of the narrative. This is supported by the characterization of Shechem. For example, in 39.224, there is a list of vices which are illustrative of the kind of man Shechem was: "of irrational nature," "the son of Hamor ... the name Hamor means "an ass; giving himself up to folly and being bred up with shamelessness and audacity; infamous man that he was, attempted to pollute and to defile the judicial faculties of the mind ... these men, having ravished a virgin soul, hoped to escape notice."[29] Furthermore, the next verse continues the allegations against Shechem et al., describing the men as "those who violate treaties," depicting them as "wicked," having perpetrated "unrighteous actions," and lastly, they had "defile[d] virtue."[30]

Like the HB narrative,[31] the onus falls squarely on the shoulders of Shechem and the men of the city which bore his infamous name. To use Parry's language, "The man Shechem symbolises [sic.] the opposite kind of work from the noble work which the oak represents."[32]

One physical aspect of that group was their state of being uncircumcised. When Philo referred to Shechem he allegorized this condition too. He wrote disparagingly of the "uncircumcised" in 39.224 that they were, "involved in the labour devoted to pleasure and to the indulgence of the passions and uncircumcised."[33] Elsewhere in his writings, Philo wrote that circumcision was "a symbol of the excision of the pleasures which delude the mind; for since of all the delights which pleasure can afford, the association of man with woman is the most exquisite, it seemed good to the lawgivers to mutilate the organ which ministers such connections ..."[34] Their attempt to defile the virgin soul of Dinah illustrated their corrupt state of mind and soul. Their attempt to get away with this offense (39.224) was even further illustration of their corruption. Philo alleged, using language of sexual violation, if not rape, "the tribunal of the soul, by name Dinah, for the interpretation of the name Dinah is 'judgment' may not be seized by the exertions of that man, who being a plotter against prudence, is labouring in an opposite direction."[35] Dinah and Shechem were diametrically opposed. In the end, the wronged person was righted. Dinah herself, who survived an attempted defilement, returned to her virginal state; she became as she was when she first went forth to investigate, out of a curiosity to learn—a seeking virgin soul.

Philo employed allegorical notions of "virgin daughter" and "virginity" in other sections of his writings. For example, in *Migration* 7.31, he wrote: "How then should any good thing be wanting when the all-accomplishing God is at all times present with his graces, which are his virgin daughters, which he, the Father, who begot them, always cherishes as virgins, free from all impure contact and pollution?"[36] Graces, or virtues, are likened to God's virgin daughters.

The second reference to Dinah, which continues along a number of the lines discussed above, and it comes from another of Philo's writings, *On the Change of Names*.

> XXXV. (186) Abraham therefore believed in God; but he believed as a man; that you may be aware of the peculiar attribute of mortals, and may learn that his fall did not happen to him in any other way than in consequence of the ordinances of nature. And if it was of short duration and only momentary, it is a thing to be thankful for: for many other men have been so overturned by the violence and impetuosity of error, and by its irresistible force, that they have been utterly destroyed for ever. (187) For know, my good man, that, according to the most holy Moses, virtue is not perfect in the human body, but it suffers something like torpor, and is often ever so little lame. For says the scripture, "The broader part of his thigh became torpid, on

which he was Lame." (188) And perhaps some man of an over-confident disposition may come forward and say that this is not the language of one who disbelieves, but of one praying, so that if that most excellent of all the happy feelings were about to be produced, it would not be brought forth according to any other number than that of ninety years, that so the perfect good might arrive at its production according to perfect numbers. (189) But the aforesaid numbers are perfect, and especially according to the sacred scriptures. And let us consider each of them: now first of all there is the son of the just Noah and the ancestor of the seeing race, and he is said to have been a hundred years old when he begat Arphaxad, and the meaning of the name of Arphaxad is, "he disturbed sorrow." At all events it is a good thing that the offspring of the soul should confuse, and disorder, and destroy that miserable thing iniquity, so full of evils. (190) But Abraham also planted a field, using the ratio of an hundred for the measurement of the ground: and Isaac found some barley yielding a hundred fold. And Moses also made the vestibule of the sacred tabernacle in a hundred arches, measuring out the distance towards the east and towards the west. (191) Moreover the ratio of a hundred is the first fruit of the first fruit which the Levites assign to those who are consecrated to the priesthood; for after they have taken the tenth from the nation they are enjoined to give unto the priests a sacred tenth of the whole share, as if from their own possessions. (192) And if a person were to consider, he might find many other instances to the praise of the aforesaid number brought forward in the law of Moses, but for the present what have been enumerated are sufficient. But if from the hundred you set aside the tenth part as a sacred first fruit to God who produces, and increases, and brings to perfection the fruit of the soul—for how can it be anything but perfect, inasmuch as it is on the confines between the first and the tenth, in the same manner in which the Holy of Holies is separated by the veil in the middle. [...] by which those things which are of the same genus are divided according to the differences in species?

XXXVI. (193) Therefore the good man was speaking and saying things which were really good in his mind. But the bad man at times interprets good things in a very excellent manner, but nevertheless does shameful things in a most shameful one, as Shechem does who is the offspring of folly. For he is the son of Hamon his father, and the name Hamon, being translated, means "an ass," but the Shechem means "a shoulder" when interpreted, the symbol of labour. But that labour of which folly is the parent is miserable and full of suffering, as, on the other hand, that labour is useful to which prudence is related. (194) Accordingly the holy scriptures tell us that, "Shechem spake according to the mind of the virgin, having first humbled Her." It is not said then, with great purpose and accuracy, that he spake according to the mind of the damsel, for the purpose of showing distinctly that he acted in a contrary manner to that in which he spoke? For Dinah means "incorruptible judgment:" justice the attribute seated by God, the everlasting virgin; for the name Dinah, being interpreted, means either thing, "judgment" or "justice." (195) Fools, then, laying violent hands upon and attempting to defile her, by means of their daily designs and practices, by their plausibility of speech escape conviction. Therefore they must either act in a manner consistent with the language that they hold, or else they must hold their tongues while committing iniquity. For it is said, "Silence is one half of evil:" as Moses says when rebuking the man who accounted the creature worthy of the principal honour, and the immortal God worthy only of the second place, "Thou has sinned, be silent." (196) For to use bombastic language, and to boast of one's evil deeds, is a double sin: and men in general are very prone to this; for they are constantly saying what is pleasing to the ever-virgin virtue, and such things as are just: but they never omit any opportunity of insulting and violating her when they are able. For what city is there which is not full of those who are continually celebrating the praises of virtue?—(197) men who weary the ears of those who hear them by everlastingly dwelling on such subjects as these; wisdom is a necessary good; folly is pernicious; temperance is desirable; intemperance is hateful; courage is a thing proper to be cultivated; cowardice must be avoided; justice is advantageous; injustice is disadvantageous; holiness is honourable; unholiness is shameful; piety towards the gods is praiseworthy; impiety is blameable; that which is most akin to the nature of man is to design, and to act, and to speak virtuously; that which is most alien from his nature is to do the contrary of all these things. (198) By continually stringing together these and similar aphorisms they deceive the courts of justice, and the council chambers, and the theatres, and every assembly and company which they meet; as men who put beautiful masks on ugly faces, with the intention of not being discovered by those who see them. (199) But it is of no use; for some persons will come endowed with great vigour, and occupied with a real zeal and admiration for virtue, and who will strip them of all their coverings, and disguises, and appendages which they had woven round themselves by the evil artifice of plausible speeches, and will display their soul naked by itself as it really is, and will make themselves acquainted with the secret things of their nature which are hidden as it were in recesses. And then having brought to light all its shame and all the reproaches to which it is liable, they will display them in broad daylight to every one, and show what sort of thing it is, how disgraceful and ridiculous, and what a spurious kind of beauty it has disguised itself with by means of its appendages and coverings. (200) And those who are prepared to avenge themselves on such profane and impure dispositions are Simeon and Levi, two indeed in number, but only one in mind; on which account, in his blessings of his sons, their father numbers them together under one classification, on account of the harmonious character of their unanimity and of their violence in one and the same direction. But Moses does not make any mention of them afterwards as a pair, but classes the whole tribe of Simeon under that of Levi, combining together two essences, of which he made one impressed as it were with one idea and appearance, hearing to doing.[37]

Note that in this passage, particularly in *Names* 36.193, Shechem is used as the prototype[38] of the "bad man," the antagonist, who did shameful things. This is consistent with how Shechem had been portrayed in *Migration*. Philo's writings held Shechem fully liable for the offense against Dinah. Throughout this section, Philo negatively wrote about the man Shechem. Once again, he is presented as the "offspring of folly."[39] In *Migration* 39.224, Philo had also mentioned that Shechem/Sichem had given "himself up to folly and being bred up with shamelessness audacity." The reference to folly (heinous offense) coalesces with Gen 34:7 and the biblical narrator's point of view that Shechem had committed a heinous offense by lying with Dinah.[40] Furthermore, Philo pointed out that "Hamor/Hamon" means "ass."[41] "The labour of which folly is the parent is miserable and full of suffering." Shechem is again referred to in a very negative light.

When Philo wrote of Shechem's verbally addressing Dinah (Gen 34:3), that too is used as evidence that his intentions and his actions were incongruous with one another; his speech and actions were askew.[42] Furthermore, upon on reading *Names* 36.195–96, modern readers may conclude that Shechem attempted to "smooth talk" Dinah. Philo wrote for the second time that Shechem hoped to "escape conviction" by their "plausibility of speech." He had written that Shechem "hoped to escape notice in *On the Migration of Abraham* 39.224. Returning to *Names* 36.194, Philo went on to write that Shechem had acted/spoken in ways which represented something opposed to the Divine. Men, he claimed in 36.196 were inclined to this double-nature, "saying what is pleasing to the ever-virgin virtue and never omit[ting] any opportunity of insulting and violating her when they are able." On the other end of the spectrum, Dinah (AKA judgment or justice) and God were allies.

Simeon and Levi were also construed positively (v. 200); they could be considered protagonists.[43] They were said to have been willing to avenge the wrong done to Dinah. They were of the same mind with one another; because of this, their father, Jacob, treated them as one.[44] However, Moses, the archetypal hero/protagonist throughout Philo's works, saw things differently than Jacob.[45] The Levites were lauded in the earlier sections of the above passage, as those who assign and share proper offerings with the priests. Bringing Moses into the argument, Philo garners even more support for Simeon and Levi. The Levites were said to have acted in accordance with the Law of Moses (35.190–92). They served as representatives of the law; i.e., what people should do. Shechem was one anti-model: he acted and spoke with duplicity. Simeon and Levi were heroes: their thoughts and actions were in alignment.

The astute reader of Genesis 34 might disagree. Simeon and Levi there are portrayed equally duplicitously. In the biblical account, the reader is clearly told that "they spoke with deceit because he had defiled their sister." Their speech led the Hivites to expect one thing. Their actions proved otherwise. Such a portrayal of Simeon and Levi is missing from Philo.

The next and final reference is an indirect reference to the Dinah event; it tells more about the passing of the city of Shechem from Jacob's to Joseph's hands. The narrative involving Jacob's burying the foreign gods and accoutrements under the tree at Shechem may be found in Genesis 35. The tradition about how Joseph received Shechem may be found in Gen 48:22.[46] The following is from yet another writing of Philo, *Allegorical Interpretation* 3.8:

VIII. (23) But Moses speaks thus, "And they gave to Jacob the foreign gods which were in their hands, and the earrings which were in their ears; and Jacob hid them under the turpentine tree which was in Shechem." These are the gods of the wicked, but Jacob is not said to have taken them, but to have concealed and destroyed them, for every case being most accurately described, for the virtuous man will take nothing from wickedness for his own advantage, but will conceal all such things and destroy them secretly. (24) Just as Abraham tells the king of Sodom, when he was proposing to give him things of irrational nature in exchange for rational animals, namely, horses in exchange for men, "that he would take nothing that belonged to him, but that he would stretch out "the action of his soul," which, speaking symbolically, he called "his hand," to the most high God; "for that he had not taken from a thread even to a shoe-latchet of all that was his (the king of Sodom's), in order that the king might never say that he had made the discerning man," namely Abraham, "rich," exchanging poverty for wealthy virtue. (25) The passions are always concealed and guarded in Shechem; and the name Shechem being interpreted means "the shoulder;" for he who labours concerning pleasures is inclined to preserve them. But the passions are concealed and destroyed by the wise man, and that too not for a brief space of time, but up to this present day, that is to say, for ever, for all time is measured by the present day, for the cycle of one day is the measure of all time. (26) On which account Jacob gives Joseph Shechem, as an especial portion beyond the rest of his brethren, meaning thereby the bodily things which are the objects of the outward senses, since he had gone through labour in respect of them; but to Judah the confessor he gave not presents but praise, and hymns and divine songs, in which he should be celebrated by his brethren. And Jacob did not receive Shechem as a gift from God, but he took it with his sword and with his bow, that is to say, by words, which had the power of cutting and repelling; for the wise man subjects all secondary things to himself, and when he has so subjected them he does not retain them, but makes a present of them to him who is by nature adapted to them. (27) Do you not see that also, when he appeared to take the gods, he did not take them but concealed them and put them out of the way, and destroyed them out of his sight for ever. Now to what soul could it have happened to conceal vice and to put it out of the way, except to that soul to which God was revealed, and which he considered worthy to receive the revelation of his unspeakable mysteries? For he says, "shall I hide from Abraham my son that thing which I am Doing?" Well done, O Saviour, in that thou showest thy works to the soul which desires good things, and has concealed from it no one of thy works: and by reason of this conduct of thine he is able to avoid evil, and to conceal it and keep it out of sight, and to destroy for ever the passions which are injurious.[47]

Jacob is here presented as someone who acted piously, not wanting to benefit from the wicked (Shechem). Jacob was represented as the "good man," who could put away that which was injurious to one's self (and one's family). On the proverbial journey of life, Shechem is the place where passions are to be concealed and guarded. This is in direct contrast to the uncircumcised man Shechem, whose passions ran amuck. Unlike the man Shechem, the righteous seeker of Wisdom is to be wary of such unrestrained passions. Jacob is illustrative of such a person; he is a protagonist.

Philo preserved the piety of Jacob. The way in which he described Jacob's actions asserted that Jacob and God had a special relationship; God had revealed "unspeakable mysteries" to him. One may also note the piety of Jacob, when, according to Philo he did not take Shechem with sword and bow, i.e., militantly, but via his words. Genesis 48:22 preserved the tradition of Jacob taking Shechem with his sword. A number of the other texts have included a militant assault upon the Amorites, with Jacob at the helm.

Conclusion to Philo

Philo used the Dinah incident to refer allegorically to every person's spiritual journey. Because he used the episode from Genesis 34 in this allegorical/hypothetical way, he began by presenting Dinah as the subject in the passive voice, "the man fond of learning is taken up to the field of Sichem" (*Migration* 39.221) and "the man who wishes to be perfect ... in order that the tribunal of the soul, by name Dinah ... may not be seized" (*Migration* 39.223). Dinah is the one on the journey—"the man fond of learning" and the "one who wishes to be perfect." As Philo continued this illustration, "Dinah" stood for the tribunal of the soul and judgment (*Migration* 39.223). This metaphorical woman/person met Sichem/Shechem, who "attempted to pollute and to defile the judicial faculties of the mind" (*Migration* 39.224).

Her brothers intervened, coming to Dinah's defense, so that scripture might be upheld: "There should be no harlot among the daughters of the seer, Israel." Dinah, Simeon, and Levi stood on one side of the metaphorical battle; Shechem and all his men were the opponents. This group of opposing men, having ravished a virgin soul, hoped to escape notice (*Migration* 39.224). The narrative may be paused at this juncture, the "virgin soul" Dinah had been "ravished" by the "plotter against prudence" (*Migration* 39.223) "of irrational nature" "giving himself up to folly and being bred up with shamelessness and audacity" (*Migration* 39.224).

Because Dinah had either committed no wrong or had unintentionally done so, her virginity was restored. *Migration* 39.225 spelled out that the soul had only appeared to be defiled and it changed and returned to its virgin state. In this particular section, Philo also spoke of Dinah as "the patient."

In his second primary reading or interpretation of the incident from Genesis 34, in *On the Change of Names,* Philo again presented Dinah as a virgin (*Names* 36.194). In this passage he developed the reference from Gen 34:3, which dealt with Shechem speaking to the heart of Dinah. Dinah is referred to both as a virgin and damsel. Philo used the verb "humbled her" to express the sentiment he had described in *Migration* 39.224 as "polluted and defiled."

In a manner that parallels his depiction of Dinah in *Migration* 39, Philo in *Names* 36:194 referred to Dinah as "incorruptible judgment," "justice, the attribute seated by God," "the Everlasting Virgin," and "judgment or justice."

He continued to speak about the offense against Dinah, that "fools, then laying violent hands upon and attempting to defile her ... by the plausibility of their speech escape conviction." He wrote of the plural attempt to defile Dinah. He also used this opportunity to develop the characterization of Shechem, who represented all whose speech and actions are incongruous. Throughout, Dinah is the "ever-virgin virtue." Such men miss no "opportunity of insulting and violating her when they are able" (*Names* 36.196). Modern readers would be inclined to conclude that this was either a successful (i.e., completed) or an attempted rape. The language of "violent hands" leads to that impression. Dinah was a victim/survivor of wrongs that were of not her fault. She had gone out from her father's house to find wisdom; folly found her, through no fault of her own. She was vindicated. People were encouraged to continue their journeys, regardless of what they meet en route. So concludes Philo's positive and laudatory presentation of Dinah.

JOSEPHUS

Introduction to Josephus

Josephus made a profound contribution to the ancient and modern understanding of his time. His writing is unparalleled as the source of historical information of and about the Greco-Roman period. Besides being a prolific writer, he has been referred to as; historian, seer/prophet, politician, soldier, priest, and apologist.[48]

Josephus was born Yosef ben Mattityahu "in Jerusalem in 37/38 C.E. into a priestly family that traced its lineage back to Jonathan, the first of the Hasmonean high priests."[49] His parents were influential and affluent,[50] as Josephus' education and knowledge indicative. Furthermore, as Josephus grew and became increasingly curious, he gained exposure to the teachings of the Pharisees, Saducees, Essenes; he also learned with and from a desert ascetic or hermit by the name of Bannus.[51]

Josephus, somewhat akin to Philo, was respected enough by his community that he served as a political advocate. On one occasion, he went to Rome, where he advocated successfully to Nero and Nero's wife/mistress Poppaea, for the release of Jewish priests whom Felix had charged and imprisoned. His connections and his finesse quickly acquainted him with actors, the emperor, and the empress at Rome.[52]

Virtually all scholars note the difficulty of deciphering with clarity Josephus' political allegiances.[53] Although certainly a "friend of Rome," by 66/67 C.E. Josephus was appointed a general, in command of an army in Galilee that was in revolt against Rome. According to some accounts (even his own writings conflict with one another), he surrendered to Rome, most specifically to Vespasian.[54] It seemed as though Rome was impressed with him and his abilities. At first he was kept under guard, in Caesarea; he later

> accompanied the Roman army to Jerusalem, where he served as an adviser and interpreter for Titus during the siege that resulted in the destruction of the temple and the city. Thus he was an eyewitness of and a participant in many of the events in the Jewish War. At the end of the war, Josephus accompanied Titus back to Rome. There Vespasian gave him an apartment in his former residence, honored him with the privilege of Roman citizenship, and granted him a pension and a large tract of land in Judea ... Thus honored and well looked after by the Romans, Josephus had the leisure to produce his substantial corpus of writings ... He died late in the last decade of the first century or early in the second century C.E.[55]

Josephus was highly invested in educating the non-Jewish world about Judaism and Jewish history. For him, this history went back as far as the biblical story, including creation. He sought to retell or recount the biblical narrative, at times referring to Dinah and the incident at Shechem. His first reference to her and this episode may be found in *Antiquities of the Jews (Ant.)*. David M. Rhoads concluded that this writing was completed later in Josephus' life, ca. 93–94 C.E.[56]

As has been the case with each of the texts studied thus far, this writing gives the contemporary reader an insight into how biblical thinking and hermeneutics was done at the time. It will be obvious that his general story line comes from the HB; however, like the midrashic tradition, Josephus felt comfortable expounding upon the actual text of the HB or LXX. He did indeed retell the story, adding significant portions and interpretations to the text. Nickelsburg wrote, "His *Jewish Antiquities* provides a window into first-century Jewish exegesis that interprets Scripture by recasting its narratives."[57] Some scholars are of the opinion that this text was written primarily for Greek-speaking Gentiles, to acquaint them with the history of the Jews.[58] The following is *Ant.* 1.21:

> Chapter 21: Concerning the Violation of Dina's Chastity
>
> 1. Hereupon Jacob came to the place till this day called Tents, (Succoth) from whence he went to Shechem, which is a city of the Canaanites. Now as the Shechemites were keeping a festival, Dina, who was the only daughter of Jacob, went into the city to see the finery of the women of that country. But when Shechem, the son of Hamor the king, saw her, he defiled her by violence; and, being greatly in love with

her, desired of his father that he would procure the damsel to him for a wife:—to which desire he condescended, and came to Jacob, desiring him to give leave that his son Shechem might, according to law, marry Dina. But Jacob, not knowing how to deny the desire of one of such great dignity, and yet not thinking it lawful to marry his daughter to a stranger, entreated him to give him leave to have a consultation about what he desired him to do. So the king went away, in hopes that Jacob would grant him this marriage. But Jacob informed his sons of the defilement of their sister, and of the address of Hamor, and desired them to give their advice what they should do. Upon this the greatest part said nothing, not knowing what advice to give. But Simeon and Levi, the brethren of the damsel, by the same mother, agreed between themselves the action following:—It being now the time of a festival, when the Shechemites were employed in ease and feasting, they fell upon the watch when they were asleep, and, coming into the city, slew all the males, as also the king and his son with them, but spared the women; and when they had done this without their father's consent, they brought away their sister.

2. Now while Jacob was astonished at the greatness of this act, and was severely blaming his sons for it, God stood by him, and bid him be of good courage; but to purify his tents, and to offer those sacrifices which he had vowed to offer when he went first into Mesopotamia, and saw his vision. As he was therefore purifying his followers, he lighted upon the gods of Laban, (for he did not before know they were stolen by Rachel, and he hid them in the earth, under an oak, in Shechem; and departing thence, he offered sacrifice at Bethel, the place where he saw his dream, when he went first into Mesopotamia.

3. And when he was gone thence, and was come over against Ephrata, he there buried Rachel, who died in child-bed: she was the only one of Jacob's kindred that had not the honour of burial at Hebron; and when he had mourned for her a great while, he called the son that was born of her Benjamin, because of the sorrow the mother had with him. These are all the children of Jacob, twelve males and one female;—of them eight were legitimate—viz., six of Lea, and two of Rachel; and four were of the handmaids, two of each; all whose names have been set down already.[59]

Here in Josephus, the "Dinah incident" is set at the time of a Shechemite festival. Josephus was not the only ancient writer familiar with this tradition; Theodotus and Ginzburg also mention the festival setting.[60] This has been addressed previously.[61] Some read this as Josephus' attempt to portray Simeon and Levi more positively. For example, referring to Rappaport's work, Bernard Heller wrote that Josephus' change—alleging that the Shechemites were celebrating and partying and not in pain because of their recent demanded circumcision—presented Simeon and Levi in a "favorable light."[62]

Dinah/Dina is clearly identified as the only daughter of Jacob. This has been one of the recurring themes explored in this book.[63] In Josephus' later naming Dinah as one who went down to Egypt with Jacob (*Ant.* 2.7.4), she is also presented as the only named daughter of Leah and Jacob.[64] Louis Feldman referred to the tradition in *Baba Batra* which alleged that Dinah was a twin.[65] That same tradition was seen in *Jub.* 28:23.[66] Josephus ended *Ant.* 1.21.3 by returning to this point: "These are all the children of Jacob, twelve males and one female." He seemed to exclude Dinah from the accounting of legitimate or illegitimate children of Jacob; that appeared to apply only to Jacob's sons.

A little more explanation is given here for Dinah's going out; according to Josephus, she went into the city to see the finery of the foreign women.[67] Thibodeau claims this is but a "small touch, suggesting frivolity and heedlessness, which is absent in both Genesis and Theodotus."[68] Josephus certainly makes it sound as though Dinah was curious about the women's dress, accessories, etc. One might link this comment with Theodotus' account, which spoke of Dinah as one who worked with wool, she might have been doing some business exploration, not something "heedless and frivolous." Nowhere does Josephus portray Dinah as the above (heedless or frivolous).[69] Neither does Josephus hold Dinah accountable for a wrong. In fact, his account makes it clear that this was an instance of rape; he alleged that Shechem "defiled her by violence." Josephus offered no value judgment of Dinah's actions.

Josephus makes it clear that Jacob was uncertain about what he should do. The patriarch's state of mind is much more fully developed here than it is in Genesis 34. Josephus wrote about the dilemma in which Jacob found himself. He did not think it was lawful or appropriate to allow Dinah to marry a stranger/foreigner; yet, he did not know how to refuse the king's demands.[70] No such information is given about Jacob in Genesis 34. This could reflect Josephus' own stance or his readers' sensitivities on intermarriage.[71] To furthermore illustrate this, please note that Josephus makes no mention of the prospect of full intermarriage between the Shechemites/Hivites and Jacob's clan that is so prevalent in Genesis 34.[72] In contrast to the HB, here in Josephus, Jacob is portrayed as being in control of the marriage negotiations involving his daughter, Dinah. In the HB, his sons take over immediately, giving the reader the impression that Jacob appeared to be comfortable allowing the inter-marriage negotiations to progress.

The details, as presented by Josephus, help the reader gain sympathy for Jacob; the reader of Genesis 34 may conclude that Jacob was indecisive or passive. Heller wrote of the "tendency in the Hellenistic scriptural exegetes ... to justify biblical characters."[73] Another example is here in Josephus, it is clearly said that Jacob "informed his sons of the defilement of their sister."[74] In Genesis 34, there are no specific details about how the sons heard this information; i.e., it is not clarified that Jacob was the one who told them of the offense.[75] Furthermore, in terms of Josephus' attempt to "clean up" Jacob, the above text makes it clear that Jacob had not given his consent to the act of Simeon and Levi. It portrays him as having reservations about giving Dinah to Shechem in marriage—i.e., it portrays him as being against intermarriage.[76] Josephus also later claimed that "God stood by" Jacob (*Ant.* 1.21.2).

Here Jacob is also said to have asked Hamor for time to think about the marriage proposal involving Dinah. The reader soon discovers that he consulted with his sons, specifically asking for their input and advice. Thus again, Jacob seems very rational and collegial. In the context of this "family meeting," most of Jacob's sons did not know what to do or say; however, Simeon and Levi, the two maternal brothers of Dinah agreed with one another. Josephus hesitated, ever so briefly, to tell the reader of their plan. Instead, Josephus claimed that they carried out their conspiracy with celerity, killing all the men of Shechem, including Shechem and Hamor. They saw the festival as an opportune time to commit this act of revenge; the Shechemites were involved in "ease and feasting," and had fallen asleep during one of the watches. Note that here in Josephus, the festival itself helped facilitate the plan of Simeon and Levi; nothing here is said that this happened on the third day of their being in pain (from circumcision)(Gen 34:25).[77] Like Theodotus, Josephus omitted the reference to the mass circumcision of the Shechemites.[78] It is simply not an element in the Josephan account.

Josephus also omitted the reference to the tradition that the sons of Jacob had taken captive the women and children. Here it is only said that they "spared the women" from slaughter. Josephus clarifies that Simeon and Levi had done this without the consent of Jacob. He also wrote that the two maternal brothers of Dinah "brought away their sister" out of the city of Shechem.

As Josephus continued, he, again, unlike the HB account of this story, included God as a character.[79] In *Ant.* 1.21.2, Josephus wrote, "God stood by him ... bid him be of good courage; but to purify his tents ..." God intervenes and supports Jacob.[80] As Jacob rid his camp of the foreign elements, the Josephan text clarifies that it was the gods Rachel had stolen which were purged from the assembly. Other accounts would lead the reader to believe that it was spoils of war taken from Shechem.[81]

The other reference to Dinah may be found in Josephus, *Ant.* 2.7.4. Here Josephus listed her among those "belonging to the sons of Jacob" who went down to Egypt with Jacob and Leah:

> 4. Jacob, encouraged by this dream, went on more cheerfully for Egypt with his sons, and all belonging to them. Now they were in all seventy ... Now Jacob had twelve sons ... So far is the posterity of Lea, with whom went her daughter Dinah. These are thirty-three.[82]

Thus the closing reference to Dinah is familiar. Many ancient texts mention Dinah as one of the people who accompanied Jacob to Egypt.

Conclusion to Josephus

Josephus' presentation of the episode from Genesis 34 is much closer to the MT than is Philo's account. There are, however, a few discrepancies. The first is that Josephus set the event at the time of a Shechemite festival. Also in variance with the HB, Josephus claimed that Dinah "went into the city to see the finery of the women of that country." In this opening introductory section, Dinah is referred to as "the only daughter of Jacob."

As Philo also had, Josephus claimed that violence was a factor in the sexual congress of Shechem and Dinah. Josephus wrote, "when Shechem … saw her, he defiled her by violence." Philo had written, "Fools, then, laying violent hands upon and attempting to defile her."

In accordance with the MT account, Josephus included Shechem's desire to marry Dinah. When he wrote about this, he referred to Dinah as a "damsel." Dinah is portrayed as Jacob's daughter; the patriarch is presented with a troubling situation. He apparently thought it inappropriate to give his daughter in marriage to a stranger (i.e., a foreigner), but he was not sure how to refuse Hamor or Shechem. The patriarch is here said to have asked Hamor for some time to consider what he would do. In that space of time, Josephus recorded that "Jacob informed his sons of the defilement of their sister" and asked them what they (including Jacob) should do.

As is the case in the HB account, Simeon and Levi quickly come to the forefront of the narrative. In both cases, the HB writer and Josephus reiterate that these two men were the maternal brothers of Dinah. Josephus used the noun "damsel" to refer to Dinah. With the air of an omniscient narrator, Josephus told the reader of these two brothers' strategy. The strategy is at the same time presented and completed. In partial accordance with the HB, Dinah was removed from the city of Shechem by her two brothers. In Gen 34:26, "they took Dinah from the house of Shechem, and they went out." Thus ends the episode involving Dinah. Neither the HB nor Josephus provides additional information about her fate back in Jacob's household.

In both cases, the reader is informed that Dinah went to Egypt with the rest of Jacob's clan. She is the only daughter of Jacob, named in some accounts alongside her twelve brothers, the sons of Jacob. Six of these twelve were born of Leah, Dinah's mother.

CONCLUSIONS

Whereas Philo wrote allegorically about the event related in Genesis 34, Josephus stayed closer to the HB account, with a number of divergences. Neither exegete blamed Dinah for what had transpired at and with Shechem. Philo and Josephus claimed that there was an element of violence in the sexual encounter between Shechem and Dinah, thus helping the modern reader to conclude that the intercourse involving Dinah and Shechem was not consensual. Dinah's name or reputation was cleared. Shechem was held liable for his actions.

Conclusion

The exploration conducted within this book has shown that the gaps of Genesis 34 were filled by ancient interpreters in a number of varying ways. This concluding material is organized chronologically, in terms of Dinah's life.

Two of the midrashic sources explored commented that Dinah's birth was surrounded by miracles. *Genesis Rabbah* 72.6 relays that Rachel began praying and exhorted the other matriarchs to do likewise. They proclaimed that they had had enough males (baby boys); Leah then gave birth to Dinah. *Tanhuma* 8.18 relates a similar tradition; however, in that passage it was Leah who had prayed. Accordingly, the gender of the fetus she was carrying was changed to female. Although Dinah had been conceived male, there had been a gender switch while she was *in utero*. *Tanhuma* 8.18 asserts that because of this alteration of gender, Dinah was more associated with Leah.

The midrashic passages make the most of the fact that Leah was Dinah's mother. Much of this is spun or portrayed very negatively. A number of passages contain the phrase, "Like mother, like daughter." In not one instance was this comparison for the good. All attempted to besmirch both Dinah and Leah, daughter and mother, by this analogy. The following two passages could be cited to substantiate that claim: *Gen. Rab.* 80.1 and *Tanh.* 8.14. Furthermore, *Tanhuma* 8.15 alleged that "the corruption had begun with her mother."

Dinah was also presented as the daughter of Jacob. In most passages, for example, *Gen. Rab.* 84.21, *Pirqe R. El.* 36 and 39, and Josephus' *Ant.* 1.21.1, 1.21.3, and 2.7.4, she is spoken of as Jacob's only daughter. Most frequently, it is furthermore presumed that her birth was a single birth, i.e., that she was the only child born at the time. Genesis 30:21 certainly gives the reader that impression. However, *Legends* V:319 n. 309 shows that there were conflicting ideas about whether or not Dinah had a twin. *Jubilees* 28:23 asserts that she had been born with Zebulun; however, it also speaks of Dinah as Jacob's only daughter (44:18).

Many texts have sought to explicate why Dinah went out that fateful day. The following clarifying phrases may be found within this literature: "Dinah went abroad to see the dancing and singing women, whom Shechem had hired to dance and play in the streets to entice her forth" (*Legends* I;395); she "wished to see the city" (Theodotus, Fragment 4); "went into the city to see the finery of the women of that country" (*Ant.* 1.21.1); she "went out to let herself be seen with the daughters of the people of the land" (*Tg. Neof.*); she "went out to look at the women of the land" (*Tg. Onq.*); she "went out to see the customs of the daughters of the people of the land" (*Tg. Ps.-J.*). A few passages, such as *Targum Neofiti* and *Tanhuma*, change the voice of the verb from the active "to see," and allege that Dinah went out "to be seen" (the passive voice).

Much was made about her intentions. Some pointed blaming fingers at Dinah's going out, of her wanting to see (and therefore get to know others or others' ways), and of her wanting to be seen. This was particularly true of the midrashic texts, which viewed her "going out" to be problematic.

Those wanting to clear Dinah of any potential or accused wrongdoing, made it clear that she was lured out of her tent(s) by Shechem. That is most precisely what *Pirqe R. El.* 38 alleged happened. That passage even further attempts clears her name by stating overtly, "the daughter of Jacob was abiding in tents, and she did not go into the street. And what did Shechem the son of Chamor do? He brought dancing girls who were (also) playing on piples in the streets. Dinah went forth to see those girls who were making merry; and he seized her …"

Legends I:395 is not as strong in clearly Dinah of transgression; while it holds Shechem responsible for "setting Dinah up," it allows a significant portion of the blame/responsibility to fall on Dinah. That passage reads, "While Jacob and his sons were sitting in the house of learning, occupied with the study of Torah, Dinah went abroad to see the dancing and singing women, whom Shechem had hired to dance and play in the streets to entice her forth. But she was a woman, and all women like to show themselves in the street."

Some texts allege that the setting of Dinah's misfortune was a festival. That is stated in Theodotus' Fragment 4 and in Josephus' *Ant.* 1.21.1 (twice). One might also interpret *Legends* 1:395 above to describe a festival.

Some passages provide a larger theological setting for why this affront happened. Three people are generally held responsible: Jacob, Leah, and Dinah. Strangely, Shechem is "let off the hook" in many of these texts. Jacob was frequently said to have erred; that is a recurrent theme in *Legends*, most often paired with a Divine curse upon Jacob. Jacob was said to have either broken a vow that he made with the Divine (*Lev. Rab.* 37.1 and *Tanh.* 8.20 and 8.22); expressed too much pride/hubris, which challenged the Divine (*Gen. Rab.* 73.9, 79.8, and 80.4); or he had concealed Dinah from Esau (*Gen. Rab.* 76.9 and *Tanh.* 8.19). In the latter case, he is said to have allegedly withheld her in marriage from Esau. Because of any one of these three infractions, he incurred the wrath of the Divine. It was the Divine who pronounced that because of this, "to- morrow thy daughter will go out and be violated." The refrain may be found numerous times throughout the midrashic material in ch. 2.

Quite a few passages of the *midrashim* place the blame on Dinah. Another midrashic refrain is "And what caused this? The fact that Dinah went out." Furthermore, *Eccl. Rab.* X.8.1 made the claim, "she brought upon herself the violation." *Tanhuma* 8.12 expresses a sentiment that is very close to *Eccl. Rab.* X.8.1. It (the former *Tanhuma* passage reads), "as soon as she went out into the marketplace, she caused herself to come to corruption."

In addition to such outright expressions of blame, these texts also included rhetoric which sought to paint a negative picture of Dinah. For example, she was consistently referred to as a "gadabout" in *Legends* (I:66 and V:298–99) and in the *midrashim*. That noun may be found in: *Gen. Rab.* 80.5 and 18.2 and *Tanh.* 8.17. Furthermore, she was referred to as "immodest" in *Gen. Rab.* 18.12 and 80.5; "immoral" in *Gen. Rab.* 80.1, *Pirqe R. El.* 38, *Lev. Rab.* 37.1, and *Tanh.* 8.14 and 15. "Unchastity" was one of her marks according to *Tanh.* 8.20. In *Targum Job*, Job uses the following phrase in speaking with his wife, Dinah, "You talk as any woman who acts shamefully from the house of her father talks."

Many of the references which likened her to Leah, her mother, may also be cited here. Such parallelism may be found in *Gen Rab* 80.1 and *Tanh.* 8.14 and 15. Most of these references above have been from the *midrashim*, that body of literature spoke most negatively of Dinah's character. *Targum Job*, which contained the phrase, Dinah had "acted disgracefully from the house of [her] father," may be paralleled to the *midrashim*.

As part of the exploration of "who did what," this next section considers the actions of Shechem. What do the Targums say about this? *Targum Neofiti* 34:2 reads, "Shechem … saw her and took her and abused her and disgraced her." The text continues on to allege that: "he [Shechem] had defiled Dinah" (v. 5); "he had done an abomination in Israel in having intercourse with the daughter of Jacob" (v. 7). "They spoke thus because he had violated Dinah their sister" (v. 13). "The sons of Jacob went in upon the slain and plundered the city because they had defiled their sister" (v. 27). The text repeats the phrase, "defiled Dinah" in v. 31.

Targum Onqelos 34:2 reads, "Shekhem … saw her; whereupon he took her and lay with her, and thus abused her." It goes on to say that "he had defiled his [Jacob's] daughter Dinah" (v. 5). Furthermore, "he had committed a disgraceful act in Israel by lying with Jacob's daughter (v. 7). Verse 13 alleges that Shechem had defiled Dinah.

Targum Pseudo-Jonathan 34:2 reads, "Shechem … saw her and took her by force and lay with her and afflicted her." It continues, "Jacob heard that he had defiled his daughter Dinah" (v. 5). Furthermore, "Shechem had done a disgraceful deed in Israel in lying with Jacob's daughter" (v. 7). Verses 13 and 31 allege that he had defiled Dinah. Verse 31 additionally contains the phrase "polluted the daughter of Jacob."

The *Testament of Levi* 6:3 alleges that he had done an "abominable thing;" 7:3 clarifies that he defiled Dinah, thus committing folly in Israel. *L.A.B.* 8.7 used the language that Shechem had "raped and humiliated." *Joseph and Aseneth* 23:14 made the claim that he "defiled" Dinah and "insulted the sons of Jacob." Theodotus, Fragment 4 reads, "he seized her as his own, carried her off, and ravished her." Fragment 6 calls it a "violent attack." Josephus' *Ant.* 1.21.1 also claimed that "he defiled her by violence."

Along similar lines, *Jubilees* 30:2 alleged that Shechem, "Dinah was snatched away to the house of Shechem … he lay with her and defiled her, but she was little, only twelve years old." The verb "defile" is repeated in v. 3 Verse 4 uses the language, "they polluted Dinah." Verses 5 and 6 repeat the verb "defile." Verse 5 asserts that the men of Shechem had "caused a shame in Israel." This offense was deserving of the death penalty. Demetrius refers to the offense as a "defilement" (Fragment 2:9); he also there asserts, "Dinah was defiled by Shechem."

The rhetoric found in Judith is similar to that of *Jubilees*: "defile" and "pollute" were often used. For example, Judith 9:2 reads, "those strangers … had torn off a virgin's clothing to defile her, and exposed her thighs to put her to shame, and polluted her womb to disgrace her." In Jdt 9:4, there is a reference to the "pollution of their blood."

Furthermore, a number of texts allege that Shechem's deed against Dinah/her brothers/Israel demanded or justified vengeance. *T. Levi* 2:2 and 5:3 and *Legends* II:194, III:199, and IV:259, may be cited as supporting that thought. The way in which the character of Judith speaks/prays also shows that the writer of that book considered Simeon to be justified in and lauded for his revenge (Jdt 9:2-6). The same may be said of *Jub.* 30:18.

In a number of the preceding chapters, the following possible interpretation investigated: Was Dinah abducted by Shechem? Did the Shechemites practice marriage by abduction? That was explored in *Legends* (I;403) and in the Pseudepigrapha chapter, when dealing with the books of Theodotus, Fragment 4 and *Jubilees* 30.2. Theodotus alleged that Dinah was "snatched away." These references give the modern reader the impression that Dinah was taken away against her will.

In his allegorical interpretation of this incident, Philo also uses language of "seizing," but with very different implications. He wrote in *Migration* 39.223, "the tribunal of the soul, by name Dinah … may not be seized by exertions." In *Migration* 39.224, he says that "Sichem … attempted to pollute and defile the judicial faculties of the mind …" Again, one may note the pairing of "pollute" and "defile." That same verse also shows that Philo was aware of the prohibition of there being a "harlot among the daughters of the seer, Israel." That adage served to provide the impetus or incentive for the brothers to carry out their revenge. Lastly, in *Migration* 39.225, Philo used the verb "defile" to describe what some think had happened to Dinah (and others). Using this incident as allegory, Philo continued to talk about the way in which Dinah's state reverted back to virginity. He classified what had happened as an "involuntary accident" on Dinah's part.

In *Names* 36, Philo again referred to the Dinah-Shechem incident. Here his language was somewhat different from that of *Migration*. For example, in *Names* 36.195, he wrote, "laying violent hands upon and attempting to defile her ..." Using Shechem as an archetype of a horrible person, he wrote, "they never omit any opportunity of insulting and violating her when they are able." He did, however, consistently talk about an "attempted" defiling of Dinah. Part of this may be because of how he perceived and evaluated Shechem. He resolutely presented Dinah as virtue (incorruptible judgment/justice or everlasting virgin) and virtuous. One could contrast this interpretation with that of midrashic material. Whereas a number of the midrashic passages held Dinah liable for her "infraction" of going out, Philo presents her as a model of investigation and inquiry. In short, her "going out" was admirable.

Josephus' *Ant.* 1.21.1 is reminiscent of *Names* 36.195 in that it, too, alleged, "he defiled her by violence." The reference from *Ant.* gives the reader the impression that the act was completed or carried out, not only "attempted," as *Names* might lead one to conclude.

A few paragraphs above, mention was made of the adage found in Philo about there not being a harlot among the daughters of Israel. The examined texts vary greatly in their depictions of Dinah in this regard. When one even scans the *midrashim*, it is clear that they come close to alleging that Dinah was a prostitute because she transgressed a social boundary or border; i.e., she went out. The *targumim* may be seen as opposing the midrashic interpretation. They uphold Dinah's reputation vehemently. If one were to scan the Pseudepigrapha, it is striking that not once is the word "prostitute," "harlot," or "whore" found in reference to Dinah.

In both allegorical interpretation and the more literal or typical style of writing, Dinah either represented (in the allegorical) or was presented as a virgin. That kind of rhetoric was prevalent throughout the material explored. Interestingly, it is not found in *Legends,* the *midrashim,* or Josephus. It is found in *Targums Neofiti* and *Pseudo-Jonathan* (both 34:31). In the Pseudepigraphal works, it is attested in Theodotus, Fragment 4 and *Jub.* 30:6. It may be found in Jdt 9:2. Both Philo's *Migration* 39.224–25 and *Names* 36.194 referred to Dinah as a virgin. She is referred to as a damsel (*Legends* I:396, *Gen. Rab.* 80.7, *Ant.* 1.21.1) or a maiden (*Tg. Neof.* 34:3, 4, and 12; *Tg. Ps.-J.* 34:3, 12), girl (*Tg. Onq.* 34:3, 4, 12; *Tg. Ps.-J.*

34:4) or a woman (*Legends* I:395, 396, and 398; *Gen. Rab.* 8.12. 19.12, 57.4, 80.11; and *Tg. Job* 2:10).

When it came to describing Dinah, Theodotus gave the fullest narrative account. Her livelihood, looks, and disposition were all mentioned. In Fragment 3, Theodotus claimed that "Dinah ... had a beautiful form, and admirable frame, and a noble spirit." He also went on, in Fragment 4, to speak of Dinah as a one who worked with wool and was a virgin. However, only *Jub.* 30:2 and Demetrius mentioned her age. *Jubilees* stated that she was twelve when this happened; Demetrius recorded her age as 16 years and four months old.

There has been some attestation of a tradition which states that Dinah did not want to leave Shechem—*Gen. Rab.* 80.11 and *Legends* II:37–38. Stated reasons for her not wanting to leave focus either on the shame she would feel (this is true in both *Gen. Rab.* 80.11 and *Legends* II:37–38) or upon her not wanting to leave an uncircumcised man (*Legends* bore no attestation to this tradition). In both passages, Dinah's refusal or inhibitions to leave prompted Simeon's vow to marry her.

Thus, there are numerous accounts of Dinah's marriages. *Legends* II:38 and *Gen. Rab.* 80.11 claim that she had married Simeon. Of course, Shechem was also her husband. *Genesis Rabbah* 76.9 and 80.8 write as if that was indeed a *fait accompli*. There are quite a few references to Dinah and Job as wife and husband. This occurs within *Legends* I:396, II:225 and II:241, *Gen. Rab.* 19.12, 57.4, and 80.4; *Tanh.* 8.19, *Tg. Job* 2:10, *T. Job* 1:5, and *L.A.B.* 8:8.

As might be expected with a married woman, ancient texts often turned their attention to enumerating the children Dinah bore. There are at least three distinct streams of tradition here. The first claims that Aseneth was the daughter born to Dinah and Shechem (*Legends* II:38 and 138–39)[*Legends* II:76 makes the claim that "Hamor" was the father of Aseneth]. *Pirqe Rabbi Eliezer* 36 refers to Aseneth as Dinah's daughter; *Pirqe R. El.* 38 clarifies that Aseneth was conceived when Shechem seized Dinah and slept with her.

The second tradition is that Dinah and Simeon had a child. This may be found in *Legends* II:38 and *Gen. Rab.* 80.11.

The third stream of tradition surrounding Dinah's children is that she and Job had numerous offspring. *Legends* II:241 asserts that Dinah was the mother of ten children with Job, seven sons and three daughters. The *Testament of Job* alleges that Dinah had ten children with Job after his first wife and ten children had died. *L.A.B.* 8:11 claims that Dinah had twenty children with Job: ten before his miseries (who had perished) and ten after. She had given birth to a total of fourteen sons and six daughters.

So whatever became of Dinah? *Legends* I:396 is the only passage which asserts that Jacob tried to extricate his daughter from Shechem's household, by sending servants or maidens to "fetch her" and to eventually stay with her. The vast majority of passages lead the reader to conclude that Dinah was taken out of Shechem's house when either her two maternal brothers or all her brothers (full- and half-) came upon the city of Shechem. *L.A.B.* 8:7 claims that "Simeon and Levi ... took their sister Dinah and went away from there [Shechem]." *Jubilees* 30:24 claims that the "children of Israel brought forth Dinah ... from the house of Shechem ... to Jacob." Theodotus' Fragment 8 gives the reader a very similar understanding; it reads, "after rescuing their sister, they carried her off with the prisoners to their father's quarters." *Antiquites* 1.21.1 gives a similar impression; it reads, "they (Simeon and Levi) brought away their sister."

Only two remaining pieces of data are left to be considered. A number of texts offer similar ideas to the HB in terms of Dinah's being a part of Jacob's clan who went to Egypt. Genesis 46:15 agrees with *Pirqe R. El.* 39. *Jub.* 44:18, Demetrius 2:17, and *Ant.* 2.7.4, in that regard. Demetrius clarified that Dinah was thirty-nine years old at this time.

Lastly, it was important for these ancient writers to note where Dinah died and/or was buried. Commentary about this may be found in *Legends* V:336 n. 96 and *Legends* II:37, *Gen. Rab.* 80.11, and *Jub.* 34:15–17. One may interpret both references from *Legends* to mean that Dinah had died in Egypt; her body was taken from there to Israel/Palestine/Canaan.

Thus one can see that various stories about Dinah grew out of the HB. It is clear that this narrative of Dinah continued to be grappled with and altered. There are narratives and legends about her birth—whether that includes a change in her gender and/or whether or not she had been born alone or had a twin.

Many stories dealt with her intentions or her motivations for going out. A multitude of reasons are given for why she went out on that fateful day. Some writers widen the scope of the background of this story to assert that the Divine was "punishing" Jacob.

Texts vary regarding the details of what Shechem did to or with Dinah. Some ancient interpreters sought to describe Dinah physically; this included various details about her age, virginity, and daily lifestyle (i.e., that she and the matriarchs had worked with wool).

In some instances, writers/narrators gave Dinah voice. That is, she spoke and expressed her desire to stay with Shechem or her concern that she would be shamed. In other instances, she conversed with later husbands (Simeon and Job). As this sentence suggests, there are prevalent legends about Dinah's subsequent marriages and the children she bore.

As they variously developed the character of Dinah, narrators included information about her migration to Egypt as well as details about her death and her burial place. Thus the modern reader is given sundry portraits of the biblical figure who was violated by Shechem.

Notes

INTRODUCTION

1. Mary Anna Bader, Sexual Violation in the Hebrew Bible: A Multi-Methodological Study of Genesis 34 and 2 Samuel 13 (New York: Peter Lang, 2006).
2. For this discussion, please see Bader, Sexual Violation, 104–5, 109–10, and Appendix A, 178–82.
3. Genesis 34 as I translated it for Sexual Violation in the Hebrew Bible. For further information, please see Bader, Sexual Violation, ch. 2.

CHAPTER 1

1. For more information on Louis Ginzberg's life and work, please consult: Arthur Hertzberg, "Ginzberg, Louis," *EJ* 7:584–85 and Rebecca Schorsch, "Ginzberg, Louis," in *Reader's Guide to Judaism*, ed. Michael Terry (Chicago: Fitzroy Dearborn, 2000), 210–11.
2. Hertzberg, "Ginzberg," *EJ* 7:584–85.
3. Rebecca Schorsch, "Louis Ginzberg," 210. Hertzberg refers to Ginzberg and his work very similarly to Schorsch; Hertzberg, "Ginzberg," *EJ* 7:584.
4. In accordance with the standard way of referring to passages from *Legends of the Jews*, I will consistently use the page numbers as points of reference; I have added the page numbers within the cited text for easier reference. Please know that "I:394" refers to volume I, page 394.
5. Louis Ginzberg, *The Legends of the Jews*, trans. Henrietta Szold (Philadelphia: Jewish Publication Society of America, 1913), I:394–403.
6. **Bold indicates that Dinah is the subject**; regular font indicates that Dinah is the object; ***bold italics indicate where Dinah is presented grammatically in the passive voice***; and *regular italics indicate that Dinah is the passive object.*
7. I made this point with regard to Jacob in Genesis 34; Bader, *Sexual Violation*, 114.
8. One may certainly wonder whether "time" refers more to the time of composition/redaction than the story time itself.
9. Please refer to the conclusion of this chapter for further attestations of this thought.

10. *Midrash Rabbah: Ecclesiastes*, trans. A. Cohen (London: Soncino Press, 1961), 268–9. In the passages that follow, there is reference to the commerce that Jacob began at Shechem; one may note the parallelism between this and the tradition in *Legends* that Jacob sold merchandise at reasonable prices.
11. It is possible, as one of my students pointed out, to interpret "Shechem" here to mean the city. This would, of course, explain the shared responsibility for what happened to Dinah.
12. In the biblical narrative, there are times in Genesis, Judges, and 2 Samuel that festivities such as sheep-shearing and the festival at Shiloh provided an opportunity for questionable sexual activity (in the case of Judah in Genesis 38), for mass marriage by abduction (in Judges 21), and for Absalom kill his half-brother Amnon over the rape of Tamar (2 Samuel 13). In Judges 21:21, the dancing women are the ones abducted.
13. Please note that *Legends'* mention that Shechem had spoken with his friends about wanting Dinah as his wife is also a new piece of information, compared with Genesis. If one does construe him in a most negative light, one could notice that in some ways, his involving friends in his ploy to "get Dinah" may be comparable to the role Amnon played in employing his friend-cousin Jonadab in his attempt to get Tamar alone. For more on the later, please see Bader, *Sexual Violation*, 123–41, 168–69.
14. For more information, please see Bader, *Sexual Violation*, 1–36.
15. It is intriguing that in *Legends*, when the Noahide law is mentioned by the sons of Jacob, it is inferred that Shechem had committed adultery with Dinah (I:396–97).
16. Louis Ginzberg, *The Legends of the Jews*, trans. Henrietta Szold (Philadelphia: Jewish Publication Society of America, 1925), V: 313.
17. See *Gen. Rab.* 80:1, found in the next chapter of this book.
18. Ginzberg, *The Legends of the Jews*, I:66. See also *Gen. Rab.* 18.2.
19. *Midrash Rabbah: Genesis in Two Volumes*, vol 1, trans. H. Freedman (London: Soncino Press, 1961), 141–42. Note 193 in *Legends* V:298–99 refers to *Gen. Rab.* 18.2 and states that "... Dinah ... is described by this expression" [gadabout]. See Ginzberg, *Legends*, V:298–99 for the full citation.
20. Ginzberg, *Legends*, I:396. Please see *Gen. Rab.* 74.9, found in ch. 2, as it expresses similar sentiments.
21. *Midrash Rabbah: Genesis in Two Volumes*, vol. 2, trans. H. Freedman (London: Soncino Press, 1961) 743.
22. Ibid.
23. Ginzberg, *Legends*, I:396.
24. For more information, please see Bader, *Sexual Violation*, 9–10, 60–69, and 100–101.
25. As is also the case in Genesis, Ginzberg, the narrator of *Legends*, is silent about Dinah's reaction to Shechem's sexual advances.
26. Dinah is also referred to in the active voice on I:396, where her marriage to Job is referenced; "she will have to marry Job ..." Ginzberg, *Legends*, I:396. The traditions regarding Dinah's marriage(s) will be addressed later.
27. Simeon's wife Bunah is also referred to in Ginzberg, *Legends* II:38; this is addressed later in this chapter. Some interpreters have struggled with the thought that Simeon had intermarried. For more details, please see: Louis Ginzberg, *The Legends of the Jews*, trans. Henrietta Szold (Philadelphia: Jewish Publication Society of America, 1913), II:38.

28. Ginzberg's note 96 on *Legends* V:336 asserts that "older sources would not admit that any one of Jacob's sons married a Canaanitish woman ... this gave rise to the view that *k'na-anit* (Gen. 46.10) refers to Dinah." Ginzberg, *Legends*, V:336.
29. This point will be expanded upon later.
30. Please see Bader, *Sexual Violation*, 61–69.
31. The proper name "God" is used fourteen times: "Lord" is referred to in eight passages. On three occasions, there is reference to "Lord God."
32. Please see Bader, *Sexual Violation*, 102–5 for a discussion of this point.
33. If one's focus the various portrayals of the sons of Jacob, one could pursue tracking where and when individual sons come to the foreground of the narratives. This, for example, is one of the few instances in which Judah is featured. As one of my students pointed out, this could be a tradition that originated in the South of Israel.
34. This is also true in Ginzberg, *Legends* II:195; see that section of this same chapter.
35. Ginzberg, *Legends* I:401.
36. See, e.g., Ginzberg, *Legends* I:399–401, and 403.
37. Ginzberg, *Legends*, II:93. One may also consult *Gen. Rab.* 93.6, found on *Genesis in Two Volumes*, II:860, for further attestation of the tradition that two of the sons entered and destroyed a large city by themselves. *Midrash Rabbah. Genesis*: II:860.
38. Ginzberg, *Legends*, II:84–85.
39. Louis Ginzberg, *The Legends of the Jews*, trans. Henrietta Szold (Philadelphia: Jewish Publication Society of America, 1911), III:199.
40. Louis Ginzberg, *The Legends of the Jews*, trans. Henrietta Szold (Philadelphia: Jewish Publication Society of America, 1913), IV:259.
41. Please see *The Testament of Levi* 6:8, found in chapter 3 of this book.
42. "And thus they did to all strangers, taking away their wives by force."
43. Please see the subsequent discussion of this in the next chapter, as it is pertinent to *Tanhuma*. Please also see the excursis at the end of ch. 2.
44. That note reads "BR 82.8, which states that each of the other sons of Jacob was born with one twin-sister, Benjamin with two. Comp. note 170. *Baba Batra* 123a objects to the idea of "twin-sisters," and admits it only in the case of Dinah. See however, Jub. 33.22, which reads: Dinah the only daughter of Jacob." Ginzberg, *Legends*, V:319. For the passage from Jubilees, consult the chapter on the Pseudepigraphal references to Dinah.
45. "Talmud," *The New Encyclopedia of Judaism*, editor-in-chief Geoffrey Wigoder; coeditors Fred Skolnik and Shmuel Himelstein (New York: New York University Press, 2002), 747.
46. *Baba Batra* 123a. *The Babylonian Talmud: Seder Nezikin in Four Volumes*, vol. 2, trans. I. Epstein (London: Soncino Press, 1935), 511. This particular chapter of *Baba Batra* was translated by Israel W. Slotki.
47. Ginzberg, *Legends*, II:194–96. One may note the parallelism between this account and *T. Levi*, found in the chapter dealing with Pseudepigrapha. The Sanhedrin Tractate of the Talmud also demonstrates a parallel tradition regarding the negative reputation of Shechem. *Sanhedrin* 102a reads: "[It was] a place predestined for evil; in Shechem Dinah was ravished; in Shechem his brethren sold Joseph; and in Shechem the House of David was divided." For more details please consult: *The Babylonian Talmud: Seder Nezikin in Four Volumes*, vol. 3, trans. I. Epstein (London: Soncino Press, 1935), 692. This particular

chapter of *Sanhedrin* was translated by H. Freedman. Please also note that in the quote from *Sanhedrin* as well as that below (from *Legends* II:10), Dinah is spoken of in the passive: she "was ravished" and "was dishonored."
48. There is further attestation of the ill-repute of Shechem: *Legends* II:10 reads, "... Joseph reached Shechem, where he expected to find his brethren. Shechem was always a place of ill omen for Jacob and his seed—there Dinah was dishonored, there the Ten Tribes of Israel reveled against the house of David while Rehoboam, ruled in Jerusalem, and there Jeroboam was installed as king ..." Ginzberg, *Legends*, II:10.
49. Please see Chapter 1 of *Sexual Violation in the Hebrew Bible*, for an in-depth word study of "heinous offense" and a report of the frequency with which such deeds resulted in the perpetrator's death. I deal there with the sense of democratization of this offense; Bader, *Sexual Violation*, 39, 106, and 119.
50. This may also be evidenced in Ginzberg, *Legends*, I:397.
51. Ginzberg, *Legends*, II:142–43. We see similar themes in *Legends* II:195.
52. Fraternal loyalty to Dinah is ascribed to Simeon in III:199, a passage discussed later in this chapter.
53. Please see the reference to this in the Introduction.
54. *Legends* V:331 n. 65 reminds readers, "Dinah is mentioned in Gen. 46.15 among the members of Jacob's family who emigrated to Egypt many years after Joseph had been sold into slavery." Ginzberg, *Legends*, V:331.
55. Ginzberg, *Legends*, II:114-15.
56. Ginzberg, *Legends*, II:27.
57. *Midrash Rabbah. Genesis*, II:829.
58. *Midrash Rabbah. Genesis*, II:829.
59. *Legends* II:84–85, in which Joseph and his brothers were conversing, contains a very similar sentiment. Joseph said to them, "Report hath told us that two of you did massacre the people of Shechem on account of the wrong done to your sister, and now have ye come down into Egypt (85) to kill the Egyptians for the sake of your brother." Ginzberg, *Legends*, II:84–85. The two events of retribution for wrong done to Dinah and wrong done to Joseph are also connected in III:199. "Just as Reuben interceded to save his brother Joseph's life so did Simeon rise up for his sister Dinah when he took vengeance upon the inhabitants of Shechem for the wrong they had done her." Ginzberg, *Legends*, III:199. Consistently connected throughout are the wrong done to Dinah and the massacre at Shechem. This may be seen in II:93; the context of this is in a letter that Jacob had written to the viceroy of Egypt. Jacob asks, "Or hast thou not heard what my two sons Simon and Levi did to the eight cities of the Amorites, which they destroyed on account of their sister Dinah?" Ginzberg, *Legends*, II:93. It is also evident in IV:259, where the fates of the various later kings of Judah are recounted. The pertinent passage reads: "At first Joash sought to turn Amaziah aside from his purpose by a parable reminding him of the fate of Shechem, which the sons of Jacob had visited upon him for having done violence to their sister Dinah. Amaziah refused to be warned." Ginzberg, *Legends*, IV:259.
60. Ginzberg, *Legends*, II:37–38.
61. *Legends* V:336 n. 96 refers to the issues which some sources had regarding the possibililiy that any of Jacob's sons might have intermarried; "this gave rise to the view that *k'na-anit* (Gen. 46:10) refers to Dinah ..." Ginzberg, *Legends*, V:336.

62. Please see *Gen. Rab.* 80.11 and the ensuing discussion in ch. 2.
63. Ginzberg, *Legends*, II:38.
64. This is the only attestation naming Hamor as a sexual consort of Dinah.
65. Ginzberg, *Legends*, II:76–77.
66. Ibid., II:138–39.
67. *Genesis Rabbah* 90.4 n. 4 might also be included in this category; please see *Gen. Rab.* 90.4 and the note in chapter 2.
68. These legends, whether biblical or extra-biblical, may shed light on the origin of the city of Shechem. One could look at these texts to determine what traditions existed regarding who had "rightful" possession of the city of Shechem.
69. This might reflect the tradition possibly seen in Gen 48:22, where Jacob passed the city of Shechem to Jacob. The older patriarch claims that he had taken some territory "from the hand of the Amorites with my sword and with my bow."
70. *Genesis Rabbah* 19.12 and 57.4, found in chapter 2, refer to Dinah and Job's marriage.
71. Ginzberg, *Legends*, II:225.
72. Ibid., II:241.
73. This parallels a tradition regarding Hannah, who was also said to have had ten children. For more details on Hannah, please see Ginzberg, *Legends* VI:220.
74. Ginzberg, *Legends*, II:242.
75. Ibid., V:375 n. 436 reminds readers that more information about Dinah's burial may be found in Jubilees and in the Testaments of the Twelve Patriarchs. For these references, please consult the chapter on the Pseudepigrapha.
76. *Midrash Rabbah. Genesis in Two Volumes*, II:744.
77. Ginzberg, *Legends*, II:37.
78. Ibid., V:375.
79. For another quotation containing a similar tradition, please see *Lev. Rab.* 37.1 in the next chapter. Like *Legends* I:411–12, *Lev. Rab.* asserts that Jacob neglected to fulfill a vow.
80. Ginzberg, *Legends*, I:411–12.
81. Please see the next chapter in this book for that quote.
82. One could also consider the biblical evidence of the patriarchs' fear that the matriarch be seen and taken by a foreign ruler in Egypt and Gerar. Genesis 12, 20, and 26 address this. For more on this, see Bader, *Sexual Violation*, 32, 38–39.
83. For more on this point, please see: Bader, *Sexual Violation*, 183–86.

CHAPTER 2

1. See Porton's article, "Defining Midrash," for an overview of work that has been done in this field. Gary G. Porton, "Defining Midrash," in *The Study of Ancient Judaism*, ed. Jacob Neusner; vol. 1: *Mishnah, Midrash, Siddur* (New York: Ktav, 1981), 55–103. For a more detailed overview of scholars' contributions to the study of midrash, please see Timothy H. Lim, "Origins and Emergence of Midrash in Relation to the Hebrew Bible" in *Encyclopaedia of Midrash: Biblical Interpretation in Formative Judaism*, ed. Jacob Neusner and Alan J. Avery-Peck; vol. 2 (Boston: Brill, 2005), 595–612.

2. Porton, "Defining Midrash," 58. Richard S. Sarason expresses a thought very similar to Porton's. Richard S. Sarason, "Midrash," *DBI* 2:155–57. See note 11 below.
3. For a discussion of such scholars, see Porton, "Defining Midrash," 59–60. Please also see Jacob Neusner, *Invitation to Midrash: The Workings of Rabbinic Bible Interpretation* (New York: Harper & Row, 1989), 3–4.
4. Mishael Maswari Caspi, "The Story of the Rape of Dinah: The Narrator and the Reader," *Hebrew Studies* XXVI:1 (1985), 43. Jacob Neusner also speaks of the midrash as forming a bridge between the written and oral Torah; see, e.g., Neusner, *Invitation to Midrash*, 11–12. For a more complete discussion of the dual Torah, see Jacob Neusner, *Introduction to Rabbinic Literature*, Anchor Bible Reference Library (New York: Doubleday, 1994), ch. 1.
5. Porton, "Defining Midrash," 78–79. See also Sarason, "Midrash," *DBI* 2:156.
6. Porton, "Defining Midrash," 78. For a very similar identification of exegetical midrashim, please see Jacob Neusner, *Introduction to Rabbinic Literature*, 229.
7. For the sake of defining and thus narrowing the scope of this book, I am considering "early" to be no later than the ninth century C.E. I have relied on the dates given in Strack and Stemberger's *Introduction to the Talmud and Midrash* and in the corresponding articles in *Encyclopaedia Judaica (EJ)*. I fully realize that scholars have debated these issues and that there are immense complexities to issues of dating and redaction. I will provide only the most basic introductions to each midrashic text. For more information, please see H. L. Strack and G. Stemberger, *Introduction to the Talmud and Midrash*, trans. Markus Bockmuehl (Edinburgh: T & T Clark, 1991). One may also consult the corresponding articles in *Encyclopedia Judaica* on: *Genesis Rabbah, Pirkei de Rabbi Eliezer, Ecclesiastes Rabbah, Tanhuma,* and *Leviticus Rabbah*. The precise references (i.e. locations/page numbers of these articles) are forthcoming in subsequent footnotes. Most of the sources mentioned also provide bibliographies for additional research. I have excluded from this study the relatively later midrashic texts, particularly those written after the ninth century and well into medieval times. There are references to Dinah in some of these texts. For example, *Yashar WaYishlah, Seder Olam,* and *Midrash HaGadol* are a few of the sources which mention Dinah. For details about these later midrashic references to Genesis 34, see Caspi, "The Story of the Rape of Dinah," 25–45.
8. For this designation, please see: Strack and Stemberger, *Introduction to the Talmud*, 303; Moshe David Herr, "Genesis Rabbah," *EJ* 7:399–401; and Neusner, *Introduction to Rabbinic Literature*, 11. Porton would use the classification "expositional" instead of "exegetical;" see e.g., Porton, "Defining Midrash," 78.
9. Lucille Claire Thibodeau, *The Relation of Peter Abelard's 'Planctus Dinae' to Biblical Sources and Exegetical Tradition: A Historical and Textual Study* (PhD diss., Harvard University. Ann Arbor, Mich.: UMI, 1990), 70.
10. Strack and Stemberger, *Introduction to the Talmud*, 303. So too Porton, "Defining Midrash," 78–79.
11. For example, when introducing the concepts and content of midrash, Sarason wrote: "A Midrash is simultaneously exegesis and eisegesis: The rabbinic value system and worldview are read into the text, by the textual details themselves associatively generate or trigger the reading." Sarason, "Midrash," *DBI* 2:156.
12. Strack and Stemberger, *Introduction to the Talmud*, 304. For confirmation of this date, please see Herr, "Genesis Rabbah," *EJ* 7:400 and Neusner, *Invitation to Midrash*, 101.

13. Strack and Stemberger, *Introduction to the Talmud*, 304.
14. Neusner, *Invitation to Midrash*, 101.
15. Ibid.
16. Ibid.
17. For confirmation of this conclusion and for further elaboration, please see Herr, "Genesis Rabbah," *EJ* 7:399–400.
18. Strack and Stemberger, *Introduction to the Talmud*, 302; Herr, "Genesis Rabbah," *EJ* 7:400.
19. Ibid.
20. *Midrash Rabbah. Genesis*, II:666–67.
21. Ibid., II:667.
22. A close parallel may be found in *Tanhuma* 8.18.
23. Please note the discussion on the pairing of Dinah and Leah from ch. 1 in *Legends of the Jews*. Other scholars have pointed out the way in which the rabbis connected mother and daughter: see for example Thibodeau and Parry. Thibodeau, *Relation*, 73 and Robin Allinson Parry, *Old Testament Story and Christian Ethics: The Rape of Dinah as Case Study* (Bletchley: Paternoster Press, 2004), 97. Parry also notes Leah's transgression, Jacob's pride, and Dinah's going out as places of blame; Parry, *OT Story*, 97–98.
24. This reference may have been the source of information for *Legends* I:394–46 etc., found in ch. 1 of this book. In many of these passages, Dinah's violation is directly connected with Jacob's lack of righteousness.
25. *Midrash Rabbah. Genesis*, II:673.
26. The complete text of both of these passages, 79.8 and 80.4, may be found later in this same chapter.
27. This may have been a source of the material found in *Legends* I:396.
28. *Midrash Rabbah. Genesis*, II:709.
29. This passage may be found toward the end of this chapter.
30. This point was made by one of my students in the context of a class discussion.
31. Thibodeau has written about the way in which the rabbis perceived or constructed the roles of Simeon and Levi with regard to proselytism. This may be connected back with the opening comments about how midrash was a way of interpreting biblical texts in light of one's own historical/societal issues.; see Thibodeau, *Relation*, 71–73.
32. *Gen. Rab.* 19.12 in *Midrash Rabbah. Genesis*, I:157.
33. *Midrash Rabbah. Genesis*, I:157, n. 5.
34. *Midrash Rabbah. Genesis*, I:505. A note (n. 8) indicates that the bracketed passage has been added from the cur. edd.
35. Bader, *Sexual Violation*, 55–57.
36. Porton would argue against this idea, maintaining that the bulk of *midrashim* were not meant for the "common man." See Porton, "Defining Midrash," 60.
37. *Midrash Rabbah. Genesis*, I:63.
38. For comment on this passage, please consult: Bader, *Sexual Violation*, 32–33.
39. Broede Young, "Dinah in Midrash" (class paper, Dinah in Scripture and Literature, Women's Studies class at the College of Wooster, Wooster, Ohio, submitted March 1, 2007).
40. I have excised section 9, regulations about circumcision.
41. *Midrash Rabbah. Genesis*, II:727–44.

42. Ibid., II:771.
43. *Midrash Rabbah. Genesis*, II:785–86. The footnote to this passage says of Jacob, "He had experienced so much sorrow and trouble through his daughter Dinah." *Midrash Rabbah. Genesis*, II:786.
44. The material found in *Legends* I:395 might be derived from this source.
45. Thibodeau also addressed the trend that *Genesis Rabbah* regarded Dinah's "plight ... as ... punishment for her father Jacob's pride." Thibodeau, *Relation*, 73. We may indeed connect this point back to the previous discussion regarding *Legends of the Jews*' similar portrayal; there it was stated that because Jacob had erred, Dinah was humbled or violated. Please see the previous chapter.
46. For details on where this trend may be evidenced, please see the conclusion to this chapter.
47. A very similar tradition may be found in *Tanhuma* 8.14 and 15.
48. One might wonder if Dinah's making Leah immoral was done post-humously for Leah. The texts (both biblical and midrashic) are unclear if Leah was still alive at this point of the story.
49. Thibodeau wrote that the rabbis portrayed "Dinah as the 'cause' of the massacre in Shechem and the loss of Simeon and Levi's honor ... she is accused of being 'responsible' for the deaths of Hamor and Shechem ... and her plight is interpreted as the proper punishment for her father Jacob's pride." Thibodeau, *Relation*, 73.
50. The same point is made in *Tanhuma* 8.20.
51. We will return to this thought later in this chapter.
52. Naomi Graetz, *Unlocking the Garden: A Feminist Jewish Look at the Bible, Midrash, and God* (Piscataway, N.J.: Gorgias Press, 2005), 31–33. Graetz also places pieces of *Ecc. Rabbah* within this tradition; see pages 34–35. This article was previously published in *A Feminist Companion to Genesis*. Feminist Companion to the Bible. Edited by Athalya Brenner (Sheffield: Sheffield, 1993), 306–317.
53. Ibid., 35–36.
54. Thibodeau asserted "Dinah, the virgin daughter of Israel, is restored by her marriage to Job." Thibodeau, *Relation*, 75.
55. Graetz, *Unlocking the Garden*, 36.
56. Neusner, *Invitation to Midrash*, 102–3.
57. This is one of the main themes of the works of both Thibodeau and Parry.
58. *Legends* II:138, quite likely drawing upon this passage, identifies Shechem as a city which Jacob had taken with his sword and bow.
59. Parry also pointed this out and connected this point with the rabbinic assertion that it was Dinah who was the Canaanite woman Simeon married. Parry, *OT Story*, 98–99.
60. Young, "Dinah in Midrash."
61. See, for example, Bader, *Sexual Violation*, 9–10.
62. *Midrash Rabbah. Genesis*, II:855.
63. *Midrash Rabbah. Genesis*, II:952. The corresponding note at this verse reads, "They avenged Dinah, yet themselves counselled evil against Joseph." *Gen. Rab.* 98.5 n. 3, *Midrash Rabbah. Genesis*, II:952.
64. Ibid., II:953.
65. Ibid., II:979.
66. Strack and Stemberger, *Introduction to the Talmud*, 315; Joseph Heinemann, "Leviticus Rabbah," *EJ* 11:148; and Porton, "Defining Midrash," 79.

67. Neusner, *Invitation to Midrash*, 235. For an introduction to this type of midrash, please see Neusner, *Invitation to Midrash*, 231.
68. Strack and Stemberger, *Introduction to the Talmud*, 317 write of the different scholarly conclusions that are confined to these two centuries; Heinemann clearly identifies it as having been composed in the fifth century. Heinemann, "Leviticus Rabbah," *EJ* 11:147. Please also note that Heinemann, as Porton has succinctly put it, "has argued that Leviticus Rabbah is the first midrash of this type and the precursor of the 'literary homily' as a new literary genre." Porton, "Defining Midrash," 79. Neusner also claimed that "Leviticus Rabbah was the first major rabbinic composition to propose to make topical and discursive statements, not episodically … but systematically and in a disciplined framework." Neusner, *Invitation to Midrash*, 235.
69. Strack and Stemberger, *Introduction to the Talmud*, 316–317 and Joseph Heinemann, "Leviticus Rabbah," *EJ* 11:147.
70. *Midrash Rabbah. Leviticus*, trans. Judah J. Slotki (London; Soncino, 1961), 465.
71. *Legends* drew upon this tradition for its information.
72. Please see the conclusions to this chapter for more on the connection between Dinah and sexual immorality.
73. Please see Moshe David Herr, "Pirkei de-Rabbi Eliezer," *EJ* 13:558 and Strack and Stemberger, *Introduction to the Talmud*, 356.
74. Strack and Stemberger, *Introduction to the Talmud*, 356; Herr dates the document more in the "first half of the eighth century." Herr, "Pirkei de-Rabbi Eliezer," *EJ* 13:559.
75. Herr, "Pirkei de-Rabbi Eliezer," *EJ* 13:559 and Strack and Stemberger, *Introduction to the Talmud*, 357.
76. Ibid.
77. *Pirke De Rabbi Eliezer: The Chapters of Rabbi Eliezer the Great According to the Text of the Manuscript Belonging to Abraham Epstein of Vienna*, trans. Gerald Friedlander (New York: Hermon Press, 1965), 272–73. Henceforth, this source will be referred to as *Pirqe R. El.*
78. This may have influenced or been one of the sources of Ginzberg's parallel passages in *Legends of the Jews*, considered.in the previous chapter.
79. *Pirqe R. El.*, 234.
80. *Pirqe R. El.*, 287–89.
81. *Gen. Rab.* 79.6 may be found in this same chapter. In *Ecclesiastes Rabbah*, it was Dinah, not Jacob, who "was bitten" by the snake.
82. This is in direct opposition to the many traditions found in numerous passages in *Gen. Rab.*, *Lev. Rab.*, *Eccl. Rab.*, and *Tanhuma*.
83. We may also note a similarity between this and the Hagar-Ishmael narrative. One line of Israel's race is sent away from the rest of the encampment and there is angelic intervention.
84. This too may be contrasted to *Legends* and other traditions which tell of the ensuing Amorite clash with the Hebrew people. We certainly note the various ways of recounting this incident. Some segue into militant action; others, such as *Pirqe R. El.*, do not.
85. *Pirqe R. El.*, 303–4.
86. Strack and Stemberger, *Introduction to the Talmud*, 345 and Moshe David Herr, "Ecclesiastes Rabbah," *EJ* 6:355.
87. Strack and Stemberger, *Introduction to the Talmud*, 345.
88. Herr, "*Ecclesiastes Rabbah*," *EJ* 6:355.

89. *Midrash Rabbah. Ecclesiastes*, 268–69. In the passages that follow this citation, there is reference to the commerce that Jacob began at Shechem; one may note the parallelism between this and the tradition in *Legends* that Jacob sold merchandise at reasonable prices.
90. Quite possibly influenced by excerpts such as this, Ginzberg made the same assertion in *Legends*.
91. One could place this alongside interpretations of the serpent and Eve in Genesis 3, where the words of the wise/crafty serpent "seduce" Eve.
92. Strack and Stemberger, *Introduction to the Talmud*, 330; Moshe David Herr, "Tanhuma Yelammedenu," *EJ* 15:794; and *Midrash Tanhuma: S. Buber Rescension* (trans. John T. Townsend. Vol. 1: Genesis (Hoboken, N.J.; Ktav Publishing House, 1989), xi.
93. Strack and Stemberger, *Introduction to the Talmud*, 333. The Buber rescension is thought to have originated from or been compiled in Southern Italy. For more information please see *Midrash Tanhuma: S. Buber Rescension*, xii.
94. Strack and Stemberger, *Introduction to the Talmud*, 332–333; Herr, "Tanhuma Yelammedenu," *EJ* 15:795; and *Midrash Tanhuma: S. Buber Rescension*, xii.
95. *Midrash Tanhuma: S. Buber Rescension*, xii.
96. *Midrash Tanhuma: S. Buber Rescension*, 216–23.
97. See note 50; Ibid., 216.
98. In numerous passages, *Tanhuma* connects Dinah with corruption: 8.12, 13, and 15.
99. See note 52; *Midrash Tanhuma: S. Buber Rescension*, 217.
100. Michelle Lydenberg, "Dinah in Midrash" (class paper, Dinah in Scripture and Literature, Women's Studies class at the College of Wooster, Wooster, Ohio, submitted March 1, 2007).
101. For specific references to this, please see Bader, *Sexual Violation*, 105.
102. Jazmin McNeal, "Dinah in Midrash" (class paper, Dinah in Scripture and Literature, Women's Studies class at the College of Wooster, Wooster, Ohio, submitted March 1, 2007).
103. This is the litany of women presented in *Gen. Rab.* 80.5 and 18.2 and *Tanhuma* 8.17.
104. Note 56, *Midrash Tanhuma: S. Buber Rescension*, 218.
105. *Midrash Rabbah. Genesis*, I:141–42. For the text of *Gen. Rab.* 80.5, please see earlier in this chapter. Note 193 on *Legends* V:298–99 referred to *Gen. Rab.* 18.2 and stated, "... Dinah ... is described by this expression" [gadabout]. See Ginzberg, *Legends*, V:298–99 for the full citation.
106. Please note the previous discussion of this point in ch. 1. Parry made a very similar assertion; Parry, *OT Story*, 98.
107. Elizabeth Bennett, "Dinah in Midrash" (class paper, Dinah in Scripture and Literature, Women's Studies class at the College of Wooster, Wooster, Ohio, submitted March 1, 2007).
108. Ibid.
109. See note 58; *Midrash Tanhuma: S. Buber Rescension*, 219.
110. See note 60; Ibid.. Thibodeau also drew the parallel between the rabbis' portrayal of Dinah as both a gadabout and a "pound of meat." Thibodeau, *Relation*, 74. Parry also noticed this; Parry, *OT Story*, 98.
111. See note 61; *Midrash Tanhuma: S. Buber Rescension*, 219.
112. See note 62; Ibid., 220.

113. Catherine Grandgeorge, "Dinah in Midrash" (class paper, Dinah in Scripture and Literature, Women's Studies class at the College of Wooster, Wooster, Ohio, submitted March 1, 2007).
114. Grandgeorge, "Dinah in Midrash."
115. See the earlier comment that Dinah was paired with Leah because Dinah had originally been conceived male; that tradition, again, is in *Tanhuma* 8.18.
116. Grandgeorge, "Dinah in Midrash."
117. *Leviticus Rabbah* is excluded from that group.

CHAPTER 3

1. See, e.g., Bernard Grossfeld, *The Targum Onqelos to Genesis. The Aramaic Bible*. Volume 6 (Wilmington, Del.: Michael Glazier, Inc., 1988), 1. See also Bernard Grossfeld, "Bible: Translations: Ancient Versions: Aramaic," *EJ* 4:841–42.
2. Grossfeld, *Targum Onqelos to Genesis*, 3 and Grossfeld, "Bible: Translations," *EJ* 4:842. For additional details on Mishnaic references, please see Martin McNamara, *Targum Neofiti 1: Genesis. The Aramaic Bible*. Volume 1A (Collegeville, Minn.: Michael Glazier, Inc., 1992), 44.
3. See for example, McNamara, *Targum Neofiti 1*, 41–42. For more information on the use of the targumim in worship and in school/academic settings, see: Anthony D. York, "The Targum in the Synagogue and in the School," *JSJ* Vol. X, No.1, 74–86.
4. Philip S. Alexander, "Targum, Targumim," *ABD* 6:323. So too Bruce Chilton, "Targumim," *DBI* 2:532.
5. Alexander, "Targum, Targumim," *ABD* 6:323. So too Chilton, "Targumim," *DBI* 2:532.
6. Alexander, "Targum, Targumim," *ABD* 6:323.
7. Ibid.
8. Ibid.
9. Ibid.
10. Alexander, "Targum, Targumim," *ABD* 6:323. Chilton puts forward a third century date: Chilton, "Targumim," *DBI* 2:532.
11. McNamara, *Targum Neofiti 1: Genesis*, 162–64.
12. McNamara notes that a marginal gloss to *Tg. Neof.* reads: "The daughter of Leah who was born." McNamara, *Targum Neofiti 1: Genesis*, 162. From this point on, I will use McNamara's abbreviation "Nfmg" for a Neofiti marginal gloss; McNamara, *Targum Neofiti 1: Genesis*, xii.
13. McNamara comments regarding this phrase, that the HT (Hebrew text) has "to look at." He also notes Ginzberg's *Legends*, V, 313. For more on that please see the chapter on *Legends of the Jews*.
14. McNamara observes that an interlinear gloss identifies Shechem and Hamor to be "of the nations of the world." McNamara, *Targum Neofiti 1: Genesis*, 162. Note that the expression found in the gloss reveals a larger world view, reflecting the religious-political situation of the first few centuries C.E. (as opposed to that seen in the biblical era, for example).
15. In note 2, McNamara commented that this verb could be translated literally as "used." He notes that the HT reads, "lay with." See n. 2, McNamara, *Targum Neofiti 1: Genesis*, 162.

16. McNamara notes that a marginal gloss reads, "and joined (sexually) with her." Ibid. The language found within this gloss is very delicate, especially compared to *Tg. Neof.*'s rhetoric of "abused her and disgraced her." One may still note that the Targum tradition here is more delicate, in turn, than the HB.
17. McNamara observes that a marginal gloss here reads, "the girl." McNamara, *Targum Neofiti 1: Genesis*, 162. Modern interpreters are more likely to conclude that "a girl" is younger and therefore more innocent than "a maiden." This was certainly the impression of the traditional college-aged group which I taught in the Spring of 2007 at The College of Wooster. The language of some of these glosses helps to present a younger, more innocent Dinah than do other traditions.
18. McNamara notes that a marginal gloss reads, "of peace to the heart of the girl." He also notes that the phrase "words of peace" is not in the HT. McNamara, *Targum Neofiti 1: Genesis*, 162.
19. In all three of these instances, vv. 3 and 4 (twice in v. 3) McNamara has noted that the marginal glosses have the noun "girl," which McNamara has translated here as "maiden." McNamara, *Targum Neofiti 1: Genesis*, 162.
20. McNamara notes that a marginal gloss reads, "herds." Ibid.
21. McNamara comments that a marginal gloss reads, "he abandoned." McNamara, *Targum Neofiti 1: Genesis*, 162. This gloss may be interpreted as being judgmental of the patriarch and his reaction to the sexual violation of his daughter. The primary text of *Tg. Neof.*, above, protects the reputation of the ancestors.
22. A marginal gloss reads, "there had been done." McNamara, *Targum Neofiti 1: Genesis*, 162.
23. McNamara points out that one of the marginal glosses translates this phrase as, "in joining (sexually) with." All seem to be synonymous with "lying with," as found in the MT. Ibid.
24. McNamara notes that the HT reads, "thus it was not done" and that *Tg. Neof.* "translates [the] passive of 'to do' with the negative in similar fashion elsewhere." McNamara, *Targum Neofiti 1: Genesis*, 162.
25. A marginal gloss reads, "give her to him, I pray, as wife." McNamara, *Targum Neofiti 1: Genesis*, 162.
26. McNamara comments that the HT reads, "intermarry." McNamara, *Targum Neofiti 1: Genesis*, 162.
27. A marginal gloss reads, "You shall give." McNamara also notes that one of the Cairo Genizah manuscripts reads with *Tg. Neof.* McNamara, *Targum Neofiti 1: Genesis*, 162.
28. McNamara notes that a marginal gloss reads, "Reside in it." He also notes that one of the Cairo Genizah manuscripts reads, "reside and trade in it." Ibid.
29. McNamara observes that a marginal gloss reads, "we (= I) have found," or "let us (= me) find." McNamara, *Targum Neofiti 1: Genesis*, 162.
30. McNamara notes that the Paris (P), Vatican (V), and Nürnberg Fragments read, "(make very great for me) the dowry and the marriage contract (*ketuba*, as in Nf)." Furthermore, he comments: "'dowry' in Nf *prn*; in VN *pwrn*; in CTgC: *pryn*; = Greek loan word *phernê*." He continued, the HT has "marriage present and gift; 'dowry'; Greek loan work *phernê* also used here in the LXX." Ibid.
31. McNamara made note of a marginal gloss reading, "all (that you say)." McNamara, *Targum Neofiti 1: Genesis*, 162.
32. McNamara's comments that the HT here has "with guile." He also notes that "the same translation occurs again in Nf, in the only other occurrence of the word in the Pentateuch

(Gen 27:35). McNamara, *Targum Neofiti 1: Genesis*, 163. Genesis 27:35 reads, "And he [Isaac] said: 'Your brother came with a plentitude of wisdom and took your blessing." Note again, the substitution of "wisdom" for deceit/cunning."
33. A marginal gloss reads, "he spoke." McNamara, *Targum Neofiti 1: Genesis*, 163.
34. A marginal gloss reads, "they had violated; so too does one of the Cairo Genizah fragments." Ibid. Please note that more than one tradition attests to the plural form of the verb (i.e., "they had violated"). This may be placed alongside the plural form of "they had defiled" in v. 27 of both the HB and *Tg. Neof.*
35. A marginal gloss reads, "to give …" McNamara, *Targum Neofiti 1: Genesis*, 163.
36. McNamara notes this phrase is missing in the text and in glosses. It is in one of the Cairo Geniza fragments, however. McNamara, *Targum Neofiti 1: Genesis*, 163.
37. McNamara comments that a marginal gloss reads, "an abomination;" so too does one of the Cairo Geniza fragments. Ibid.
38. McNamara observes that the HT is rended "we will consent; the expression is found only in Gen 34:15, 22, and 23, and rendered in like manner in Nf in all occurrences." McNamara, *Targum Neofiti 1: Genesis*, 163.
39. A marginal gloss reads, "looked good." McNamara, *Targum Neofiti 1: Genesis*, 163.
40. McNamara notes the marginal gloss: "boy," as does one of the Cairo Geniza fragments. McNamara, *Targum Neofiti 1: Genesis*, 163.
41. A marginal gloss reads, "the people of the city." McNamara also made note of the fact that one of Cairo Geniza fragments (CT_g) reads, "the wise men of their city." McNamara, *Targum Neofiti 1: Genesis*, 163.
42. McNamara records that the "HT reads 'perfect.' He comments further, "The transliation is in accord with HB practice. See note to 33:18." McNamara, *Targum Neofiti 1: Genesis*, 163.
43. McNamara notes that a marginal gloss reads, "when he circumcises." McNamara, *Targum Neofiti 1: Genesis*, 163.
44. A marginal gloss reads, "the herds (or: riches) and their possessions." CT_g reads, "their wealth and their possessions." McNamara, *Targum Neofiti 1: Genesis*, 163.
45. McNamara notes that the HT has "when they were sore." Ibid.
46. McNamara observes a marginal gloss here reading, "they had defiled Dinah." McNamara, *Targum Neofiti 1: Genesis*, 163. The marginal gloss mentions the proper name of Dinah. Regarding the plural form of this verb, both in the gloss and in the primary text, please see my comments in note 34. This is most often interpreted as the democratization of the blame/responsibility for the offense. For more, please see Bader, *Sexual Violation*, 106.
47. McNamara notes that this is missing from the text. McNamara, *Targum Neofiti 1: Genesis*, 163.
48. McNamara observes that the HT reads, "might." Ibid., 164.
49. A marginal gloss here reads, "my reputation." McNamara suggests that this be compared with *Tg. Ps.-J.* McNamara, *Targum Neofiti 1: Genesis*, 164.
50. McNamara comments that this is missing in the text and has been supplied from a marginal gloss. McNamara, *Targum Neofiti 1: Genesis*, 164.
51. A marginal gloss here reads, "and they shall kill and destroy the mothers with the children." McNamara, *Targum Neofiti 1: Genesis*, 164. The language of the gloss shows Jacob fearing a total obliteration of his household.
52. McNamara notes, "This elaborate aggadic supplement in Nf Gen 34:31, which is also present in the Frg. Tgs. and in a shorter form in Ps.-J., 'finds no reflection in any known

rabbinic literature' (Grossfeld, Neofiti, note 24 to Gen 34)." McNamara, *Targum Neofiti 1: Genesis*, 164.
53. McNamara observes the variant traditions: PVNL all correspond with Nf. Ibid. See the next note for more details on the variants.
54. McNamara notes "VNL: 'the two sons of Jacob answered together, and said to Israel'; P: 'Simeon and Levi answered and said to Jacob.'" McNamara, *Targum Neofiti 1: Genesis*, 164.
55. A marginal gloss here reads, "'that it be said'; = VNL." McNamara, *Targum Neofiti 1: Genesis*, 164.
56. McNamara observes that a marginal gloss here reads, "'in their school houses; this is the same reading as PVNL." McNamara, *Targum Neofiti 1: Genesis*, 164.
57. McNamara notes that this was erased by a censor; it is in PVNL. Ibid. This is one of three times that McNamara wrote of a censored erasure. See notes 59 and 63. The writer who made the amendments deleted references to "uncircumcised" and "idols." This primary uncensored text therefore created a much more negative picture of the Hivities. Some have proposed that, depending upon the congregational or academic setting in which these texts were used, writers/editors may have striven to avoid language which might have been considered "questionable" by their audience. This could explain such censureship and altering of the text.
58. McNamara attests that others have also noted a marginal gloss "which clarifies this expression: "virgins with regard to virginity," i.e., with regard to the hymen, as opposed to menstruation, this being the formula of *j. Nid.* I, 49a. ..." McNamara, *Targum Neofiti 1: Genesis*, 164. McNamara includes a textual apparatus note which indicates, "P: 'uncircumcised (*s' s'ybw*) defiled virginity' (*btwln*); Nfmg: *s'(s'ybw=* defiled?; or: sepher 'aher= varant readings) 'virgins with regard to virginity' (*btwln lbtwlt'*). J. Nid. 49a bot. speaks of: 'a *betulah* (virgin) as to virginity (*lbtwlyn*), 'i.e., a virgin with regard to the hymen as opposed to menstruation (lit." 'bloods'). See Jastrow, I, 200." Ibid.
59. McNamara notes that this was erased by a censor; it is in PVNL. McNamara, *Targum Neofiti 1: Genesis*, 164.
60. McNamara observes that a marginal gloss reads, "they have violated the daughter of." McNamara, *Targum Neofiti 1: Genesis*, 164.
61. A marginal gloss reads, "'that is should be said in the congregations of:' = VNL." McNamara, *Targum Neofiti 1: Genesis*, 164.
62. McNamara notes that a marginal gloss reads, "'in their (school) houses' = P." Ibid.
63. McNamara observes that this phrase had been "erased by censors; in PVNL." McNamara, *Targum Neofiti 1: Genesis*, 164.
64. McNamara notes that an interlinear gloss of *Tg. Neof.* reads, "they have defiled Dinah; Nfmg: "because of the daughters of Jacob and not only (this) but lest." Ibid.
65. McNamara's note reads, "Nfmg: 'after this it is not fitting for Shechem'; P: 'from now it is not fitting for Shechem.'" McNamara, *Targum Neofiti 1: Genesis*, 164.
66. McNamara's observes that there is more than one marginal gloss. Ibid. His note reads, "Nfmg 1^0: '(like a) lost woman, a prostitute who has no avenger, has it been done to my sister Dinah. Because of this have we done this thing'; Nfmg 2^0: '(who has no) avenger of blood nor avenger of humiliation, thus did it happen to Dinah, the daughter of Jacob. And he said: Like a whoring woman and a prostitute he has reckoned our sister'; cf. VNL: 'like a woman who has no man to avenge her humiliation, thus was it done to Dinah

the daughter of Jacob, and they said" Like a whoring woman and a prostitute have they reckoned our sister'; P almost identical. McNamara, *Targum Neofiti 1: Genesis*, 164.
67. McNamara, *Targum Neofiti 1: Genesis*, 9.
68. Note that like the HB, *Tg. Neof.* has Dinah as the object of four verbs which come in rapid succession.
69. Bader, *Sexual Violation*, 91–95.
70. McNamara, *Targum Neofiti 1: Genesis*, 163.
71. For more information on this, please see Bader, *Sexual Violation*, 103.
72. Céline Mangan, *The Targum of Job. The Aramaic Bible.* Volume 15 (Collegeville, Minn.: The Liturgical Press, 1991), 16. This is also the case in the HB book of Ezekiel, where the expression in oftentimes rendered "mortal."
73. The expression "avenge(r) of humiliation" may be found in marginal gloss 2°, V, N, L, and P. See the primary text above and McNamara, *Targum Neofiti 1: Genesis*, 164.
74. See, e.g., n. jj. McNamara, *Targum Neofiti 1: Genesis*, 164, which refers to the marginal gloss with its tradition of "school houses."
75. Grossfeld, *Targum Onqelos to Genesis*, 30.
76. See Alexander, "Targum, Targumim," *ABD* 6: 321–22 and Grossfeld, *Targum Onqelos to Genesis*, 31–35.
77. Grossfeld, *Targum Onqelos to Genesis*, 31–32.
78. Alexander, "Targum, Targumim," *ABD* 6: 321–22.
79. For more detail, please see Grossfeld, *Targum Onqelos to Genesis*, 30–31. Please also note that Grossfeld, as others, has proposed actual persons, e.g., Rab, who lived both in Palestine and Babylonia in the third century C.E. who might have carried these traditions between the two Jewish centers. Please see, for example, Grossfeld, *Targum Onqelos to Genesis*, 34–35. For additional information on the debate regarding the Babylonian vs. Palestinian origin(s) of *Targum Onqelos*, please see Alexander, "Targum, Targumim," *ABD* 6: 321. See also Grossfeld, "Bible: Translations," *EJ* 4:843–44, where he discussed the provenance of the Targum.
80. Alexander, "Targum, Targumim," *ABD* 6: 321.
81. Alexander, "Targum, Targumim," *ABD* 6: 322 and Grossfeld, "Bible: Translations," *EJ* 4:844.
82. Alexander, "Targum, Targumim," *ABD* 6: 321.
83. See Alexander, "Targum, Targumim," *ABD* 6: 321; Grossfeld, "Bible: Translations," *EJ* 4:842–843; and Grossfeld, *Targum Onqelos to Genesis*, 4–5.
84. Grossfeld has also made this point; Grossfeld, "Bible: Translations," *EJ* 4:844.
85. The following translation comes from Bernard Grossfeld, *Targum Onqelos to Genesis*, 118–21.
86. Grossfeld notes this may be translated, "Lit. 'his soul." Ibid., 118.
87. Grossfeld observes, "The Hebrew 'clung to' is idiomatic and accordingly explained by its intended meaning. Grossfeld, *Targum Onqelos to Genesis*, 119.
88. Grossfeld notes, "E and b add: 'comfortably,' a common type of insertion in the Targum, supplying an object (here the noun tanhumin, functioning as an adverb) implied in the Hebrew." Grossfeld, *Targum Onqelos to Genesis*, 118. "E" stands for l and n, *Biblia Hebraica*, *Ixar* and *Biblia Sacra Complutensis*. Grossfeld's sigla correspond to A. Sperber's. See Alexander Sperber, *The Bible in Aramaic: The Pentateuch According to Targum Onqelos* (Leiden: E. J. Brill, 1959), 1:vi–vii.

89. Grossfeld notes, "The Hebrew *'et* is here understood as the accusative particle as this Targum renders *yat*, in contrast to b, k, l, all of which understood the Hebrew to be the preposition 'with' and accordingly render *'im*." Ibid. Here b refers to "The First Biblia Rabbinica"; "k" to *Biblia Hebraica*, Lisbon; see above note for "l." Sperber, *Bible in Aramaic*, vi
90. Grossfeld observes, "An insertion that is implied in the Hebrew phrase ..." Grossfeld, *Targum Onqelos to Genesis*, 119.
91. Grossfeld comments, The Hebrew has: 'and traverse it.'" He also adds in his commentary that Speiser had pointed out "the connotation 'to trade in' for Hebrew *shr* used in the verse, 'is a late secondary development in Heb. and Jewish Aramaic based on the noun *sōhēr*—'merchant,' 'peddler, one who makes the rounds.' Accordingly, this Targum's translation, paralleled by *Tg. Ps.-Jon.* is based on this Post-Biblical meaning of *shr*." Grossfeld, *Targum Onqelos to Genesis*, 121.
92. Grossfeld notes, "l has 'before you.'" Ibid., 120. See previous notes for the meaning of "l."
93. Grossfeld observes, "The Hebrew has: 'with deceit' or 'with guile.' This approach—translating the Hebrew text in a way that would reflect creditably on the character of the Patriarchs—is common in the Targum ... Likewise Tg. Neof. ('with much wisdom') and Tg. Ps.-Jon ..." Grossfeld, *Targum Onqelos to Genesis*, 121.
94. Grossfeld notes, "i has 'this.'" Ibid., 120. "I" refers to "Mss. Or. 2228, 2229 and 2230 (one ms. in three volumes) of the British Museum." Sperber, *Bible in Aramaic*, vi.
95. Grossfeld comments, "Lit. 'complete.'" Grossfeld, *Targum Onqelos to Genesis*, 121.
96. Grossfeld observes, "Lit. 'breadth of hands.'" Ibid.
97. Grossfeld comments, "The Hebrew simply has 'when they were in pain.' This closer description of their state of being is in agreement with the Rabbinic view that the pain reached its climax on the third day after circumcision." He procedes to note a number of rabbinic sources of this thought, included in the list are *Gen. Rabbah* 80.9 and *Pirqe R. El.* 29. Grossfeld, *Targum Onqelos to Genesis*, 121.
98. Grossfeld notes, "c and k omit it, and the Hebrew does not have it, as the next word 'in security' (Hebrew *bétah*) refers to Simeon and Levi, i.e., they committed their act with confidence. The insertion of *déyatbā'*—"which dwelt" in the text of our Targum would make 'in security' refer to the (inhabitants of the) city of Shekhem instead. According to Tg. Neof., the Syr. And Gen. Rab. LXXX; 10, p. 965, 'in security' refers to Simeon and Levi. Ibid., 120. "C" refers to "Ms. Or. 9400 of the British Museum;" Sperber, *Bible in Aramaic*, vi; see above notes for "k". This does, in effect, change the MT Genesis account.
99. Here Grossfeld comments, "The Hebrew has: 'came upon the slain." The Targum adds the purpose of their coming which was 'to strip' the slain (of their valuables and weapons). Tg. Ps.-Jon likewise makes this addition." Grossfeld, *Targum Onqelos to Genesis*, 121.
100. Grossfeld notes, "b and g have 'took,' the literal rendering of the Hebrew." Ibid., 120. "B" has been used above and "g" refers to the Second Bibla Rabbinica; Sperber, *Bible in Aramaic*, vi.
101. Grossfeld comments, "The idiomatic Hebrew, 'to make me have a bad odor' is here paraphrased into its intended meaning, especially out of respect to the Patriarch Jacob. Ibid., 121.
102. Grossfeld notes, "L has 'should he make our sister a harlot,'" which is a literal translation of the Hebrew." Grossfeld, 120. He also comments, "The term employed by the Targum for 'harlot' *nāpqat brā'* is one of three used in Targumic terminology. Another term *zānîtă* (Aramaic for Hebrew *zônāh*) is used by the Syr, here, by the Frg. Tg. (P, V), which also

uses *nāpqat brā'*, as well as by Tg. Neof. m; a third term *t'āāyyā'* occurs in Tgs. Neof. and Ps.-Jon. to this verse … The selection of *nāpqat brā'* in Onqelos here and in 38:35 below, may just be related to the comment that the Rabbis made on Gen. 34:1 "Just as Leah was a gadabout, so was this one (Dinah) a gadabout." Tanh[A]*Wayyišlah* VII. The term for 'gadabout' *yosānît* for *ys'*, a root which is rendered in Aramaic by npq …" Ibid., 121. "L" here in the beginning of this note refers to a group of three texts: g', l, and n. Sperber, *Bible in Aramaic*, vii; where "g" is the Second Biblia Rabbinica; "l" is the Biblia Hebraica, Ixar; and "n" is the Biblia Sacra Complutensis. Sperber, *Bible in Aramaic*, vi–vii.

103. Michael Maher, *Targum Pseudo-Jonathan: Genesis. The Aramaic Bible*. Volume 1B (Collegeville; Minn.: Michael Glazier, Inc., 1992), 1.
104. Maher, *Targum Pseudo-Jonathan: Genesis*, 1; Alexander, "Targum, Targumim," *ABD* 6:324; and Grossfeld, "Bible: Translations," *EJ* 4:846.
105. Maher, *Targum Pseudo-Jonathan: Genesis*, 1.
106. Maher, *Targum Pseudo-Jonathan: Genesis*, 1 and Alexander, "Targum, Targumim," *ABD* 6:324.
107. Maher, *Targum Pseudo-Jonathan: Genesis*, 1. For a more extensive review of others' conclusions regarding the issue of language in this Targum, please see Maher, *Targum Pseudo-Jonathan: Genesis*, 8–11. Grossfeld concluded that the language was Galilean Jewish Aramaic; Grossfeld, "Bible: Translations," *EJ* 4:845.
108. Maher, *Targum Pseudo-Jonathan: Genesis*, 7.
109. Maher, *Targum Pseudo-Jonathan: Genesis*, 7. Furthermore, on this basis, Maher concludes that it was unlikely that author-editor intended the text to be used in synagogue reading.
110. Maher, *Targum Pseudo-Jonathan: Genesis*, 12. Please see Maher, *Targum Pseudo-Jonathan: Genesis*, 11–12 for a review of scholarly conclusions regarding dating *Tg. Ps.-J*. Grossfeld's dating agrees with Maher; Grossfeld, "Bible: Translations," *EJ* 4:845.
111. Alexander, "Targum, Targumim," *ABD* 6:325, where Alexander pinpoints the final redaction to the 4th/5th centuries.
112. Maher, *Targum Pseudo-Jonathan: Genesis*, 117–19.
113. At this verse, Maher has a note referring the reading to "PRE 38." Maher, *Targum Pseudo-Jonathan: Genesis*, 117.
114. Maher again refers the reader to "PRE 38." He comments further "HT says that Shechem 'took' Dinah. Ps.-J.makes it clear that she did not consent to go with him." Ibid.
115. Maher connects this to Gen. R. 80.7 and Qoh. R. 1.16, 1. Maher, *Targum Pseudo-Jonathan: Genesis*, 117.
116. Maher notes the parallelism between this expression here and *Tg. Onq*. Maher, *Targum Pseudo-Jonathan: Genesis*, 117. Maher also points out that similar expressions to "not proper" appear elsewhere; for more details see: Ibid., 73.
117. Maher observes the parallelism between this verse and *Tg. Onq*. Furthermore he comments, "In our present verse Nf, Ps.-J., and Onq., but not CT_gC, avoid the biblical statement that the sons of Jacob spoke deceitfully or with guile. *Gen. R.* 80, 8 says that Jacob's sons were not guilty of deceit, because the fact that Shechem had defiled their sister justified their proposal. *Jubilees* 30.3, on the other hand, stressed the brothers' treacherous intentions." Maher, *Targum Pseudo-Jonathan: Genesis*, 118.
118. Maher notes, "… In our present verse the Targums (see also Pesh. And LXX) translate Heb. *shr* 'trade' (RSV), according to the meaning it had in late Hebrew and in Aramaic

(cf. Speiser ...). See also v. 21. (Nf. CTg C, Ps.-J., Onq.) ..." Maher, *Targum Pseudo-Jonathan: Genesis*, 117.
119. Maher comments, "= Onq; Ps.-J. and Ong. take Heb. *bth*, lit. 'in security,' (RSV: 'unawares') to refer to the city of Shechem rather than to Simeon and Levi." Maher, *Targum Pseudo-Jonathan: Genesis*, 118.
120. Maher observes the parallelism between this and vs. 28's "plundered" and Onq. Ibid.
121. Maher notes that the expression "their wives" is omitted in two manuscripts: Lond. and ed. pr. Ibid. ("Lond." stands for the British Library MS 27031 of Pseudo-Jonathan [Ibid., xii] and "ed. pr." refers to Editio princes of Tg. Ps.-J. [Ibid., xi].)
122. Maher comments, "Lit.: 'causing a bad reputation to go forth.'" He proceded to list a number of other biblical references in which this same expression may be found. Maher, *Targum Pseudo-Jonathan: Genesis*, 118.
123. Maher has pointed out, "Ed. Pr.: 'in the congregation of Israel.'" Maher, *Targum Pseudo-Jonathan: Genesis*, 119.
124. Maher instructs the reader, "Compare Nf., Nfmg, P. V, N, L, Ps.-J. uses the same verb (*tb'*, lit.: 'seek, demand') as these Targums, but it does not have a direct object ('blood, shame') for this verb. Maher, *Targum Pseudo-Jonathan: Genesis*, 119.
125. Maher notes, "There are no parallels in rabbinic literature to the long addition which the Pal. Tgs. and Ps.-J. make to this verse ..." Ibid.
126. Philo, for example, in *On the Migration of Abraham* XXXIX.216 and ffg., as we shall see in ch. 6, interpreted curiosity and investigation very positively.
127. For information on the Aramaic behind these translations and the patterns that may be visible within each of the *targumim*, please see McNamara, *Targum Neofiti 1*, 27.
128. Please note the similarity between v. 11 in this text, in *Tg. Onq.*, and in the HB; all read "'her' father and brothers." *Tg. Neof.* has the pronoun "his" at this juncture.
129. See, for example, Bader, *Sexual Violation*, 14–37.
130. Maher, *Targum Pseudo-Jonathan: Genesis*, 7.
131. Alexander, "Targum, Targumim," *ABD* 6:325.
132. See, e.g., Alexander, "Targum, Targumim," *ABD* 6:325.
133. Alexander, "Targum, Targumim," *ABD* 6:325; Mangan, *Targum of Job*, 5–6.
134. Alexander, "Targum, Targumim," *ABD* 6:325; Mangan, *Targum of Job*, 5–6. Scholars frequently refer to the 476 C.E. fall of Rome as a significant marker for the dating of this Targum; e.g., Mangan, *Targum of Job*, 7 and Grossfeld, "Bible: Translations," *EJ* 4:848.
135. Mangan, *Targum of Job*, 26–27.
136. Mangan notes, "*B.B.* 15a also links Job with the Patriarchs and has him marry Dinah the daughter of Jacob: see Gen 34; Gen. R. 73.9 ..." Ibid., 27. A textual note of Mangan's corresponding to this verse comments "A omits" the name "Dinah." Ibid., 26. Note that "A" refers to "*Biblia Regia*: The Antwerp Polyglot." Ibid., 10. Mangan classifies both A and M (below) as "The most important of the early printed editions used by Fernández Vallina in his apparatus." Mangan, *Targum of Job*, 10.
137. Mangan comments, "The complaint of Job's wife is greatly expanded in the LXX." Mangan, *Targum of Job*, 27.
138. A textual note of Mangan's corresponding to this verse comments, "M 'in.'" Ibid., 26. "M" refers to "*Miqra'ot Gedolot*." Mangan, *Targum of Job*, 10.

139. Mangan observes, "'Foolish ones' of Hebrew expanded; see *Test. Job.* 26:6." Mangan, *Targum of Job*, 27.
140. Mangan notes, "*B.B.* 16a quoted Raba as saying, 'With his lips he did not sin, but he did sin within his heart.' …" Mangan, *Targum of Job*, 27
141. *Genesis Rabbah* 80.8 may be compared to the HB and the *targumim;* it claims that the brothers' answer was not a "case of deceit." Rather, their actions were justified because of what Shechem had done to Dinah, i.e., he defiled her.

CHAPTER 4

1. James H. Charlesworth, "Pseudepigrapha, OT," *ABD* 5:537–540. Please also see the Table of Contents of the two volumes of James H. Charlesworth, *Old Testament Pseudepigrapha*, 2 vols. (New York: Doubleday, 1983 and 1985).
2. Charlesworth "Pseudepigrapha, OT," *ABD* 5:538.
3. How and when the individual testaments were collected into one unit is another matter that has, of course, received scholarly attention. See, for example, G. J. Brooke, "Testaments of the Twelve Patriarchs," *DBI* 2:538.
4. For more information, please see Brooke, "Testaments of the Twelve Patriarchs," *DBI* 2:539; H. C. Kee, "Testaments of the Twelve Patriarchs," *OTP* 1:777; and Marinus De Jonge, "Testaments of the Twelve Patriarchs," *ABD* 5:182.
5. Kee, "Testaments of the Twelve Patriarchs," *OTP* I:777.
6. Ibid., and De Jonge, "Patriarchs, Testaments of the Twelve," *ABD* 5:183–84.
7. De Jonge, "Patriarchs, Testaments of the Twelve," *ABD* 5:182; George W. E. Nickelsburg, *Jewish Literature between the Bible and the Mishnah*, 2d ed. (Minneapolis: Fortress, 2005), 164; Kee, "Testaments of the Twelve Patriarchs," *OTP* 1:777–78.
8. Kee, "Testaments of the Twelve Patriarchs," *OTP* I:777 and De Jonge, "Patriarchs, Testaments of the Twelve," *ABD* 5:182.
9. De Jonge, "Patriarchs, Testaments of the Twelve," *ABD* 5:183; Brooke, "Testaments of the Twelve Patriarchs," *DBI* 2:540
10. Kee, "Testaments of the Twelve Patriarchs," *OTP* 1:778. This expectation was also attested at Qumran. See also D. S. Russell, *The Old Testament Pseudepigrapha: Patriarchs and Prophets in Early Judaism* (London: SCM Press, 1987), 88.
11. Kee, "Testament of Levi, the third son of Jacob and Leah," *OTP* 1:788.
12. Ibid., *OTP* I:790.
13. I am not the first to note the tendency of the writers of this era to portray Simeon and Levi positively. See, for example, John J. Collins "The Epic of Theodotus and the Hellenism of the Hasmoneans," *HTR* 73 (1980), 95–97.
14. Kee, "Testament of Levi, the third son of Jacob and Leah," *OTP* 1:790.
15. See, for example, Numbers 25. For references linking Numbers 25 with the pseudepigraphical portrayal of the Genesis 34 episode, please see Collins, "The Epic of Theodotus," 96 n.14 and the Hellenism of the Hasmoneans," *HTR* 73 (1980), 96 n. 14 and Parry, *Old Testament Story*, 88. Both link Numbers' description of Phineas to *Jubilees'* characterization of Levi's zeal. See also Reinhard Pummer, "Genesis 34 in Jewish Writings of the Hellenistic and Roman Periods," *HTR* 75 (1982), 180–81.

16. Kee, "Testament of Levi, the third son of Jacob and Leah," *OTP* 1:790. Thibodeau also noted how unique *T. Levi* is in this regard. Thibodeau, *Relation*, 49.
17. In note 6 c., Kee described Levi's "roles of priest and instructor of the Law of God." Kee, "Testament of Levi, the third son of Jacob and Leah," *OTP* 1:790.
18. I am not the first to note that *T. Levi* portrays the circumcision differently from Genesis. See, for example, note 6 b. in Kee, "Testament of Levi, the third son of Jacob and Leah," *OTP* 1:790.
19. DeJonge, "Patriarchs, Testaments of the Twelve," *ABD* 5:184 also noticed this. Kee noted also that neither *Jub.* 30 nor Josephus' Antiquites 1.21 mentions circumcision. Kee, "Testament of Levi," *OTP* 1:790.
20. Parry, *Old Testament Story and Christian Ethics*, 89.
21. Collins, "Epic of Theodotus," 96. Collins also sites Ben Sirach.
22. In Sirach 50:26, the people of Shechem are referred to as degenerate or foolish. For details on this larger pattern of referring to Shechem/the Shechemites as senseless/foolish, please see Thibodeau, *Relation*, 50–51.
23. Kee, "Testament of Levi, the third son of Jacob and Leah," *OTP* 1:790.
24. Bader, *Sexual Violation*, ch. 1; most particularly pp. 37–38.
25. Kee, "Testament of Levi, the third son of Jacob and Leah," *OTP* 1:792.
26. Ibid., *OTP* 1:788.
27. Comments about Demetrius' work may be found in this same chapter.
28. His royal status is referred to frequently throughout the testament; e.g., 28:7, 31:5, 31:7.
29. Nickelsburg, *Jewish Literature*, 316. In *T. Job* 28:7, Job spoke of how all the kings came to encourage Job as he was plagued; one of them had asked, "Where is Jobab, the king of all Egypt?"
30. Nickelsburg, *Jewish Literature*, 320–21; Russell, *Old Testament Pseudepigrapha*, 60; R. P. Spittler, "Testament of Job," *OTP* 1:833.
31. For a more detailed discussion of the implications of this, please see Nickelsburg, *Jewish Literature*, 321 and Russell, *Old Testament Pseudepigrapha*, 60.
32. Nickelsburg, *Jewish Literature*, 321.
33. Spittler, "Testament of Job," *OTP* 1:833.
34. Nickelsburg, *Jewish Literature*, 321. See Spittler, "Testament of Job," *OTP* 1:830 for more discussion on this.
35. Nickelsburg, *Jewish Literature*, 321; Spittler, "Job, Testament of" *ABD* 3:870 and Spittler, "Testament of Job," *OTP* 1:831.
36. Spittler identified a number of the places where Dinah is presented as Job's wife: *L. A. B.* 8:7 and following; *T. Job* 2:9; *Gen. Rab.* 57.4. Spittler, "Testament of Job," *OTP* 1:839.
37. See, for example, Russell, *Old Testament Pseudepigrapha*, 59.
38. For more on women's roles in the *Testament of Job*, see Nickelsburg, *Jewish Literature*, 319–20.
39. For more, please see: Nickelsburg, *Jewish Literature*, 321; Russell, *Old Testament Pseudepigrapha*, 60; Spittler, "Job, Testament of," *ABD* 3:870 gives an excellent summary of the different scholarly opinions of the origins of the testament as does Spittler, "Testament of Job," *OTP* 1:833.
40. In some ways this is reminiscent of the account found in Numbers 27 and 36, where the daughters of Zelophehad requested their rightful paternal inheritance and married endogamously.

41. Spittler, "Testament of Job," *OTP* 1:834.
42. Ibid., *OTP* 1:839–40.
43. See both Ginzberg, *Legends*, II:225, in chapter 1, for further information.
44. Daniel J. Harrington, "Philo, Pseudo-," *ABD* 5:344.
45. Ibid.
46. See Harrington, "Philo, Pseudo-," *ABD* 5:344 and D. J. Harrington, "Pseudo-Philo" in *OTP* 2:297–302; and Nickelsburg, *Jewish Literature*, 265–66; and F. J. Murphy, "Pseudo-Philo," *DBI* 2:334.
47. Harrington, "Philo, Pseudo-," *ABD* 5:344 and Nickelsburg, *Jewish Literature*, 269.
48. Harrington, "Philo, Pseudo-" *ABD* 5:344–45 and Harrington, "Pseudo-Philo," *OTP* 2:299–300; Murphy, "Pseudo-Philo," *DBI* 2:334; and Nickelsburg, *Jewish Literature*, 269.
49. Harrington, "Philo, Pseudo-," *ABD* 5:345; Murphy, "Pseudo-Philo," *DBI* 2:334–35; and Nickelsburg, *Jewish Literature*, 269.
50. Harrington, "Philo, Pseudo-" *ABD* 5:344–45; Harrington, "Pseudo-Philo," *OTP* 2:298–300; Murphy, "Pseudo-Philo," *DBI* 2:334; and Nickelsburg, *Jewish Literature* 269.
51. Harrington, "Pseudo-Philo," *OTP* 2:298–300.
52. Ibid. and Murphy, "Pseudo-Philo," *DBI* 2:335. One may also find a similar emphasis against exogamy in *Jubilees*.
53. Nickelsburg, *Jewish Literature*, 269.
54. Harrington, "Pseudo-Philo," *OTP* 2:313–14.
55. This has been noted by Harrington, "Pseudo-Philo," *OTP* 2:314; see also *L.A.B.* 8:7, note h.
56. Harrington, "Pseudo-Philo," *OTP* 2:314.
57. Pummer, "Genesis 34 in Jewish Writings," 179.
58. See C. Burchard, "Joseph and Aseneth," *OTP* 2:181. Burchard also notes that some of the language found in *Jos. Asen.* bears similarity to that of the LXX (Burchard, "Joseph and Aseneth," *OTP* 2:185). Randall D. Chesnutt, "Joseph and Aseneth," *ABD* 3:969 agrees, as does Nickelsburg, *Jewish Literature*, 337.
59. Burchard, "Joseph and Aseneth," *OTP* 2:181.
60. Ibid., *OTP* 2:187.
61. Chesnutt, "Joseph and Aseneth," *ABD* 3:970.
62. Burchard, "Joseph and Aseneth," *OTP* 2:181 and 187–88. See also Chesnutt, "Joseph and Aseneth," *ABD* 3:969.
63. Chesnutt, "Joseph and Aseneth," *ABD* 3:969.
64. Burchard, "Joseph and Aseneth," *OTP* 2:187 and Chesnutt, "Joseph and Aseneth," *ABD* 3:970.
65. Burchard, "Joseph and Aseneth," *OTP* 2:187 and Chesnutt, "Joseph and Aseneth," *ABD* 3:970.
66. Burchard, "Joseph and Aseneth," *OTP* 2:183.
67. Chesnutt, "Joseph and Aseneth," *ABD* 3:969.
68. We see this characterization of Joseph in 8:5, check 21:21. His insistence prompted Aseneth's conversion. Joseph is portrayed as a virgin in 7:7–8:1.
69. Much has been written of the feminine imagery found in *Jos. Asen.*; Burchard, "Joseph and Aseneth," *OTP* 2:187–88 and 191.
70. 23:4 of *Joseph and Aseneth* in Burchard, "Joseph and Aseneth," *OTP* 2:240.
71. Burchard, "Joseph and Aseneth," *OTP* 2:240–41.

72. Ibid., *OTP* 2:240.
73. Ibid., *OTP* 2:240, note o.
74. Nickelsburg, *Jewish Literature*, 334.
75. Ibid., 334–35.
76. Burchard, "Joseph and Aseneth," *OTP* 2:240.
77. Ibid.
78. Ibid., *OTP* 2:241.
79. We may also insert Amnon into this group. The depiction of the pharoah's son in *JosAsen* 23:1–2 is reminiscent of Amnon in 2 Sam 13:2.
80. Burchard, "Joseph and Aseneth," *OTP* 2:184 raised the possibility that pharoah's son was "modeled upon Shechem;" Nickelsburg expressed the same idea; Nickelsburg, *Jewish Literature*, 334.
81. For more information on this, please see Bader, *Sexual Violation*, 26. Fleishman has also written on the ANE practice of marriage by abduction. Joseph Fleishman, "Why Did Simeon and Levi Rebuke Their Father in Genesis 34:31?," *JNSL* 26/2 (2000), 102–3.
82. Burchard, "Joseph and Aseneth," *OTP* 2:241.
83. For more information on hypotheses regarding the identity of the writer, please see the following: F. Fallon, "Theodotus," *OTP* 2:785–89; Collins, "Epic of Theodotus," 102–104; and Pummer, "Genesis 34 in Jewish Writings," 177–78, 187–88.
84. Fallon, "Theodotus," *OTP* 2:785.
85. For more details, please see Fallon, "Theodotus," *OTP* 2:788 and Collins, "Epic of Theodotus," 99–103.
86. Fallon, "Theodotus," *OTP* 2:786.
87. For further discussion on the expression "sacred town," please see: Collins, "Epic of Theodotus," 93–94.
88. Fallon, "Theodotus," *OTP* 2:791. Fallon notes that some "manuscripts read, *at ree* 'improvident' rather than *ateriree*, 'stubborn.' For more information see note b.
89. Fallon, "Theodotus," *OTP* 2:791.
90. Ibid., *OTP* 2:791.
91. Fallon, "Theodotus," *OTP* 2:791–92.
92. Ibid., *OTP* 2:792; Fragment 4, note b.
93. Fallon, "Theodotus," *OTP* 2:791–92.
94. Fallon, "Theodotus," *OTP* 2:792.
95. Fallon, "Theodotus," *OTP* 2:792.
96. Ibid.
97. Fallon contrasts this detail to the MT Genesis account; he also claims that by presenting Jacob as the one who proposed circumcision, "Theodotus would remove the appearance of treachery on the part of the sons of Jacob ..." Fallon, "Theodotus," *OTP* 2:792, note e. See also note b on the same page. For similar ideas, see Collins, "Epic of Theodotus," 96.
98. Fallon has also noted the way in which this account differs in this regard from Genesis; for more information, please see Fallon, "Theodotus," *OTP* 2:792; Fragment 6, note b and Fragment 4, note e. For similar ideas, see Collins, "Epic of Theodotus," 95–96 and Thibodeau, *Relation*, 37.
99. Fallon, "Theodotus," *OTP* 2:791–92; Fragment 4, note a. Thibodeau makes some of the same points as Fallon. Thibodeau, *Relation*, 36.

100. Fallon, "Theodotus," *OTP* 2:792–93.
101. For more on Josephus, please see ch. 6. Fallon also noted this connection; Fallon, "Theodotus," *OTP* 2:792, note c. See also Collins, "Epic of Theodotus," 97 for this same connection.
102. In commenting on this passage, Fallon notes that Simeon was the one who was said to have taken the initiative both here and in Judith. Fallon, "Theodotus," *OTP* 2:792–93, note c. He concludes therefore that "Theodotus ... does not represent a sympathy of the priestly or Levitical group." Ibid., *OTP* 2:793. Regarding the introduction of the divine into this situation, Fallon notes, "Later Jewish tradition was evidently concerned to show that the killing of the Shechemites was not simply an act of revenge but was in accord with the will of God." Ibid. Thibodeau also makes a similar point that Theodotus adds God into the narrative. Thibodeau, *Relation*, 38.
103. Fallon, "Theodotus," *OTP* 2:792.
104. Ibid.
105. Fallon, "Theodotus," *OTP* 2:793. Fragment 7, note a. This observation was also made by Collins, "Epic of Theodotus," 95.
106. Fallon noted that this was also the case in Jdt 9:2, *Jub.* 30:6–7, and *T. Levi* 5:1–5; 6:8, and 11. Fallon, "Theodotus," *OTP* 2:786, 793.
107. Fragment 7 is found on Fallon, "Theodotus," *OTP* 2:793. Collins also noted that "The account of Theodotus differs from the biblical story in ... the claim that God prompted Simeon and Levi to act ... [and] the allegation that the Shechemites were wicked." Collins, "Epic of Theodotus," 95.
108. Fallon, "Theodotus," *OTP* 2:793.
109. Collins, "Epic of Theodotus," 98. Thibodeau made a very similar point: Thibodeau, *Relation*, 35.
110. Fallon, "Theodotus," *OTP* 2:786.
111. Ibid.
112. Ibid., *OTP* 2:793.
113. I am not the first/only one to make this observation. For example, see Collins, "Epic of Theodotus," 95.
114. So too J. C. VanderKam, "Jubilees, Book of," *DBI* 1:634; Nickelsburg, *Jewish Literature* 69; and O. S. Wintermute, "Jubilees," *OTP* 2:35.
115. Wintermute, "Jubilees," *OTP* 2:112–113.
116. Ibid., *OTP* 2:113.
117. Wintermute, "Jubilees," *OTP* 2:113. Thibodeau uses some of these same quotations to show that one of the main points of *Jubilees* is the author's "clear, emphatic, and unrelenting (law) prohibiting intermarriage." Thibodeau, *Relation*, 45. See also Collins, "Epic of Theodotus," 97.
118. See, for example, Bader, *Sexual Violation*, 9–10, 61–69.
119. VanderKam, "Jubilees, Book of," *DBI* 1:632.
120. Wintermute, "Jubilees," *OTP* 2:37.
121. VanderKam, "Jubilees, Book of," *DBI* 1:634, speaks of Israel's "separation from the peoples." See also James C. VanderKam, "Jubilees, Book of," *ABD* 3:1030–31 and Nickelsburg, *Jewish Literature* 70–71. For more on the issues of circumcision and the ban on intermarriage, see Thibodeau; Thibodeau, *Relation*, 42–43.

122. So too Nickelsburg, *Jewish Literature*, 70; Wintermute, "Jubilees," *OTP* 2:48; and Collins, "Epic of Theodotus," 96–97.
123. VanderKam, "Jubilees, Book of," *ABD* 3:1030; Nickelsburg, *Jewish Literature*, 74; and Wintermute, "Jubilees," *OTP* 2:45.
124. Please see VanderKam, "Jubilees, Book of," *DBI* 1:633; Wintermute, "Jubilees," *OTP* 2:38 and 44.
125. VanderKam, "Jubilees, Book of," *DBI* 1:633; VanderKam, "Jubilees, Book of," *ABD* 3:1030; Nickelsburg, *Jewish Literature*, 73–74; and Wintermute, "Jubilees," *OTP* 2:43–44.
126. VanderKam, "Jubilees, Book of," *DBI* 1:634.
127. Ibid., *DBI* 1:632 and Wintermute, "Jubilees," *OTP* 2:41.
128. Wintermute, "Jubilees," *OTP* 2:45.
129. Nickelsburg, *Jewish Literature*, 74 and Wintermute, "Jubilees," *OTP* 2:42.
130. Wintermute, "Jubilees," *OTP* 2:41.
131. Ibid., *OTP* 2:110.
132. Wintermute, "Jubilees," *OTP* 2:135.
133. Collins, "Epic of Theodotus," 96–97. For details about how the issue of intermarriage impacts our reading of Genesis 34, please see Bader, *Sexual Violation*, 61–69.
134. Nickelsburg, *Jewish Literature*, 70. See also Parry, *Old Testament Ethics*, 88.
135. Collins cites this same verse. Collins, "Epic of Theodotus," 96–97.
136. This is a slight paraphrase from the translation found in *OTP*; Wintermute, "Jubilees," *OTP* 2:112.
137. Thibodeau, *Relation*, 43.
138. Wintermute, "Jubilees," *OTP* 2:113.
138. Ibid.
139. Wintermute, "Jubilees," *OTP* 2:113. Thibodeau devoted at least a paragraph to developing *Jubilees*' affinity for Levi. Thibodeau, *Relation*, 46–47.
140. Wintermute, "Jubilees," *OTP* 2:114.
141. Fallon, "Theodotus," *OTP* 2:793.
142. Please consult ch. 2 for this midrashic text.
143. Wintermute, "Jubilees," *OTP* 2:121.
144. Ibid., *OTP* 2:112.
145. Ibid.
146. Ibid., *OTP* 2:113.
147. Ibid., *OTP* 2:112
148. J. Hanson, "Demetrius the Chronographer," *OTP* 2:843.
149. Ibid., *OTP* 2:844–45.
150. Ibid., *OTP* 2:844.
151. Ibid., *OTP* 2:844–45.
152. Ibid., *OTP* 2:846.
153. Hanson notes that "the traditions in Gen 34 do not explicitly mention "10 years." Hanson, "Demetrius the Chronographer," *OTP* 2:848, note 9a. Hanson also notes that the chronology of Demetrius and *Jubilees* differs in that "according to Jub. 30:2, Dinah is 12 years old at the time of the rape." Ibid., *OTP* 2:850.
154. Hanson, "Demetrius the Chronographer," *OTP* 2:850.
155. Ibid., *OTP* 2:849.

156. Ibid., *OTP* 2:850.
157. Demetrius' account mentions the 3624 years that had transpired between Adam and Joseph's brothers' entry into Egypt; see Fragment 2:18. Hanson, "*Demetrius*," *OTP* 2:851.
158. *L.A.B.*, Theodotus' Fragments 3 and 4, *Jub.* 28:23, and Demetrius' Fragment 2, v. 9.
159. Fallon, "Theodotus," *OTP* 2:792.
160. Wintermute, "Jubilees," *OTP* 2:112.
161. Fallon, "Theodotus," *OTP* 2:791.
162. Kee, "Testaments of the Twelve Patriarchs," *OTP* 1:790.
163. Ibid.
164. Ibid.
165. Harrington, "Pseudo-Philo," *OTP* 2:314
166. Ibid.
167. Burchard, "Joseph and Aseneth," *OTP* 2:240–241.
168. Fallon, "Theodotus," *OTP* 2:792.
169. Fallon, "Theodotus," *OTP* 2:792.
170. Wintermute, "Jubilees," *OTP* 2:112.
171. For verses 2–6, see Wintermute, "Jubilees," *OTP* 2:112.
172. Ibid., *OTP* 2:113.
173. Ibid., *OTP* 2:114.
174. Ibid., *OTP* 2:121.

CHAPTER 5

1. For further details, please see Carey A. Moore, "Judith, Book of," *ABD* 3:1117; Yehoshua M. Grintz, "Judith, Book of," *EJ* 10: 451; and Denise Dombkowski Hopkins, "Judith," in *Women's Bible Commentary* (Expanded Edition. Carol A. Newsom and Sharon H. Ringe, ed. Louisville: Westminster John Knox, 1998), 279.
2. Moore, "Judith," *ABD* 3:1119–20.
3. For further discussion regarding the possible location/identity of Bethulia, see, e.g., Carey A. Moore, *Judith: A New Translation with Introduction and Commentary* (AB 40; Garden City: Doubleday, 1985), 51; Charles C. Torrey, "The Site of Bethulia," *JAOS* 20 (1899):160–72; and Thibodeau, *Relations*, 32.
4. David A. deSilva, *Introducing the Apocrypha: Message, Context, and Significance* (Grand Rapids, Mich.: Baker, 2002), 105. Listed in the genealogical introduction of Judith are also names that are reminiscent of those found in connection with Job: Ox/Uz, Elihu, Uzziah. For more on the form and function of genealogies, see Moore, *Judith*, 187–88. The general theme of a faithful pious widow (in Judith's case) and/or widower (in the case of Job) bears mentioning. Both Judith and Job were said to have "feared the Lord" (see for example, Jdt 8:8 and Job 1:9). When one becomes familiar with both the characters of Job and Judith, it is clear that they were examples of wisdom and devotion. For example, the magistrates of Bethulia laud Judith's piety; Job's friends speak about how upright he was. Clearly, there were times when that righteousness was tested, either directly by God, or in the experience of life. Both characters talked of the Divine's "testing" people (Jdt 8:13, 25, and 26 and

Job 7:18). There is indeed a wisdom-based piety exhibited by Job and Judith. For more on Judith as "Woman Wisdom," please see Hopkins, "Judith," 279–85.

5. See for example, Moore's sections: "'Explanations' for the Book's Errors" and "The So-Called 'Imbalance' of the Book;" Moore, "Judith, Book of," *ABD* 3:1120.
6. Moore, "Judith, Book of," *ABD* 3:1120–21 and Moore, *Judith*, 71–76. See also Grintz, "Judith, Book of," *EJ* 10: 452.
7. Moore, "Judith, Book of," *ABD* 3:1121.
8. Hopkins, "Judith," 279.
9. Toni Craven, *Artistry and Faith in the Book of Judith* (SBLDS 70. Chico: Scholars Press, 1983), 2.
10. For example, please see: deSilva, *Introducing the Apocrypha*, 90; Moore, *Judith*, 70–71; and Hopkins, "Judith," 280.
11. Moore, "Judith, Book of," *ABD* 3:1122–23 and Moore, *Judith*, 70–71. So too A. Cowley and W. Oesterley as per W. P. Brown, "Judith, Book of," *DBI* 1:649. Brown provides a summary of the scholars who have disagreed with Moore, Cowley, and Oesterley. Please see deSilva's work, as he does not embrace Pharisaic origins of Judith. He views the text as representing a much less "sectarian or partisan" line than others have alleged; deSilva, *Introducing the Apocrypha*, 104–5. On the other hand, for examples of scholar who spoke of likely Pharisaic authorship of Judith, see Hopkins, "Judith," 281 and Craven, *Artistry and Faith*, 118–22.
12. Moore, "Judith, Book of," *ABD* 3:1123. See Brown's summary of scholarship about dating issue; Brown, "Judith, Book of," *DBI* 1:648–49. Harrington's general dating agrees with Moore's; Daniel J. Harrington, *Invitation to the Apocrypha* (Grand Rapids, Mich.: William B. Eerdmans Publishing Company, 1999), 29. For further discussion about debates around dating Judith, see Thibodeau, *Relations*, 28 and Hopkins, "Judith," 280–81.
13. Harrington, *Invitation to the Apocrypha*, 29 and Moore, "Judith, Book of," *ABD* 3:1123.
14. Harrington, *Invitation to the Apocrypha*, 29. So too: deSilva, *Introducing the Apocrypha*, 90; Nickelsburg, *Jewish Literature*, 99; and Grintz, "Judith, Book of," *EJ* 10: 451.
15. Moore, "Judith, Book of," *ABD* 3:1122 and Moore, *Judith*, 66–67; so too, e.g., Brown, "Judith, Book of," *DBI* 1:647. For an excellent handling of introductory issues such as dating, textual issues, and scholarship regarding Bethulia/Shechem, please see Craven, *Artistry and Faith*, 1–9.
16. Hopkins referred to Judith as both "priest" and "judge"; Hopkins, "Judith," 284–85.
17. All quotes in this chapter from Judith and 4 Maccabees are from *The New Oxford Annotated Bible: New Revised Standard Version with the Apocryphal/Deuterocanonical Books*, 3d ed. (New York: Oxford University Press, 2001).
18. Collins, "The Epic of Theodotus," 97.
19. The word may be found in Jdt 1:12, 2:1, 6:5, 8:27 and 35, 9:2, and 16:17. God is the subject of the verb in 2:1 and the references in chs. 8 and 16. Indirectly God is also the subject in 9:2, when the Divine equips Simeon to take vengeance on the Shechemites.
20. Hopkins, "Judith," 283. See also Amy Jill Levine, "Sacrifice and Salvation," in *"No One Spoke Ill of Her": Essays on Judith*, ed. James C. VanderKam (SBL *Early Judaism and Its Literature* (Atlanta: Scholars Press, 1992), 18.
21. Hopkins, "Judith," 283. A similar comment has been made by Moore/Freedman; Moore, *Judith*, 190–91, where Moore credits this statement to D. N. Freedman from a private conversation.
22. Moore, "Judith, Book of," *ABD* 3:1118. Harrington also referred to the "rape of Dinah" in his commentary; Harrington, *Invitation to the Apocrypha*, 36.

23. deSilva, *Introducing the Apocrypha*, 87. For a more detailed analysis of past scholarship and conclusions about whether Dinah was raped, see Bader, *Sexual Violation*, chapter 1.
24. deSilva, *Introducing the Apocrypha*, 96–99.
25. Moore, *Judith*, 179. Thibodeau once again made a statement which closely paralleled Moore; Thibodeau, *Relations*, 30.
26. Thibodeau has written that the book and character of Judith represents the "reverse reenactment of the episode in Genesis 34." Thibodeau, *Relations*, 30–32.
27. Thibodeau, *Relations*, 29. See also Moore, *Judith*, 190, for a parallel comment. See Thibodeau, *Relations*, 31–32 for more comparisons between Judith and Dinah.
28. This democratizing of the offense may also be seen in Gen 34:27, where it is said that "they" had defiled Dinah.
29. See for example, Gen 34:14, 30:23; I Kg 11:2; and Job 19:5.
30. This same word may also be found in Jdt 1:14, 5:21, 8:22, and here at 9:2.
31. Moore, *Judith*, 152, 191, 192. For similar assumptions of the dangers women and children faced in the time of war, see Hopkins, "Judith," 281.
32. Deuteronomy 20:14 is one of the few other places where the objects of this verb include human beings. For further details, please see Bader, *Sexual Violation*, 103. This specific Greek verb does not appear in the LXX version of Gen 34:27 or 29. The plundering of the city is καὶ διήρπασαν τὴν πόλιν and their wives and their little ones they took captive and made their prey (καὶ τὰς γυναῖκας αὐτῶν ἠχμαλώτευσαν καὶ διήρπασαν). A Greek word with similar derivation may be found in Jdt 2:7, where Nebuchadnezzar was sharing his intentions with Holofernes.
33. See Moore, *Judith*, 191, where Moore explores the probability that Simeon and Levi had raped the women of Shechem. As Moore indicates the same expression may be found in 4:12 and in 9:4.
34. Moore, *Judith*, 193.
35. The verb may also be found in the earlier points of the narrative: 2:27, 5:12, and 6:3.
36. Pummer, "Genesis 34 in Jewish Writings," 181. See also Parry, *Old Testament Story*, 90, where Pummer's quote helped Parry come to the conclusion that "the story is seen as having moral import—in defence of Israel, deceit and violence are justified in the name of Yahweh." This conclusion that Genesis 34 legitimates Judith's ruse quite common; see also Thibodeau, *Relation*, 30.
37. Jubilees 30:6 is more of an insinuation, not an outright statement, that Dinah was a virgin at the time Shechem had violated/polluted her. For more information, please see the previous chapter's discussion of this verse.
38. Hopkins, "Judith," 279.
39. Levine, "Sacrifice and Salvation," 18.
40. Please consult my book, *Sexual Violation*, 183–84 for theological considerations of this point.
41. Bader, *Sexual Violation*, ch. 1.
42. James H. Cone, *God of the Oppressed* (New York: Seabury Press, 1975).
43. This was true in the wife-sister incidents and in the case of Dinah. For more information, please see Bader, *Sexual Violation*, 91.
44. For more on the parallels between Judith and Jael and for how Judith's widowhood and wealth may have played a part in her story, see Hopkins, "Judith," 282, 284–85. Levine concluded "Judith had to be a widow—that is, sexually experienced but unattached—in

order for her to carry out her plan." Levine, "Sacrifice and Salvation," 20. Levine also wrote about the ways in which Judith's widowhood and wealth were essential elements in the narrative; for further details, please see Levine, "Sacrifice and Salvation," 21–22.
45. For more on these comments, please consult chs. 2 and 3. A discussion of this may be found in ch. 2, in the section on *Tanh.* 8.12, where it is alleged that an adorned woman would attract the stare/sexual gaze of men.
46. In both instances there are additional phrases that allow the informed reader to make other connections back to Genesis 34. For example, 10:6 is set at the city gate; we can remember how much of the negotiations between Hamor and Shechem and the men of their city took place at the gate of their city (Gen 34:20). Also 10:10 mentions "men of the city" as had Genesis 34:20. Yet another link is all the mention of circumcision as a way to "become one of us" in Genesis 34 (vv. 15, 17, 22 [2x], and 24). In the book of Judith, Achior is circumcised (14:10) and becomes a part of Israel.
47. Harrington noted that "the narrator makes ample use of speeches and dialogues to give liveliness to the plot." Harrington, *Invitation to the Apocrypha*, 28.
48. Thibodeau, *Relations*, 33 noted that Judith was "held up as a model of Jewish piety and courage which no Gentile can assail or overcome."
49. Both Jdt 9:2 and Gen 34:3 refer to Dinah as a virgin (parqe,noj). Judith uses the noun again at 16:4 to speak of the threat that Holofernes, the Assyrian, had posed: her virgins would be seized as spoil.
50. Moore, *Judith*, 45.
51. Moore, "Judith, Book of," *ABD* 3:1119.
52. Nickelsburg, *Jewish Literature*, 100; see also Thibodeau, *Relations*, 31.
53. Moore, *Judith*, 190. Thibodeau's remarks closely parallel those of Moore; Thibodeau, *Relations*, 29.
54. Obviously one can wonder why the Divine protected some (Judith) and not others (Dinah). As I stated in *Sexual Violation*, this certainly is a question that many survivors of sexual violation raise; "Why is it that some never face this and others do?" That question is often asked by the survivor in much more pointed and personal ways.
55. Collins, "Epic of Theodotus," 97.
56. See for examples: deSilva, *Introducing the Apocrypha*, 102 and Collins, "Epic of Theodotus," 97.
57. Quoted from Moore, *Judith*, 190–191, where Moore credits this statement to D.N. Freedman from a private conversation. See Levine's work for both a development of how Judith identified with Simeon, the avenger, and for more about Judith's return. Levine, "Sacrifice and Salvation," 17–30.
58. Moore, "Judith, Book of," *ABD* 3:1122. See also deSilva, *Introducing the Apocrypha*, 99 for a summary of commentators who have come to this same conclusion. Harrington repeatedly uses the phrase; Harrington, *Invitation to the Apocrypha*, 40 and 42.
59. Both phrases come from Moore, "Judith, Book of," *ABD* 3:1122 and Moore, *Judith*, 61.
60. For an example of how scholars have treated irony in the book of Judith, see Moore, Judith, 78–85.
61. Moore, "Judith, Book of," *ABD* 3:1119; deSilva, *Introducing the Apocrypha*, 87.
62. deSilva, *Introducing the Apocrypha*, 99.
63. Harrington, *Invitation to the Apocrypha*, 28.

64. See for example: Bader, *Sexual Violation*, 1 and 5.
65. Harrington's reference to Genesis 34 is found on p. 36, as it regards Judith's prayer to her ancestor Simeon. The above quote is from Harrington, *Invitation to the Apocrypha*, 29.
66. deSilva, *Introducing the Apocrypha*, 96.
67. deSilva, *Introducing the Apocrypha*, 85, 102–3. For others who have noted the strong Deuteronomic ties in Judith, see Harrington, *Invitation to the Apocrypha*, 29; Moore, "Judith, Book of," *ABD* 3:1122; Moore, *Judith*, 60–61; and Thibodeau, *Relations*, 30.
68. In mentioning that Judith was a widow, the same Greek word is used to refer to Tamar, after she had been raped by her half-brother Amnon. It is said that she remained "desolate" in her brother's house (2 Sam 13:20). I will later make a point that Judith exhorts God as the "God of the lowly" (9:11); these points connect with regard to survivors of sexual violation.
69. Parry, *Old Testament Story*, 90.
70. Noah Lyons, "Dinah in Apocryphal/Deuterocanonical Texts" (class paper, Dinah in Scripture and Literature, Women's Studies class at the College of Wooster; Wooster, Ohio, submitted May, 2007).
71. For a more complete discussion of the various manuscripts of the LXX which include 4 Maccabees, please see any of the introductions referred to in the footnotes below. Robin Darling Young notes, "Fourth Maccabees, however, is found only as an appendix to some manuscripts of the Septuagint, and thus is not considered canonical in any of the branches of Christianity." Robin Darling Young, "4 Maccabees," in *The Women's Bible Commentary* Expanded Edition. Carol A. Newsom and Sharon H. Ringe, ed. (Louisville: Westminster John Knox, 1998), 317.
72. The tradition of ascribing 4 Maccabees erroneously to Josephus is found consistently throughout even introductory comments on this book. See for example, H. Anderson, "4 Maccabees," *OTP* 2:531; Yehoshua Amir, "Maccabees, Fourth Book of (IV Maccabees)," *EJ* 11:661; and deSilva, *Introducing the Apocrypha*, 355.
73. Anderson, "4 Maccabees," *OTP* 2:532; Hugh Anderson, "Fourth Maccabees," *ABD* 4:452. Other examples of those who have concluded that the work was originally composed in Greek by a Jewish author, please see L. H. Shiffman, "Maccabees, Fourth Book of," *DBI* 2:105; and deSilva, *Introducing the Apocrypha*, 355.
74. An example of another scholar who has come to this conclusion is deSilva, *Introducing the Apocrypha*, 366–69 and 372–73.
75. This point may be found in many introductions: see for example, Amir, "Maccabees," *EJ* 11:661–62; Harrington, *Invitation to the Apocrypha*, 207; Nickelsburg, *Jewish Literature*, 256; and deSilva, *Introducing the Apocrypha*, 352 and 359–64. The latter has a discussion of the comparison/contrast of the philosophy of 4 Maccabees vis-à-vis Roman/Greek philosophy.
76. Anderson, "4 Maccabees," *OTP* 2:533.
77. Anderson, "4 Maccabees," *OTP* 2:533–34; Anderson, "Fourth Maccabees," *ABD* 4:453; Shiffman, "Maccabees, Fourth Book of," *DBI* 2:105; and deSilva, *Introducing the Apocrypha*, 355–56.
78. Young, "4 Maccabees," 330.
79. Anderson, "4 Maccabees," *OTP* 2:533–34; Anderson, "Fourth Maccabees," *ABD* 4:453; and Shiffman, "Maccabees, Fourth Book of," *DBI* 2:105.
80. Anderson, "4 Maccabees," *OTP* 2:534–35. So too Shiffman, "Maccabees, Fourth Book of," *DBI* 2:105 and deSilva, *Introducing the Apocrypha*, 356. Young identifies the provenance as Antioch. Young, "4 Maccabees," 330.

81. Shiffman, "Maccabees, Fourth Book of," *DBI* 2:104 and deSilva, *Introducing the Apocrypha*, 356–58.
82. This is a fairly common starting point for understanding the book of 4 Maccabees; see, for ex., Anderson, "Fourth Maccabees," *ABD* 4:452 and Young, "4 Maccabees," 330.
83. Amir, "Maccabees, Fourth Book of (IV Maccabees)," *EJ* 11:661.
84. I have found no other scholar who links 4 Macc 18:7–8 with Dinah or Genesis 34.
85. deSilva had made this point; deSilva, *Introducing the Apocrypha*, 96.
86. The contrasting ideas of wisdom/wise in 4 Maccabees and Judith could be studied more. For example, note how Jacob is here referred to as "wise" because he reprimanded his sons' lack of control. That could be contrasted with Judith's portrayal as wise as she wielded her deadly sword.
87. Recall the discussions of sections of *Genesis Rabbah* and *Leviticus Rabbah* and *Tanhuma* 8.19.
88. This may be found in *Gen. Rab.* 80.6 and *Tanh.* 8.13.
89. I am not the first to make this assertion; see, for example, Anderson, "4 Maccabees," *OTP* 2:532 who also notes that Eusebius and Jerome may have known this work as *On the Supremacy of Reason*.
90. deSilva's previous quote had referred to the contrast between 4 Maccabees and Judith and had enumerated a few, but not all, of these post-HB texts. deSilva, *Introducing the Apocrypha*, 96.
91. Anderson notes that rabbinic traditions ascribed the mother a name. See Anderson, "4 Maccabees," *OTP* 2:541. Anderson's articles indicate that numerous traditions referred to her as "Miriam" or "Hannah." Amir's article speaks of her as "Hannah;" Amir, "Maccabees," *EJ* 11:661.
92. Note b of Anderson's work states, "Staying at home was of course a means of ensuring the protection of chastity." Anderson, "4 Maccabees," *OTP* 2:563. Earlier, in reference to midrashic texts, the fallacy of this line of thinking was addressed, using, for example, incest or domestic violence. The thought that "staying at home" was or might be safer, particularly in *Tanh.* 8.12 was noted. There is frequently the sense that the woman who crosses boundaries is asking for trouble. The mother of seven praises herself that she, unlike Dinah, never left her father's house and the safety that provided. There is a level on which the woman in 4 Maccabees is holding Dinah partially liable for what happened to her.
93. We could also consider HB legislation that spoke of a woman who transgressed such boundaries as one who had "played the whore in her father's house;" see, for example, Deut 22:13–21. In some instances, such as Deut 22:13–21, it was a capital offense for the woman. See Bader, *Sexual Violation*, 32–33 and 73–74. One may also recollect the ways in which the rabbis construed womanhood as consistently disappointing the Divine (see ch. 2 for these examples).
94. deSilva, *Introducing the Apocrypha*, 354.
95. Harrington, *Invitation to the Apocrypha*, 215.

CHAPTER 6

1. For an example of a scholar who has addressed situating Philo among the Judaisms of his day, please see, Peder Borgen, *Philo of Alexandria: An Exegete for His Time*, Vol. LXXXVI in Supplements to Novum Testamentum, ed. C. K. Barrett et al. (New York: Brill, 1997), 1–9.

2. Peder Borgen, "Philo of Alexandria," *ABD* 5:333; Nickelsburg, *Jewish Literature*, 212–13; Yehoshua Amir, "Philo Judaeus," *EJ* 13:409; and D. Winston, "Philo of Alexandria," *DBI* 2:283.
3. Borgen, "Philo of Alexandria," *ABD* 5:333–34; Nickelsburg, *Jewish Literature*, 212–13 and 215; Amir, "Philo Judaeus," *EJ* 13:409–10; and Winston, "Philo of Alexandria," *DBI* 2:283.
4. Borgen, "Philo of Alexandria," *ABD* 5:333–34; Nickelsburg, *Jewish Literature*, 214–15; and Amir, "Philo Judaeus," *EJ* 13:409.
5. Nickelsburg, *Jewish Literature*, 214.
6. Winston, "Philo of Alexandria," *DBI* 2:283–84.
7. Winston, "Philo of Alexandria," *DBI* 2:283; so too Amir, "Philo Judaeus," *EJ* 13:409 and Nickelsburg, *Jewish Literature*, 217.
8. For more on Philo's allegorical perspective, see, "Philo, Alexandrian and Jew" in David T. Runia, *Exegesis and Philosophy: Studies on Philo of Alexandria* (Hampshire, Great Britain: Variorum, 1990), 5–8. Other chapters in Runia's book address allegory in Philo's works. Nickelsburg also gives an excellent summary of allegory in Philo's contemporary Greco-Roman period; Nickelsburg, *Jewish Literature*, 219.
9. See also Borgen, *Philo of Alexandria*, 70–71; Nickelsburg, *Jewish Literature*, 220; and Parry, *Old Testament Story*, 91.
10. For similar ideas developed in light of issues of proselytism, please see Borgen, *Philo of Alexandria*, 217–23.
11. *The Works of Philo: Complete and Unabridged*, trans. C. D. Yonge, New Updated Edition (Peabody, Mass.: Hendrickson, 1993), 274. "On the Migration of Abraham," 39:216.
12. Yonge, *Works of Philo*, 274.
13. Parry, *Old Testament Story*, 92.
14. Neither Parry, Pummer, nor Thibodeau mentions Philo's *Allegorical Interpretation* with regard to the incident involving Dinah. As Pummer pointed out, Collins includes no reference to Philo's works; Pummer, "Genesis 34 in Jewish Writings," 178–79.
15. Yonge, *Works of Philo*, xii.
16. Borgen, "Philo of Alexandria," *ABD* 5:334.
17. Yonge, *Works of Philo*, 274–75.
18. Yonge, *Works of Philo*, 275.
19. Yonge, *Works of Philo*, 274.
20. Thibodeau wrote that "Shechem, the emblem of folly and shame ... is said ... to have spoken to Dinah, the emblem of justice." Thibodeau, *Relation*, 61.
21. Yonge, *Works of Philo*, 275.
22. The translation is from: Bader, *Sexual Violation*, 87.
23. Yonge, *Works of Philo*, 275.
24. Yonge, *Works of Philo*, xix.
25. Yonge, *Works of Philo*, 275. Parry wrote, "Because the soul did not intend the wrongdoings then the unwilled sufferings are not real defilements." Parry, *Old Testament Story*, 93.
26. Noah Lyons, "Dinah in Philo and Josephus" (class paper, Dinah in Scripture and Literature, Women's Studies class at the College of Wooster, Wooster, Ohio, submitted March 1, 2007). See also Parry, *Old Testament Story*, 94, where Parry writes of Dinah, "In no way is she to blame for the attack although Philo does not think that a genuine ravishing took place (at least in the spiritual reality)."

27. Much of Thibodeau's work on Philo addressed the issues of conversion/personal salvation. For example, she wrote, "Philo's allegorized Dinah is thus the violated soul which can regain its lost virginity through conversion." For more information, see Thibodeau, *Relation*, 62–64.
28. See, for example, *On the Migration of Abraham* II.9; Yonge, *Works of Philo*, 253. Pummer also concluded that in this account of Philo's "the role of Simeon and Levi is a praiseworthy one. Pummer, "Genesis 34 in Jewish Writings," 179.
29. Yonge, *Works of Philo*, 275.
30. Yonge, *Works of Philo*, 275. Pummer also wrote of the negative way in which the Shechemites were developed by Philo. Pummer, "Genesis 34 in Jewish Writings," 178.
31. Especially, but not exclusively, Gen 34:2, 5, 7, 13, and 27.
32. Parry, *Old Testament Story*, 92.
33. Yonge, *Works of Philo*, 275. Others have noted that Philo omits the account of the Shechemites' circumcision; e.g., Pummer, "Genesis 34 in Jewish Writings," 178; Parry, *Old Testament Story*, 92–93; and Thibodeau, *Relation*, 64–65.
34. Yonge, *Works of Philo*, 534.
35. Yonge, *Works of Philo*, 275.
36. Yonge, *Works of Philo*, 256.
37. Yonge, *Works of Philo*, 357–58.
38. Parry refers to Shechem as an "archetype." Parry, *Old Testament Story*, 93.
39. Pummer also noted this repetition. Pummer, "Genesis 34 in Jewish Writings," 179.
40. For a discussion on the term "heinous offense," please see Bader, *Sexual Violation*, ch. 1, especially pages 37–38.
41. For more on this, see Bader, *Sexual Violation*, 48.
42. See Parry, who wrote, "his actions were the opposite of his words." Parry, *Old Testament Story*, 93. Thibodeau interpreted this passage similarly; Thibodeau, *Relation*, 61.
43. For more on the positive portrayal of Simeon and Levi here, please see Pummer; he refers to the two as "champions of truth." Pummer, "Genesis 34 in Jewish Writings," 179. For very similar sentiments, see also Parry, *Old Testament Story*, 94 and Thibodeau, *Relation*, 61.
44. Pummer interpreted this as an allusion to Gen 49:5, but a reference to that passage without its judgment of Simeon and Levi. For further details, see Pummer, "Genesis 34 in Jewish Writings," 179.
45. Philo demonstrated a slight antipathy or leaning against Jacob. We have noted that the texts explored in this book vary on their empathy with or antipathy against Jacob.
46. In that passage, Jacob says to Joseph, "I now give to you one portion more than to your brothers, the portion that I took from the hand of the Amorites with my sword and with my bow." The Hebrew word for portion here is "Shechem." Some have read this as a reference to the passing of Shechem from Jacob's to Joseph's hands.
47. Yonge, *Works of Philo*, 52–53.
48. Louis H. Feldman, "Josephus," *ABD* 3:981 and Nickelsburg, *Jewish Literature*, 288. David M. Rhoads classified Josephus as a seer: David M. Rhoads, *Israel in Revolution: 6–74 C.E.: A Political History Based on the Writings of Josephus* (Philadelphia: Fortress Press, 1976), 8–11. Tessa Rajak wrote that Josephus had "prophetic status:" Tessa Rajak, *Josephus: The Historian and His Society* (Philadelphia: Fortress Press, 1983), 18–19.

49. Nickelsburg, *Jewish Literature*, 289. The information presented in Feldman's article agrees; see Feldman, "Josephus," *ABD* 3:981. Similar details may be found in the articles by Abraham Schalit, "Josephus Flavius," *EJ* 10:251; L. H. Feldman, "Josephus, Flavius," *DBI* 1:622; Rajak, *Josephus*, 1, 14–20; and J. Goldin, "Josephus, Flavius," *IDB* 2:987–88.
50. Rajak, *Josephus*, 7, 14–20. Rhoads wrote, that the "priestly ruling class ... cooperated most directly with the Romans and ... had the most to lose by a war with Rome." Rhoads, *Israel in Revolution*, 5.
51. Nickelsburg, *Jewish Literature*, 289; Feldman, "Josephus," *ABD* 3:982; Louis H. Feldman, "Josephus, Flavius," *DBI* 1:622; Schalit, "Josephus Flavius," *EJ* 10:251; and Rhoads, *Israel in Revolution*, 5.
52. This information may be found in: Nickelsburg, *Jewish Literature*, 289; Feldman, "Josephus," *ABD* 3:982; Feldman, "Josephus, Flavius," *DBI* 1:622–23; Schalit, "Josephus Flavius," *EJ* 10:251; and Per Bilde, *Flavius Josephus Josephus between Jerusalem and Rome*. Journal for the Study of the Pseudepigrapha Supp Series (JPSP) 2 (Sheffield: Sheffield/JSOT Press, 1988), 20–21.
53. See, for example, Rajak, *Josephus*, 1–2, 4; Bilde, *Flavius Josephus*, 16; Rhoads, *Israel in Revolution*, 8–13.
54. For this information, please see Nickelsburg, *Jewish Literature*, 288–89; Feldman, "Josephus," *ABD* 3:982–83; and Feldman, "Josephus, Flavius," *DBI* 1:623.
55. Nickelsburg, *Jewish Literature*, 288–89; similar information may also be found in Schalit's article: Schalit, "Josephus Flavius," *EJ* 10:252–54 and in Feldman's: Feldman, "Josephus, Flavius," *DBI* 1:623.
56. Rhoads, *Israel in Revolution*, 4.
57. Nickelsburg, *Jewish Literature*, 289.
58. See, for example, Feldman, "Josephus, Flavius," *DBI* 1:623 and Bernard Heller, "Ginzberg's Legends of the Jews" *JQR* New Ser., Vol. 24, No. 2 (Oct. 1933): 183. Heller wrote of Josephus' tendency to "exalt and glorify the past history of the Jews."
59. *The Works of Josephus: Complete and Unabridged. New Updated Edition*, trans. William Whiston (Peabody, Mass.: Hendrickson Publishers, 1987), 51–52.
60. Louis H. Feldman noted that Theodotus had set this incident at the time of a festival. Furthermore, Feldman cites two later rabbinic writings, namely *Sefer Hayashar* and *Sekel Tov*, which refer to "a festival of women." Steve Mason, ed. *Flavius Josephus: Translation and Commentary*. Louis H. Feldman, *Judean Antiquities 1–4*. Vol. 3. (Boston: Brill, 2000), 123. According to Strack and Stemberger, the two aforementioned writings may be dated to the 11–16th centuries and the 12th centuries respectively; Strack and Stemberger, *Introduction to the Talmud and Midrash*, 359–60 and 390. Others have noted that the festival setting links Josephus and Theodotus. Collins, "The Epic of Theodotus," 97; Parry, *Old Testament Story*, 90; and Thibodeau, *Relation*, 69.
61. See chs. 1 and 4.
62. Heller, "Ginzberg's Legends of the Jews," 183.
63. Chapters 1 and 2 deal with this at length.
64. This reference, *Ant.* 2.7.4 may be found later in this same chapter.
65. Feldman, *Judean Antiquities*, 179.
66. For more on *Jubilees*, see ch. 4.
67. Parry also noted this line of Josephus' text; Parry, *Old Testament Story*, 91.

68. Thibodeau, *Relation*, 69.
69. One might conclude that some of the midrashic texts had portrayed Dinah in this manner.
70. For more details, see Feldman, *Judean Antiquities*, 123.
71. See Feldman, *Judean Antiquities*, 123–24.
72. Feldman also noted this difference: Feldman, *Judean Antiquities*, 123.
73. Heller, "Ginzberg's Legends of the Jews," 165.
74. Parry also noted this line of Josephus' text; Parry, *Old Testament Story*, 91.
75. For more details, please see Bader, *Sexual Violation*, 93–95 and 114–15.
76. Parry also noted this line of Josephus' text; Parry, *Old Testament Story*, 91.
77. Feldman makes a similar point: Feldman, *Judean Antiquities*, 123.
78. Others have noted this. Feldman, *Judean Antiquities*, 123; Whiston, *Works of Josephus*, 52; Collins, "The Epic of Theodotus," 97; Parry, *Old Testament Story*, 91; and Thibodeau, *Relation*, 68.
79. See also Feldman, *Judean Antiquities*, 124.
80. Collins interpreted this as God's reassuring Jacob. Collins, "The Epic of Theodotus," 97. Parry also used the word "support" to speak of God's siding Jacob's sons. Parry, *Old Testament Story*, 91.
81. So too Feldman: Feldman, *Judean Antiquities*, 124.
82. Whiston, *Works of Josephus*, 64.

Bibliography

Alexander, Philip S. "Targum, Targumim." Pages 320–31 in vol. 6 of *The Anchor Bible Dictionary*. Edited by David Noel Freedman. 6 vols. New York: Doubleday, 1992.

Amir, Yehoshua. "Maccabees, Fourth Book of (IV Maccabees)." Pages 661–62 in vol. 11 of *Encyclopaedia Judaica*. Edited by Cecil Roth. 16 vols. Jerusalem: Keter Publishing House, 1972.

———. "Philo Judaeus." Pages 409–15 in vol. 13 of *Encyclopaedia Judaica*. Edited by Cecil Roth. 16 vols. Jerusalem: Keter Publishing House, 1972.

Anderson, H. "4 Maccabees." Pages 531–64 in vol. 2 of *Old Testament Pseudepigrapha*. Edited by James H. Charlesworth. 2 vols. Garden City, N. Y.: Doubleday, 1985.

———. "Fourth Maccabees." Pages 452–54 in vol. 4 of *The Anchor Bible Dictionary*. Edited by David Noel Freedman. 6 vols. New York: Doubleday, 1992.

The Babylonian Talmud: Seder Nezikin in Four Volumes. Translated I. Epstein. London: Soncino Press, 1935.

Bader, Mary Anna. *Sexual Violation in the Hebrew Bible: A Multi-Methodological Study of Genesis 34 and 2 Samuel 13*. New York: Peter Lang, 2006.

Bennett, Elizabeth. 2007. "Dinah in Midrash." Class paper. Dinah in Scripture and Literature, Women's Studies class at The College of Wooster, Wooster, Ohio.

Bilde, Per. *Flavius Josephus between Jerusalem and Rome*. Journal for the Study of the Pseudepigrapha Supplement Series 2. Sheffield: Sheffield/JSOT Press, 1988.

Borgen, Peder. *Philo of Alexandria: An Exegete for His Time*. Vol. LXXXVI in Supplements to Novum Testamentum, ed. C. K. Barrett et al.; New York: Brill, 1997.

———. "Philo of Alexandria." Pages 333–42 in vol. 5 of *The Anchor Bible Dictionary*. Edited by David Noel Freedman. 6 vols. New York: Doubleday, 1992.

Brooke, G. J. "Testaments of the Twelve Patriarchs." Pages 538–41 in vol. 2 of *The Dictionary of Biblical Interpretation*. Edited by John H. Hayes. 2 vols. Nashville: Abingdon, 1999.

Brown, W. P. "Judith, Book of." Pages 647–50 in vol. 1 of *The Dictionary of Biblical Interpretation*. Edited by John H. Hayes. 2 vols. Nashville: Abingdon, 1999.

Burchard, C. "Joseph and Aseneth." Pages 177–201 in vol. 2 of *Old Testament Pseudepigrapha*. Edited by James H. Charlesworth. 2 vols. Garden City, N.Y.: Doubleday, 1985.

Carroll, Scott T. "Theodotus." Page 448 in vol. 6 of *The Anchor Bible Dictionary*. Edited by David Noel Freedman. 6 vols. New York: Doubleday, 1992.

Caspi, Mishael Maswari. "The Story of the Rape of Dinah: The Narrator and the Reader," *Hebrew Studies* XXVI:1 (1985), 25–45.

Charlesworth, James H. *Old Testament Pseudepigrapha*. 2 vols. Garden City, N.Y.: Doubleday, 1983 and 1985.

———. "Pseudepigrapha." Pages 331–34 in vol. 2 of *The Dictionary of Biblical Interpretation*. Edited by John H. Hayes. 2 vols. Nashville: Abingdon, 1999.

———. "Pseudepigrapha, OT." Pages 537–40 in vol. 5 of *The Anchor Bible Dictionary*. Edited by David Noel Freedman. 6 vols. New York: Doubleday, 1992.

Chesnutt, Randall D. "Joseph and Aseneth." Pages 969–71 in vol. 3 of *The Anchor Bible Dictionary*. Edited by David Noel Freedman. 6 vols. New York: Doubleday, 1992.

Chilton, Bruce. "Targumim." Pages 531–34 in vol 2 of *The Dictionary of Biblical Interpretation*. Edited by John H. Hayes. 2 vols. Nashville: Abingdon, 1999.

Collins, John J. "The Epic of Theodotus and the Hellenism of the Hasmoneans." *Harvard Theological Review* 73 (1980): 91–104.

Cone, James. *God of the Oppressed*. New York: Seabury Press, 1975.

Craven, Toni. *Artistry and Faith in the Book of Judith*. Society of Biblical Literature Dissertation Series 70. Chico: Scholars Press, 1983.

De Silva, David A. *Introducing the Apocrypha: Message, Context, and Significance*. Grand Rapids, Mich.: Baker, 2002.

Fallon, F. "Theodotus." Pages 785–93 in vol. 2 of *Old Testament Pseudepigrapha*. Edited by James H. Charlesworth. 2 vols. Garden City, N. Y.: Doubleday, 1985.

Feldman, Louis H. "Josephus." Pages 981–98 in vol. 3 of *The Anchor Bible Dictionary*. Edited by David Noel Freedman. 6 vols. New York: Doubleday, 1992.

———. "Josephus, Flavius." Pages 622–25 in vol. 1 of *The Dictionary of Biblical Interpretation*. Edited by John H. Hayes. 2 vols. Nashville: Abingdon, 1999.

———. *Judean Antiquities 1–4*. Vol. 3. Mason, Steve, ed. *Flavius Josephus: Translation and Commentary*. Boston: Brill, 2000.

Fleishman, Joseph. "Why Did Simeon and Levi Rebuke their Father in Genesis 34:31?" *Journal of Northwest Semitic Languages* 26/2 (2000): 101–16.

Ginzberg, Louis. *The Legends of the Jews*. Translated by Henrietta Szold. 7 vols. Philadelphia: Jewish Publication Society of America, 1909–1938.

"Ginzberg, Louis." No Pages. Cited 24 January 2006. Online: http://www.britannica.com/eb/article-9036875.

Goldin, J. "Josephus, Flavius." Pages 987–88 in vol. 2 of *The Interpreter's Dictionary of the Bible*. Edited by George Arthur Buttrick. 5 Vols. Nashville: Abingdon Press, 1962.

Graetz, Naomi. "Dinah the Daughter." Pages 306–17 in *A Feminist Companion to Genesis*. Feminist Companion to the Bible. Edited by Athalya Brenner. Sheffield: Sheffield, 1993.

———. "Dinah the Daughter." Pages 27–40 in *Unlocking the Garden: A Feminist Jewish Look at the Bible, Midrash, and God*. Piscataway, N.J.: Georgias Press, 2005.

Grandgeorge, Catherine. 2007. "Dinah in Midrash." Class paper. Dinah in Scripture and Literature, Women's Studies class at The College of Wooster, Wooster, Ohio.

Grintz, Yehoshua M. "Judith, Book of." Pages 451–59 in vol. 10 of *Encyclopaedia Judaica*. Edited by Cecil Roth. 16 vols. Jerusalem: Keter Publishing House, 1972.

Grossfeld, Bernard. "Bible: Translations: Ancient Versions: Aramaic." Pages 841–51 in vol. 4 of *Encyclopaedia Judaica*. Edited by Cecil Roth. 16 vols. Jerusalem: Keter Publishing House, 1972.

———. *The Targum Onqelos to Genesis. The Aramaic Bible*. Volume 6. Wilmington, Del.: Michael Glazier, Inc., 1988.

Hanson, J. "Demetrius the Chronographer." Pages 843–54 in vol. 2 of *Old Testament Pseudepigrapha*. Edited by James H. Charlesworth. 2 vols. Garden City, N. Y.: Doubleday, 1985.

Harrington, Daniel J. *Invitation to the Apocrypha*. Grand Rapids, Mich.: William B. Eerdmans Publishing Company, 1999.

———. "Philo, Pseudo-." Pages 344–45 in vol. 5 of *The Anchor Bible Dictionary*. Edited by David Noel Freedman. 6 vols. New York: Doubleday, 1992.

———. "Pseudo-Philo." Pages 297–378 in vol. 2 of *Old Testament Pseudepigrapha*. Edited by James H. Charlesworth. 2 vols. Garden City, N. Y.: Doubleday, 1985.

Hatch, Edwin and Henry A. Redpath. *A Concordance to the Septuagint and the Other Greek Versions of the Old Testament (Including the Apocryphal Books)*. 2d ed. Grand Rapids, Mich.:Baker, 1998.

Heinemann, Joseph. "Leviticus Rabbah." Pages 147–50 in vol. 11 of *Encyclopaedia Judaica*. Edited by Cecil Roth. 16 vols. New York: Macmillan, 1971.

Heller, Bernard. "Ginzberg's *Legends of the Jews*." *Jewish Quarterly Review* New Series, Vol. 24, No. 2 (Oct. 1933): 165–90.

Herr, David Moshe. "Ecclesiastes Rabbah." Pages 355–56 in vol. 6 of *Encyclopaedia Judaica*. Edited by Cecil Roth. 16 vols. New York: Macmillan, 1971.

———. "Genesis Rabbah." Pages 399–401 in vol. 7 of *Encyclopaedia Judaica*. Edited by Cecil Roth. 16 vols. New York: Macmillan, 1971.

———. "Pirkei de-Rabbi Eliezer." Pages 558–60 in vol. 13 of *Encyclopaedia Judaica*. Edited by Cecil Roth. 16 vols. New York: Macmillan, 1971.

———. "Tanhuma Yelammedenu." Pages 794–96 in vol. 15 of *Encyclopaedia Judaica*. Edited by Cecil Roth. 16 vols. New York: Macmillan, 1971.

Hertzberg, Arthur. "Ginzberg, Louis." Pages 584–85 in vol. 7 of *Encyclopaedia Judaica*. Edited by Cecil Roth. 16 vols. Jerusalem: Keter Publishing House, 1972.

Hopkins, Denise Dombkowski. "Judith." Pages 279–85 in *Women's Bible Commentary*. Expanded Edition. Edited by Carol A. Newsom and Sharon H. Ringe. Louisville:Westminster John Knox, 1998.

Jonge, Marinus De. "Patriarchs, Testaments of the Twelve." Pages 181–86 in vol. 5 of *The Anchor Bible Dictionary*. Edited by David Noel Freedman. 6 vols. New York: Doubleday, 1992.

———. *Testaments of the Twelve Patriarchs: A Study of their Text, Composition and Origin*. 2d ed. Assen, Amsterdam: Van Gorcum, 1975.

Kee, H. C. "Testaments of the Twelve Patriarchs." Pages 775–828 in vol. 1 of *Old Testament Pseudepigrapha*. Edited by James H. Charlesworth. 2 vols. Garden City, N. Y.: Doubleday, 1983.

Levine, Amy Jill. "Sacrifice and Salvation." Pages 17–30 in *"No One Spoke Ill of Her": Essays on Judith*. Edited by James C. VanderKam. Society of Biblical Literature. Early Judaism and Its Literature. Atlanta: Scholars Press, 1992.

Lim, Timothy H. "Origins and Emergence of Midrash in Relation to the Hebrew Bible." Pages 595–612 in vol. 2 of *Encyclopaedia of Midrash: Biblical Interpretation in Formative Judaism*. Edited by Jacob Neusner and Alan J. Avery-Peck. Boston: Brill, 2005.

Lydenberg, Michelle. 2007. "Dinah in Midrash." Class paper. Dinah in Scripture and Literature, Women's Studies class at The College of Wooster, Wooster, Ohio.

Lyons, Noah. 2007. "Dinah in Apocryphal/Deuterocanonical Texts." Class paper. Dinah in Scripture and Literature, Women's Studies class at The College of Wooster, Wooster, Ohio.

———. 2007. "Dinah in Philo and Josephus." Class paper. Dinah in Scripture and Literature, Women's Studies class at The College of Wooster, Wooster, Ohio.

Maher, Michael. *Targum Pseudo-Jonathan: Genesis*. *The Aramaic Bible*. Volume 1B. Collegeville; Minn.: Michael Glazier, Inc., 1992.

Mangan, Céline. *The Targum of Job*. *The Aramaic Bible*. Volume 15. Collegeville, Minn.: Michael Glazier, Inc., 1991.

Mason, Steve ed. *Flavius Josephus: Translation and Commentary*. Louis H. Feldman, *Judean Antiquities 1–4*. Vol. 3. Boston: Brill, 2000.

McNamara, Martin. *Targum Neofiti 1: Genesis*. *The Aramaic Bible*. Volume 1A. Collegeville, Minn.: Michael Glazier, Inc., 1992.

McNeal, Jazmin. 2007. "Dinah in Midrash." Class paper. Dinah in Scripture and Literature, Women's Studies class at The College of Wooster, Wooster, Ohio.

Midrash Rabbah. Edited by H. Freedman and Maurice Simon. 10 vols. London: Soncino Press, 1961.

———. *Genesis in Two Volumes*. Translated by H. Freedman. Vols. 1–2 of *Midrash Rabbah*.

———. *Ecclesiastes*. Translated by A. Cohen. Vol. 8 of *Midrash Rabbah*.

———. *Leviticus*. Translated by J. Israelstam and Judah J. Slotki. Vol. 4 of *Midrash Rabbah*.

Midrash Tanhuma: S. Buber Rescension. Translated by John T. Townsend. Vol. 1: Genesis. Hoboken, N.J.: Ktav Publishing House, 1989.

Moore, Carey A. "Judith, Book of." Pages 1117–25 in vol. 3 of *The Anchor Bible Dictionary*. Edited by David Noel Freedman. 6 vols. New York: Doubleday, 1992.

———. *Judith*. Anchor Bible 40. Garden City, N.Y.: Doubleday, 1985.

Murphy, F. J. "Pseudo-Philo." Pages 334–35 in vol. 2 of *The Dictionary of Biblical Interpretation*. Edited by John H. Hayes. 2 vols. Nashville: Abingdon, 1999.

Neusner, Jacob. *Introduction to Rabbinic Literature*. Anchor Bible Reference Library. New York: Doubleday, 1994.

———. *Invitation to Midrash: The Workings of Rabbinic Bible Interpretation*. New York: Harper & Row, 1989.

The New Oxford Annotated Bible: New Revised Standard Version with the Apocryphal/ Deuterocanonical Books. 3d edition. New York: Oxford University Press, 2001.

Nickelsburg, George W. E. *Jewish Literature between the Bible and the Mishnah*. 2d ed. Minneapolis: Fortress, 2005.

Parry, Robin Allison. *Old Testament Story and Christian Ethics: The Rape of Dinah as a Case Study*. Bletchley: Paternoster, 2004.

Pirke De Rabbi Eliezer: The Chapters of Rabbi Eliezer the Great According to the Text of the Manuscript Belonging to Abraham Epstein of Vienna. Translated by Gerald Friedlander. New York: Hermon Press, 1965.

Porton, Gary G. "Defining Midrash." Pages 55–103 in *The Study of Ancient Judaism*. Edited by Jacob Neusner. Vol. 1: *Mishnah, Midrash, Siddur*. New York: Ktav, 1981.

Pummer, Reinhard. "Genesis 34 in Jewish Writings of the Hellenistic and Roman Periods," *Harvard Theological Review* 75 (1982): 177–88.

Rajak, Tessa. *Josephus: The Historian and His Society*. Philadelphia: Fortress Press, 1983.

Rhoads, David M. *Israel in Revolution: 6–74 C.E.: A Political History Based on the Writings of Josephus*. Philadelphia: Fortress Press, 1976.

Runia, David T. *Exegesis and Philosophy: Studies on Philo of Alexandria*. Hampshire, Great Britain: Variorum, 1990.

Russell, D. S. *Old Testament Pseudepigrapha: Patriarchs and Prophets in Early Judaism*. London: SCM Press, 1987.

Sarason, Richard S. "Midrash." Pages 155–57 in vol. 2 of *The Dictionary of Biblical Interpretation*. Edited by John H. Hayes. 2 vols. Nashville: Abingdon, 1999.

Schalit, Abraham. "Josephus Flavius." Pages 251–63 in vol. 10 of *Encyclopaedia Judaica*. Edited by Cecil Roth. 16 vols. Jerusalem: Keter Publishing House, 1972.

Schorsch, Rebecca. "Louis Ginzberg." Pages 210–11 in *The Reader's Guide to Judaism*. Edited by Michael Terry. Chicago: Fitzroy Dearborn, 2000.

Shiffman, L. H. "Maccabees, Fourth Book of." Pages 104–6 in vol. 2 of *The Dictionary of Biblical Interpretation*. Edited by John H. Hayes. 2 vols. Nashville: Abingdon, 1999.

Speiser, Ephraim Avigdon. *Genesis: Introduction, Translation, and Notes*. Anchor Bible 1. Garden City, N. Y.: Doubleday, 1964.

Sperber, Alexander. *The Bible in Aramaic: The Pentateuch According to Targum Onqelos*. Vol. 1. Leiden: E. J. Brill, 1959.

Spittler, Russell. "Job, Testament of." Pages 869–71 in vol. 3 of *The Anchor Bible Dictionary*. Edited by David Noel Freedman. 6 vols. New York: Doubleday, 1992.

———. "Testament of Job." Pages 829–68 in vol. 1 of *Old Testament Pseudepigrapha*. Edited by James H. Charlesworth. 2 vols. Garden City, N.Y.: Doubleday, 1983.

Strack, H. L. and G. Stemberger. *Introduction to the Talmud and Midrash*. Translated by Markus Bockmuehl. Edinburgh: T & T Clark, 1991.

"Talmud." Pages 747–50 in *The New Encyclopedia of Judaism*. Editor-in-chief Geoffrey Wigoder; coeditors Fred Skolnik and Shmuel Himelstein. New York: New York University Press, 2002.

Thibodeau, Lucille Claire. *The Relation of Peter Abelard's 'Planctus Dinae' to Biblical Sources and Exegetical Tradition: A Historical and Textual Study*, Harvard University Disseration. Ann Arbor, Mich.: 1990

Torrey, Charles C. "The Site of Bethulia." *Journal of the American Oriental Society* 20 (1899): 160–72.

VanderKam, James C. "Jubilees, Book of." Pages 1030–32 in vol. 3 of *The Anchor Bible Dictionary*. Edited by David Noel Freedman. 6 vols. New York: Doubleday, 1992.

———. "Jubilees, Book of." Pages 632–35 in vol. 1 of *The Dictionary of Biblical Interpretation*. Edited by John H. Hayes. 2 vols. Nashville: Abingdon, 1999.

Winston, D. "Philo of Alexandria." Pages 283–86 in vol. 2 of *The Dictionary of Biblical Interpretation*. Edited by John H. Hayes. 2 vols. Nashville: Abingdon, 1999.

Wintermute, O. S. "Jubilees." Pages 35–142 in vol. 2 of *Old Testament Pseudepigrapha*. Edited by James H. Charlesworth. 2 vols. Garden City, N. Y.: Doubleday, 1985.

The Works of Josephus: Complete and Unabridged. New Updated Edition. Translated by William Whiston. Peabody, Mass..: Hendrickson Publishers, 1987.

The Works of Philo: Complete and Unabridged. New Updated Edition. Translated by C. D. Yonge. Peabody, Mass.: Hendrickson, 1993.

York, Anthony D. "The Targum in the Synagogue and in the School." *Journal for the Study of Judaism in the Persian, Hellenistic, and Roman Periods* Vol. X, No. 1, 74–86.

Young, Broede. 2007. "Dinah in Midrash." Class paper. Dinah in Scripture and Literature, Women's Studies class at The College of Wooster, Wooster, Ohio.

Young, Robin Darling. "4 Maccabees." Page 317 in *Women's Bible Commentary*. Expanded Edition. Edited by Carol A. Newsom and Sharon H. Ringe. Louisville:Westminster John Know, 1998.

Index

abduction
    of Dinah, 104, 105, 166
    marriage by, 18, 166
"abomination," connotations of, 73
activity, of Dinah, 81
"afflicted," use of in *Targum Pseudo-Jonathan*, 81–82
age
    of Dinah, 46, 78, 108, 110–11, 113
    of Levi, 46, 94–95, 110–11
    of Simeon, 46, 111
agency
    of Dinah, 8, 14
    Dinah's lack of, 8, 27, 103, 104
    of Judith, 127
aggressors, women as, 121
Alexander, Philip S., 70
Alexander Polyhistor, 110
Alexandria, Jews in, 143–44
Allegorical Interpretation (Philo), 152–54
allegory, Philo's use of, 144
Amir, Yehoshua, 138
Amnon, 27
Amorites, 17, 47
Anderson, H., 137
antagonist, Shechem as, 148, 151
Antiquities of the Jews (Josephus), 156–60
apocryphal writings. *see* Judith (book of)

Asenath
    conversion of, 100
    Dinah's role as mother of, 45
    marriage to Joseph, 21, 22, 23, 50
    parallels with Dinah, 101
    as Shechem's daughter, 168
    Simeon and Levi as protectors of, 100
    story of, 23

Baba Batra, 18
beauty, 126–27
Biblical Antiquities. see Liber Antiquitatum Biblicarum
birth
    of Dinah, 50, 107, 110, 112, 150, 163
    of Joseph, 50, 110
Bissell, E. C., 118, 134
blame
    of Dinah, 55, 65, 67–68, 164, 165
    Job's of Dinah, 85–86
    of Shechem, 87
    of victim, 12, 44, 45, 54, 67–68
    of women, 12, 35
body, dichotomy of with soul, 148
Burchard, C., 100
burial site, Dinah's, 26, 68, 114, 169
business, importance of, 82–83

212 | INDEX

Caligula, 144
Canaanite/Canaanites
    Dinah referred to as, 23, 47
    relationship with Jacob's family, 111
    Simeon's intermixing with, 15, 23
    Simeon's marriage with, 48
Charles, R. H., 90
Charlesworth, James H., 90
children
    of Dinah, 2, 22, 24, 25–26,
        95, 96, 97, 98–99, 102, 168
        (*see also* Asenath)
    of Jacob, 66, 108 (*see also* Dinah; Levi;
        Simeon; sons of Jacob)
Christianity, Roman Empire's
    conversion to, 45–46
chronography, 110–12
circumcision
    and harmony with covenant, 107
    lack of as identifying characteristic of
        outsiders, 133
    Philo on, 149
    and shame, 12–13
    Shechemites' lack of, 149
    Shechem's lack of, 133
circumcision of Shechemites
    Jacob as instigator of, 104
    and Jacob's willingness to give Dinah to
        Shechem, 93
    lack of account of in Theodotus, 104
    Levi's opposition to, 92, 93
    omission of in book of Judith, 136
    theologization of, 105
    use of in deceit, 131
Collins, John, 105, 117
commerce, importance of, 82–83
conversion
    of Hivites, 61
    of Job, 86
    of Roman Empire, 45–46
counselor, Levi as, 92–93
covenant
    harmony with, 107
    intermarriage as infraction of, 108
Craven, Toni, 116

creation of women, 11–12, 40, 57, 62
criticism, 11

daily life, 103
"damsel," Dinah referred to as, 160, 167
daughters
    inheritance by, 25, 26, 96
    of Jacob, 18, 53, 66, 157–58
    of Job and Dinah, 25, 26, 96, 97
death, Dinah's, 22, 68, 110
deceit
    as acceptable, 134
    in Genesis, 152
    by Judith, 122, 131, 136
    by Simeon and Levi, 131, 134, 152
    use of religious rituals in, 131
    victory through, 122
    vs. wisdom, 73–74, 135
"defile," use of by Philo, 167
Demetrius, 94–95, 110–12
descriptions of Dinah, 8–9, 102, 168
De Silva, David, 118, 134–35, 141
detail, lack of in Demetrius, 111–12
deuterocanonical writings
    Judith, book of, 116–37
    Maccabees, Fourth Book of, 137–41
Dinah
    age of, 46, 78, 108, 110–11, 113
    association with Jacob, 9, 32, 163
    association with Leah, 32, 63, 66, 111,
        163, 165
    biblical references to, 18, 21
    birth of, 50, 107, 110, 112, 150, 163
    as blessing to Job, 99
    burial site, 26, 68, 109–10, 114, 169
    children of, 2, 22, 24, 25–26, 95, 96, 97,
        98–99, 102, 168 (*see also* Asenath)
    contrasts with mother of seven sons,
        140, 141
    death of, 22, 68, 110
    description of, 8–9, 102
    fate of, 21, 22
    gender of, 31, 63, 66, 163
    as Jacob's only daughter, 66, 108,
        157–58, 163

Joseph's gifts to, 21
juxtaposition to males, 10
lured out by Shechem, 164
marriages of, 68, 168
marriage to Job, 25, 33, 85, 97, 98, 112, 113
marriage to Simeon, 22–23, 47–48
as metaphor in Philo's writings, 154
migration to Egypt, 52, 53, 68, 108, 114, 159, 169
naming of, 50
need for rescue, 106
as one of two wives, 26
passivity of, 66
referred to as Canaanite, 23, 47
referred to as "damsel," 160, 167
referred to as "girl," 82, 131
referred to as "maiden," 167
referred to as vile, 33–34
relationship with Joseph, 21–22
removal from Shechem (man), 52–53, 168–69
sent away from Jacob's house, 52
sexualization of, 47, 63
as Shechem's wife, 50
as twin, 107–8, 112, 163
unwillingness to leave Shechem (man), 13
used as type, 62
virginity of, 75, 84, 103, 104, 112, 113, 122, 148, 149, 154–55, 167, 168
voice given to, 169
"Dinah the Daughter" (Graetz), 45
disgrace
giving Dinah to uncircumcised man as, 73
Judith's of Holofernes, 133
Shechem as, 73
Divine
affinity for male characters, 62
compared to Shechem (man), 44–45
defense of God's people, 137
as God of lowly/humbled, 124–25
intervention in plans of Holofernes, 121

involvement in massacre, 16, 19–20, 105, 114, 117, 118
Jacob's link with, 9
Judith as agent of, 132
as justification for Judith's deceit, 122
Levi as agent of, 92, 135
love for Israel, 66
matriarchs' relationship with, 62–63
presence of in Genesis, 16
presence of in *Legends,* 16
protection of Jacob's clan by, 123–24
punishment of Jacob, 9, 10, 26–27, 32–33, 43, 64–65, 67, 108
relationship with Levi, 91–92, 101
relationship with Simeon, 101
role in beheading of Holofernes, 122
role in vengeance, 122
sanctioning of Levi's actions, 92
Simeon as agent of, 118, 135
support of Jacob, 159
use of sexual crimes against women as punishment against men, 27
vengeance upon Shechemites, 121

Ecclesiastes Rabbah, 10, 53–54
Egypt
Dinah's migration to, 52, 53, 68, 108, 114, 159, 169
migration of Jacob's clan to, 21, 53
emotions, reason as sovereign over, 138–40
Esau, 26, 27, 32–33
exogamy, 15

Fallon, F., 102, 103, 104, 105, 106
females, 9–10
. *see also* women
festival, 103, 156, 157, 164
"folly," 152
footnotes in *Tanhuma,* 60, 61
"force," use of in *Targum Pseudo-Jonathan,* 83

gender
Dinah's, 31, 63, 66, 163
Judith's cross-gender identification, 133

214 | INDEX

Genesis
    deceit in, 152
    intermarriage in, 15–16
    Jacob's views of massacre at Shechem in, 16
    Josephus's similarity to, 160
    Judith's differences with, 118, 132, 135
    Judith's similarities to, 134–35
    Legends' differences with, 10–11
    presence of Divine in, 16
    silence of Divine in, 34, 135
    Theodotus's differences with, 104–6
Genesis Rabbah
    blame of victim in, 44, 45
    date of, 30, 45–46
    as exegetical *midrash*, 30
    first-person perspective of Jacob in, 43
    introduction of idea of marriage of Simeon and Dinah in, 47–48
    Job's references to Dinah in, 33–34
    meat analogy in, 64
    negative evaluation of Shechem (city) in, 44–45
    passage regarding Dinah in, 36–43
    portrayal of Dinah in, 47
    portrayal of Jacob in, 46
    portrayal of Simeon and Levi in, 46, 48
    portrayal of women in, 11
    provenance of, 30–31
    punishment of Jacob in, 32–33, 43
    on ramifications of "going out," 44
gifts, Joseph's to Dinah, 21
Ginzberg, Louis, 1
    . *see also Legends of the Jews*
"girl"
    Dinah referred to as, 82, 131
    implications of, 82
    Judith referred to as, 131
God. *see* Divine
gods, foreign, 109
"going out"
    by Dinah, 127
    Dinah's intent for, 72, 163–64
    Dinah's reasons for, 158
    focus on in *midrashim*, 113
    by Judith, 127
    ramifications of, 44
    sparse reference to in Pseudepigrapha, 113
Graetz, Naomi, 45
Grossfeld, Bernard, 76

Hadakkum, 15
Hamor
    gullibility of, 78–79
    as Hurrite, 98
    intent to take Dinah as Shechem's wife, 73
    as rapist of Dinah, 118
    Theodotus's description of, 102
    as thistle, 61
    view of in *Tanhuma*, 61
Hanson, J., 110
harlotry, 61, 167
Harrington, Daniel, 97, 134
Hellenism, Philo's openness to, 146
Heller, Bernard, 157
heroism, 133
Herr, Moshe David, 31
Hertzberg, Arthur, 1
Hivites
    intermarriage as way of converting, 61
    relationship with Jacob's family, 111
    Targum Neofiti's portrayal of, 73
    threats to matriarchs, 93
Holofernes
    desire for Judith, 131
    discourse with Achior, 136
    Divine intervention in plans of, 121
    Judith's disgrace of, 133
    lack of circumcision, 133
    referral to Judith as "maiden" or "girl," 131
honor/shame, semantic domain of, 120, 133
Hopkins, Denise Dombkowski, 115–16, 123
Hurrites, Hamor and Shechem as, 98

inheritance by daughters, 25, 26, 96
integrity, 86
intermarriage

acceptability of, 46
concern for in *Joseph and Asenath*, 100
as distasteful to Divine, 97
in Genesis, 15–16
invectives against in *Jubilees*, 106–7, 108
Jacob's willingness to consider, 107
Josephus's lack of mention of, 158
in *Legends*, 15–16
prohibition of, 108
of Simeon with Canaanite, 23
in *Tanhuma*, 61
as way of converting Hivites, 61
irony in book of Judith, 131, 133–34
Israel, Divine's love for, 66

Jacob
acquisition of land by, 103
age of, 111
attempts to remove Dinah from Shechem's household, 168
bond with Dinah, 33
character development in narratives, 14
children of, 108 (*see also* Dinah; Levi; Simeon; sons of Jacob)
desire to retrieve Dinah, 13–14
Dinah associated with, 9, 32, 163
emotional state of, 43
first-person perspective of, 43
God's support of, 159
indictment of in *midrashim*, 32
intervention to save life of Dinah, 52
involvement in events at Shechem, 20
liability for Dinah's fate, 51, 64–65, 164 (*see also* punishment)
link with Divine, 9
in negotiations with Hamor and Shechem, 104, 160
number of daughters of, 18, 53, 66, 157–58
as out of sync with family, 103
piety of, 154
portrayal of by Philo, 153–54
portrayal of in *Genesis Rabbah*, 46
portrayal of in Josephus, 158–59
portrayal of in *Legends*, 9–10

portrayal of in *Tanhuma*, 64, 66
praise of in 4 Maccabees, 139–40
as protagonist, 154
punishment of, 9, 10, 26–27, 32–33, 43, 64–65, 67, 108
reaction to Dinah's rape, 158
reaction to massacre at Shechem, 16, 20, 74, 79, 83
refusal to give Dinah to Esau, 26, 27, 32–33
role in *Joseph and Asenath*, 101
severance from sons, 20–21
silence of, 61, 66
transgressions of, 32–33, 67, 164 (*see also* punishment)
willingness to consider intermarriage, 93, 107

Job
blame of Dinah by, 85–86
children of by Dinah, 98–99, 168
conversion of, 86
Dinah as blessing to, 99
Dinah as wife of, 25, 33, 85, 97, 98, 112, 113
Dinah compared to in *Tanhuma*, 65–66
negative attitude toward Dinah, 85–86, 99
references to Dinah in *Genesis Rabbah*, 33–34
royal status of, 95–96
Testament of Job, 95–97
Jobab, 95–96
see also Job
Jonge, Marinus De, 90, 91
Joseph
ability to control passions, 139
birth of, 50, 110
death of, 22
Dinah's relationship with, 21–22
gifts to Dinah, 21
marriage to Asenath, 21, 22, 23, 50
possession of Shechem (city), 24–25, 152–53
prince's plan to murder, 100
Joseph and Asenath, 99–102

Josephus
   Antiquities of the Jews, 156–60
   on Dinah incident, 167
   festival setting in, 156, 157
   introduction to, 155–56
   portrayal of Jacob in, 158–59
   references to Dinah in, 156–57, 159
   similarity to Genesis 34, 160
journey, Philo on, 144, 154
Jubilees
   author of, 107
   characterization of Shechemites in, 110
   date of, 107
   on Dinah incident, 166
   as divine revelation to Moses, 107
   invective against intermarriage in, 106–7, 108
   language of, 107
   limited information about Dinah in, 109–10
   portrayal of Simeon and Levi in, 109, 110
   provenance of, 107
   reference to Dinah in, 107–8
   similarities to Genesis, 109
   support of rape theory, 108
Judah
   in *Genesis Rabbah*, 48
   kings of, 17
Judith (book of)
   as apocryphal, 115
   centrality of faith in, 116
   claim of Divine as God of lowly/humbled, 124–25
   date of, 116
   differences with Genesis, 118, 132, 135
   genre of, 115–16
   introduction to, 115–16
   irony in, 131, 133–34
   language of, 116
   links with Dinah narrative, 115, 119–20, 121–22, 124, 125–26, 131, 132
   omissions from, 136
   rhetoric in, 166
   similarities to Genesis, 134–35
   theocentric grounding of, 135
   use of Deuteronomic ideas, 135–36
Judith (woman)
   ability to go out, 137
   actions of, 125–30
   agency of, 127
   as agent of Divine, 132, 135, 136–37
   beauty, use of, 126–27
   contrast with Dinah, 132–33
   deceit by, 122, 131, 136
   faith in God's protection, 123–24
   faith of, 116
   in foreground, 134
   as fully developed character, 127
   heroism of, 133
   identification with Simeon, 115, 118, 123, 133
   intertextual reference to incident at Shechem, 116–18
   men's desire for, 131
   piety of, 130–31, 135–36
   portrayal of Dinah, 122–23
   prayer of, 116–18, 124
   as prophetess/sage, 136
   prophetic role of, 116, 136
   as protector-avenger, 123
   purification of, 131
   referred to as "maiden" or "girl," 131
   refusal to name Shechem, 118
   religious rituals, use of, 133–34
   theme of vengeance in narrative of, 117–18
   vulnerability of, 120
   wealth of, 120
   widowhood, 120
   wisdom of, 127, 135

Kee, H. C., 91, 92

L.A.B. *see Liber Antiquitatum Biblicarum*
land, Jacob's acquisition of, 103
Leah
   adorned as prostitute, 44
   Dinah associated with, 11, 32, 63, 66, 163, 165

Dinah referred to as daughter of, 9
liability for Dinah's fate, 61, 164
as not responsible for Dinah's rape, 87
portrayal of, 11, 55
prayer of, 66
reflection of Dinah's actions on, 44
legal material, 107
The Legends of the Jews (Ginzberg)
    agency of Dinah in, 14
    attitude toward intermarriage in, 15–16
    clear reference to rape in, 10
    criticism of Dinah in, 11
    deaths of Joseph and Dinah in, 22
    development in Jacob's character in, 14
    development of Dinah's character in, 27
    difference with Genesis narrative, 10–11
    Dinah presented as one of two wives in, 26
    Dinah's burial site in, 26
    Dinah's close affiliation with Jacob in, 9
    fate of Dinah in, 22
    females contrasted with males in, 9–10
    God's intervention in events at Shechem in, 19
    Jacob's desire to retrieve Dinah in, 13–14
    on Jacob's errors, 27
    Jacob's severance from sons in, 20–21
    Jacob's views of massacre at Shechem in, 16
    marriage between Job and Dinah in, 25
    nouns in, 8–9
    as point of entry, 1
    portrayal of Jacob in, 9–10
    portrayal of Leah in, 11
    portrayal of Shechem (city) in, 20
    portrayal of women in, 11
    presence of Divine in, 16
    reference to Rebekah in, 18
    reference to Sarah in, 18
    sources for, 1
    text of Dinah narrative in, 2–6
    threat of Hivites to matriarchs in, 93
    verbs in, 6–8
Levi
    as agent of Divine, 135
    age of, 46, 94–95, 110–11
    concern for Dinah's reputation, 74
    as counselor, 92–93
    deceit of, 131, 134, 152
    desire to redeem Dinah's name, 83–84
    emphasis on Dinah as sister of, 112
    as exacting God's judgment, 19–20
    in forefront of massacre, 93
    in foreground, 134
    as heroic, 119
    as illustration of non-temperance, 140
    Jacob's severance from, 20–21
    in *Joseph and Asenath*, 100–101
    massacre attributed to, 16–17, 48–49
    opposition to circumcising Shechemites, 92, 93
    portrayal of by Philo, 152
    portrayal of in Genesis, 152
    portrayal of in *Genesis Rabbah*, 46, 48
    portrayal of in *Jubilees*, 109, 110
    portrayal of in *Leviticus Rabbah*, 49
    portrayal of in *Testaments of the Twelve Patriarchs*, 91
    as priest, 48, 91–92
    as prophet, 101
    as protagonist, 152
    as protector of endangered woman, 100
    reaction to Shechem's actions, 75
    recounting of events at Shechem, 19
    relationship with Divine, 91–92, 101
    as sage, 136
    Testament of Levi, 18, 91–95
    wisdom of, 147
Leviticus Rabbah, 49–50
Liber Antiquitatum Biblicarum, 97–99, 166

Maccabees, Fourth Book of, 137–41
Maher, Michael, 79
"maiden"
    Dinah referred to as, 72, 82, 167
    implications of, 82
    Judith referred to as, 131
males contrasted with females, 9–10
Mangan, Céline, 75
Mangey, Thomas, 147

marketplace, 34, 35
marriage
    by abduction, 18, 166
    in business-relations, 82–83
massacre at Shechem
    attributed to Simeon and Levi, 16–17, 48–49
    Dinah as justification for, 91, 98, 102
    Divine's involvement in, 16, 19–20, 105, 114, 117, 118
    Jacob's views of, 16, 20, 74, 79, 83
    justification of, 91, 98, 102, 108
    Levi's recounting of, 19
    linked to Dinah, 17–18
    reprisal for, 17
    as retribution, 17–18
    as righteousness, 109
    Simeon as instigator of, 105
    in Theodotus, 105–6
    theologization of, 105
mastery of women, 34, 60–61, 65
matriarchs
    Dinah linked to, 11
    negative portrayal of, 31, 62–63
    relationship with Divine, 62–63
    spiritual/magical influence of, 31
    threat of Hivites to, 93
McNamara, Martin, 71, 72
meat analogy, 64
Meili, Trisha, 12
men
    admonishment to master wives, 34
    social role of, 65
midrashim
    advice to women in, 34–36
    blame of Dinah in, 165
    blame of women in, 35
    contrast with Philo's writings, 167
    Dinah as prostitute in, 167
    Ecclesiastes Rabbah, 53–54
    focus on Dinah's "going out" in, 113
    indictment of Jacob in, 32
    introduction to, 29–30
    Leviticus Rabbah, 49–50
    passages regarding Dinah in, 36–43
    Pirqe Rabbi Eliezer, 50–53
    portrayal of Dinah in, 163–65
    types of, 29–30
    verbs in, 62
    warnings in, 34
    . see also Genesis Rabbah; Tanhuma
mind, dichotomy with body, 148
Miriam, 11
misogyny, 12
Montanist movement, 96
Moore, Carey, 115, 116, 118, 119, 121, 132, 133
Mosaic Law, 107
Moses, 107, 152
mother of the seven sons, 140–41

naming of Dinah, 50
Neusner, Jacob, 49
Nickelsburg, George W. E., 96, 98, 100, 108, 156
nouns
    in *Legends of the Jews* narrative, 8–9
    in *targumin,* 86

object of verb, Dinah as, 7, 72, 78, 81, 95, 98, 99
On the Change of Names (Philo), 149–51
On the Migration of Abraham (Philo)
    references to Dinah in, 145–46
    use of allegory in, 144
outsiders
    ease of tricking, 132
    lack of circumcision as identifying characteristic of, 133

Parry, Robin, 136, 144, 149
passivity of Dinah, 8, 66
Philo
    acquittal of Dinah, 148
    Allegorical Interpretation, 152–54
    contrast with *midrashim,* 167
    as descendant of tribe of Levi, 147
    dichotomy between body and mind in writings of, 148
    Dinah as metaphor in writings of, 154

on Dinah incident, 166–67
encouragement of readers to seek wisdom, 146, 148
introduction to, 143–44
on journey, 144, 154
On the Change of Names, 149–51
On the Migration of Abraham, 144, 145–46
openness to Hellenism, 146
portrayal of Dinah, 146, 155, 167
portrayal of Jacob, 153–54
portrayal of Shechem (city), 147, 153
portrayal of Shechem (man), 147, 148–49, 151–52, 167
portrayal of Simeon and Levi, 147, 152
references to Dinah, 144–46, 149–51, 152–54
use of allegory, 144
use of "defile," 167
on virginity, 149, 154–55
on wisdom, 153
piety
    of Jacob, 154
    of Judith, 130–31, 135–36
Pirqe Rabbi Eliezer, 50–53
pollution, 119, 120
Porton, Gary G., 29–30
Potiphar, 23
priest
    Levi as, 48, 91–92
    Simeon as, 48
prince, Egyptian, 100, 101
prophet, Levi as, 101
prophetess, Judith as, 136
prostitute
    Dinah as, 167
    lack of reference to Dinah as in Pseudepigrapha, 113
    Leah adorned as, 44
protagonists, 152, 154
Pseudepigrapha
    Demetrius, 110–12
    introduction to, 89–90
    Joseph and Asenath, 99–102
    Jubilees, 106–10
    lack of focus on Dinah's "going out" in, 113
    lack of reference to Dinah as harlot/prostitute in, 113
    Liber Antiquitatum Biblicarum, 97–99, 166
    Testament of Job, 95–97
    Testament of Levi, 91–95, 166
    Testaments of the Twelve Patriarchs, 90–95
    Theodotus, 102–6
Pummer, Reinhard, 122
punishment
    of David, 27
    of Jacob, 9, 10, 26–27, 32–33, 43, 64–65, 67, 108
    sexual crimes against women as punishment against men, 27
purification, 130–31

Rachel, 12, 31, 66
rape
    laws regarding, 83
    setting of, 83
    as stratagem of war, 121
rape of Dinah
    clear reference to in *Legends of the Jews*, 10
    Hamor as perpetrator of, 118
    as insult to sons of Israel/Jacob, 101–2
    in Josephus, 158
    as justification for massacre, 91, 98, 102, 166
    portrayal of in book of Judith, 122–23
    as punishment of Jacob, 67
    Shechem held responsible for, 148–49
    spiritualizing of, 148
    in Theodotus, 105
    and use of "afflicted" in *Targum Pseudo-Jonathan*, 81–82
reason as sovereign over emotions, 138–40
Rebekah, 18
reputation, Dinah's, 74, 75–76, 167
rescue, Dinah's need for, 106
retribution
    linked to Dinah, 19
    massacre as, 17–18
    see also vengeance

revenge theme in Judith, 117–18
Rhoads, David M., 156
ribands of celestial girdle, 25
rituals, religious, 131, 133–34
Roman Empire, 45–46
Russell, D. S., 96

sage, 136
Sarah, 12, 18
"scoffing," meaning of, 94
"seeing" of Dinah by Shechem, 63
serpent/snake
    Dinah portrayed as, 54
    in *Ecclesiastes Rabbah*, 54
    Shechem (man) as, 51, 54, 141
sexuality, democratization of leader's, 131
sexualization of Dinah, 63
shame
    and circumcision, 12–13
    semantic domain of, 120, 133
Shechem (city)
    attitude toward Hebrew women, 15
    democratization of guilt to, 14, 20, 93–94, 108, 148
    described as sacred, 102
    Dinah's desire to see, 103
    festival in, 103, 156, 157
    Jacob's clan historically situated in, 102
    Judith's refusal to name, 118
    massacre at (*see* massacre at Shechem)
    negative portrayal of in *Genesis Rabbah*, 44–45
    negative portrayal of in *Legends*, 20
    negative portrayal of in *Testament of Levi*, 94
    passed to Joseph, 24–25, 152–53
    portrayal of by Philo, 147, 153
    possession of, 24–25
Shechemites
    characterizations of, 105, 110, 113
    circumcision of, 92, 93, 104, 105, 131, 136
    Divine vengeance upon, 121
    Judith's portrayal of, 117–18
    lack of circumcision, 149
    relationship with Jacob's family, 111
    . *see also* Shechem (city)
Shechem (man)
    age of, 74
    blame of in *targumin*, 87
    compared to Divine, 44–45
    as Dinah's husband, 168
    Dinah's removal from, 52–53
    Dinah's unwillingness to leave, 13
    as disgrace, 73
    graveness of offense of, 73
    gullibility of, 78–79
    held responsible for actions, 63
    held responsible for rape, 148–49
    as Hurrite, 98
    intent to take Dinah as wife, 73
    lack of circumcision, 133
    love for Dinah, 65, 66, 103, 104
    luring out of Dinah, 164
    parallels with Egyptian prince, 101
    portrayal of by Philo, 147, 148–49, 151–52, 153, 167
    portrayal of in *Pirqe Rabbi Eliezer*, 50, 51
    portrayal of in *Tanhuma*, 61
    as serpent, 51, 54, 141
    son of, 74
    Theodotus's description of, 102
    use of speech, 152
sheep, 103
Sichem. *see* Shechem
silence
    of Divine in Genesis 34, 135
    of Jacob, 61, 66
Simeon
    as agent of Divine, 118, 135
    age of, 46, 111
    characterized as heroic, 119
    concern for Dinah's reputation, 74, 83–84
    deceit of, 131, 134, 152
    in foreground, 134
    heroism of, 133
    as illustration of non-temperance, 139, 140
    intermarriage with Canaanite woman, 15, 23, 48

Jacob's severance from, 20–21
in *Joseph and Asenath,* 100–101
Judith's identification with, 115, 118, 123, 133
marriages of, 15
marriage to Dinah, 19, 22–23, 47–48
massacre attributed to, 16–17, 48–49, 105
portrayal of by Philo, 147, 152
portrayal of in Genesis, 152
portrayal of in *Genesis Rabbah,* 46, 48
portrayal of in *Jubilees,* 109, 110
portrayal of in *Leviticus Rabbah,* 49
positive portrayal of, 22–23
as priest, 48
promise to marry Dinah, 13, 168
as protagonist, 152
as protector of endangered woman, 100
reaction to Shechem's actions, 75
relationship with Divine, 101
as sage, 136
wisdom of, 73–74, 147
snake. *see* serpent
sons of Jacob
described by Theodotus, 102
Dinah's rape as insult to, 101–2
Jacob's severance from, 20–21
names of, 108
in *Targum Neofiti,* 73–74
testaments attributed to, 90–95
as wise *vs.* deceitful, 73–74
. *see also* Levi; Simeon
soul, dichotomy of with mind/body, 148
Spittler, Russell, 96
status, women's, 15, 96
Stemberger, G., 30
Strack, H. L., 30
subdue, Divine imperative to, 65
subject of verb, Dinah as, 7–8, 14, 72, 78, 81, 89

Talmud, 18
Tamar
collapse of Dinah's character with, 47
parallelism with Dinah, 13
rape of as David's punishment, 27

Tanhuma
blame of Dinah in, 55, 65, 67–68
Buber rescension of, 60
date of, 54
Dinah compared to Jacob in, 65–66
Dinah linked with harlotry in, 61
on Dinah's conception as male, 63
Dinah used as type in, 62
footnotes in, 60, 61
hiding of Dinah in, 64
Jacob's silence in, 61
Leah's liability for Dinah's fate in, 61
portrayal of Dinah in, 65, 68
portrayal of Jacob in, 64, 66
portrayal of Leah in, 55
portrayal of matriarchs in, 62–63
portrayal of Shechem (man) in, 61
provenance of, 54
text regarding Dinah, 55–60
view of Hamor in, 61
targumin
blame of Shechem in, 87
on Dinah incident, 165–66
intentions of, 84
introduction to, 69
language in, 84
nouns in, 86
Targum Job, 84–86
Targum Neofiti, 69–76
Targum Onqelos, 76–79
Targum Pseudo-Jonathan, 79–84
Targum Job, 84–86
Targum Neofiti
date of, 70
on Dinah incident, 165
on Dinah's virginity, 167
language of, 69–70
portrayal of Dinah in, 72, 73, 75
portrayal of Shechem (man) in, 73
portrayal of sons of Jacob in, 73
provenance of, 69
redaction of, 70
references to Dinah in, 70–71
safeguarding of Dinah's reputation in, 75–76

textual errors in, 74
textual variants in, 71–72
Targum Onqelos, 76–79, 165
Targum Pseudo-Jonathan
    authority of, 80
    author of, 79
    date of, 79
    delicacy of language in, 84
    on Dinah incident, 165–66
    on Dinah's virginity, 167
    introduction of Dinah in, 81
    language of, 79
    passage relating to Dinah in, 80–81
    simplicity of, 84
    use of "afflicted" in, 81–82
    use of "force" in, 83
    use of "maiden" *vs.* "girl" in, 82
    verbs in, 81
Testament of Job, 95–97
Testament of Levi, 18, 91–95, 166
Testaments of the Twelve Patriarchs, 90–95
textual errors in *Targum Neofiti*, 74
Theodotus
    characterization of Shechemites, 105
    description of Dinah, 168
    description of Dinah incident, 102–3
    description of Hamor, 102
    differences with Genesis, 104–6
    on Dinah's virginity, 167
    lack of account of circumcision, 104
    on massacre, 105–6
    portrayal of Dinah, 104
    use of verbs, 103–4
Therapeutae, 96
Thibodeau, Lucille Claire, 120, 158
thistle, Hamor as, 61
"took," use of in Theodotus, 106
Torah
    centrality of in Judaism, 69
    and measurement of other texts, 118
    obedience to, 137
    translation of, 69
transgressions, Jacob's, 32–33, 67, 164
    . *see also* punishment

trickery, 132
    . *see also* deceit
twin, Dinah as, 107–8, 112, 163

Uzziah, 134

VanderKam, James C., 107
vengeance
    Dinah's rape as justification for, 166
    Divine's role in, 122
    as male characteristic, 123
    theme of in Judith, 117–18
    . *see also* retribution
verbs
    Dinah as object of, 7, 72, 78, 81, 95, 98, 99
    Dinah as subject of, 7–8, 14, 72, 78, 81, 99
    in *Legends*, 6–8
    in *midrashim*, 62
    order of in *Ecclesiastes Rabbah*, 54
    used by Theodotus, 103–4
victim
    blame of, 12, 44, 45, 54, 67–68
    Dinah as, 10, 72, 78
victory through deceit, 122
vile, Dinah referred to as, 33–34
virginity
    Dinah's, 75, 84, 103, 104, 112, 113, 122, 148, 149, 154–55, 167, 168
    Philo on, 149, 154–55
    restoration of Dinah's, 148, 154
virgins, defloration of by uncircumcised, 74–75
voice, given to Dinah, 169
vow, ramifications of failure to fulfill, 49–50
    . *see also* punishment

warnings, 34
wealth, Judith's, 120
widowhood, Judith's, 120
Wintermute, O. S., 107
wisdom
    of Judith, 127, 135
    and need to be wary of unrestrained passions, 153–54

Philo on, 153
Philo's encouragement of seeking of, 146, 148
of sons of Jacob, 73–74, 147
use of in *Targum Neofiti*, 73–74
vs. deceit, 73–74, 135
wisdom literature, 86
women
advice to in *midrashim*, 34–36
as aggressors, 121
blame of, 12, 35
boundaries of, 140–41
considered inherently sinful, 63
creation of, 11, 40, 57, 62
criticism of, 11
danger in being seen, 34–35
Hebrew, Shechemites' attitude toward, 15
indictment of in *midrashim*, 32
inheritance by, 25, 26, 96
within Jacob's household, 18
L.A.B.'s attitude toward, 98
Legends' criticism of, 11
need to master, 34, 60–61, 65
portrayal of in *Genesis Rabbah*, 11–12
portrayal of in *Legends*, 11
sexual crimes against as punishment against men, 27
social role of, 65
status of, 96
in *Testament of Job*, 96
wool, 103

Zebulun, 107–8, 112, 163

Studies in Biblical Literature

This series invites manuscripts from scholars in any area of biblical literature. Both established and innovative methodologies, covering general and particular areas in biblical study, are welcome. The series seeks to make available studies that will make a significant contribution to the ongoing biblical discourse. Scholars who have interests in gender and sociocultural hermeneutics are particularly encouraged to consider this series.

For further information about the series and for the submission of manuscripts, contact:

>Peter Lang Publishing
>Acquisitions Department
>P.O. Box 1246
>Bel Air, Maryland 21014-1246

To order other books in this series, please contact our Customer Service Department:

>(800) 770-LANG (within the U.S.)
>(212) 647-7706 (outside the U.S.)
>(212) 647-7707 FAX

or browse online by series at:

>WWW.PETERLANG.COM